A History of British National Audit

A History of British National Audit

The Pursuit of Accountability

David Dewar
Warwick Funnell

OXFORD
UNIVERSITY PRESS

OXFORD
UNIVERSITY PRESS

Great Clarendon Street, Oxford, OX2 6DP,
United Kingdom

Oxford University Press is a department of the University of Oxford.
It furthers the University's objective of excellence in research, scholarship,
and education by publishing worldwide. Oxford is a registered trade mark of
Oxford University Press in the UK and in certain other countries

First Edition published in 2017

Impression: 1

Published in the United States of America by Oxford University Press
198 Madison Avenue, New York, NY 10016, United States of America

British Library Cataloguing in Publication Data
Data available

Library of Congress Control Number: 2016942457

ISBN 978–0–19–879031–0

Printed in Great Britain by
Clays Ltd, St Ives plc

'People will not look forward to posterity who never look backward to their ancestors.'

Edmund Burke, *Reflections on the Revolution in France* (1790)

Foreword

by
Sir Amyas Morse, KCB
Comptroller and Auditor General
National Audit Office

Living in a modern democracy it is easy to take for granted that the Executive will keep proper records of how it has used the resources at its disposal and be accountable to Parliament for the way it conducts its business. But as the meticulous research by the authors of this book shows, instilling effective financial control and accountability for the use of public funds and the proper conduct of public business has been an incremental process that has taken centuries. My predecessors in this office and its forerunners, supported by enlightened parliamentarians, have been key players in promoting financial accountability for government spending and the need for it to be audited independently on behalf of Parliament.

The scope of that audit has developed over the years from a focus on the presentation and accuracy of accounts to ensuring that funds are spent only for purposes approved by Parliament and that resources have been used efficiently, effectively, and with economy. As a result, the National Audit Office and its predecessors have long played a vital role supporting Parliament to hold government to account for the value for money of public spending and the services it delivers. While this is the Office's ultimate purpose, it also aims to use its work to help the organizations it audits to improve performance and service delivery.

The significant financial constraints that departments face today requires them to recognize that short-term cost-cutting measures will not be enough. Fundamental changes will be needed requiring departments to identify and implement new ways of delivering their objectives with a permanently lower cost base. Responses to this challenge are likely to include service transformation, digitization, further use of private and third sector providers, and more integration of services at a local level. While there have been some positive developments in terms of the civil service acquiring and developing the skills and capabilities required to make these complex changes and protect public value, they do not yet match the scale of the challenge. The weaknesses we still see in the public sector—services delivered in silos, short-term decision making, and a lack of organizational learning from experience—are all ones that would be familiar to many of my predecessors.

Complementing our existing charges of helping Parliament hold government to account, and helping to drive improvement in public services, our new roles relating to the audit of local public bodies under the Local Audit and Accountability Act 2014 substantially increase the breadth of our work. These responsibilities mark a significant extension in the reach of our work, enabling us to take an end-to-end view from national policy through to local delivery and the effect on citizens.

At the heart of the National Audit Office are the expertise and passion of the people who work there, who are engaged on tasks that are challenging and satisfying and continue to reflect individual initiative. I, like my predecessors, am indebted to them for their dedication and hard work in the service of the public.

Table of Contents

1

A Sense of History

'The student who knows no history thinks each continent new to him a continent newly discovered.'

Sir Joshua Reynolds

Public accountability is a cornerstone of democracy. This was firmly recognized in the cradle of democracy itself when Athens in the fourth century BCE had well-established procedures for holding all office holders publicly accountable for their propriety and stewardship.[1] In Britain, ensuring that the Executive—that is the government, whether elected or appointed by a ruling monarch—is held accountable to Parliament has over the centuries been a barometer of fundamental constitutional struggles between monarch and Parliament. Today it remains a key element in relationships between Parliament and the Executive.

Political power and Executive dominance were crucially dependent upon control over public finances, especially in the ability to marshal and use military force, either against external foes or to stifle internal revolution or discontent. Constitutional controls over finance were therefore a bulwark against oppressive use of Executive power. This nexus between political hegemony and public finances lay at the heart of the constitutional battles between Parliament and the Executive in the evolution of the English Constitution. John Morley, politician, biographer, and political writer, noted that 'Under other governments a question of expense is only a question of economy, and it is nothing more; with us, in every question of expense, there is always a mixture of constitutional considerations.'[2] Prime Minister William Gladstone believed that 'finance of the country is ultimately associated with the liberties of the country.... (I)t is a powerful leverage by which English

---

[1] Aristotle, 325 BCE, *Constitution of Athens*. The orator Demosthenes complained that throughout his career he had been subject to public audit in all the posts he had held.
[2] Morley, 1909, p. 92.

liberty has been gradually acquired.'[3] From the late seventeenth century until the late nineteenth century the constitutional importance of Executive financial accountability provided the core rationale for reforms to government accounting and the nature and extent of parliamentary audit.

Throughout the eighteenth and early nineteenth centuries reforms of government accounting and auditing were often responses to the political crises of war and revolution and their financial demands and priorities. Repeated calls by the Executive for increased funding and greater powers over spending then jeopardized key elements of the constitution, the powers of Parliament, and the liberties and rights these protected.[4] From these ferments came the impetus for accounting and audit reforms to strengthen constitutional safeguards for holding the Executive accountable to Parliament. In the late eighteenth century the political and economic crisis engendered by the American War of Independence (1775–83) was especially significant in prompting government accounting and audit reforms, which laid the foundations for developments in British public sector audit in the middle decades of the nineteenth century. The last decades of the eighteenth century were the crucible of modern Westminster constitutional audit.

For parliamentarian Edmund Burke the 'distinguishing part' of the English constitution was its liberty. To 'preserve that liberty inviolate', he warned, 'seems the particular duty and proper trust of a member of the House of Commons'.[5] Indeed, the Act of Settlement in 1701 had sought to reinforce the constitutional relationship between Crown and Parliament, which had been forged in the Declaration of Rights (1689), and later the Bill of Rights, by affirming the need 'for the further limitation of the Crown and better securing the rights and liberties of the subjects'.[6] Protection of this liberty was the 'sacred, illimitable obligation' of those who inherited the benefits of the Glorious Revolution of 1688–9. According to Burke, the 'only security for law and liberty' was a strong, independent, and vigilant parliament.[7] The constitution would endure only so long as parliamentary sovereignty remained its keystone, especially in matters of finance.[8] The people, Burke emphasized, 'took infinite pains to inculcate, as a fundamental principle, that in all monarchies the people must in effect themselves . . . possess the power of granting their own money, or no shadow of liberty could subsist'.[9] Arthur Onslow, Speaker of the House of Commons 1728–61, confirmed that Parliament's exclusive authority to grant money was:

---

[3] Einzig, 1959, p. 3.   [4] Funnell, 1996, 2004.
[5] Edmund Burke, Speech at Bristol 1774 in Burke, 1942, p. 66.
[6] Stephenson and Marcham, 1937, p. 610.
[7] Burke 1790, quoted in Roberts, 1977, p. 59.   [8] Dicey, 1926, pp. xvii, xviii.
[9] Speech on Conciliation with the Colonies, 22 March 1795, in Burke, 1942, p. 92.

the great and most important Right of this House.... It is a Right...that never ought to come into doubt; it is a Right which we cannot part with the sole Exercise of, without giving up our own power, without betraying the Liberties of our constituents.[10]

Against this background, public accountability has been a complex amalgam of institutions, practices, and requirements where patterns changed to reflect movements in the scale and distribution of public expenditure and developments in the objectives, priorities, management, and delivery of departmental programmes and projects. Although the pursuit of better accountability has been a dominant force in shaping parliamentary financial control, the evolution of modern public sector audit has been 'cautious and at times faltering', rather than following an 'orderly march towards carefully considered, defined and agreed objectives'.[11] Improvements have often depended on a combination of opportunism and determination, against a background of wider developments in constitutional and political manoeuvring.

The earliest opportunities to strengthen the accountability of the Executive to Parliament came when reductions in the royal estates and revenues and the heavy costs of wars and other adventures meant that the King, or Queen, could no longer afford 'to live of his or her own' and had to seek parliamentary grants and aids. Additional funds inevitably came with conditions and restrictions attached. Accordingly, 'parliamentary control of expenditure was strong when the Executive was weak, as under the Lancastrians, and weak when the Executive was strong, as under the Tudors'.[12] The King's need for additional funds was a feature of developments towards wider accountability in the fourteenth century, which were given added weight by the financial demands of the Hundred Years War. Similarly, the seventeenth-century wars against the Dutch, the American War of Independence of 1775–83, and the South African War of 1899–1902 all gave rise to successful pressure for more detailed parliamentary scrutiny of military expenditures. Although accountability was pursued with some success against the waste and extravagances of the Stuarts, there was a failure to follow this through when Parliament gained direct power following the Glorious Revolution of 1688–9.[13]

Public accountability was often notably absent when abuses were greatest. For example, it took many years to tackle the corruption and waste of the powerful and lucrative public sinecures that flourished amongst the Whig aristocracy until belatedly removed by reforms in the closing years of the eighteenth century with examinations and reports by the Commissioners of Audit (1780–5). Despite these improvements it was not until the middle of the

[10] Speaker Onslow, House of Commons 11 February 1740, quoted in Thomas, 1971, p. 65.
[11] Normanton, Evidence before Select Committee on Procedure (1978) First Report, p. 133.
[12] Davenport, 1918, p. 34.　　[13] Funnell, 2007.

nineteenth century that Parliament established a consistent system of accountability, accounts, and audit. Roseveare considered the 'arid technicalities' of public sector audit as the reason for the slow progress of audit reform.[14] In the early nineteenth century George Harrison, of the British Treasury, referred to the 'dry and irksome details' of audit while Sir Francis Baring,[15] who in 1861 was to become the first chairman of the British Committee of Public Accounts, thought audit's arcane details made it a 'wearying and uninteresting subject'.[16] Along the path to improved accountability, the procedures and priorities for examining accountability, first to the King and later to Parliament, had to adjust to enormous changes in the nature and scale of public sector activities and expenditures.

Ultimately, accountability is sustained by the provision of information. Financial accountability in particular depends upon information that is relevant, reliable, and regular. It depends upon the facts and analysis provided by an annual cycle of accounts, validated by independent examination and report: an audit. Audit in turn depends on a regular cycle of accountability to give it focus and purpose. This symbiosis lies at the heart of audit in its original sense as a hearing, a bringing to account in person before a judicial court or council.[17] Auditors themselves were sometimes vigorous in extending their independence, remit, and responsibilities while at other times they seemed reluctant to move beyond traditional roles and concerns. Advance and retreat depended not only on audit skills and determination but also on the climate of resistance in departments and other audited bodies. Whereas in the past the relationship between the auditor and the auditee was often confrontational, since the 1990s there has been a welcome recognition of the benefits of a more collaborative relationship, the importance of audit providing added value to those audited, and the need to use audit experience and findings to encourage improvements more widely across the public sector.

The emphasis on broader issues of financial accountability and not just the preparation and submission of accounts has over time produced the three main concerns of public sector audit. The overriding concern is appropriation, to ensure that funds are spent within the amounts voted and only on services and for purposes approved by Parliament. This includes verifying that

---

[14] Roseveare, 1969, p. 142.

[15] Select Committee on Finance (1819), Fifth Report, p. 208.

[16] House of Commons debates, 24 April 1856, col. 1450; also see similar comments by the Chancellor of the Exchequer on the same day, col. 1458.

[17] The court structure, with associated legal powers, has long disappeared from modern audit in the United Kingdom, as it has in other countries where arrangements are based directly or indirectly on the Westminster parliamentary system. However, the national audit courts of some countries in Europe and elsewhere, such as the Cour des Comptes in France, the Corte dei Conti in Italy, and the Cuentas and Contralorias in Spain and Latin America, retain important judicial traditions and powers.

expenditures have been made consistent with relevant rules and regulations. Complementing these two enduring concerns of public sector audit is the need to examine the economic, efficient, and effective use of resources—that is, achieving value for money. Appropriation and regularity are often considered together and remain central to the annual examination and certification of public sector accounts. Although value for money is today more often the focus of separate, distinct audit reports, these different elements of public sector audit are often best planned and carried through in close association, not as separate activities conducted by separate audit bodies.

There are strong links between sound financial control, accounting, and reporting systems, and economical, efficient, and effective administration. Ensuring probity, propriety, and regularity in the conduct of public business, avoiding waste and extravagance, and pursuing wider issues of value for money are common objectives. The most widely recognized single achievement after the 1866 Audit Act, the ground-breaking legislation that created the post of Comptroller and Auditor General (C&AG) and established the Exchequer and Audit Department (E&AD), was the progressive introduction of examinations of value for money in all its aspects. Starting from modest beginnings in the 1880s, it developed, without statutory authority and against strong opposition, into major reports on a wide range of programmes and projects, especially those arising before, during, and after the First and Second World Wars. Originally these audit reports were mainly about criticisms of individual failings and failures, but later reports sought to be more balanced and more positive in findings and recommendations for improvement, while retaining where necessary a critical edge.

The concerns and priorities of modern public sector audit are not new. Their discovery and rediscovery has been a feature of developments in public sector audit for at least the last 900 years. Concern for the proper conduct of public business, for accountability for resources, for stewardship and good management can be traced back beyond Parliament itself into the earliest controls over the King's revenues and expenditures. Some of the audit boards and commissioners that operated at various times before a permanent framework of audit was introduced in the nineteenth century also recognized the need to pursue waste and extravagance, although their examination of such matters was often limited, uncertain, and variable. The public sector has additional expectations and priorities that are not readily captured in the cold terms of economy and efficiency and need to be recognized when evaluating results. Social and welfare considerations, and ethical factors such as fairness, natural justice, equality of treatment, transparency, and similar values have to be taken into account when judging performance. There can be a tension between the importance of recognizing such values and pressures to be efficient and cost-conscious. Edmund Burke's warning that 'The service of the public is not a thing to be put to auction and struck down to the highest bidder' has a continuing resonance today.

Until the 1866 Audit Act, for many centuries the Treasury and its priorities were allowed to dominate the audit work and auditor powers. The finances and staffing of public sector audit bodies—and even the audits to be conducted—were subject to Treasury approval. Although the 1866 Act substantially reduced the Treasury's dominance over all aspects of audit, continuing vigilance was needed to maintain and enhance the C&AG's independence by ensuring that it applied not only to statutory safeguards on appointment and removal but to all aspects of the day-to-day conduct of audits. This determination brought with it the need to ensure that necessary boundaries between auditor and auditee did not become rigid or embattled, and to respond positively to legitimate criticisms. Also, rights of access to, and inspection of, public bodies where the C&AG is not the appointed auditor have always been important to ensure coverage of all public expenditure, however dispersed. Securing such rights has not always been straightforward, but they have become increasingly necessary for examinations across the growing number of non-departmental bodies responsible for increasing levels of public expenditure, including some in the private sector.

The close relationship with, and enthusiastic support of, the Public Accounts Committee (PAC) has from 1866 been a key factor in both the effectiveness of the C&AG's reports and the effectiveness of the Committee. This close involvement was enhanced by provisions in the 1983 Audit Act. In such a close relationship there is a balance to be maintained between the views and priorities of the PAC and the powers and responsibilities of the C&AG. Though the PAC remains the main focus of relationships with Parliament as a whole, in more recent years working relationships have been developed with other Select Committees.

From the early 1970s onwards there was a growing recognition within the E&AD of the need to improve important aspects of the planning, management, objectives, and the conduct of audits. It was increasingly accepted within the E&AD, in government, and in Parliament that further and wider changes should be pursued by a reconstituted audit body under fresh legislation. The establishment of the National Audit Office (NAO) in 1983, replacing the E&AD, was a further significant development in this continuing process of challenge and change. The NAO's developments built upon and extended the legacy left by the E&AD. Similar responsibilities and objectives remain key elements in the work of the NAO today.

The creation of the NAO, with strong new powers, marked an important next stage in the development of public sector audit. The widening range of audit developments was accentuated by legislation in 2001 which replaced departmental appropriation accounts prepared on a cash basis with resource accounts on an accruals basis and, most significantly, by legislation in 2011 which fundamentally altered the organization and allocation of powers within a restructured NAO. Coincident with, and stimulated by, these changes there were shifting emphases in the NAO's range and conduct of business and also in relationships with Parliament, with the Treasury, and with departments and other audited bodies. The powers and responsibilities of departmental and other Accounting Officers are central in many of these areas. These relationships have been enduring, fundamental determinants of the independence and powers of the public sector auditor.

Changes in government policies and priorities will continue to influence the scale, range, objectives, organization, management, and delivery of government programmes and projects and require the NAO to respond to ensure a modern audit for modern circumstances. In discharging their responsibilities auditors have not been concerned with only narrow professional concerns. Rather, the issues pursued have often been an integral part of developments in democratic and constitutional accountability. On this historical timescale, many challenges had to be overcome. This book charts the progress through that odyssey to its present success.

2

Medieval Beginnings

'Is this the Court of the Exchequer? Be firm, be firm my pecker.'

W. S. Gilbert, *Trial by Jury*

The 900-year history of the audit of British government finances began in the organization and operations of the twelfth-century King's Exchequer, the centre of medieval accounting and accountability. For centuries it was at the heart of public finance with a country-wide network of accounting officers, which gave it strong and immediate powers of enforcement. Woven into the fabric of the feudal economy, the Exchequer was the focus for the discharge of financial responsibilities and the clearing house for business between the King, his barons, sheriffs, tenants, and vassals.

The Court of Exchequer was created to administer revenue collection and the control of expenditure following the Norman Conquest in 1066. It was revised substantially and strengthened around 1110 under Henry I (1100–35), the main features of which are described in the *Dialogus de Scaccario*, the seminal twelfth-century treatise on the operations of the Exchequer.[1] Although previous Saxon administration had some broadly similar features, for example in the work of sheriffs and the day-to-day custody and accounting for receipts, stricter Norman imperatives required new measures and more complex organization that were swiftly put in place.

Origins of the Exchequer

There continues to be some uncertainty as to whether the Exchequer was introduced from Normandy or whether its operations were developed in

[1] The two earliest copies of the *Dialogus* are held in the Public Record Office. Both are illuminated manuscripts produced in the thirteenth century. The earliest copy is contained in the Red Book of the Exchequer and the slightly later version in the Black Book of the Exchequer.

England and then re-exported to Normandy. Poole concluded that, certainly on the introduction of improved procedures, the process was from England to Normandy.[2] The *Dialogus* states, however, that the Exchequer 'is said to have begun with King William's Conquest and to have borrowed its constitution from the Exchequer of Normandy'.[3] Historian Thomas Madox also favoured a Norman origin.[4] Further anecdotal support for the 'Normandy first' school is the reported presence of a tablet on the old Exchequer building at Caen proudly declaring it to be 'Le père de l'échiquier à Londres' (the father of the London Exchequer). Nevertheless, by 1176 the Norman Exchequer was in such disarray that two officials of the English Exchequer, Richard of Ilchester and Richard Fitz-Nigel, had to be sent to address the problems and reorganize it on more modern and efficient lines. Whichever came first, there were certainly exchequers at London, Caen, and Rouen in the early part of the twelfth century, working in close liaison and with some sharing of staff.

The strengthening of the Exchequer in the twelfth century was the direct result of pressures to provide efficient controls and better accountability for the increasingly varied financial dealings between the King and his subjects. Strong financial systems and procedures were particularly important to deal with the complications arising from the emergence of a monetary economy. Originally, many of the debts and duties owed to the King were discharged by a variety of payments in kind. These ranged from military service and the raising of troops to the supply of meat, corn, cloth, accommodation, and household and sporting necessities demanded by the King on his travels throughout the country. However, such services, though useful to an itinerant court, became increasingly inconvenient to a more settled administration. More importantly, payments in kind provided less flexible resources to a King engaged in foreign wars and needing substantial liquid funds to meet the heavy costs of recruiting and maintaining a mercenary army over long periods. The *Dialogus* clearly records the growing pressures to switch from payment in kind to payment in cash. It emphasizes in particular that 'when King Henry was engaged in suppressing armed rebellion in distant places overseas, coined money became of the utmost necessity to him for that purpose'.[5] Commutation of payments in kind to rents, fees, and other cash payments made it essential to reorganize the Exchequer and strengthen its staffing and procedures. The successful completion of this task was largely the achievement of Roger le Poer, Bishop of Salisbury.

A Norman from Caen, Roger le Poer was Chancellor and Justiciar under Henry I. He was recognized as the most knowledgeable and skilful administrator of his day. It is believed that he first came to the attention of the ruling

---

[2] Poole, 1912, pp. 57–69. [3] *Dialogus de Scaccario*, p. 14.
[4] Madox, 1796, pp. 177–83. [5] *Dialogus de Scaccario*, pp. 40–1.

powers when, as a little-known parish priest, he impressed Henry, then Duke of Normandy, by saying the quickest Mass he had ever heard. Recognizing that such a man was no time-waster, Henry promptly made him his chief adviser. Roger served as Justiciar for more than thirty years, during which time he transformed the Exchequer into a body of trained administrators, working to consistent procedures and standards, thereby creating the first recognizable civil service. He was also the uncle of Nigel, Bishop of Ely, and thus the great-uncle of Richard Fitz-Nigel, author of the *Dialogus*. This was a line of descent to which Richard Fitz-Nigel made frequent and proud reference.

Commutation, however, did not involve an immediate or total relinquishment of payments in kind. The power of tradition ensured that a number of smaller services and tributes were retained for many years on historical or token grounds. The importance of hunting, for example, was reflected in gifts of hounds, hawks, and falcons to the King and his Court.[6] Within the King's household other continuing services included 'the supply of a cook for a year for the King's kitchen'. Similarly, the King's Treasurer received an annual gift of 'two barrels of wine and 200 apples'. The longevity of some token payments was evident in the annual rent which was paid from 1235 until the nineteenth century by the mayor and citizens of London in the form of six horseshoes and nails for a piece of land in London's Strand, originally used for a forge.[7] Until recent years the Comptroller and Auditor General (C&AG) received each year a haunch of venison from the culling of deer in the royal parks.[8] Even where services in kind were replaced by commutation there was sometimes an echo of their original nature in the names of the fees and taxes that instead were levied. For example, scutage, from the Latin *scutum* or shield, was the fee paid to discharge a knight's former liability for personal military service. Other taxes such as hidage and carucage similarly reflected their agricultural origins and medieval systems of land tenure.[9]

Although the trend of medieval financial business was to replace feudal obligations to provide labour-service by a commensurate payment in money, there were periods when labour was the more valuable commodity. The trend towards commutation and monetary discharge was then slowed down or even reversed. For example, the agricultural boom and expanding markets of the

---

[6] *Dialogus de Scaccario*, pp. 121–2 refers specifically to 'royal birds promised to the King for various reasons, that is hawks or falcons' and deals with their treatment at some length.

[7] *Public Income and Expenditure 1688–1869*, pp. 347–9.

[8] The haunch of venison was for many years shared out amongst senior staff, and was known inevitably as 'passing the buck'. C&AG Sir John Bourn later democratized the arrangement by hosting an annual 'Venison Lunch' to recognize special achievements by individual junior members of staff.

[9] Hides and carucates, both measures of land of around 100 acres, were the basis for several taxes and were calculated as being the area that could be ploughed in a normal farming season by the standard team of eight oxen. By the same etymology, a 'bovate' was one-eighth of a carucate.

thirteenth century offered the King and his Lords opportunities for greater profits if they could reduce costs of production. This created pressures to exploit to the full the free labour of their peasants instead of hiring extra labour to farm an increased arable acreage, particularly in the heavily-farmed lands of the Midlands and the south-east of England, where the need for extra labour was greatest and labour-service therefore more valuable. However, the extent of the movement towards commutation depended on economic and social circumstances in different parts of the country.[10]

The continuing theme and primary concern of the Exchequer was to maximize the revenues raised on the assessed rents and produce of the King's estates, the services of his tenants and vassals, and the activities carried out on his behalf or at his favour. Inevitably this involved looking beyond simple accounting to examining questions of economical husbandry, efficient management, and effective stewardship. Such 'value for money' concerns were woven into the management and control of the King's business at a number of levels. The importance of land and property made it natural that the primary examination of the sheriffs and other accounting officers before the Barons of the Exchequer should be conducted on the premise that they were expected to be good managers of the King's resources as well as reliable accountants. Value for money was also pursued as a matter of course in more detailed day-to-day matters. For example, the building accounts of Henry III (1216–72) record that in 1265 William the Hermit was to be paid one mark for whitewashing the walls of the Exchequer 'by task', that is at a fixed-price lump sum, a less costly method than traditional payment at daily rates.

Emphasis by the Exchequer on the management of the lands and properties that were the bedrock of the King's revenues and wealth meant that the natural starting point for medieval accountability was the detailed inventory of possessions and rents chronicled in the Domesday Book. For centuries the Domesday Book was so important in Norman financial administration and, thus, in the workings of the Exchequer, that it was officially lodged at the Exchequer as a continuing source of reference. Only in the eighteenth century was it moved to Westminster Abbey, and then in 1859 to the Public Record Office. Although over time the values of individual estates quoted in the Domesday Book became out of date, it was still a valuable source of reference. This was particularly so on questions of land distribution and ownership, which remained the ongoing basis of most taxation and associated labour services. Although this information also became unreliable with changes in title and the splitting up of estates, the Domesday Book remained of continuing interest and relevance to litigants, historians, and others. The Domesday

---

[10] See Myers, 1971, pp. 58–9.

Book's strong links with the Exchequer makes it particularly appropriate that the first reference to the name 'Domesday' is contained in the *Dialogus*, which describes William the Conqueror's survey in suitably apocalyptic terms:

> It is metaphorically called by the native English, 'Domesday', that is the Day of Judgement. For as the sentence of that strict and terrible last account cannot be evaded by any skilful subterfuge, so when this book is appealed to on those matters which it contains, its sentence cannot be quashed or set aside with impunity. That is why we have called the book 'the Book of Judgement', not because it contains decisions on various difficult points, but because its decisions, like those of the Last Judgement, are unalterable.[11]

The emphasis on judicial finality was not just extravagant language. Rather, it was central to the processes of the Exchequer, the status of its decisions, and the exactitude of its accounting records. The Exchequer was a high court, part of the Curia Regis, and its ultimate discharge of those accountable before it were documents of record with full legal authority. The decisions of the Barons of the Exchequer on rights, duties, debts, and acquittances were given in the King's name and were rarely open to challenge or appeal. The *Dialogus* confirmed that 'these records and judgements may not be impugned',[12] adding that:

> The Exchequer has its own rules. They are not arbitrary but rest on the decisions of great men; and if they are observed scrupulously, individuals will get their rights and Your Majesty will receive in full the revenues due to the Treasury, which your generous hand, obeying your noble mind, may spend to the best advantage.[13]

The author of the *Dialogus*, Richard Fitz-Nigel, was appointed as Treasurer of the Exchequer around 1158 when only twenty-eight years old. Richard was the illegitimate son of Nigel, Bishop of Ely, who was himself an influential former Treasurer and later a Baron of the Exchequer. Medieval nepotism made it inevitable that Nigel should use his influence and pay £400 to purchase the treasurership for his son. Richard's good fortune was to be a member of 'the most characteristic official family of his time',[14] whose stranglehold on the key Exchequer posts was established under Henry I. When Stephen became King (1135–54), and Roger of Salisbury was Justiciar, his son Richard succeeded him as Chancellor and his nephew Nigel became Treasurer. Another nephew with great influence was Arnold, Bishop of Lincoln. When the family fell from favour under Stephen, the imprisonment of Roger and persecution of his family helped to bring Stephen's reign to an end. Though the family's fortunes later recovered they never regained their former eminence and political power.

---

[11] *Dialogus de Scaccario*, pp. 63–4.   [12] *Dialogus de Scaccario*, p. 3.
[13] *Dialogus de Scaccario*, p. 3.   [14] Poole, 1912, p. 6.

The interweaving of Church and state meant that regular ecclesiastical advancement was the standard accompaniment to high administrative service. Richard Fitz-Nigel therefore served as Treasurer of the Exchequer at the same time as he rose steadily up the Church hierarchy, becoming successively Archdeacon of Ely, Canon of St Paul's, Dean of Lincoln, and finally Bishop of London in 1189. He continued to serve as Treasurer until his forty-year tenure ended with his death in 1198. This ecclesiastical pedigree was not reflected in any religious other-worldliness; the *Dialogus* is a severely practical treatise whose God was essentially Mammon. Underlining St Matthew's dictum that 'Where your treasure is, there shall your heart be also', Richard made his pragmatism very clear:

> Power indeed rises and falls as portable wealth flows or ebbs. However questionable may be or appear to be the origin or the method of acquisition of wealth, those whose duty is to guard it have no excuse for slackness, but must give anxious care to its collection, preservation and distribution. Sound and wise schemes take effect earlier through the agency of money, and apparent difficulties are smoothed away by it, as though by skilful negotiation. Money is no less indispensable in peace than in war. The glory of princes consists in noble action in peace and war alike, but it excels in those in which is made a happy bargain, the price being temporal and the reward everlasting.[15]

Although receipt and issue of funds was the main day-to-day business of the Exchequer, accountability was its fundamental responsibility. Richard Fitz-Nigel, despite his concern for financial rectitude, and his repeated endorsement of detailed and traditional Exchequer procedures, was well aware that the needs of true accountability could not be secured by mere arithmetic and the niceties of accounting. He pointed out in one of the most quoted passages in the *Dialogus* that:

> It is easy enough to set down the sum due, and to set underneath for comparison the sums paid, and find by subtraction whether the debt has been paid or what is the balance due. But when complicated questions arise ... the King's assessors are among the greatest and most prudent in the realm, whether clerks or courtiers. *For the highest skill at the Exchequer does not lie in calculations, but in judgements of all kinds.*[16] (emphasis added)

'Course of the Exchequer'

The term 'exchequer' referred specifically to the twice-yearly process of accountability and its supporting procedures, known as the 'course' of the

---

[15] *Dialogus de Scaccario*, Dedication.   [16] *Dialogus de Scaccario*, p. 15.

Exchequer. Events and decisions were thus described as having taken place 'at the Exchequer of such and such a year'. In straightforward physical terms, the name derived from the chequered cloth covering the table on which the regular counts of revenue were displayed and around which the Head Justiciar, the Barons of the Exchequer, and their supporting officers sat in judgement on the sheriffs and other accounting officers appearing before them to seek acquittance. Set on a rectangular table some ten feet by five feet, with 'a rim round it about four finger-breadths in height to prevent anything set on it from falling off',[17] this dark, specially ruled cloth used by the official known as the Calculator served as an abacus on which counters in various lines confirmed the progress of the count to those witnessing it. This physical demonstration by display and simultaneous calling over was an important element of public accountability in an age when some of those attending could be unskilled in the calculations involved.

The use of the abacus, with the empty column available to represent zero, made the addition and subtraction more intelligible to the layman since it avoided the clumsiness and complication involved in strict Roman arithmetic. Although the *Dialogus* describes the calculation as 'a confusing and laborious process', it adds that 'without it the business of the Exchequer would be interminable, or nearly so'. Nevertheless, the deft hands and quick arithmetic of the Calculator brought its own risks and the *Dialogus* warns that 'he must take care that his hand does not outrun his tongue or vice versa'.[18] Though the function of the counters on the Exchequer table was strictly utilitarian, their progress around the squares in ritual and predetermined moves has provoked analogies with chess. Asked why the court was called the 'exchequer' Richard Fitz-Nigel replies:

> I can think, for the moment, of no better reason than that it resembles a chess-board. For as on the chess-board the men are arranged in ranks, and move or stand by definite rules and restrictions, some pieces in the foremost rank and others in the foremost position. Again, just as on a chess-board, battle is joined between two kings; here too the struggle takes place, and battle is joined, mainly between two persons, the Treasurer and the sheriff who sits at his account, while the rest sit by as judges to see and decide.[19]

These judicial processes in the Upper Exchequer were accompanied by more utilitarian activities in the Lower Exchequer, or Exchequer of Receipt. Here money was paid in, counted, and entered in various parchment rolls, and wooden tallies cut and issued as receipts. The Lower Exchequer also paid out the amounts approved by the Upper Exchequer on behalf of the King, which

---

[17] *Dialogus de Scaccario*, p. 6. [18] *Dialogus de Scaccario*, pp. 24–5.
[19] *Dialogus de Scaccario*, p. 7.

were authorized by the issue of writs specifying the payee and the purposes for which the money was required. No funds could be released from the Exchequer without these express instructions. It was therefore one of the most significant privileges of the Justiciar, and confirmation of the King's personal trust, that he could authorize writs to be issued in the King's name, with his own as witness, or even in his own name. Writs were generally issued in the King's name when he was in England and in the Justiciar's name only when the King was abroad. This underlined the King's trust and the extent of the Justiciar's power, especially when it is remembered that Henry II (1154–89) was out of England for twenty-one years of the total thirty-five years of his reign.

The main Exchequer writs were those of *liberate, computate,* and *perdono.* Writs of *liberate* were for issues of cash to specified persons, carefully counted and witnessed. It was a quirk of Exchequer procedure that the payee was allowed to challenge the amount received only if he had not left the counting room; 'but if after fair warning he has passed the door of the Treasury, his application must be refused, however great a personage he may be, and however great his loss'.[20] This is the same idea as the modern notice 'Please check your change before leaving, for mistakes cannot afterwards be rectified'. Writs of *computate* were issued to allow those appearing before the Exchequer to claim credit for expenditure they had already incurred on the King's behalf. Writs of *perdono* authorized waiver of specified debts and acquittances or remissions of various other charges.

Throughout these processes the Upper and Lower Exchequers worked closely together: 'Both spring from the same root, because whatever is found in the Upper Exchequer to be due is paid in the Lower, and what is paid in the Lower is credited in the Upper'.[21] Despite its subordinate position, the Lower Exchequer had older pre-Norman roots, with some of its operations linked with those of earlier Saxon tallies. Certainly Richard Fitz-Nigel recognized that the term 'exchequer' and its methods of accounting were a relatively recent innovation, pointing out that 'where we now say "at the Exchequer" of such a year, they used to say "at the Tallies"'.[22] The Lower Exchequer also became ultimately the main focus of day-to-day financial business and accountability as the judicial character of the Upper Court of Exchequer, the development of its common law activities, and handling of personal actions moved it progressively over the centuries to become essentially a part of the main law court structure.

As the Lower Exchequer grew in power and influence it developed a growing range of professional and administrative responsibilities. This in turn spawned its own bureaucracy and the conduct of Exchequer business became increasingly complicated and time consuming, resulting in long delays. Inevitably

---

[20] *Dialogus de Scaccario,* p. 10. [21] *Dialogus de Scaccario,* p. 8.
[22] *Dialogus de Scaccario,* p. 7.

this provided opportunities for officials to benefit financially from their position. Consequently, those dealing with the growing army of Exchequer officials quickly discovered that cutting through the spreading web of inefficiency, and receiving prompt and favourable treatment, had to be accompanied by appropriate 'sweeteners'. Bribery and corruption became commonplace, involving almost everyone at the Exchequer, from the barons to the doorkeepers, with the result that poor customer service became an abiding characteristic of Exchequer business. The bruising and expensive experience of John Bell, a customs collector appearing before the Exchequer in the early fifteenth century, produced a heartfelt poetic complaint about the extensive gifts required to receive favourable treatment, or indeed any treatment at all. Bell is forced to reward the Cutter of Tallies and his clerks, 'otherwise their quills will break and their inkwells run dry so that they cannot attend to business until given a suitable bribe'.[23] His verses warned that:

> Oh the Court of the Exchequer is a wondrous place as I shall truly tell. There are a thousand extortioners there... the Auditor who is a demon unless propitiated with large gifts... and make yourself agreeable to the Chancellor by means of a gift... and don't forget the Keeper of the counter-roll sitting nearby for he too is a great lover of gifts... and the writing clerks are more attentive to money than to prayer, for truly all the clerks are willing to do little without gifts.[24]

The origins of modern financial posts such as the Chancellor of the Exchequer and the Comptroller and Auditor General (C&AG) are to be found not amongst the barons who were the King's principal appointees and judges in the Upper Exchequer but within the lower orders of supporting clerks and officials, including those in the Lower Exchequer. As the judicial functions of the Upper Exchequer were separated from the Lower Exchequer's executive and administrative responsibilities, these subordinate officials were increasingly called upon to discharge important responsibilities in the absence of their masters. As a result, in time they became high officials in their own right.[25] The post of Comptroller General of the Exchequer is normally traced back to 1314, the first identified date for the establishment of permanent auditors within the Exchequer. Thomas Madox, the earliest historian of the Exchequer, records that:

> In process of time there were officers at the Exchequer who were called *Auditores Computorum Scaccarii*. In the reign of King Edward II, certain clerks were appointed

---

[23] Gladwin, 1974, pp. 256–60.   [24] Gladwin, 1974, pp. 256–60.

[25] The movement of the Upper Exchequer towards a wider and more independent judicial role had developed substantially by the end of the fourteenth century and was almost fully in place by Tudor times. (See Poole, Chapter VIII, and Myers, 1971, p. 45.) The Court of Exchequer was finally translated into a division of the High Court of Justice in 1875 and is now merged in the Queen's Bench Division.

to audit the foreign accounts in the Exchequer, who seem to have been settled officers, because on the death or removal of one of them another was put into his place.[26]

Madox, when making specific reference to the appointment of a certain Richard de Luda 'in the 7th year of King Edward II', that is in 1314, concluded that such posts 'were officers then newly introduced. ... Before that time particular Exchequer transactions were usually audited by the Justiciar or some of the Barons, or by other persons specially appointed by them or by the King.'[27] The line of such officials can be traced back further still, to the special appointment of Master Thomas Brown by Henry II around 1160.[28]

Driven back to England by intrigues at the court of King Roger II of Sicily, where he had been a trusted financial adviser, Thomas Brown was appointed to maintain a third roll and record of business to provide a further personal and independent check for the King on the two separate rolls maintained simultaneously on behalf of the Treasurer and the Chancellor. The *Dialogus* emphasizes that this extra control was introduced 'contrary to the ancient constitution of the Exchequer' and on the biblical premise that 'a threefold cord is not easily broken'.[29] To discharge his special responsibilities on the King's behalf, Thomas Brown had a clerk in the Lower Exchequer 'who sits next the Treasurer's Clerk, and has full freedom to take notes of all the receipts and expenses of the Treasury'.[30] As functions developed and shifted over the years, this clerk became ultimately the Auditor of the Receipt, one of several posts that were merged in 1834 into the office of Comptroller General of the Exchequer. In 1867 this post was in turn merged into the present post of C&AG. This direct descent from the operations of the medieval Receipt is reflected in the C&AG's full title of 'Comptroller General of the Receipt and Issue of Her Majesty's Exchequer and Auditor General of Public Accounts'. The title 'comptroller' rather than 'controller' reflects an old error arising from the assumption that the name was somehow derived from the French 'compte' or account. Instead, the 'comptroller' was the 'contrarotulator', an official who keeps a counter-roll as a double check on transactions.[31]

---

[26] Madox, 1796, p. 290.   [27] Madox, 1796, p. 290.

[28] Thomas Brown's title of 'Magister' emphasized his importance and authority. Hoskin and Macve (1986, pp. 113–15) view the creation of his special post and its monitoring function, both originating in the English Exchequer, as reflecting developments in medieval 'power-knowledge' relationships that were spreading outwards from universities and their processes of disciplined examination, and were to lead in time into new accounting and audit methodologies.

[29] Ecclesiastes 4:12.   [30] *Dialogus de Scaccario*, p. 35.   [31] Poole, 1912, p. 9.

Accountability of Sheriffs

Examination of Accounts

Accountability in the medieval Exchequer was centred around the formal periodic examinations of the sheriffs, who were the King's principal agents for the management and collection of the revenues of the various counties. The examination was essentially a confrontation, with the Barons of the Upper and Lower Exchequer and their army of officials on the attacking side, while opposite them, on the defending side, sat the sheriff who was accompanied by his clerks armed with the accounts, tallies, documents, and explanations that he hoped would secure the final acquittance, or *quietus*, on which his financial, or even physical, wellbeing depended. This could be a bruising encounter.

The post of sheriff, originally 'shire reeve', had grown in importance during centuries of Saxon administration and was central to the management of local government well before the Norman Conquest. William I was content to allow this established system to continue largely unchanged when he realized how effective the arrangements were in meeting his key objective of maximizing his revenues. One of his first moves was to secure the allegiance of his sheriffs by filling the posts with his Norman followers, thereby rewarding them for their part in his military victories. Only under Henry I were those of Saxon blood gradually allowed back into the fold, though later most of King John's sheriffs were of English heritage. The office of sheriff has always been a formal royal appointment, with the name of the chosen individual 'pricked' with a silver bodkin from a list of potential appointees submitted by the Privy Council. The process of 'pricking' is said to have originated with Queen Elizabeth I (1558–1603) who was one day embroidering in her garden when approached with the list and, unwilling to go inside, simply pricked the names of the new sheriffs with her needle.

The bulk of the King's treasure was originally stored at Winchester, where for a time extensive Exchequer hearings were held and, less frequently, at York. By the middle of the twelfth century the regular sessions were almost always held at Westminster. Richard Fitz-Nigel introduces the *Dialogus* 'sitting at a turret window overlooking the Thames'.[32] The Court of Exchequer originally operated within Westminster Hall itself but subsequently moved to adjacent buildings. The main location was on the east side of Westminster Hall, as part of a two-storey complex next to New Palace Yard and close to the medieval line of the Thames. The Upper Exchequer occupied the first floor and the Exchequer of Receipt was directly below. The Upper Exchequer later

---

[32] *Dialogus de Scaccario*, p. 5.

moved elsewhere while the Receipt continued to occupy buildings in this same location until the 1820s, in the process giving its name to a nearby coffee house.

The Exchequer year ran from Michaelmas to Michaelmas, that is from September to August, with various mid-term breaks and holidays. The broad pattern was for the sheriff or his representative to make a preliminary or interim settlement, or 'proffer', at Easter in respect of half the agreed revenue for which he was to be held directly accountable, with the full account at Michaelmas. This full account was set in hand by a formal 'Summons of the Pipe' issued by the officers of the Exchequer. The sheriff was always required to appear in person to obtain his final acquittance for the year. The imperious form of the official summons clearly underlined the direct personal nature of the sheriff's accountability, and the depth of his impending examination. He was summoned in the following terms:

> Henry, King of the English, to such-and-such a sheriff, greeting. See that, as you love yourself and all that you have, you be at the Exchequer at such a place on the morrow of Michaelmas, or on the morrow of Low Sunday, and have with you whatsoever you owe of the old farm or of the new and in particular these debts underwritten (then listed). And have all these with you in money, tallies, writs and acquittances, or they will be deducted from your farm. Witness so-and-so, at such a place, at the Exchequer.[33]

The importance and authority of this summons was such that it could not be issued if sullied with any alteration or erasure. Any mistake in drawing it up required the preparation of a fresh writ. As the summons was an open document this also safeguarded its integrity against any attempted deletion or alteration by the sheriff. However, the *Dialogus* warned that it would be:

> a proof of madness [for the sheriff] to expose himself wilfully to such grave risks, especially as he could not thus annul the debts to the King. For all the debts included in the summons have been previously noted and are kept on record; so that even with the sheriff's connivance, nobody could be freed from them by this method.[34]

The sheriff's appearance was not just a matter of form or procedural nicety. He was only too well aware that when he came before the Exchequer he was delivering himself into physical custody. He was detained at the King's disposal until he had satisfied the Barons of the Exchequer as to the full and proper discharge of his responsibilities. The wording of the summons was a firm threat to the sheriff: 'Your absence, whoever you are who receive the summons, unless it can be excused by necessary causes within the legal

---

[33] *Dialogus de Scaccario*, p. 70. [34] *Dialogus de Scaccario*, p. 74.

definition, will endanger your head.'[35] Similarly, the writs issued for the recovery of the King's debts further emphasized that the sheriff was to pursue them 'on penalty of his body and goods and of the King's wrath'.

At his final account for the year, the sheriff had ranged around him the full forces of public accountability, with the formal examination being conducted by the Treasurer and other officials. The Barons of the Exchequer were also present to give final judgements as necessary. The sheriff was fully aware of his direct personal responsibilities and knew that he had to be well versed in all the financial details of his stewardship. He had to be ready with the answers and explanations on which his future position and personal safety depended. Failure to appear on exactly the due date, with all the appropriate documents, brought heavy penalties. These included seizure of his estates or imprisonment. Breaching the network of obscure Exchequer regulations, or too much hesitation or evasion in his responses, were also punishable by instant hefty fines, particularly if the barons hearing his account were in an unforgiving mood.

In many respects, in both form and substance but with less stringent penalties, there are clear parallels between this medieval tableau and the scene facing today's departmental accounting officers appearing before the Public Accounts Committee (PAC). The nervousness of some modern accounting officers was also shared by their medieval predecessors. One notable exception was the experienced Gilbert of Surrey, sheriff of Surrey, Cambridgeshire, and Huntingdonshire. Of his appearances at the Exchequer in the middle of Henry I's reign it was recorded that:

> When the sheriffs from all over England assembled at the Exchequer they trembled to a man from their extreme fear, Gilbert alone arrived fearlessly and cheerfully and, when called by the receivers of money, came up to them straight away and sat down brisk and composed, the only one amongst them to be so.[36]

The central, though not necessarily the largest, part of the sheriff's accountability was the collection of rents and other payments due for the King's demesne lands and estates and other properties. Sometimes the sheriff paid these over on the basis of the individual rents collected, although until the later part of the thirteenth century they were more generally 'let to farm' to the sheriff at a composited fixed sum. The gross annual amount for which he was then accountable was the 'farm of the county' or '*corpus comitatus*'. Once he had delivered that predetermined sum he was free to pocket the often substantial difference between the actual rents he was able to extract and the amounts to be remitted to the Exchequer. It was this potentially lucrative arrangement that made the post of sheriff so financially attractive.

---

[35] *Dialogus de Scaccario*, p. 79.   [36] Original source quoted in Gladwin, 1974, p. 52.

The arrangement didn't always work in the sheriff's favour. Sometimes the King would arbitrarily and without notice increase the amount of the farm because his funds were low or his expenses high or simply from envy of the rich pickings in the shires. For example, Henry II in the 1150s raised the farms of several counties by more than 50 per cent. Other monarchs followed suit and added annual increments as well. The sheriff could also suffer as a result of delays in adjusting his liability to take into account any lands sold off or otherwise disposed of by the King, or for various other reductions in the rents to be collected. Determined not to suffer financially, the sheriff promptly passed responsibility for countering the impact of these measures down the line to his underlings. Inevitably the extra funds were extracted forcibly from the defenceless peasants and other taxpayers. Some sheriffs also sold off parts of their 'farm' to other collectors who, in turn, extracted a further return. In these circumstances, the scope for oppression, bribery, and corruption was almost limitless.

Abuse of their position by the sheriffs and their officers was an ever-present reality throughout the twelfth and thirteenth centuries, the main period of their financial and judicial powers. Occasionally an upsurge of concern over shortfalls in the King's finances, or flagrant misappropriation or malfeasance, prompted remedial action against the sheriffs. Public reaction and opposition to particular taxes or arbitrary impositions could also bring matters to a head and prompt royal intervention. All taxes were naturally unwelcome but, by their nature or by the oppressive manner of their implementation, some taxes demonstrated a special capacity to provoke resentment and unrest. Poll taxes in particular were widely perceived as discriminatory and regressive and were one of the causes of the violent response of the Peasants' Revolt in 1381.

Abuses of Office

Oppressing the peasants was something that did not bother the King or his officials. Abusing your accountability to the King himself was quite another matter. Periodic royal purges of corrupt, inefficient, or recalcitrant sheriffs were therefore hazards of the post. For example, when Henry II returned to England in 1170 from one of his long periods abroad he held a council at Westminster at the time of the sheriffs' Easter proffers and announced their entire dismissal pending full inquiry into their conduct. The resulting 'Inquest of Sheriffs', widened to cover all aspects of local administration and the work of all those handling public money, was conducted by independent barons over the next few weeks. Eventually, the evidence produced led to the permanent expulsion of twenty-two out of the twenty-nine sheriffs originally dismissed. The vacancies were then filled with selected Exchequer officials, whose financial skills during the rest of Henry's reign successfully built up the royal revenues.[37]

Despite the sanctions imposed and improvements introduced, the effects of occasional investigations diminished gradually over the years. By 1274 a rising tide of inefficiency and corruption had once more brought the royal finances to such a perilous level that, on his return to England after a four-year absence, King Edward I (1272–1307) was similarly forced to appoint a commission of inquiry into the discharge of the country's financial and judicial administration. This was known as the 'Ragman Quest' because of the ragged and dishevelled appearance of the commissioners' records as a result of their winter travels around the country.[38] Hundreds of sheriffs and other royal officials were criticized and charged with corruption and abuse of their position. Although this time there were fewer immediate and penal sanctions against individuals there were, for a period at least, some wider-ranging organizational and other benefits.[39]

Despite the uncertainties surrounding the post of sheriff, the financial rewards remained a magnet for greedy men. Accordingly, very large fees were paid to secure access to the personal profits to be made. The incentives to become sheriff of a rich and profitable county meant that the sums offered to secure the post were often several times higher than the amount of the annual farm. The worldly temptations of tax collection extended even to those senior members of the Church who 'loved their purse better than their bible'. In 1194, for example, the Archbishop of York topped all other offers with an enormous bid of 3,000 marks to become the sheriff of Yorkshire. He was the first archbishop to buy the position of sheriff, although several bishops had previously done so. In some cases the clergy's greed continued to outrun their honesty and they had to face the ignominy of being summoned before the Exchequer for failing for several years to pay the sums they had originally bid to become sheriffs. The Gadarene rush of the rich and powerful continued until the post of 'farmer' sheriff started to be phased out with the introduction of salaried 'custodian' sheriffs in the latter part of the thirteenth century.

A similar wide-ranging and oppressive system of tax farming continued in France until brought to a bloody end in 1791 during the Revolution. It was controlled by the *Ferme Générale*, a body of rich and powerful men who paid annual amounts to purchase from the government the power to impose and collect a wide range of dues and taxes. Heavy and increasing taxes and oppressive collection methods made them widely detested. Their most notorious

---

[37] Gladwin, 1974, pp. 78–80.
[38] See Gladwin, 1974 (Chapter VI) for details of the Ragman Quest.
[39] Gladwin, 1974, pp. 179–86.

imposition was the introduction of the *gabelle*, or salt tax, which was based on presumed rather than actual levels of consumption and set at artificially high levels. This and other taxes impacted particularly upon the poor, with the nobility, clergy, and other privileged groups being exempt.

During the Revolution the *Ferme Générale* was suppressed and its members arrested and sent for trial. A prominent and enthusiastic *fermier* was Antoine Laurent Lavoisier, the father of modern chemistry, whose energetic pursuit of enormous profits provided him with funds to pursue his research. His fame meant that Lavoisier became a special target of the revolutionary mob. Despite his many services to France, and the pleas of his friends, his taxation activities and the personal enmity of Jean Marat, whose scientific credentials Lavoisier had mocked, led to his execution during the Terrors in 1794. He went calmly to the guillotine, noting philosophically: 'It will save me from the troubles of old age, and I shall die in full possession of my faculties.' His death confirmed Edmund Burke's warning that: 'To tax and to please, no more than to love and to be wise, is not given to men.'[40]

As the gross amount of the sheriff's farm was largely fixed in advance and specified at the head of the summons, the immediate business of the Exchequer hearing was to identify and allow the various expenditures and expenses claimed by the sheriff to offset the amount for which he was formally accountable and, thus, after taking into account his Easter 'proffer', to arrive at the net sum to be remitted or the amount he was owed. Increasingly the sheriff was also held accountable for the collection of a range of other demands and impositions. These included the substantial sums from fines and fees arising from the King's prerogatives or imposed by the courts. There was also a wide range of casual revenues passing through the sheriff's hands. For all these 'foreign' amounts he was accountable in full and in detail, outside the terms of his farm. The range of financial matters enforced or otherwise handled by the sheriff was therefore extensive and complex. The rents from royal lands were only the starting point. These were constantly added to by estates that fell to the King by escheats, where owners died without heirs or were convicted of felony. Vacant churches, bishoprics, and abbeys could also come to the King. In principle the revenues from escheated estates and ecclesiastical property accrued only temporarily, yet they were often deliberately kept vacant for many years to enable the King to secure the income.

There were also reliefs and aids granted to the King for specific purposes, and general and special taxes such as scutage, carucage, and Danegeld. Fees, termed fines, were payable for many activities such as approving wardships and marriages, and granting charters. Fines, termed amercements, and other

---

[40] Edmund Burke, *On American Taxation* (1775).

penalties were imposed not only for larger crimes but also for breaches of the multitude of rules and regulations surrounding everyday medieval business. Many of these impositions continued to reflect the dominance of agriculture in the economy. For example, the importance attached to protecting the royal forests and their hunting and other rights was reflected in 'assarts' and 'pru-prestures' imposed as financial penalties for infringing on the forests and clearing land for cultivation. Commerce was also being brought into the tax net, and charges linked with land and property were in time increasingly supported by taxes on income and chattels, based on various proportions of their assessed value. Aids of this kind were also particularly attractive to the King because large sums of cash could be realized relatively quickly.

Particular wealthy groups were also targeted. For example, heavy and wide-ranging taxes were levied on the Jews to such an extent that a special section of the Exchequer, the *Scaccarium Judeorum*, had to be set up to manage and account for them. The Jewish community and their businesses paid heavily for the King's special 'protection'. Individual wealthy Jews were also singled out. For example, the heavy taxes and other charges imposed on Aaron of Lincoln and the forfeiture of his estates led to a special sub-section of the Exchequer, the *Scaccarium Aaronis*, being set up to deal solely with his affairs.[41] The anti-Semitism involved was open and unambiguous. It was bluntly justi-fied on the basis that: 'As they fleeced the subjects of his realm, so the King fleeced them.'[42] Persecution, both physical and financial, continued until the Jews were expelled from England around 1290 when all their assets were promptly taken into the King's hands.

Throughout the Middle Ages the growing demands on the royal resources meant that the ingenuity of the King and his officials in devising new aids and taxes was almost endless. The array of taxes required a growing army of officials to administer and enforce them, and in time the sheriff was only one of the many administrators and collectors appointed to cope with the work. Customs officers in particular multiplied with the growth in inter-national trade. In addition to the sheriff's tax-collection responsibilities, large profits arose from his judicial and enforcement functions within the Hundred and shire courts. These were a key part of his responsibilities and powers for several centuries until the legal system was reorganized and a separate and powerful judiciary introduced. The sheriff was also generally responsible for law and order within the county. In particular, he was empowered to call on citizens to form the *posse comitatus*, or 'force of the county', to pursue and arrest felons and other lawbreakers. When the post of sheriff was later exported to the American colonies these law-enforcement

---

[41] Madox, 1796, pp. 190–1.   [42] Madox, 1796, Chapter VII.

functions became predominant. The iconic Hollywood image of the western sheriff riding out after the bad guys at the head of the town 'posse' is therefore directly following medieval English precedent.

Exchequer Controls

During the sheriff's examination the Exchequer officers carefully checked all his transactions against supporting writs, tallies, and vouchers, with the relevant additions and subtractions and changing position of the count displayed on the table. The main elements of the audit were at the same time meticulously set out in the Great Pipe Rolls, which were the full and final official record of Exchequer transactions and the sheriff's acquittance or the surplus or deficit to be met. The 'Pipe' derivation has been variously explained. The more pedestrian view is that the word simply reflected the cylindrical, pipe-like shape of a rolled-up parchment scroll. Poole, for example, insists that:

> The pipe roll is a roll of pipes, just as a pine wood is a wood of pines; and any fanciful interpretation, such as that which traces the name to the resemblance of the bulky roll to a pipe or cask of wine, or to the pipe or channel through which the King drew his revenue, must be dismissed as unhistorical.[43]

Sir Francis Bacon in 1598 referred to 'That office of Her Majesty's Exchequer which we, by a metaphor, do call the pipe...because the whole receipt is finally conveyed into it by the means of diverse small quills or pipes.' The Public Record Office later took a similar, but more grandiose, line by stating that the Pipe Office derived its name from the fancied resemblance of its functions to those of a pipe or conduit:

> For as water is conveyed from many fountains and springs by a pipe into the cistern of a house and from thence into the several offices of the same, so this golden and silver stream is drawn from several courts, as fountains of justice and springs of revenue, reduced and collected into one pipe and by that conveyed into the cistern of His Majesty's Receipt.[44]

The Lower Exchequer administered detailed procedures and controls for the custody and handling of cash, carrying out assays of coinage, recording receipts and payments in a variety of books and records and cutting tallies. These activities in time acquired a network of increasingly specialist officials to carry them out, which often degenerated into lucrative sinecures. Posts such as the Clerk of the Nichils, the Foreign Apposer, the Clerk of the Pipe, the Comptroller of the Pipe, the Surveyor of the Green Wax, the Rembrancer of

---

[43] Poole, 1912, p. 51.   [44] *A Guide to the Public Records*, 1908, p. 228.

the First Fruits and Tenths, Filacers, and the Clerk of the Estreats were mostly historical but expensive curiosities long before they were belatedly abolished, together with various subordinates, in the nineteenth century. The sheriffs accounts were reckoned in pounds and shillings, or in marks (13s. 4d.) or, rarely, in gold marks (£6), but the only Norman currency was the silver penny produced at more than fifty mints throughout England and, in theory at least, to a consistent weight and purity. In practice debasement of coinage was common, from poor control during manufacture, through wear and tear, by forgery or by deliberate clipping of the coinage.

Concern to protect trade from deterioration of the coinage prompted periodic attempts at reform, which included redesigned coinage and sanctions against counterfeiters, such as loss of the right hand or castration. Despite these measures the problems continued. Thus, rather than accepting money at its face value it became standard practice in Exchequer business to compensate for known or assumed deterioration in the coinage by making an appropriate deduction from the sums involved. Typically this was done by making the sheriff accountable '*ad scalam*', by discounting his payments into the Exchequer by a standard amount, generally at sixpence or a shilling in the pound. In some cases, either on certain classes of account or as a random check, or if there were particular grounds for suspicion, the amount to be deducted was arrived at after testing the purity of a sample of pennies by assay, a process termed 'blanching'. Assays to test the purity of the coinage had been carried out well before the Norman Conquest and settlement of debts on 'blanch farm' terms, despite a denial in the *Dialogus*, was mentioned in the Domesday Book. It was given added emphasis and became fully established when it was introduced as a standard practice in Exchequer business, probably starting around 1110, and linked with Roger of Salisbury's reforms.[45]

The discipline of discounting was designed primarily to protect the Exchequer. Its potential impact on the sheriff's profit also provided him with a strong encouragement to ensure that tighter standards and controls were imposed on money coiners and others at the local level. The care taken to safeguard the King's financial interests against a debased coinage was also implemented so as to provide reasonable protection for the sheriff. There were therefore elaborate sampling and assay procedures and controls, carefully witnessed and recorded.[46] It underlined the importance attached to these procedures that the Knight Silversmith (Pesour) and the Melter were regarded

---

[45] In practice there remained a mixture of approaches. Generally the trend over time was to move from accepting coins at face value towards verifying them by assay. (For further analysis see Johnson's introduction to the *Dialogus*, pp. xxxvii–xli.)

[46] *Dialogus de Scaccario*, pp. 36–9.

as important officials associated with the Upper rather than the Lower Exchequer.

The traditional importance of the medieval Exchequer assay is still commemorated today in the annual ceremony of the Trial of the Pyx at the Royal Mint, where the purity of the coinage is formally tested against a standard set of gold and silver coins. This is a direct re-enactment of the procedure described by Richard Fitz-Nigel in which the coins presented at the Exchequer were carefully weighed against 'the Exchequer pound'.[47] The custody and trial of these standard coins, and indeed other standard weights and measures, remained an Exchequer responsibility until statutorily transferred to the Board of Trade by the Standards Act 1866. The Pyx Chamber within the Exchequer, near Westminster Abbey, was also the scene of a massive break-in and theft of the King's treasure in 1303, the first of only two recorded thefts throughout its history. The Treasury was then holding the proceeds of a tax on every ninth lamb and ninth fleece, imposed by Edward I to provide funds to fight the Scots, together with jewels and other treasure.

The enormous sum of £100,000 was taken in the theft as well as other items of immense value. The culprits were found to be eleven monks from Westminster Abbey, who were charged together with assorted servants and accomplices, including goldsmiths employed to melt down the plate. Having planned the robbery for more than four months, when they broke through the walls they were so unprepared for the volume of treasure that they left a great deal behind and failed properly to conceal what they removed. The second recorded theft took place in 1729, when the chest of one of the Tellers was broken into and £4,000 stolen. This time the culprits were not found, nor was the money ever recovered. None of the thieves involved in these two cases appeared to have been dissuaded by the tradition that the white 'leather' that covered the studded door of the Pyx Chamber was in fact the skin of those flayed for sacrilege and other crimes, and by custom used to line the doors of sacred treasuries as a warning to others.[48]

The Later Exchequer

The twelfth-century 'Course of the Exchequer', as described in the *Dialogus*, was simple in principle, although strains were developing. Business for many years remained relatively straightforward and orderly while it was conducted largely in cash terms and was centred on revenues and expenditure that were

---

[47] *Dialogus de Scaccario*, pp. 7, 11.
[48] For a full account see *Public Income and Expenditure 1688–1869*, pp. 343–5.

reasonably stable. During the thirteenth century, and increasingly thereafter, Exchequer operations became more varied and more complex. This was partly the result of changes in the medieval economy as domestic and international trade increased and the potential for a variety of taxes on goods and customs duties rose accordingly. The move away from feudal revenues based on land and property brought in the interests and concerns of a rich and powerful merchant class alongside the traditional powers of the nobles, magnates, and the Church. These centres of power shifted as the King surrendered, recovered, and again lost elements of his prestige and financial powers due to a persistent shortage of funds. The course of financial business was directly affected by the terms that the King could arbitrarily or unilaterally impose on the country, or by the conditions the nobles and burgesses could instead demand from him as the price for their aid.

Given fluctuations in resources and in funding, the complications of international and domestic borrowing became an increasing feature of Exchequer business. For example, the Florentine merchant banking families of Frescobaldi, Bardi, and Peruzzi were extensive lenders to the first three King Edwards. The inability or unwillingness of Edward III (1327–77) to repay his heavy borrowings in the early years of the Hundred Years War (1337–1453) was the main cause of the bankruptcy of both the Bardi and the Peruzzi. When the Italian bankers then became wary and began to withdraw their support, Edward turned to borrowing heavily from rich Englishmen, aristocratic and otherwise, who were prepared to lend at high interest rates in return for trading concessions and monopolies in key commodities such as wool. The uncertainties and risks of the times meant that some of these financiers themselves ran into serious financial difficulties, often from being undercapitalized. Perhaps the most capable was William de la Pole, a Hull merchant of modest background who became an ambitious and successful entrepreneur and a Baron of the Exchequer. He was an extensive manipulator of the wool trade, both to enrich himself and to provide the King with funds for military operations. His business acumen and, despite some falls from grace, his continuing usefulness to the King enabled him and his descendants to build up extensive landed estates, with his son becoming Earl of Suffolk and his grandson Duke of Suffolk.

Although fourteenth-century England was still in many respects a feudal society it was also developing sophisticated financial mechanisms and a wealthy and influential business class. Customs duties were farmed out to wealthy merchants, similar to the way in which land revenues had been farmed out to the sheriffs. Future revenues were assigned in advance. Monopolies were created and sold and royal debts were traded at substantial discounts. All these changes impacted on Exchequer operations by broadening the range of the work and making business more complex in both substance and form.

Accounting became more complicated and technical, with obscure procedures deliberately helping to blur accountability.

It was not only the nobles, magnates, and Barons of the Exchequer such as William de la Pole who made great profits from public funding. At lower levels, Exchequer officials were prepared to lend their own moneys temporarily, at handsome interest rates, to meet payments falling due for which Exchequer funds were not immediately available. Sometimes these transactions were recorded as official loans. The position was blurred further by the accounting methods adopted, which were carefully designed to avoid disclosing penal rates of interest that would have been prohibited under canon laws against usury. For example, a loan of £1,000 would be recorded as £1,250 to allow for the 25 per cent interest that was being charged. Or a tally of assignment for £1,000 would be issued for which the lender paid the Exchequer only £800 cash down, later taking the balance as interest. There were also 'forced' loans when those entitled to a payment at the Exchequer could not at the time be paid because funds were short, requiring them to wait for their money.

Sometimes tallies of assignment and other payment instruments were discounted officially at the Exchequer. There was also a variety of other lenders, again including individual Exchequer officials, who were prepared to take these off the recipients' hands for a price. Such immediate cash-in-hand arrangements could be very attractive to someone who might otherwise have an uncertain wait for their money or be required to travel a long way to collect it. Transactions of this kind and the complicated bookkeeping they produced had become a regular feature of Exchequer accounting by the latter part of the fourteenth century,[49] thereby enhancing the power over the public purse strings of those well versed in Exchequer practices. Whilst it continued to profess its concern for the King's interests, the Exchequer became characterized by a determination to protect its own position and primacy in financial matters through a mastery of intricate detail and opposition to any change. The processes surrounding 'the ancient course and custom of the Exchequer' were defended fiercely and used as the excuse for keeping the formalities of medieval procedure obstinately in place until the middle of the nineteenth century.

The Exchequer's determination to protect its pre-eminence in financial business, and the position of its officials, was also demonstrated by its resolve to see off other challengers. For example, the extensive building works of Henry III made it useful to have payment facilities on the construction sites rather than passing everything through Westminster. As a result, several informal and largely independent 'exchequers' were set up. Persistent pressure

[49] An exhaustive analysis of these matters is contained in Steel's *The Receipt of the Exchequer 1377–1485*, summarized in his Introduction, pp. xxix–xl.

over several years finally succeeded in bringing these back under main Exchequer control, and the experiment was not repeated. From time to time there were other 'inferior' or 'subordinate' exchequers.[50] These appear, however, to have been temporary collection points in different parts of the country or for specific purposes, and represented no challenge to the Exchequer.

Ironically, a far more serious challenge to the Exchequer arose as a direct consequence of the Exchequer's own stranglehold on financial business, which by the end of the thirteenth century was sufficiently powerful to act as a brake on the King's activities. Pressing circumstances, the need for urgent action, and royal impatience were not always well served by the Exchequer's attachment to restricting and elaborate routine and its unwillingness to change its ways. While sometimes this recalcitrance was innocent, the excuse of needing to follow established procedures was also used deliberately by powerful voices within the Exchequer to frustrate or delay unwelcome royal initiatives and activities. Accordingly, the King began to look elsewhere for the speed, flexibility, and control he wanted. He found it by building up the strength and resources of the department of the Wardrobe within the royal household. Traditionally the King's Wardrobe, opening off his private apartments, was where the royal treasures were kept and it had become the best place to ensure privacy, confidentiality, and speed of business. The powers of the Wardrobe were thus progressively strengthened during the thirteenth century and by the time of Edward I substantial amounts of royal revenues and expenditure were bypassing the Exchequer. The Wardrobe was particularly involved in funding military operations and other urgent or secret matters. Many financial matters that had previously been authorized by the Great Seal within the Exchequer were now dealt with under the authority of the Privy Seal. The barons came to see that this development of the King's power was a direct threat to their own interests, driving them to re-establish their control over both administration and finance.

By 1315 the power of the barons and the relative weakness of the King had effectively overturned his arrangements for funding through the Wardrobe. Though the King subsequently made various attempts to re-create private funding operations by using the Wardrobe, or similar bodies, these were never really successful and came to an end under the severe financial pressures of the Hundred Years War. Although the great power of Richard II (1377–99) meant that at the end of the fourteenth century he was able to restore the influence of the Wardrobe, particularly in military administration, he had less need to build up its separate financial powers since he had by then established effective control over the Exchequer. However, the Exchequer's innate resistance

---

[50] Madox, 1796, pp. 190–1.

to change, and the delays from its reluctance to depart from traditional procedures, continued to threaten its prestige and authority. In a changing world these, over time, would bring further challenges to its financial primacy.

Conclusion

For centuries medieval accountability was effectively a one-way process. There was a complex framework of accountability to the King for the efficient and effective collection of his revenues but the King was not in turn held accountable for subsequent expenditures. The detailed accountability that was imposed on officers and officials at lower levels was not accompanied by what would later be regarded as basic features of wider parliamentary and public scrutiny. From around the middle of the thirteenth century knights representing the shires had from time to time been summoned by the King for consultation on the raising of specific taxes but there was not an established forum for consolidating such processes until Simon de Montfort's Parliament of 1265. In practice the early parliaments were not a consistent or effective vehicle for holding the King accountable on financial matters. Nor did they reflect a wider and more democratic public interest, for the early constitutional struggles were essentially between the vested interests of the King and the vested interests of the barons and magnates. They were part of the battle for power rather than a campaign conducted in the interests of the people as a whole.

The dominance of the King in financial matters could not last. Medieval monarchs, whatever their position in theory, were not in full autocratic control of policy, administration, and finance. Their powers grew and waned in line with other forces and interests. Shortage of funds, in particular, was often at the heart of these struggles, with a King in chronic financial difficulties frequently in a place where refusal or delay in granting funds was the single most effective weapon used against him. Even more important, if possible, was to secure control over the King's spending, especially on the Army, which was his main source of power. Increasing demands for accountability to Parliament to encompass both the raising of revenues and subsequent spending were inevitable. Yet, there were centuries still to go before such accountability became fully effective and an integral part of the democratic process.

3

Advance and Retreat in the Financial Supremacy of Parliament

'The perception of your new accountability might well impress you with an awful concern.'

J. Harris, *Great Teacher*

'No taxation without representation' was the clarion call of the American colonists fighting to free themselves from British rule in 1776. This basic constitutional demand echoed a similar call within England itself more than 450 years earlier. At the end of the thirteenth century the principle of *de tallagio non concedendo*, no taxation without consent, was being pressed on Edward I in reaction to his arbitrary imposition of increasingly heavy taxes to fund the mounting costs of his expeditions against France. Known as the 'Hammer of the Scots', Edward was also engaged in costly operations across the border, as well as facing the recurring expenditure of maintaining peace in an insurgent Wales and an intractable Ireland. He was being forced to yield more and more to the demands of the wider cross-section of interests that were being asked to provide the increasingly heavy resources needed to pursue these recurring conflicts. The King's continuing inability to 'live of his own' meant that his freedom to raise extra revenue and to spend without accountability was being eroded. The concept of appropriation, specifying the purposes for which funds granted by Parliament were to be used, was also being pressed.

In 1297 and again in 1306 financial pressures and the growing need to enlist parliamentary support forced a statutory promise from Edward I that, apart from some ancient aids and subsidies, no further aids or taxes would be imposed without the 'common assent' of the powerful voices of the nobles and burgesses within these early parliaments. Despite such measures, and associated royal assurances, it was always difficult to hold a medieval King to his promises after an immediate crisis was past and he regained a position of strength. Nor was he in a position to bind his successors. Assurances of this kind, even when expressed in statute, were acts of temporary expediency, not fundamental commitment. They were a convenient practice shaped and directed by events. Only much later would they be developed into a constitutional principle. Whilst there was the practical necessity for the King to give such undertakings it did not represent an irrevocable step towards the ascendancy of Parliament in financial control. Still less did it recognize any wider role for the people in such matters, for early parliaments were a focus for powerful vested interests rather than democratic and genuinely representative assemblies. Edward I's stated belief that 'what touches all should be approved by all' was strictly limited in practice. Nevertheless, the King's recognition of the need for 'common assent' within Parliament was a first step towards the emergence and naming of the House of Commons, with the raising of revenue becoming its financial prerogative. Securing a greater voice in royal spending would be the next prize.

Financial pressures on the King were far less significant under Edward II (1307–27) who, despite his excesses in other directions and his personal extravagances, did not burden either himself or the country with the crippling costs of long-standing military operations, particularly after the Scots decisively won their independence under Robert the Bruce at Bannockburn in 1314. Under Edward III (1327–77) not only the monarchy but also its external financial needs were brought to their lowest ebb. The costs of continuing military operations would, however, again drive the King into increasing financial dependence on the barons and magnates.

Accountability to Parliament

Introduction of Appropriation

The resurgence of operations against the Scots and, in 1337, the financial demands with the onset of the Hundred Years War, allowed Parliament to take its powers to a further stage by insisting upon a provision requiring appropriation of the funds raised. A statute of 1340, after granting Edward III additional funds by a two-year subsidy of a ninth part of a range of agricultural produce and business goods, added that: 'All the profits arising of the said aid . . . and other profits arising of the said realm of England . . . shall be put and spent upon the maintenance and the safeguard of our said realm of England, and of our wars in Scotland, France and Gascony, *and in no places elsewhere during the same wars*' (emphasis added). Similar provisions to strengthen control by putting a time limit on taxation and, significantly, by appropriating revenues to specified purposes were incorporated into subsequent statutes in 1344, 1348, and 1353. These early developments signalled the growing importance of the concept of appropriation and its value to

Parliament as a constraint on the King's powers to spend at will. Such provisions were at first attached only to the extra-ordinary grants and taxes needed for military purposes and not to the King's ordinary revenues, which he remained free to spend as he pleased. However, they were at least a start in moving forward from controlling the raising of revenue towards controlling the purposes for which that revenue was spent.

Attempting control by appropriation could not be fully effective without subsequent follow-up to ensure that statutory commitments and stated intentions were complied with in practice. It did not take long for those in Parliament to recognize that to be effective their control needed to include three elements: appropriation of grants; audit of accounts; and the power to criticize expenditure. Accordingly, various attempts were made from 1340 onwards to introduce some form of parliamentary audit of accounts, with the appointment at various times of commissioners of accounts.[1] One examination that is recognized as a more direct accountability to Parliament arose in 1340 when William de la Pole and John Charnels were called before 'certain persons assigned by Parliament' and required to give an account of their receipts and expenditures as treasurers. This was considered to be 'the first occasion on which money given in Parliament was by them ordered to be accounted for to persons appointed by themselves'.[2] Auditors were also appointed for particular examinations in 1406, 1625, and 1675.

The cotillion of advance and retreat continued throughout the later years of the fourteenth century, with Parliament gradually becoming pre-eminent as the Hundred Years War dragged on and fading memories of the military triumphs of Crecy and Poitiers could not sustain the King's crumbling administration.[3] Pressures for greater control and accountability, in principle at least, were still largely directed towards the periodical extra-ordinary grants approved for military purposes and to Parliament's growing control over customs and other duties. Although Parliament was initially less successful in influencing the wider range of the King's expenditures this changed as it continued to secure greater financial and political leverage.

Growing dissatisfaction and anger against the corruption, financial misappropriation, and inefficiency of the later years of Edward III came to a fierce, though short-lived, head under the 'Good Parliament' of 1376, which attempted to impose stringent controls on administration and finance, including the establishment of an effective parliamentary audit. These moves were suppressed but the discontent simmered on as financial burdens increased and began to

---

[1] Davenport, 1918, pp. 39–40.
[2] Noted by early historian James Tyrrell and in *'Hatsell's Parliamentary Precedents'* by John Hatsell, Clerk to the House of Commons (1768–97) and the foremost authority on early parliamentary procedure.
[3] Davenport, 1918, pp. 41–6.

affect the landed nobility and the increasingly powerful merchant classes as well as the people as a whole. As the century drew to a close an increasingly belea-guered Richard II (1377–99) found himself, like his grandfather before him, facing renewed calls for greater financial accountability and a more powerful voice for Parliament in the direction of financial affairs. Richard's arrogance and high-handedness in dealing with these and other demands were to lead to his downfall in the revolution of 1399. The circumstances of his removal meant that his successors were in a particularly weak position to resist parliamentary pressures, as the latter quickly realized.

Developments under the Lancastrians

The strengthening of Parliament's position under the later Plantagenets was reinforced almost from the outset under the Lancastrians. Appropriation, audit, and general powers to criticize expenditure were consolidated and extended. Doubts over the legitimate right of Henry IV (1399–1413) to suc-ceed Richard II meant that he had effectively been elected by Parliament and, therefore, started from a position of fatal disadvantage. Weak and uncertain administration, costly military failures, and excessive royal expenditures con-tinued to provoke public and parliamentary criticism, which further under-mined Henry's position. His heavy dependence on the goodwill of Parliament led to a succession of measures to tighten financial control and accountability throughout the early years of his reign. These not only consolidated parlia-mentary control over raising revenue and taxation but also extended the House of Commons' powers to criticize expenditure. In 1407 the Commons obtained from the King a formal recognition of its exclusive right to initiate money grants. If it concluded that too much money was being called for, it was prepared either to refuse or to insist that its approval was accompanied by reforms and economies to cut back on the taxation and aids required.

Growing attempts were also made to distinguish the King's personal expenditure from the more general expenditures of military and civil govern-ment. This analysis and breakdown into different classes of expenditure led to sharpened parliamentary scrutiny of both financial rectitude and general economy, at the same time as audit of accounts was increasingly introduced. However, the pendulum swung too far and controls and sanctions were applied to such an exaggerated extent that they started to interfere with sensible and prudent administration. On some key services the King and his executive were given so little flexibility and were subject to such close over-sight that firm decision making was inhibited. These pressures were to some extent relaxed or suspended under Henry V (1413–22).

Henry V's successes in battle and his public popularity and prestige put him in a stronger position to make confident demands for funds for his military operations. The chronic reluctance by the Commons to release funding to Henry IV was relaxed and Parliament was mostly prepared to grant subsidies for wars whenever these were requested. This respite was short-lived. From 1422 the initially precarious, and later inept, rule of Henry VI (1422–61) provided Parliament with both opportunity and encouragement to resume its close financial control. Henry's chronic insolvency, coupled with the interest rates of 25 per cent or more that he faced on any attempts to raise additional extra-parliamentary funds, forced him into virtually total dependence on Commons grants to provide resources to augment the Crown's increasingly inadequate normal income. These grants were given grudgingly, where given at all. The end result was excessive, tight control of the royal executive instead of a sensible recognition that a reasonable level of funding was needed to encourage economic and efficient administration.

The dependence of the Lancastrians on the goodwill of Parliament increased the latter's influence in three main ways. First, the frequency of royal funding requests confirmed Parliament's prerogatives in financial issues. Second, more frequent and regular meetings helped Parliament, and the Commons in particular, to develop a more corporate, united approach and an established pattern of business and procedure. Finally, the Commons was encouraged to seek a positive role in approving legislation and to argue, with increasing effect, the need for its consent before bills were enacted. Control of taxation and the power to award grants were not pursued in isolation or as strict matters of principle; they were essentially part of the wider constitutional power struggle. Parliament's objective was to exert greater control or influence on the King, not just to control expenditure.

It would be simplistic to assume that the deep financial and administrative dependency of the Lancastrians on parliamentary grants, which extended in one form or another throughout the period 1399–1460, was wholly welcomed by Parliament. The nobles and magnates and an increasingly affluent middle class still expected sound financial governance of the country to be primarily the King's responsibility. They wanted stability rather than recurring financial crises and, predictably, disliked the imposition of unpopular and divisive taxation. In many respects, therefore, there was towards the end of the period a strong desire for a financially strong and, indeed, authoritative administration. It was not long before this wish was to be fulfilled.

Yorkist Revival and Tudor Reorganization

The increase in parliamentary control of taxation and expenditure under the Lancastrians did not last under the Yorkists. The reign of Edward IV (1461–83) saw a major shift in power back towards the King. One of the key factors in the reduction of Parliament's influence, as always, was a significant strengthening of the King's personal financial position. Edward's victories in the Wars of the Roses and the associated confiscation of the estates of his defeated enemies vastly augmented the royal fortunes. Whatever his other faults, Edward was in many ways a sound businessman as well as a financial opportunist. He developed powerful merchant connections and made substantial sums in trade. On the opportunist side he called off his invasion of France, which he had embarked upon in 1474 in pursuit of his claim to the French throne. In return he was offered a lump sum of 75,000 gold crowns by Louis XI, with an annual pension of 50,000 gold crowns for the rest of his life. Agreements such as these made Edward almost financially independent of Parliament, a position not enjoyed by any monarch since Henry II. The only Parliament held between 1475 and 1482 was not asked for any grants. When Edward died in 1483 at the age of forty he left a fortune to his successor and a regime that had firmly checked the concessions the Lancastrians had previously given for greater parliamentary financial control and accountability.

Following the defeat of Richard III at Bosworth in 1485, the King's financial independence from Parliament continued and deepened under Henry VII (1485–1509) and the later Tudors. The reasons for the effective eclipse of parliamentary accountability reflected the burgeoning extent of the King's personal wealth and resources, which meant fewer calls on Parliament for extra-ordinary grants and, therefore, less scope for parliamentary influence. Maximizing revenues from his lands, from confiscations, and from a range of other sources was one of Henry VII's primary concerns. His detailed involvement with all aspects of Exchequer business was reflected in his habit of personally carrying out regular audits of the books and signing off his examination by initialling the individual pages of the accounts, thereby anticipating modern audit practice. He was the first King of England to leave a fortune of several millions of pounds to his successor. More generally, there was a desperate wish throughout the country for an end to civil war and uncertainty and for positive government. This concern was reflected by Parliament in its dealings with the King. Parliament was circumspect in all aspects of royal relationships and was prepared to cooperate more fully in meeting the King's needs and wishes. The superior position of the monarch in matters of finance and accountability, and indeed in other areas, continued throughout the reigns of Henry VIII (1509–47) and Elizabeth I (1558–1603) and for some time afterwards.

At a lower administrative level there was growing pressure for change, particularly in the core activities of the Exchequer in the collection and issue of funds. These continued to be based on traditional and cumbersome procedures, with associated delays. As always, Exchequer officials remained wedded to the past and were determined to maintain the Exchequer's primacy in matters of finance by fiercely resisting change. At the same time, significant changes were taking place in surrounding parts of Tudor financial administration. Henry VII's success in building up his resources had involved his direct participation in matters of detail and his preferred reliance on private or semi-official bodies mainly within the royal household. However, detailed involvement and 'hands on' control was not well suited to the broader style and wider concerns of Henry VIII, or to changing circumstances. Nor did it accord with the ambitions and talents of Thomas Cromwell, Chancellor under Henry VIII from 1532 until 1540. One of the great administrator/bureaucrats, Cromwell was determined to reorganize financial business on more efficient lines. Even more importantly, he wanted to strengthen his own position by establishing more direct personal controls on access to and use of funds.

The main features of Cromwell's changes were to distinguish more clearly the different streams of revenue and to establish separate bodies to manage these different areas of the royal finances. Under these arrangements six courts or quasi-departments were set up. The Court of the Exchequer continued to account for traditional revenues, for customs, and for parliamentary grants; the Duchy of Lancaster managed its established lands; the Court of First Fruits and Tenths dealt with the fees paid by the clergy for appointment and tenure; the Court of the General Surveyors of the King's Lands took over from the Exchequer the collection and paying of rents from royal lands; the Court of Wards and Liveries dealt with inheritance issues following the death of tenants-in-chief of royal lands; and a separate Court of Augmentations was created to handle the revenues flowing from the immensely valuable lands and properties acquired following the dissolution of the monasteries. All these bodies had their own appointed officers and auditors. At the end of the sixteenth century Tudor wealth, prestige, and power had secured royal dominance on the constitutional issue of accountability and was to remain so for many years.

As well as the political objective of strengthening his personal control over the levers of financial power, an important aim of Thomas Cromwell's reforms, particularly as regards the burgeoning lands revenues, was to minimize the debilitating effects of traditional Exchequer procedures. In the face of all opposition, Exchequer officials had for centuries clung fiercely and exasperatingly to the need to keep strictly to the detailed and constipated requirements of formal Exchequer business. Cromwell was determined to introduce a more flexible and responsive system to speed up the collection and issues of funds and simplify accounting. However, the turbulent waters of Tudor politics and shifts in the balance of powers meant that the new arrangements for financial administration, accounting, and audit did not in practice operate as smoothly or as entirely as he had intended.

Following Cromwell's fall, the introduction of new bodies led to growing numbers of officials, sub-officials, clerks and auditors, more complicated procedures, delays, inefficiencies, and higher fees and charges. By 1553–4 the abuses, maladministration, and personal profiteering surrounding the handling of the land revenues had become so great that the benefits of more traditional financial controls and procedures were again recognized. Important responsibilities were therefore reassigned to the Exchequer. Land revenues were again brought largely under its control and supervision and the new court effectively abolished. Others followed. The abolition of these courts was a response to the abuses and maladministration that had taken place. Vernon notes that the reason for the change was 'in those days, notoriously known and openly declared', the revenues being 'wholly wasted and devoured by the new and unnecessary officers of those Courts'.[4] Some remnants lived on until the end of the eighteenth century, when they were either abolished or their responsibilities transferred to the Commissioners for Auditing the Public Accounts.

As well as operational failings by the Exchequer, there were serious gaps in the chain of audit and accountability. The Exchequer and the various other bodies involved were concerned primarily with the collection of revenue and the issue of funds down the line to a wide range of subordinate imprest holders. Accounting and audit were directed primarily to those initial funding operations with no regular or effective audit of the subsequent disbursement and spending of issued funds by the officials concerned. Examinations by the Auditors of the Exchequer and the Auditors of the Land Revenue were essentially internal audits with limited scope. Any further examination that might have been carried out was covered by a piecemeal system of examination by persons or groups of persons appointed for specific, and usually short-term, tasks mainly when particular difficulties arose. The expenditures and accounts of the serried ranks of imprest holders could go for long periods without effective checks, or indeed none at all. The largest imprest holders quickly took the opportunity to make enormous profits from the interest they received on the unspent funds left in their hands. It was still common at the beginning of the nineteenth century for former senior government officials to retain control of, and receive the financial benefits from, funds that had been under their control while in office but which they were yet to surrender. In many cases, there were delays of several years in providing an account of their stewardship.[5]

Many civil and military government officials acting as bankers for the government received very large amounts of money to make payments on behalf of the government.[6] From these monies they would deduct the

---

[4] *Memorandum on The Origin and History of the Exchequer of England: its Officers, Revenue, & c.* (Published 1864).

[5] Funnell, 2008.

[6] *Parliamentary History* XIX, 22 March 1778, cols. 977–8; Torrance, 1978, p. 580.

payments due to them for their services and return to government any unused funds *after* their accounts had been audited and accepted by the Exchequer's auditors on behalf of the Crown. Incredibly, an ancient statute of Henry III (1207–72), 51 Hen. III, c.5, was still held to require that accounts could not be submitted for acquittance, that is final settlement, until officials who had previously held the same position had their accounts settled and received their acquittance.[7] Any delay in the settlement of these earlier accounts delayed all subsequent finalizations, to the great financial advantage of many office holders. An early acquittance would be possible only if the officers who held profitable sinecures were required to surrender all public monies in their possession at the time that they left office rather than the finalization of their accounts being dependent upon the acquittance of their predecessors.

Auditors of the Imprests

Recognition of the need to carry examinations beyond the initial issue of funds led to the creation in 1559 of two Auditors of the Imprests, with a small number of clerks. They were primarily concerned with examining the accounts of persons receiving imprests, or authorized funding, from the Exchequer to be spent subsequently on departmental supplies and services. The auditors were entirely under the control and direction of the Treasury. The letters patent under which they were formally appointed required them to 'Audit and determine Accounts by and with the advice, authority, and consent, of the Lord High Treasurer, or Lords Commissioners of the Treasury and the Chancellor of the Exchequer'.

Although the Lords of the Treasury and the Chancellor of the Exchequer were stated to be 'parties to the audit of every account' this did not mean that the Auditors of the Imprests dealt with the accounts of all imprest holders. The accounts to be audited were distributed by the Treasury and only selected accounts were sent for examination. The Treasury could also determine the organization of the work and distribute the accounts between the auditors' divisions as it saw fit. In their examination the auditors were required to obey all Treasury directions. All audited accounts had to be submitted to the Treasury before the transactions recorded in the accounts were finally allowed and the accounts passed. The Treasury had the ultimate power to overrule any disallowances proposed by the auditors and to direct the auditors to 'declare' or pass accounts even if contrary to the auditors' recommendations. The Treasury's power to decide which accounts would be audited was used to

---

[7] 'Fourth Report of the Commissioners for Examining the Public Accounts', *Journals of the House of Commons*, 6–9 April 1781, col. 382; Torrance, 1978.

good effect to restrict examination of departmental spending, unless of course such examinations suited the Treasury's purpose. Certainly the Treasury was careful to ensure that its own accounts remained out of the reach of a mere subordinate. Given the auditors' limited powers and the fact that they were 'entirely dependent upon the Treasury', the Committee on Public Expenditure in 1810 concluded that the auditors 'could...not be considered as constituting an efficient check on the irregularities of public expenditure'.[8]

Quite apart from being entirely subordinate to the Treasury, the auditors' perception of their role and responsibilities was from the outset fundamentally flawed. The audit, in principle, was intended to ensure that the funds issued had been spent on the purposes for which they were intended and approved. In practice the examination was confined to the bank accounts of the imprest holders and, therefore, remained essentially an examination of the funding process. There was no audit of actual expenditure, even for imprest holders for major funds such as the Treasurer of the Navy or the Paymaster General for the Army. Thus, the abuses continued and the imprest holders continued to profit from the funds in their hands.

There were also excessive financial rewards for the Auditors of the Imprests themselves. They received an annual stipend but their main income was from the fees charged for the accounts they audited. The fees were based on the volume of expenditure, at rates determined by the Treasury, and thus became very large.[9] The largest profits came from the accounts of the Chief Cashier of the Bank of England, where the auditors received a fee of £100 for every £1 million of deposits, returning to each of the auditors in 1784 a total fee of £20,000. During the previous year they each earned over £16,000. Upon representations from the auditors the rates of payment could be raised by the Treasury if it was convinced that there had been a significant expansion in an imprest holder's accounts. It was not unknown for the Lord High Treasurer to grant unsolicited increases in the remuneration of the auditors 'for the pains taken' in finalizing particularly difficult accounts. Though the auditors gladly pocketed these extra fees they were not, of course, themselves inconvenienced by any additional work since this was dealt with by their six or seven low-paid clerks.

Despite the operations of the Auditors of the Imprests being widely recognized as inefficient, their enjoyment of 'high profits for little effort' became extremely attractive to the rich and powerful. By the early eighteenth century both posts had degenerated into 'a form of Executive patronage whereby very

---

[8] Committee on Public Expenditure, 1810, Fifth Report, p. 383.
[9] For a brief period after 1649 the Committee of Public Revenue had substituted a fixed salary of £500 for the generous rates determined by the Treasury. At the Restoration of Charles II in 1660 the system of payment by fees was reintroduced by the Treasury (Bromley, 1850, p. 1).

profitable sinecures were given to a fortunate few'.[10] Benefiting from what was in effect permanent tenure, both posts were to last for another forty years until they and other sinecures started to be swept away following the devastating criticisms of Edmund Burke and the Commissioners for Examining the Public Accounts appointed in 1780.

Although the Auditors of the Imprest were by far the largest and most important of the examining bodies during this period, there were also a number of other bodies examining specific areas of departmental activity, including revenue collection. Like the Auditors of the Imprests they all operated under direct Executive control. The most important of these were: the Auditor of the Exchequer established in 1314 and abolished in 1833; the Auditor of the Excise, introduced in 1643 and abolished in 1849; the Auditors of the Land Revenue, formed in 1511 and closed in 1799; the Comptrollers of Army Accounts, established in 1703, expanded in 1806 and 1815, and finally abolished in 1835; and the Commissioners for Auditing the Accounts of Ireland who operated between 1783 and 1832.

At different times other audit bodies were temporarily formed, mainly to meet the exigencies of war. For example, between 1813 and 1819 Richard Dawkins, one of the Commissioners for Auditing the Public Accounts, was seconded to the Duke of Wellington's army in Spain as Auditor General of Accounts in the Peninsula.[11] Wellington was later reported to have complained about the time army officers then had to spend dealing with essentially minor audit criticisms, 'whereas I believed my primary duty was to fulfil His Majesty's commission to defeat his enemies and drive them totally from Spain'. Some posts were also created to meet the needs arising from expansion of the Empire, including the Commissioners for West India Accounts appointed in 1806 and the Commissioners for Colonial Accounts in 1814, which absorbed the West Indian Commissioners in 1822.

Parliament and the Stuarts

The relationship between King and Parliament reached its lowest ebb under Charles I (1600–49). The first half of the seventeenth century saw fundamental conflicts over his belief in the 'Divine Right of Kings' and Parliament's demands for greater democracy. There was at the same time deepening conflict between Catholics and Protestants. Charles particularly angered Parliament with insistent and heavy demands for funding for his army. The constitutional crises these issues provoked, and the resultant upheavals of the Civil War, the

---

[10] Committee on Public Expenditure, 1810, Fifth Report, p. 382.
[11] 53 Geo.III. c.150.

Commonwealth, and the Protectorate, inevitably meant that reform of more mundane matters of financial process and procedure was largely set aside. The Exchequer and other bodies involved were therefore left to continue business as before. However, the Restoration of Charles II (1660–85) meant that financial battles with Parliament were soon to be resumed, with more positive steps towards accountability as the prize.

The defining feature of Restoration finance and accountability was Charles' chronic shortage of funds. Although his personal extravagances were one reason for his descent at times into near bankruptcy, the principal cause was the heavy costs of the wars against the Dutch. Two factors combined to make things worse. Most importantly, a fractious Parliament was increasingly reluctant to approve the extra-ordinary grants needed to meet burgeoning military expenditure, unless the King was prepared to concede some of his powers. This Charles refused to accept. The disruption of trade by the war also severely reduced revenues from customs duties and various other taxes. To meet the resulting shortfalls Charles was reduced to taking out massive loans wherever he could find them, on onerous terms and at heavy rates of interest. These hand-to-mouth arrangements became heavier and more frequent over the years 1665 to 1671.

The original loans taken out in 1665 had been intended to last for an agreed period of twenty-four months and were assigned in anticipation of a specific aid of £1¼ million that had been agreed by the Oxford Parliament and secured by tallies issued at the Exchequer. In the event, the aid, though agreed, was never voted. From 1667 onwards further loans were instead secured against more general taxes such as customs and excise, and later still against revenues in general. They could also be traded by the original lenders, with Exchequer approval. The tallies of assignment issued as security for these loans were widely taken up, encouraged by the King's personal promise that: 'We will not upon any occasion whatsoever permit or suffer any interruption to be made of our Subjects' Securities, but that they shall from time to time receive the Moneys so secured upon them.' This solemn promise of repayment was never fulfilled. In effect the loans became open-ended and out of control. Inevitably, all these temporary expediencies rebounded when repayments fell due and in 1672 there were insufficient funds to meet lenders' demands. The result was the notorious 'Stop of the Exchequer', the first and only time in more than 600 years that a bankrupt Exchequer was unable to meet its legal obligations. The losses incurred by the large number of lenders involved, and the realization that royal promises of repayment could not be trusted, dealt a further blow to the King's credit and thus added to his funding difficulties.

Shortage of funds led to mounting parliamentary discontent with the state of the King's accounts, made worse by endemic waste, mismanagement, and corruption. There were accusations that the high cost of the King's wars resulted from extravagance, fraud, and applications of money for purposes other than those approved by Parliament. This precipitated the appointment throughout Charles' reign of a series of parliamentary commissions of accounts. Some of these early commissioners had strong powers of coercion, including the authority to imprison for perjury or refusal to attend before the commissioners. In addition to pronouncing upon the accuracy and honesty of the accounts, the commissioners were also expected to suggest improvements and to report their findings to the King and both Houses of Parliament.[12] Obstruction by the King and departments meant that some of these commissions were largely ineffective.

Samuel Pepys

An unprecedented insight into the politics of the time and the operations of the royal finances is provided by the famous and vastly informative *Diary* kept by Samuel Pepys (1633–1703), the 'Saviour of the Navy'. Pepys entered the Exchequer in 1656 at the age of twenty-three. It was at the Exchequer that he started his *Diary* when he was employed as a junior clerk to Sir George Downing, of the eponymous Street. As Teller of the Receipt of the Exchequer, Downing was in the direct line of predecessors to the present post of Comptroller and Auditor General (C&AG). Rich, powerful, and ruthless, he was universally reviled for his untrustworthiness and unbridled self-interest, in both political and financial matters. It was a reputation richly deserved.[13]

Pepys' career at the Exchequer was undistinguished. His main concern was with his other position as secretary and steward to the rich and influential Edward Mountagu, a family cousin. Mountagu had promised him that 'We shall rise together', an opportunity that quickly arose. In May 1660 Mountagu was sent as General-at-Sea to escort Charles II back from exile in Holland and took Pepys with him in the special position of Admiral's Secretary and Treasurer of the Fleet. On their return the King showered Mountagu with titles and offices. He became a Knight of the Garter, Earl of Sandwich, Vice-Admiral of

---

[12] Committee on Public Expenditure, 1810, Fifth Report, p. 383.

[13] Downing joined the New Model Army in 1645 and rose rapidly during the Commonwealth and the Protectorate to become Oliver Cromwell's chief of intelligence and spymaster, a prominent and fervent member of the government, and a special envoy in negotiations with the Dutch. However, with the Restoration imminent in 1660, Downing quickly recanted his republican past and performed the same intelligence and spymaster role under Charles II. His most notorious betrayal was his willingness to gain favour with the King by securing the extradition, trial, and execution of the three regicides of Charles I: Okey (his former friend and colonel in the New Model Army), Barkstead, and Corbet. Ultimately, Downing's efforts as Secretary to the Treasury improved fiscal policy and financial management, based on his observations of the Dutch model. In particular he pursued appropriation of supply to ensure that grants were spent on the purposes for which they were approved.

the Kingdom, Master of the Great Wardrobe, and Clerk of the Privy Seal. Mountagu in turn quickly fulfilled his promise to Pepys by securing him the important post of Clerk of the Acts to the Navy Board. This provided a generous salary, the provision of official lodgings, and the prospect of further income from various gratuities and the usual bribes. As soon as his new appointment was formally confirmed Pepys promptly resigned his post at the Exchequer. To celebrate his promotion Pepys gave a lavish dinner to twelve of his closest friends at the Exchequer for which he provided 'a good chine of beefe, three barrels of oysters and three pullets and plenty of wine and mirth'.[14] Over the years he returned many times to the Exchequer to have tallies struck and his accounts passed. From the other side of the counter he then complained bitterly of high costs, obstinate officials, and long delays.

In contrast to his brief and modest career at the Exchequer, Pepys' qualities were soon noticed and appreciated at the Navy Board. Although he was by far the youngest and, initially, the junior member of the Board his influence grew quickly. Mountagu's patronage was an asset but Pepys' advancement owed much more to his well-ordered administrative skills, his capacity for hard work, his willingness to work long hours, and his boundless energy and vitality. These were attributes that could not be matched by any of the other six members of the Board, some of whom were lazy or incompetent or both. To overcome his lack of experience of nautical matters Pepys also spent many hours learning the details of the professional aspects of the Board's responsibilities to enable him to comment knowledgeably in all the Board's discussions. Within three years he was a leading member of the Board and able to persuade other members in debate and in decisions. One of his strengths was that, more than any of his colleagues and despite their greater experience, he had developed a synoptic view of the Board's wide-ranging and complex activities.

The Navy Board, independent of the Admiralty, was the civilian body responsible for the construction, maintenance, and repair of ships, and the operation of the six Royal Dockyards and other Navy establishments. It dealt with the procurement of equipment, victualling, stores, supplies, and services for the Fleet, excluding only guns and other ordnance, and used an extensive network of contractors for large areas of work. It was also responsible for naval and civilian pay and related matters. The Board of Admiralty had overarching responsibility for naval policy and for the size, disposition, and operations of the Fleet.

Pepys had a particular interest in value for money. Watching the gross overmanning at the docking of the warship *Royall James*, he produced the

---

[14] Pepys, *Diary*, 30 December 1661.

timeless aphorism about military expenditure: 'Good God, what a company there was from both yards to do it, when half the company would have done it as well. *But I see it is impossible for the King to have things done as cheap as other men'* (emphasis added).[15] On a more mundane level, Pepys referred to going 'to the shops and there enquired the price of tarr and oyle, and do find great content in it and hope to save the King money'.[16] Pepys was also a strong advocate of bulk buying and centralized purchasing. On one occasion he went outside his area of responsibility and independently arranged a £3,000 contract for a large quantity of Norwegian masts in order to avoid their being bought piecemeal and more expensively by individual dockyards. In addition to the strident, fulsome praise he gave himself for the value for money achieved, he also drew attention in quite modern terms to the absence of safeguards over the placing and pricing of contracts that should have been in place to prevent corruption by someone in his position:

> Sat all the morning making a great contract with Sir W. Warren for £3,000 worth of Masts, but good God, to see what a man might do were I a knave. The whole business, from beginning to the end, was done by me out of the office, and signed by them upon once but reading of it to them, without the least care or consultation either of quality, price, number, or need of them, only in general that it was good to have a store. But I hope my pains was such as the King hath the best bargain of Masts hath been bought these 27 years in this office.[17]

Pepys was constantly worried about his own financial affairs, which meant that despite his genuine commitment to rooting out waste, inefficiency, and corruption across the Board's activities he was not averse to benefiting personally alongside his official efforts on the King's behalf. He was therefore prepared to accept 'the usual commission' and other bribes and incentives when negotiating and placing contracts, which he often did personally in taverns with the contractors involved. The *Diary* on many occasions records Pepys' dealings with Warren, a rich timber merchant, who was a close personal friend and financial and business adviser and had become the near-monopoly supplier of timber to the Navy under a series of contracts negotiated personally with Pepys. He was also Pepys' partner in a number of other money-making projects and was a source of gifts and other favours. On one occasion, on 1 August 1665, Pepys recorded how: 'My late gettings have been very great, to my great content, and am likely to have yet a few more profitable jobs in a little while—for which Tangier and Sir W. Warren I am wholly obliged to.' Again, in July 1665 he wrote of 'Sir W. Warren coming to me by appointment discoursing about the project I have of getting some money, and doing the King

---

[15] Pepys, *Diary*, 21 July 1662.   [16] Pepys, *Diary*, 26 June 1662.
[17] Pepys, *Diary*, 10 September 1663.

good service too, about the mast dock at Woolwich.'[18] Pepys' pioneering success in pursuing efficiency and value for money was invaluable to a Navy regularly starved of funds. This was recognized in 1663 when he took on additional responsibilities as Surveyor-General of victualling with, of course, an extra salary.

Committee of Accounts 1667

Waste and extravagance was most common in the greatest spending department, the Navy. The Navy was particularly vulnerable to criticism because of the reverses and humiliation it had suffered in the Second Dutch War, especially in the capture and burning of the Fleet in the Battle of the Medway in 1667. This prompted an Act in 1667 to deal with 'the defaults, negligences, frauds, waste and abuses' in the management of the Navy.[19] The Act appointed a Committee of Accounts of nine Commissioners, chosen by Parliament, with wide powers to examine under oath all officers of the Executive who were accountable for, or received, money from the Exchequer. They were then to report to Parliament. The Committee was the successor of an earlier 'Committee of Miscarriages of the Warr' but with a wider remit and much stronger powers. The Committee of 1667 was in some respects a one-off forerunner of the Public Accounts Committee set up some 200 years later. Pepys noted that the Committee was not afraid to question the conduct and competence of those in high positions, the powerful, the rich, and, at times, the arrogant. Pepys appeared before the Commissioners on several occasions, and from hard experience described them as:

> a great council but asking impertinent questions. . . . Very strict and not easily put off. . . . Mad at going through all businesses where they can lay any fault. . . . Did ask a great many broken questions, and because my answer was not direct were not satisfied with it. . . . They do go about their business like men resolved to go through with it, and in a very good method. . . . Meanest into the meanest particulars, and had great information. . . . I find these gentlemen to sit all day and only eat a bit of bread at noon and a glass of wine, and are resolved to go through their business with great severity and method.[20]

There were a number of different strands to the Committee's work. The main line of enquiry was to question senior members of the Admiralty on the disposition, tactics, and operational conduct of the Fleet, particularly in relation to the Battle of the Medway in 1667. The Committee investigated the

---

[18] Pepys, *Diary*, 18 July 1665.   [19] 19 Caroli. c.9.
[20] Pepys, *Diary*, October 1667–February 1668.

background, appointment, and competence of the naval commanders directly involved and went much further into detailed military strategy, operations, and decision taking than would probably be regarded as appropriate in audit examinations today. Nor were they afraid to question the higher chain of command. This was a sensitive area, not least because ultimate responsibility lay with the Lord High Admiral, the Duke of York, the King's brother and future James II. It became clear that much of the Committee's inquiries in this area had wider constitutional implications, the result of which was inevitable parliamentary and political argument.

Another issue pursued by the Committee was the scandal of seamen's 'pay tickets'. When a ship was 'paid off' at the end of its period of duty the crew did not receive their wages in cash but by 'tickets', which they had to present for payment at the naval treasury office. Getting there was often inconvenient or even impossible for the seamen. Therefore, there was a brisk trade by 'ticket mongers', sometimes naval officials, to buy these tickets at a discount and redeem them later at face value. The tickets could change hands several times, which made it difficult to track down those involved. Pepys was himself accused of corruption on the production of a ticket with his name on it, although he was able to escape censure, partly on his own denials but also with the support of the King.[21] The system of tickets, was the direct responsibility of the Navy Board, and the profits made were strongly attacked by the Committee of Accounts as a miscarriage against the seamen concerned for the profits it allowed others at their expense. On this and other matters all the members of the Navy Board were called individually before the Committee, though Pepys bore the brunt of the enquiries.

The Committee of Accounts also turned its attention to the subject of prize goods and prize money. In September 1665, ships under the command of Pepys' patron Edward Mountagu, Earl of Sandwich, had captured two Dutch merchantmen returning from the East Indies with a valuable cargo of spices, silk, and other goods. The disposal of prize goods came officially under the jurisdiction of the prize court, but in this case the cargoes were particularly attractive and easy to sell. Sandwich exceeded his powers and unwisely allowed a substantial part of the goods to be distributed amongst some of his officers and men and some privileged outsiders, including Pepys. When Pepys learned the nature of the seized goods he immediately saw the opportunity to make money. Accordingly, he temporarily 'borrowed' some official funds, purchased a quantity of spices at half their worth, then quickly sold them at a handsome profit. Mountagu himself profited six times as much.[22] Pepys' prompt disposal of his share, and the passage of time, meant that his

---

[21] Pepys, *Diary*, 30 October 1667.   [22] Pepys, *Diary*, 18–23 September 1665.

involvement was easier to defend when the subject of prize goods resurfaced in the further enquiries by the Committee of Accounts. Mountagu, as the prime mover in the affair, was sent in semi-disgrace to serve some time as ambassador to Spain. The Committee's report was presented to Parliament in February 1668 and on 5 March Pepys was called before the full House of Commons to respond to the findings and conclusions. Well prepared as always, he made a closely argued speech in the Navy's defence that lasted more than three hours and successfully dismissed, explained, or mitigated many of the Committee's criticisms.[23] The work of the Committee of Accounts in 1667 was an early landmark in the long journey towards effective financial accountability to Parliament, even though it did not usher in a regime of regular audit examinations and reports.

Another attempt between 1690 and 1697 to expose Executive abuses with the appointment of Commissioners of Public Accounts quickly failed. According to Rubini, the Commissioners were considered a constitutional threat by the King,[24] and departments regarded the enquiries of the Commissioners as impertinent intrusions in departmental affairs. Consequently, departments set out to ensure that the Commissioners' work was made as difficult and as inconvenient as possible. Departments either openly refused to provide the accounts sought by the Commissioners or procrastinated by feigning ignorance. Commissioner Sir Peter Colleton, for example, complained to his diary about the difficulties in obtaining accounts from the 'great departments' of the Army and the Navy.[25] Much of the difficulties experienced by the Commissioners between 1690 and 1697, maintain Downie[26] and Roseveare,[27] can be attributed to the use of the Commissioners' mandate as a biased political weapon. It was nearly a century later before a further, and more successful, attempt was made to strengthen Executive accountability with the appointment of another Commission of Public Accounts.

Conclusion

Auditors in the Exchequer had existed in one form or another from the early years of the fourteenth century, but were generally individual appointments with limited scope. They were effectively an internal check on day-to-day transactions and the accuracy and completeness of official records. In later years small groups of outsiders were occasionally commissioned by Parliament

---

[23] Even in his usual full oratorical flood Pepys became aware that 'My speech being so long many members had gone out to dinner and come in again half drunk' (*Diary*, 5 March 1668) and proceedings had to be deferred till the following day.
[24] Downie, 1976, p. 34.   [25] Downie, 1976, p. 44.
[26] Downie, 1976, p. 43.   [27] Roseveare, 1969, p. 74.

to look into specific areas of expenditure. The operations of the auditors associated with the organizational changes introduced by Thomas Cromwell from 1532, such as the Auditors of the Land Revenue, were essentially inward looking and the work of the Auditors of the Imprests appointed in 1559 was fundamentally flawed in terms of audit and accountability for actual expenditure.

The Committee of Accounts appointed by Parliament in 1667 to look into financial mismanagement in the Navy in the Dutch War and the Commissioners of Public Accounts in 1690 were isolated, exceptional measures prompted by events and for a specific purpose. The reports of the 1667 Committee were effective in their time but its examinations left no clear legacy and did not lead to plans to continue or to develop its work. The Committee's examinations were not seen, nor did they become, a harbinger of the financial measures and controls that a more complex and higher-spending state would increasingly require.

Piecemeal assertions of Parliament's constitutional primacy in financial matters in the seventeenth century were not accompanied by any strengthening of arrangements for presentation of annual estimates for amounts to be voted by Parliament and there was little accountability to Parliament for subsequent expenditure on supplies and services. Nor were there reliable annual accounts supported by a regular and effective audit. It was not until the closing decades of the eighteenth century that a start was made towards these objectives with the appointment of the Commissioners for Auditing the Public Accounts. Even then the necessary framework for pursuing such matters more effectively and consistently would not be set in place until the middle of the nineteenth century.

4

The Commissioners and Board of Audit

'The work of the Commissioners of Audit was the dividing line between the ancient and the modern.'

> J. E. D. Binney, *British Public Finance and Administration 1774–92*

The Glorious Revolution of 1688 replaced the Catholic James II (1685–88) with the Protestant William III (1689–1702). This changed the constitutional landscape and shifted the balance of financial powers and accountability between King and Parliament. Having fought long and hard to replace Stuart autocracy, Parliament was not going to concede similar powers to the newly arrived House of Orange. However, the constitutional position was complicated. In law and in practice there was no clear constitutional distinction between the person of the monarch and the monarch as the executive government. The domestic affairs of the monarch and the operations of civil government were inextricably and—it was widely believed—properly mixed.[1] The solution was to disengage the funding of the financial needs of monarchs and their household from wider questions of government revenues and expenditure. This was done in 1697 by the introduction of the Civil List.

Introduction of the Civil List

The Civil List arrangements, introduced in 1697,[2] were intended to distinguish clearly between expenditures that were to be the monarch's responsibility and those to be funded directly by Parliament. The cost of the royal household and of the civil, as opposed to the military, departments of state was to be met primarily from the Crown's hereditary sources of income, that is

---

[1] Chester, 1981, p. 8.   [2] 9 Will.III, c.23.

from the monarch's own purse.[3] To supplement the Crown's resources the Civil List granted each monarch funding by Parliament at the beginning of his or her reign that was intended to provide sufficient income for life to meet all needs, both personal and governmental. The dignity of the Crown demanded that monarchs be master in their own household.[4] If the Crown, acting as an agent of the people, lived within its means and provided for its own needs, except during periods of emergency such as wars, Parliament was not to interfere. The reality was somewhat different. Even in times of peace Parliament was frequently called upon to vote amounts to cover large accumulated deficits in the royal budget.[5]

From the early eighteenth century until 1783, when the financial independence of the Crown was finally removed and Parliament assumed responsibility for the Civil List, a three-way balance was held to exist between the constitutional powers of the Executive, the House of Commons, and the House of Lords. Blackstone believed that the constitution would be 'at an end' if there were a threat to the independence from each other of the three parts of the legislature upon which the balance of power—so essential to the preservation of liberty—depended.[6] David Hume (1711–76) referred to the way in which:

> the Crown has so many offices at its disposal...that it will always command the resolutions of the whole so far, at least, as to preserve the ancient constitution from danger....We may call it by the invidious appellations of *corruption* and *dependence*; but some degree and some kind of it are inseparable from the very nature of the constitution, and necessary to the preservation of our mixed government.[7]

Consequently, throughout the eighteenth century the relationship between Parliament and the Executive was one of an exaggerated desire to ensure a separation of their respective powers. Only by 'destroying the equilibrium of power between one branch of the legislature and the rest' would the constitution be threatened.[8] In 1760 Lord North reminded Parliament that 'the Civil List being granted to His Majesty's use, it is not proper to require any account of the expenditure of it'.[9] He argued that the independence of the Crown was essential to the 'balanced constitution' that England enjoyed between the Crown, the Commons, and the Lords. Similarly, William Lambarde

---

[3] For a detailed list of the various officers who depended upon the King for their maintenance (*de procurationibus*) see *Liber Niger Scaccarii (Black Book of the Exchequer)* in Stephenson and Marcham, 1937, pp. 65–70.

[4] For a discussion of the 'dignified' and the 'efficient' parts of the English Constitution see Dicey, 1926.

[5] Committee on National Expenditure, 1902, Appendix 13, p. 228.

[6] Blackstone, 1803, pp. 50, 51.

[7] Hume, *Essays Moral, Political and Literary*, quoted in Foord, 1947, p. 484.

[8] Bentham, 1776, p. 73.

[9] *Parliamentary History*, XVI, 1785, column 927; Binney, 1958, p. 2.

extravagantly praised the balance of the constitution, for 'from such, and so well-tuned a base, mean and treble, there proceeds a most exquisite content, and delicious melody'.[10] If the Crown were to lose its independence there would be fewer checks and balances on the power of Parliament. Until the financial crisis created by the American War of Independence, Parliament, therefore, took no detailed and direct interest in the civil administration of the Executive.[11]

Parliament's non-interventionist role in civil government meant that the Civil List appropriation for most of the eighteenth century was made as a single vote. In 1782, however, the Civil Establishments Act divided the vote into eight sections to make the activities of the Executive more visible.[12] This was a first step towards Parliament at last starting to recognize the importance for accountability of providing improved information in estimates and accounts. However, the change still did not provide sufficient information for any effective parliamentary scrutiny. Parliament did not want to know how the King spent his money on the royal household or on civil government: it only wanted to be certain that limits were placed on the level of spending. It was the King's government and it was accepted as the King's constitutional right to govern as he saw fit.[13] Funding by the Civil List was essentially a means of reducing constitutional friction between the Crown and Parliament.[14] This became less important when in 1760 and in 1830 the scope of the Civil List was progressively reduced so as to provide only for the monarch's personal expenses and the costs of the royal household.

The Civil List arrangements meant that legislation remained primarily the responsibility of the Executive. Not until the 1830s would Parliament begin to take a close interest in legislation, with disputes over the respective constitutional prerogatives of the Executive and the legislature surfacing throughout the nineteenth century.[15] When the government proposed in 1872 to stop the purchase of commissions in the Army, Queen Victoria protested that this was an infringement by the legislature of her constitutional powers. Not wishing to precipitate a constitutional crisis in the face of the government's determination to have its way, Queen Victoria eventually relented.

Sinecures and Patronage

The high ideals of the constitution and the separation of powers it sought did not prevent the Crown from regularly attempting to influence Parliament

---

[10] Quoted in Ward, 2004, p. 184. [11] Chester, 1981, p. 34.
[12] 22 Geo III, c.82. [13] Chubb, 1952, p. 9; Blackstone in Roseveare, 1969, p. 87.
[14] Cromwell, 1968, p. 5. [15] Beales, 1969, p. 50.

through the promiscuous use of honours and sinecures. Blackstone referred to the Crown's influence as being 'most amazingly extensive',[16] while Castlereagh observed that honours and sinecures were 'more likely than any others to secure parliamentary influence'.[17] Many official posts were occupied by aristocratic or political placemen enjoying lengthy and lucrative appointments secured by letters patent, whilst the actual work, sometimes of little or no purpose, was done by minor clerks on low pay. Sinecures were not occupied on merit but simply because those concerned, or their relatives, held high office when vacancies arose. Some were allocated in infancy. Brothers, sons, and nephews of Prime Ministers, and sons of Lord Chancellors, jostled for these positions and a share of the massive sums paid to them in poundage and fees from public funds. Sinecures could be held by individuals for decades before being passed down the family line.

The royal household and the civil departments were prolific sources of sinecures and patronage. Although some appointments originally had a genuine function, by the late eighteenth century most of the senior officers in the royal household and many in other parts of the civil service no longer served any useful purpose.[18] The civil departments that provided the most valuable sinecures were the revenue departments of Customs, Inland Revenue, and Woods and Forests. The Treasury also was a fertile source of highly profitable patronage. Many of these sinecure offices had names that betrayed their ancient origins and obsolescence, including the Treasurer of the Comptroller, the Cofferer of the Household, the Master of the Household, the Groom of the Stole, Master of the Jewel Office, and, most notoriously, the Paymaster General of His Majesty's Forces.[19] Within the Exchequer the Auditor of the Receipt, the Clerk of the Pells, the four Tellers, the Chamberlains, the Tally Cutter, and many others, had also degenerated into sinecures. As already noted, the two Auditors of the Imprests were by then also sinecurists, enjoying even larger profits.

At a time when it was common for officials to receive only small salaries, many offices provided that substantial fees could be obtained from the provision of services such as signing contracts, issuing warrants for payment, and the declaration of contractor accounts. In times of war these fees rose dramatically in direct proportion to the increase in the number of transactions. Many of those favoured with appointment to a lavishly paid sinecure never attended their place of work or carried out any of the duties associated with their

---

[16] Foord, 1947, p. 484.   [17] Foord, 1947, p. 499.

[18] *Parliamentary History* XXI, 23 February 1780, columns 111–12; Prior, 1839, p. 206.

[19] The Paymaster General, a senior government official first appointed in 1662, was the Army's banker. He received from the Exchequer money voted by government for military purposes and used this to meet military expenditures.

position. The Paymaster General of the Forces and the Clerk of Pells were especially notorious in this regard, as were the two Auditors of the Imprest.

Opponents of these anachronistic and lucrative sinecures emphasized that if they were abolished the state would save money and, more importantly, the constitution would be strengthened by taking from the Crown the means by which it could extend its influence. Parliamentarian Edmund Burke was probably the strongest, and certainly the most vocal, of these opponents. He attacked the string of sinecures and patent offices in scathing terms as part of his influential speech in the House of Commons on 11 May 1780 on the need for economical reform. Following his own maxim that 'There is a point at which forbearance ceases to be a virtue', Burke argued fiercely that:

> They are sinecures; they are always executed by a deputy; the duty of the principal is as nothing. I think with the public that the profits of these places are grown enormous; the magnitude of these profits, and the nature of them, both call for reform. The nature of their profits which grow out of the public distress is itself invidious and grievous. But I fear that the reforms cannot be immediate.... My idea therefore is to reduce these offices to fixed salaries.[20]

A particular sinecure that exemplified Burke's strictures was the post of Auditor for America, which profited from duties on plantation revenues and other trading activities in the American colonies. Originally serving a useful purpose, this had deteriorated into a sinecure by 1717, when it was granted to Horatio Walpole, the younger brother of Prime Minister Robert Walpole. Horatio Walpole profited handsomely from the post for forty years until his death in 1757. It then passed to the Earl of Cholmondeley, a family relation, and was willed to his descendants as a provision 'sufficient to render all further assistance to the grandchildren unnecessary'. It only disappeared as a result of the 1765 American War of Independence. Even then the incumbent member of the Cholmondeley family received a generous pension, paid for by the Americans themselves, to compensate him for his loss of profits until his own death in 1804.[21]

Some sinecures could be bequeathed as a form of personal property, the sanctity of which was universally acknowledged. Even the most fervent advocates for abolition recognized that if the incumbent had been promised the monies from the sinecure in perpetuity, neither those who currently enjoyed the benefits of profitable sinecures nor their descendants should be disadvantaged. Burke himself advocated that any administrative reform that sought to abolish sinecures and other privileges was always to be tempered by justice to the office holder.[22] His strong belief in fairness and justice for all,

---

[20] Burke, 1780.   [21] Dewar, 1991, pp. 153–7.
[22] Burke, 15 December 1779, in Elofson et al, 1996, p. 475.

demonstrated for example by his public support of the rights of the American colonists, led him to insist that: 'If I cannot reform with equity, I will not reform at all.'[23] Similarly, the Commissioners for Examining the Public Accounts, in their Eleventh Report on sinecures in 1784, reassured all interested parties that in making their recommendations:

> they did not mean to violate in the slightest Degree, any Right vested in an officer by virtue of his Office. The Principles which secure the Rights of private property are sacred, and to be preserved inviolate; they are Land Marks to be considered as immovable. But the Public have their rights also; Rights equally sacred and as freely to be exercised.[24]

The ultimate objective of replacing sinecures with a smaller number of salaried posts was to take more than fifty years to be achieved, although there were some early successes. From their inception in 1780 the Commissioners for Examining the Public Accounts attacked some of the largest sinecures, particularly those handling large sums of public funds.

Requiring the Crown to account for its expenditures made it possible to identify spending that might be intended to buy influence in Parliament. However, the impenetrable nature of the Civil List, reflecting the principle that the monarch's spending was the monarch's business, meant that the Crown was financially answerable to Parliament only when seeking additional financing to meet the needs of the royal household and the civil government, mainly during times of war. The financial demands placed upon the finances of the Crown by the American War of Independence proved to be the catalyst that would finally and irreversibly alter the balance of influence between the Crown and its parliamentary supporters and Parliament as a whole.[25] The Crown's call for additional funding at a time when the national debt was already at record levels was incontrovertible evidence to many that there was widespread corruption in Parliament.[26] Edmund Burke insisted that:

> given the condition of the monarchy had not changed, the debt had been contracted in corrupting the representatives of the people, and...the plunder has been divided among a majority of this House, which is allowed to be the most corrupt assembly in Europe.[27]

The corruption in Parliament alleged by Burke was also symptomatic of the way in which departments of state operated. Each department headed by a

---

[23] Quoted in Morley, 1909, p. 94.

[24] 'Eleventh Report of the Commissioners for Examining the Public Accounts', *Journals of the House of Commons*, 4–5 December 1783, p. 779. See also 'Fourteenth Report of the Commissioners for Examining the Public Accounts', *Journals of the House of Commons*, 26–7 January 1786, p. 23.

[25] Funnell, 2008.   [26] Burke, 18 April 1777, in Elofson et al, 1996, p. 335.

[27] Quoted in Reitan, 1966, p. 326.

minister operated as a separate entity that senior civil servants treated as their personal fiefdom, with its own regulations, salary scales, appointment procedures, and retirement provisions.[28] Although the term 'civil service' was used in the late eighteenth century, Wright argues that it was only with the appearance of public offices with uniform conditions of service and appointment, following major reform that commenced in the mid-nineteenth century, that the civil service began to assume its modern form.[29] Cohen, however, suggests that it was the introduction of a system of audit in the late eighteenth century—to provide regular information to Parliament—that was the 'necessary prelude' to the development of the modern civil service.[30]

Burke argued that by allowing the Crown to buy loyalty to its causes, patronage exercised through the granting of sinecures and titles diminished the independence of public officers and weakened the vigilance of the constitution by threatening the separation of powers.[31] As the titular head of government, the Crown was advised by ministers who sat in Parliament, but Parliament was meant to reflect the views of the people not those of the Crown. It was therefore a danger to the constitution and a risk to Executive accountability if the Crown sought to buy influence and favour in Parliament by providing lucrative positions for its parliamentary supporters and their relatives and friends. Nevertheless, throughout most of the eighteenth century much of the business of government was carried out on the basis of privileged access to the profitable benefices of the Crown. Sir James Graham, Secretary to the Navy in the 1830s, argued that patronage had succeeded the royal prerogative as the means by which the Crown sought to maintain its supremacy in both Houses of Parliament.[32] Instead of its constitutional responsibilities as a bulwark of the public interest, Parliament was regarded by many as an accomplice in the protection of a corrupt Executive.

The turning point in these developments was Burke's wide-ranging speech on economical reform in Parliament on 11 February 1780. Entitled 'Speech presenting to the House of Commons a plan for the better security of the independence of Parliament, and the economical reformation of the civil and other establishments',[33] this set out the financial problems experienced during the American War of Independence and the further consequences likely to arise from the loss of the American colonies.

---

[28] Wright, 1969, p. xxv.

[29] Wright, 1969, pp. xxiii–iv; *Report from the Commissioners on Fees and Gratuities, BPP,* 1806, VII, p. 51.

[30] Cohen, 1965, pp. 47, 51.   [31] Burke in Cromwell, 1968, p. 6; Ward, 2004, p. 78.

[32] Graham to Gladstone, 4 January 1854, in Parker, 1907, vol. 2, p. 212.

[33] *Parliamentary History,* XXI, columns 1–73.

Economical Reform

Burke's emphasis on the need to avoid unnecessary and extravagant expenditure, like his attacks on sinecures, corruption, patronage, and the undue influence of the Crown, were not ends in themselves: his objective was not simply to criticize defects but to introduce significant improvements. Behind the reformist rhetoric, Burke's aim was to promote economy across government business and public expenditure as a whole, reinforce the separation of powers, and strengthen accountability. He urged the House of Commons to rethink its traditional arms-length and ill-informed posture towards Executive finances and public spending. Burke referred to 'people who are hungering and thirsting after substantial reformation'.[34] He condemned the inadequacies and delays in finalizing the public accounts, the lack of independence of the Auditors of the Imprest, and their inadequate audit of actual expenditures. He wanted a more independently minded Parliament, better equipped to improve scrutiny of both civil and military expenditure by the provision of better financial information and accounts, supported by an effective audit. Changes on this scale clearly would take time to introduce, but prompted by Burke's speech the first moves were shortly set in hand.

Although Burke was the economical reform movement's most prominent petitioner, it attracted many passionate advocates throughout the 1770s. A notable example was the Duke of Richmond who in late 1779 placed before Parliament a motion for 'An Economical Reform of the Civil List Establishment', which proposed a reduction in Civil List expenditure that would set an example for departments and 'would add true lustre to the Crown, from the grateful feelings of a distressed people'.[35] In the same debate Lord Rockingham criticized those who might call for isolated, individual reductions in Civil List expenditure. Instead he called for 'a reformation of the constitution' through measures of economy because its 'principles were perverted; and . . . until it was restored to its original purity, nothing great or decisive could be expected'.[36] Lord Shelburne similarly argued that:

> Influence, that is corruption, and prodigality had to be eliminated for these moved in a circle; they became reciprocally cause and effect. . . . The worst of the public prodigality is, that what is squandered is not simply lost. It is the source of much positive evil. Those who are negligent stewards of the public estate will neglect everything else. It introduces a similar inaccuracy, a kindred slovenliness, a correspondent want of care, and a want of foresight into all national management.

---

[34] Burke, January 1779, in Elofson et al, 1996, p. 467.
[35] *Parliamentary History*, XX, 7 December 1779, column 1258.
[36] *Parliamentary History*, XX, 7 December 1779, column 1260.

What is worst of all, it soon surrounds a supine and inattentive minister with designing, confident, rapacious and unprincipled men.[37]

Taking a similar line, Burke observed that his own motion for economical reform was motivated by concern about the rising expense of war resulting in public expenditure that:

> was lavish and wasteful to a shameful degree. Oeconomy, the most rigid and exact oeconomy, was become absolutely necessary...amidst the many and various matters that require reformation...before this country can rise superior to its powerful enemies; the waste of public treasure requires instant remedy...; it is become indispensably necessary to adopt that true oeconomy, which, by reforming all useless expences, creates confidence in government, gives energy to its exertions, and provides the means for their continuance.[38]

Burke made it clear on many occasions that he was opposed to any reforms that would alter existing constitutional understandings. He wanted confirmation of the relevance and authority of the constitution: he did not want it redefined to embrace demands for a popular franchise and wider representation. Although Burke was alarmed at the 'fatal and overgrown influence of the Crown' he did not, unlike some reformers, want the independence of the Crown to be entirely destroyed. Only by preserving the dignity of the Crown would the constitution be preserved.[39]

Commissioners for Examining the Public Accounts 1780–5

In response to the demands of Burke and his fellow reformers, Parliament passed an Act in 1780 appointing 'not less than five Commissioners to examine, take and state the Public Accounts of the Kingdom'.[40] Seven Commissioners of Audit were appointed by letters patent in 1780, to serve on an annual basis, with power to report the results of their audit to both the Executive and to Parliament. The initial Commissioners of Audit of 1780 were reappointed in each of the following five years, until created as a permanent Commission in 1785. Their statutory duties required them not only to identify defects in present arrangements but also to consider 'in what more expeditious and effectual and less expensive manner the services can in future be regulated and carried on for the benefit of the public'. In modern terms,

---

[37] *Parliamentary History*, XX, 7 December 1779, column 1263 and column 1297.
[38] *Parliamentary History*, XX, 7 December 1779, column 1257.
[39] For Burke, the constitution was neither the product of Locke's social contract and the natural rights that this embodied nor the means to provide for these (Burke, *Letter to the Citizens of Bristol*, 1774; Pocock, 1960, p. 128).
[40] 20 Geo.III, c.54.

they were interested, in principle at least, not just in examples of bad value for money but in measures to secure good value for money.

Prime Minister Lord North's decision to entrust the audit of Executive accounts to what he claimed were independent commissioners, and thereby take the examination out of the direct hands of Parliament, was immediately criticized by Burke and many others.[41] North's decision was clearly designed to thwart the demands of Burke and Lord Shelburne, who in December 1779 were known to be preparing a motion:

> That a Committee be appointed, consisting of members of both Houses, possess-ing neither emolument nor pension, to examine without delay into the public expenditure, and the mode of accounting for the same . . . and to take into consid-eration what savings can be made consistent with public dignity, justice, and gratitude, by an abolition of old or new created offices.[42]

North argued that a commission appointed by the Executive, rather than a committee drawn from Parliament, would have far greater powers to call for papers and to take evidence under oath.[43] Instead of a committee of the House of Commons composed of politicians, North wanted a commission of know-ledgeable and experienced individuals chosen by the government from out-side Parliament who would in effect report to the government. In the House of Lords, however, Lord Irnham argued that the inspection of public accounts was the privilege and responsibility of Parliament. Burke angrily insisted that 'a parliamentary inquiry is the only mode of obtaining parliamentary information'.[44] Lord Shelburne also had wanted a committee consisting of members drawn from both Houses of Parliament who would receive no payments for their duties, thereby providing some measure of protection of their independence from Executive influence.[45] Lord North, however, pre-ferred to select men who had served the government in high office and were therefore men of practical experience in public finance and, of course, polit-ically reliable. Given the extent of the alleged abuses by the Paymaster General of the Forces, Lord North was also determined to appoint men who had experience of army accounts.[46]

---

[41] *Parliamentary History*, XXI, 13 March 1780, column 280. For the debate over the appointment of the Commissioners see *Parliamentary History*, XXI, 1 May 1780, columns 552–70.

[42] Quoted in Norris, 1963, pp. 115–16.

[43] *Parliamentary History*, XXI, 2 March 1780, column 146.

[44] 11 February 1780 in Elofson et al, 1996, p. 535.

[45] *Parliamentary History*, XX, 15 December 1779, column 1293, also 8 February 1780, column 1331; and Foord, 1947, p. 491.

[46] Mainly on the recommendation of the Treasury, and keenly observed by George III, Lord North appointed as commissioners: Sir Guy Carelton, a career soldier and recently the Governor of Quebec who would resign as a commissioner in 1782 to become Commander-in-Chief in America; Arthur Pigott, a serving barrister who later became Solicitor General to the Prince of Wales and Attorney General in Grenada; Samuel Beachcroft, a former Governor of the Bank of England;

By locating the examination of Executive accounts outside Parliament, North contrived to diffuse the pressure that had been building for constitutional reforms and thwart the hopes of the opposition by ensuring that the achievement of economy became a professional matter of better accounting and audit and improved administrative systems, not a constitutional issue. The Commissioners of 1780–5 were not responsible for the formal audit of the accounts; this remained the responsibility of the Auditors of the Imprests. The wider-ranging financial and administrative remit of the Commissioners was clearly established in the wording of the legislation, which stated that their responsibilities were:

> to introduce that System of strict Economy in the Administration of the Public Revenue, which the Legislature has . . . determined to be necessary. By strict Economy we apprehend, is not meant such as either derogates from the Honour and Dignity of the Crown, or abridges the Servant of the Public of the due Reward of his Industry and Abilities; we mean an Oeconomy that steers between extreme Parsimony on the one Hand, and Profusion on the other; that is consistent with Justice as well as Prudence; that gives to all their full Due, and to none more; that supports every useful and necessary Establishment, but cuts off and reduces every superfluous and redundant Expence.[47]

The definition of 'oeconomy' in the Commissioners statutory duties suggested that efficiency as well as economy would come under their remit. Subsequently, the Commissioners indeed confirmed in their Fourteenth Report that their aims had been to expose and redress poor economy,[48] and to introduce greater regularity and system in government administration, but especially in the accounting for Civil List expenditures. Recognizing the circumstances that precipitated their appointment, the overwhelming preoccupation of the Commissioners in their reports was the myriad defects in executive accounting. Their Seventh and Eighth Reports were especially important for their exposure for the first time of the reasons for the

---

Richard Neave, another Governor of the Bank of England; George Drummond, a banker; William Roe, Commissioner of Customs; and Thomas Anguish, at the time the Accountant-General of the Court of Chancery, who wrote most of the fifteen Commissioners' reports and died in office (Binney, 1958, pp. 12–13).

[47] 'An Act for appointing and enabling commissioners to examine, take, and state the public accounts of the kingdom; and to report what balances are in the hands of accountants, which may be applied to the publick service; and what defects there are in the present mode of receiving, collecting, issuing, and accounting for publick money.'

[48] It was 'no mark of wisdom', noted the Commissioners, 'even in an opulent Nation, to lavish the Public Treasure in Expences unprofitable to the State' ('Fourteenth Report of the Commissioners for Examining the Public Accounts', *Journals of the House of Commons*, 26–7 January 1786, p. 23). Proclaiming both the condition of the nation's finances and affirming the demands of the movement of economical reform, the Commissioners urged that 'every Reason of Prudence demands the Reduction of . . . Emoluments, from an Excess to a reasonable limited standard' (Sixth Report, *Journals of the House of Commons*, 11 February 1782, pp. 711, 712).

astonishing delays in the surrendering of public monies appropriated to both the civil list and to the military, and in the auditing of the public accounts. These delays would not be addressed until the process of discharging the final responsibilities of office was transformed. In one particularly prominent case, as a result of their investigations of the Exchequer, the Commissioners discovered that the Pay Offices of the Navy and Army had been £75 million in arrears for more than twenty-four years.[49]

The position was made worse because there was no requirement for imprest holders to surrender all public monies in their possession when they left office. An ancient statute of 1267 was some 500 years later still regarded as requiring accounts to be dealt with in sequence.[50] Imprest holders' accounts could not be submitted for final settlement until those of their predecessors had been audited and finally cleared.[51] They were therefore able to retain unspent funds until their own accounts had been audited and accepted by the Auditors of the Imprests and they in turn had received their final acquittance. Imprest holders no longer in office, but with a balance in hand, had no incentive to pay it back into the Exchequer, indeed every incentive not to do so. They were thus able to profit substantially from funds in their hands both during and after their period of office. In some cases the previous imprest holders had died, leaving matters to be finalized with their heirs. Some of the outstanding settlements were up to seventy years overdue and involved aggregate balances of millions of pounds.

One of the largest imprest holders, well known for scandalous handling of public funds and the enormous personal profits available, was the Paymaster General of the Forces. In one notorious case, Henry Fox (Lord Holland from 1763) was Paymaster General between 1757 and 1765 but did not have his accounts audited until 1778. During this time he was estimated to have received £250,000 in interest.[52] Many years earlier an even longer delay had involved the Earl of Ranelagh, who served as Paymaster General from 1685 until dismissed in 1704 for misappropriation of public funds, but whose accounts were not finally cleared until 1737. Not only was Ranelagh notorious for profiteering from his appointment, a damning report in 1702 by commissioners specially appointed to examine his accounts disclosed a catalogue of fraud and embezzlement, alterations in accounts, ten-year delays in even drawing up accounts, and a lack of vouchers for substantial expenditures, including construction work on Ranelagh's private residences. They found

---

[49] 'Eleventh Report of the Commissioners for Examining the Public Accounts', *Journals of the House of Commons*, 4–5 December 1783, p. 45.

[50] 51 Hen. III, c.5.

[51] Fourth Report of the Commissioners for Examining the Public Accounts, *Journals of the House of Commons*, 6–9 April 1781, col. 382; Torrance, 1978.

[52] Funnell, 2008, p. 13.

that there had been £2 million of public funds for which accounts had never been provided. In pursuing these matters over several years these early commissioners met obstructions familiar to auditors then and since:

> (Ranelagh) had evinced great unwillingness to produce his accounts, and had met their inquiries with endless shuffling and evasion. In his office, too, an unusual epidemic of sudden illness, and an unprecedented multitude of pressing engagements, had rendered his clerks strangely inaccessible to examination.[53]

Two hundred years later the widespread lack of audit and accountability at this time, particularly for military expenditures, would prompt Charles Harris, Director of Finance at the War Office, to observe that:

> It is difficult for us at this distance in time to appreciate the looseness of the standard that then prevailed in matters relating to the public purse. We blush as we read of money granted by the nation for military purposes, in the reign of Charles II, being in fact devoted to the entertainment of the royal mistresses; of the great Duke of Marlborough getting into trouble for pocketing what he protested was the usual percentage on the bread contract for the army of the Low Countries and on its pay; or of the Earl of Ranelagh, Paymaster-General of the Forces under William III, being expelled from the House of Commons for paying away army monies for other than army services.[54]

He might also have added the example of Lord Clive who, when appearing before a parliamentary committee in 1773 to defend his misappropriation of funds when Governor of Bengal, felt able to protest, in all seriousness and with no sense of shame, that 'My God, Mr Chairman, at this moment I stand astonished at my own moderation.'[55]

In light of their findings the Commissioners insisted that public monies in the hands of former imprest holders 'must as soon as possible be made available to the public in their time of great financial distress'.[56] They emphasized that prompt surrender of surplus funds was wholly dependent upon removing delays in the final clearance of imprest holders' accounts. Burke supported the Commissioners by calling upon the government to legislate so as to deny government agents the ability to act as bankers or treasurers and to make them instead 'mere offices of administration and account'.[57] So damning were the Commissioners' first four reports between 1780 and 1782,

---

[53] A detailed report on all these matters is given in *The History of Parliament: the House of Commons 1690–1712*, published 2002.

[54] Memorandum on a lecture delivered at the Army Staff College, 23 November 1907, p. 4.

[55] Gleig, 1848, ch. 29.

[56] Sixth Report of the Commissioners for Examining the Public Accounts, *Journals of the House of Commons*, 11 February 1782, p. 702.

[57] Burke in Elofson et al, 1996, p. 521, emphasis in the original; Fifth Report of the Commissioners for Examining the Public Accounts, *Journals of the House of Commons*, 28 November 1781, p. 577.

in which the system of accounting used by the Executive was described as being in a state of 'Confusion and Ignorance',[58] that the North government had little choice but to legislate to remedy the problems that the Commissioners had confirmed.[59]

Pre-empting the Commissioners' report, on 13 March 1780 Lord North had introduced a Bill to compel payment of outstanding balances in the hands of government bankers and agents and to inform the House and the public as to 'the real state of the accounts of the kingdom, that the nation might be informed how and in what manner the enormous sums which had been granted by parliament have been disposed of'.[60] North's subsequent 1781 Act remedied the worst excesses of the system of delayed settlements by requiring any civilian or military official in possession of unspent balances of public monies to surrender these to the Exchequer at the time they left office.[61] In future, paymasters and others responsible for paying bills out of funds appropriated by Parliament would act as accountants on behalf of the Exchequer and not as bankers with their own private accounts.

The new provisions were extended and strengthened in 1782, when Burke himself was in government, by legislation to regulate the office of Paymaster General[62] and to reform the operations of the Civil List under the Civil Establishments Act.[63] Reitan described the Civil Establishments Act as the measure that finally ended the struggle between Parliament and the Executive for control of finance.[64] These initial reform Acts were replaced in 1783 by more effective legislation,[65] which required that all monies would first be paid into accounts at the Bank of England from which the paymasters would draw funds under Exchequer control.[66]

---

[58] Sixth Report, *Journals of the House of Commons*, 11 February 1782, p. 713.

[59] See: 22 Geo.III, c.48; 22 Geo.III, c.81.

[60] *Parliamentary History*, XXI, 13 March 1780, column 278.

[61] 22 Geo.III, c.48. 'An act to direct the payment into the exchequer of the respective balances remaining in the hands of the several persons therein named, for the use and benefit of the publick; and for indemnifying the said respective persons, and their representatives, in respect of such payments, and against all future claims relating thereto; and for other purposes therein mentioned.'

[62] 22 Geo.III, c.81.

[63] 22 Geo.III, c.82, 'An act for enabling his Majesty to discharge the debt contracted upon his civil list revenues; and for preventing the same from being in arrear for the future, by regulating the mode of payments out of the said revenues, and by suppressing or regulating certain offices herein mentioned, which are now paid out of the revenues of the civil list.'

[64] Reitan, 1966, p. 335.

[65] 23 Geo.III, c.50. 'An Act for the better regulation of the office of the paymaster general of his Majesty's forces, and the more regular payment of the Army; and to repeal an act made in the last session of parliament.'

[66] See also Fifth Report of Commissioners for Examining the Public Accounts, *Journals of the House of Commons*, 5 November 1781, pp. 575–7, and Burke, 11 February 1780 in Elofson et al, 1996, p. 522.

Other reports by the Commissioners on sinecures and similar public offices were a scathing indictment of overmanning, high costs, excessive fees, duplication of work or no work at all, and outdated and cumbersome procedures. For example, in 1780 the expenses of Exchequer operations met from public funds was £8,000, but the fees and poundage collected from government departments and the public amounted to more than £82,000. This left £74,000 to be shared out amongst the aristocratic sinecurists.[67] The Commissioners recommended that until these and other sinecures were finally abolished the emoluments and awards of sinecurists should be significantly reduced.

At a broader level, the attacks on sinecures marked a shift in culture that would become one of the foundations of the modern British civil service, in which all work was to be carried out in the public interest and not for the benefit of the office holder. Senior public office, urged the Commissioners, should be a matter of legal tenure and not a gift to which was attached the privileges of private property.[68] If an office was abolished its incumbent had no grounds to object; the only grounds to justify the continuance of an office were 'the benefit of the State' and 'the Good of the Public'. Office holders had 'no other Right than to the Reward of his Labour: He has no Right to any specific Quantity of Business; that Quantity must fluctuate according to Circumstances, or may be regulated by the Convenience of the State'.[69]

As well as criticizing the funding processes of government, the Commissioners also examined actual expenditures incurred by departments, the key area completely ignored by the Auditors of the Imprests. A particularly damning Commissioners' report on military expenditure identified substantial abuses during the American War of Independence. This revealed fraud, misappropriation, bad management, excessive provisioning, and many examples of waste and extravagance. The Commissioners took evidence from the generals and others involved, criticized poor accounting systems and inadequate contracts, identified conflicts of interest, noted breaches of trust, and emphasized risks of corruption. The Commissioners pointed particularly to the high extra costs of private contracting for transportation, where officers were hiring their own vessels and wagons and horses to the Army at excessive rates. They reported that: 'The practice of letting out for hire to Government has been highly lucrative to those engaged in it. The public

---

[67] A detailed account of these scandals and the aristocratic lineage of those involved is set out in the paper *An Old Exchequer Tally* presented by Sir Ernest Clarke to the Royal Statistical Society in December 1911.
[68] *Journals of the House of Commons*, 1782, XLII, pp. 27, 30.
[69] Eleventh Report of the Commissioners for Examining the Public Accounts, *Journals of the House of Commons*, 4–5 December 1783, p. 779.

have paid £417,592 for the single article of the hire of wagons and horses, the whole of which might have been saved had the property of these wagons and horses belonged to Government.'

In presenting their reports the Commissioners of 1780–5 seemed to share with modern auditors a clear perception of the legitimate bounds of audit work, particularly when touching on questions of policy. While the Commissioners could be vigorous in their criticisms they were equally careful not to criticize policy directly. Many of their proposals for change were then studiously submitted 'for the exercise of the wisdom of the Legislature'. They also went out of their way to show due regard to the impact of policy, the importance of practical considerations, and the need to decide between a choice of options. Their reports were therefore submitted with the standard preamble that:

> Whatever reason there may be for continuing these services, whether drawn from policy or expedience, all these are topics not within the limits of our commission, but for the discussion of the Legislature, whose deliberations comprehend arguments drawn from every source.

Similarly, the Commissioners, like their modern successors, faced the perennial problem of an administrative culture that made it difficult to persuade departments to translate audit recommendations into positive action:

> We are well aware of the difficulties that must for ever attend introducing novelty of form into ancient offices, framed by the wisdom of our ancestors and established by the experience of ages. They are considered incapable of improvement; the officers educated in and accustomed to the forms in use are insensible of their defects; or, if they feel them, have no leisure, often no ability, seldom any inclination, to correct them. Alarmed at the idea of innovation, they resist the proposal of a regulation, because it is a change, though from a perplexed and intricate to a more simple and intelligible system.

The appointment of the Commissioners of 1780–5 was an early signal of Parliament's recognition that existing arrangements for the accountability and audit of public funds were inadequate. The Commissioners' individual reports provided striking examples of long-standing abuses that needed to be addressed, based on a level of investigative information that had not previously been available to Parliament. As a result, both the Executive and Parliament recognized the need for extensive financial and administrative reforms. A permanent and more coherent framework was needed, with objectives directed towards wider accountability, less delay, better accounting systems, and a more extensive and systematic audit.

The Commissioners' findings and recommendations prompted the introduction of significant and fundamental improvements to which some key principles and procedures of present governmental financial operations can be traced. The single most important and lasting change was the establishment of the Consolidated Fund in 1787. This replaced separate flows of funds coming into and out of the Exchequer with centralized funding and accounting for all parliamentary grants by the introduction of 'One fund into which shall flow every stream of public revenue from which shall come the supply of every service.' However, the Consolidated Fund remained a control of funding: accountability for expenditure was still lacking.

The sinecures most severely criticized by the Commissioners for Examining the Public Accounts were the two posts of the Auditors of the Imprests where, as already noted, there were long-standing and well-known defects and delays in the conduct of business. The Commissioners' Twelfth and Thirteenth Reports urged the reformation of these offices 'in which the Service of the Presiding Officer bears no Proportion to the Magnitude of his Profits'. They found that between 1745 and 1781 all work of the Auditors of the Imprests had been conducted by their deputies and that neither of the Auditors had attended their office for over thirty years but in 1783 each were paid £16,565.[70] The Commissioners were:

> unable to discover . . . any solid Advantage derived to the Public from the Examination given to . . . (the public accounts) by the Auditor of Imprests, and, for that Reason, we have suggested the Propriety of exempting them from his Jurisdiction, and the urgent Necessity of relieving the Nation from so heavy, and, to all Appearance, so unnecessary an Expence.[71]

The extensive criticisms by the Commissioners of 1780–5 had given the new government under William Pitt little choice but to introduce early legislation to strengthen the audit arrangements for both civil and military expenditure. Thus, both of the Auditor of the Imprests posts were abolished in 1785 and their functions and responsibilities transferred to the five permanent Commissioners for Auditing the Public Accounts, who had just been appointed to replace the Commissioners of 1780–5.[72] Abolition of the posts, however, proved to be extremely expensive because the two office holders, Lord Sondes and Lord Mount Stewart, fought long and hard for compensation for the loss of their enormous profits. Each eventually received a 'golden goodbye' with the award of £7,000 (almost £1 million today) to compensate them for the loss of their 'profits and emoluments'.

---

[70] Twelfth Report of the Commissioners for Examining the Public Accounts, *Journals of the House of Commons*, 11 June 1784, p. 123; and Thirteenth Report, *Journals of the House of Commons*, 21 March 1785, p. 665.
[71] Quoted in Cohen, 1965, p. 37.   [72] 25 Geo. III c.52.

Commissioners of Audit 1785–1866

The preamble to the 1785 Act confirmed that, together with their office, to be known as the Board of Audit, the new Commissioners were to implement a 'more effectual method...for examining the public accounts of the kingdom, and for preventing...all delays, frauds, and abuses, in delivering in and passing' the accounts. Although the Commissioners were appointed by the Executive and the audits they performed were not carried out on behalf of Parliament, the Executive was now required regularly to declare and lay before Parliament accounts of all executive spending.

It quickly emerged that the journey towards effective parliamentary accountability and an independent audit would be longer and more difficult, and the results more contentious, than had been expected. At the heart of these difficulties would be the lack of clear agreement on the primary role of the Board of Audit. On one side were those who saw the new audit arrangements as an opportunity to improve accountability to Parliament, with auditors having clear independence and a wide remit, while others, particularly the Treasury, wanted the audit to remain a creature of the Executive under their control and direction. Despite further efforts, establishing Parliament's eventual pre-eminence in all matters of accountability and audit would take another 100 years.

Under the 1785 Act the new Commissioners took over the duties and powers of the Auditors of the Imprests and were similarly placed under firm Treasury control.[73] In particular, the Treasury continued to be responsible for executing the Commissioners' oath of office, which confirmed the narrow view to be taken on the Board's remit and the nature of the audit.[74] The Treasury appointed all audit staff and determined all conditions of employment. The Treasury could also determine the structure and organization of the Board and allocate audit work and allot staff between the Board's separate divisions. Parliament was not mentioned in the 1785 Act; the Commissioners were to audit on behalf of the Treasury and it was to the Treasury that they were required to send their reports.

The unfinished work of the two Auditors of the Imprests was transferred to the new Board of Audit on the existing basis of audit. Audit did not extend to an examination of actual expenditure and was subject to the same shortcomings and delays. The continuing level of detailed Treasury control reaffirmed

---

[73] 25 Geo.III c.52, sections VIII, XI, XIV, XVIII, XIX, XXI.

[74] Inspectors of Accounts took an oath 'not to permit, suffer, or conceal, any fraud whatsoever in any accounts intrusted to your care. In all Accounts...you shall see that they are carefully and faithfully examined, drawn, and prepared for Auditing; giving therein to no Accountant any allowance but such as shall be duly and regularly vouched and allowable according to the custom, method, and rules of the Exchequer' (Office for Auditing the Public Accounts, 1786).

the subordinate position of the Commissioners and the Board of Audit and perpetuated a basic flaw in relative accountabilities. As explained many years later in clear and correct terms by Charles Macaulay, one of the Commissioners of Audit and Secretary of the Board:

> The practice of sending the accounts of imprests to the Auditors direct has always been objectionable in principle. . . . The practice of sending imprest accounts to the Audit Office before they have been reviewed by the department which ordered the imprests, is open to serious objection and in many cases is the source of much avoidable labour and delay.[75]

The initial staffing of the Board of Audit was small and demonstrably inadequate. The large backlog of uncleared accounts inherited from the Auditors of the Imprests meant that from its very first day the Board was behind in its work. The Board's staff on 5 July 1785, excluding the five Commissioners, consisted of two inspectors general and sixteen clerks. By September 1785 an extra seven junior clerks, a solicitor, an office keeper, and two messengers had been appointed. Numbers were further expanded in 1787 and remained at a total complement of forty-three until into the nineteenth century.[76] By 1805 the growing backlog of uncleared accounts was so serious that the Select Committee on Public Monies in 1857 would later remind Parliament that 'it is difficult to realise, even in imagination, the extent of abuse which was then stated to exist'.[77] The Committee on Expenditure in 1810 would also criticize the Executive for starving the Board of resources, thereby severely limiting its effectiveness.[78]

By 1806 it had become increasingly obvious to a worried Parliament that the additional financial burdens created by the recent conflicts in Europe had shown that the existing audit arrangements were insufficient to keep the audit of accounts up to date.[79] This was despite the addition in the previous year of another Board of Commissioners to support the existing Board, comprising three Commissioners with the same powers as those previously installed.[80] At the direction of the Treasury, this auxiliary Board was to assist the existing Commissioners with the audit of 'extraordinary accounts' that

---

[75] Macaulay, *Observations on Appropriation Audit, 1863, para 43* (Appendix to the Report of the Committee of Public Accounts, H.C. Paper No 413, 1865). This paper reviewed the existing system of appropriation accounts and proposed new arrangements to be adopted following the recommendations of the Select Committee on Public Monies and the passing of the Exchequer and Audit Departments Act 1866.

[76] Establishment Rolls, Board of Audit 1785–99.

[77] Select Committee on Public Monies, 1857, Appendix 3, p. 590.

[78] Fifth Report, p. 387.

[79] HC debates, 23 June 1806; Memorandum by Sir William Anderson in Parker 1907, vol. 1, p. 167.

[80] 45 Geo.III. c.91.

had fallen into arrears. However, the position continued to deteriorate. In an attempt to remedy matters the Chancellor of the Exchequer, Lord Henry Petty, presented a motion to Parliament in 1806 for yet another reorganization of audit. The resulting 1806 Act[81] increased the establishment of auditors by separating the two Comptrollers of Army Accounts from the Commissioners for Auditing the Public Accounts and adding another four Commissioners to the Board of Audit to give a total of ten.[82] The 1806 Act further strengthened the Treasury's domination over the audit by giving it the power to subdivide the Board of Audit into as many sub-boards as it saw fit, and to allocate the Board's work and its staff between the sub-boards. During the debate on the 1806 Act Lord Petty justified this increase in the Treasury's powers on the grounds that:

> It would be expedient to leave the power with Treasury to alter it as they should see occasion, because the Treasury would have the best opportunity of observing how the different boards wrought, and what might be the most effectual mode of carrying speedily forward the great work which must be managed in some manner or other. Whatever the errors therefore might occur, the Treasury would be enabled to rectify them and to make up in some measure for any defects which might escape the notice of Parliament in passing the bill.[83]

Lord Petty assured the House that it was not his intention to augment unnecessarily the 'powers and patronage' of the Treasury and that 'if there could be any other mode by which the end proposed could be effectually answered that mode would be gladly adopted'. The Executive's record on this issue made these explanations and assurances less than convincing. There were further changes in 1809, with the Commissioners now divided into four boards. A General Board was concerned with general business, correspondence, and regulations for all the Boards while the First Board was allotted by the Treasury the ordinary and extra-ordinary accounts arising from transactions after 1 January 1806. Ordinary accounts prior to 1 January 1806, that is arrears, were the province of the Second Board while the Third Board audited extra-ordinary accounts from before 1 January 1806. Apart from the General Board, each Board had three Commissioners and a Chairman. These initial arrangements applied only to 23 December 1809 when the First and Second Boards were consolidated by a Treasury Warrant and called First Subdivision Board. At the same time the Third Board was called the Second Subdivision Board. This bewildering sequence of events and the results, or lack

---

[81] 46 Geo.III. c.141.

[82] Commissioners were not to be replaced until their number was reduced to five. The Executive was allowed to nominate and appoint the Chairman of the Commissioners and any new Commissioners, provided that at all times a minimum of six was maintained.

[83] HC debates, 23 June 1806, col. 292.

of results, it produced were extensively examined by the 1810 Committee on Public Expenditure.

The 1810 Committee was highly critical about the domination of audit by the Treasury and the Board of Audit's lack of independence on the extent of the audit and the nature of the examination carried out. Much to the disappointment of the members of the Committee, the 1785 Act marked 'in the strongest manner the intention of the legislature that . . . [the Board] should be strictly subject to the controls of the Treasury'.[84] In practice this meant that:

> The decision of the Auditors is in no instance final; but the Lords of the Treasury exercise complete authority with regard to all the articles of an Account . . . the special jurisdiction of the Treasury is constantly and habitually necessary to the final settlement and passing of the greater part of the Public Accounts which are examined by the Commissioners of Audit.[85]

The 1785 Act had done nothing to improve the independence of the Board of Audit; if anything the position had deteriorated. This continuing lack of independence was entirely consistent with Executive's intention that the 1785 Act would create a mechanism for simply checking the accuracy of accounts and the authority for expenditure as opposed to establishing an independent audit, with powers specifically freeing it from external control or influence. After criticizing the Commissioners personally for their lack of interest and initiative, and the token nature of the work of the Board, the 1810 Committee moved on to examining the changes introduced by Acts in 1805, 1806, and 1809. Unimpressed, they quickly concluded that:

> The present system of Audit may therefore with propriety be declared to have failed, in many respects, in answering the purposes contemplated by the legislature . . . notwithstanding the previous Acts which have since been passed for the more effectual examination of the Public Accounts, most of the original evils are still permitted. . . . The system itself in all material aspects is precisely the same as it was more than a century ago.[86]

The 1810 Committee was particularly concerned about Treasury inaction in responding to the recommendations in the Board of Audit's reports.[87] It was even more disturbed that, because the Board's reports were directed solely to the Treasury, Parliament had no knowledge of the Board's findings and recommendations. There was no information about the Treasury's response, nor on any remedial measures introduced. Not only did the Treasury dominate the work of the Board, the Treasury was the gatekeeper for all audit

---

[84] Committee on Public Expenditure, 1810, Fifth Report, p. 388.
[85] Committee on Public Expenditure, 1810, Fifth Report, p. 388.
[86] Committee on Public Expenditure, 1810, Fifth Report, p. 389.
[87] Committee on Public Expenditure, 1810, Fifth Report, p. 388.

information to Parliament. In a rare and oblique, yet clear, criticism of the oppressive role of the Treasury, the Board of Audit themselves suggested to the 1810 Committee that the accounts would not have fallen into arrears, or the existing deficiencies of audit allowed to continue, if the Board had been allowed to address Parliament directly on the results of the audit, instead of always requiring the permission of the Treasury to do so.[88] The 1810 Committee was in no doubt that the accounts had fallen so seriously into arrears because the Board of Audit was 'entirely destitute' of the necessary authority to force departments to produce accounts.[89]

The Committee was greatly concerned that the limited authority and uncertain status of the Board and its staff affected its relationships with the bodies it audited. The powers given to the Commissioners confined 'the exercise of their discretion in matters of account *within rules more rigid than in any other great department intrusted with similar duties*' (emphasis added).[90] Given the responsibilities and tasks set for the Board, the Committee considered it anomalous that the Board should have more restrictions on its powers than the departments it examined. Tied and bound by the decisions of the Treasury, and facing departments with far greater powers of self-regulation, the Board was faced with a situation where: 'The power of acting is almost entirely denied to them, they are subject to such a variety of restrictions . . . as tends to impede all sufficient progress in the discharge of their functions, and renders them wholly subservient to the Board of the Treasury.'[91]

The 1810 Committee concluded that relegating the Board of Audit to such an inferior status meant that it was neither independent nor, in the absence of powers superior to those it was auditing, influential.[92] The subordinate position of the Board when compared to other public departments frequently impeded its proceedings. This weakness was compounded by the high situation of some public accountants with connections to persons in high office, which could at times threaten the Board's authority. The importance attached at the time to rank, social position, and class meant that, when faced with strong opposition from a high official in a department, the Board's more junior officers were at a disadvantage. It was more difficult to have unwelcome findings and criticisms accepted in a milieu that perpetuated the legitimacy of social rankings and the attendant respect that higher levels presumed as their right from 'lesser classes'.

In drawing up its report, the 1810 Committee was anxious to dispel a perception in Parliament, fostered by the Treasury despite the clear evidence

---

[88] Committee on Public Expenditure, 1810, Fifth Report, p. 388.
[89] Committee on Public Expenditure, 1810, Fifth Report, p. 388.
[90] Committee on Public Expenditure, 1810, Fifth Report, p. 388.
[91] Committee on Public Expenditure, 1810, Fifth Report, p. 388.
[92] Committee on Public Expenditure, 1810, Fifth Report, p. 388.

to the contrary, that the Board of Audit 'was purported to be an independent authority...and was supposed to be placed beyond the party and political influences of the day'. The Committee was also concerned about the 'received opinion' that the Board's audit covered all the public accounts. In practice, Treasury directions meant that the Board's detailed examination extended only to the smaller departments. All the major departments audited their own expenditure and the Board's audit was little more than a token scrutiny of total departmental expenditure.[93] Despite this long list of criticisms the Treasury was not prepared to introduce major changes. It was content simply to reorganize the Board in 1813 when the Commissioners of Audit were reduced to five.[94] The First Board was designated the Board of Audit, Somerset Place and the Second Board became the Audit Office, Adelphi. In 1822 a further change combined both bodies as the Board of Audit, Somerset Place.[95]

Consolidation of Audit

A few remaining specialist audit bodies continued to operate concurrently with the Board of Audit until their work was progressively brought within the Board's responsibilities. The last of these was the Comptrollers of Army Accounts in 1835. From 1835, therefore, the Commissioners and the Board of Audit were solely responsible for the audit of all the public accounts. This process of audit consolidation in the period 1785 to 1835 was consistently opposed by the Treasury, even though the 1810 Committee on Expenditure had seen great merit in a single Board of Audit with responsibility for 'the superintendence and control over the whole of the accounts of the receipts and expenditure of the kingdom, in all its various branches'.[96] The Treasury had objected strongly, arguing that to contemplate combining audit into one office 'would be a measure of imprudence and rashness'. It argued that the only safe course was to 'innovate as little as possible, and to retain the existing establishments'. Any other course of action was 'so replete with difficulties as to be utterly impracticable in its execution...(and) would be highly... objectionable in principle'.[97]

At the root of the Treasury's vehement opposition was the 1810 Committee's recommendation that the status of the Board should be raised and that

---

[93] Committee on Public Expenditure, 1810, Fifth Report, pp. 382, 391.

[94] Treasury Warrant, 25 August 1813.

[95] Treasury Warrant, 19 July 1822, *Summary of Commission of Audit and Exchequer and Audit Department Minutes*, Treasury internal information paper, no date, pp. 131–4.

[96] Committee on Expenditure, 1810, Fifth Report, referred to in *British Parliamentary Papers*, 1821, (517) XIV, pp. 51–2.

[97] Treasury Minute, 1 February 1811, referred to in *British Parliamentary Papers*, 1821, (517) XIV, pp. 51–2.

the discretionary powers of the Board should be widened at the expense of the Treasury. According to the Treasury, not only was the Board 'utterly incompetent to exercise' these enhanced powers, it could not do so 'with justice to the public or to the individual accountant'.[98] When the severe limits on the Board's independence were again questioned by the Select Committee on Finance in 1819, the Treasury still maintained its strong opposition to giving the Commissioners more authority. George Harrison, the Treasury representative appearing before the Committee, set out the Treasury's view of the constitutional arguments at some length:

> To vest in ... [the Board of Audit] a power to judge of the propriety or expediency of expenditure, would be to introduce a perfect anomaly into the state, and to alter the whole constitutional functions and responsibility of the highest departments in it. If a power were vested in an independent board of audit of entering into consideration of the objects or motives of this expenditure for the purpose of questioning its propriety ... it would, in effect, be placing ... a board of check and control over the Lord High Treasurer ...; it would, in effect, be investing in this independent board a power of questioning all the acts of the Crown, and of trying the whole executive government in regards to its expenditure. In short, it would amount to a delegation by parliament ... of those powers and functions which constitutionally belong ... to parliament and to parliament alone.[99]

Harrison insisted that 'It would not be advisable at any time, or under any circumstances, to hazard such an experiment.' He argued strongly in favour of relying almost entirely on the audit carried out by the departments themselves, which he maintained was far more satisfactory than 'any independent office of audit which human ingenuity could devise'.[100] In stark contrast to this supremely confident assertion, Sir Henry Parnell in particular later dismissed complete reliance on departmental self-audit as 'highly objectionable'.[101] Harrison also pointed out that extending the Board's audit would require a greater number of clerks and suggested, without explaining why, that therefore it would be less efficient. Any proposal to strengthen the Board's independence was to be discouraged on the grounds of both economy and efficiency. He also questioned suggestions by the 1819 Committee that the Board of Audit should be represented by a high officer of state who had a seat in Parliament. It was most doubtful, he intoned, that this would be of any advantage because 'The dry and irksome details of so uninteresting and so invidious an office' would be insufficient to maintain the interest and enthusiasm of a sitting

---

[98] Treasury Minute, 1 February 1811.

[99] Select Committee on Finance, 1819, Appendix to the Fifth Report, Minutes of Evidence, p. 205.

[100] Select Committee on Finance, 1819, Appendix to the Fifth Report, Minutes of Evidence, pp. 205–9.

[101] HC debates, 17 February 1831, col. 625.

Member of Parliament.[102] Obviously the last thing the Treasury wanted was to have a highly placed competitor for its authority over the audit. Harrison's comments clearly exposed the Treasury's disparaging opinion of the Board of Audit and its determination that the Board should remain, in effect, a subordinate arm of the Treasury.

The Treasury and the Civil Service in Nineteenth-Century Britain

The increasing complexity of government made it necessary to have an experienced, knowledgeable, and permanent civil service to administer government policies. Parliament was therefore prepared to sanction the rise of a strong and influential civil service, despite earlier reservations. Prior to the early nineteenth century Parliament had been reluctant to extend the powers of the Executive by allowing it an effective civil administration. This reflected underlying suspicions of Executive motives born out of the constitutional conflicts of the seventeenth century. Parliament's latent distrust of the Executive was also reflected in a preference for specific-case legislation rather than general statutes. For example, there were separate statutes for each Board of Health and Board of Education. This began to change in the 1830s. The waning of Parliament's constitutional distrust of the Executive meant that general statutes became more prominent, and these wider-ranging statutes could only be put into practice with the aid of an effective civil service.

The investigations into the civil service in the 1850s by Stafford Northcote MP, later Chancellor of the Exchequer, and Sir Charles Trevelyan, Permanent Secretary of the Treasury, and their final damning report in 1854 (hereafter the Northcote-Trevelyan Report)[103] confirmed that Executive departments were a loose collection of feifdoms, each of which was responsible for appointing its own staff. As a result, departments:

> became the habitation of the unambitious, and the indolent or incapable.... Those whose abilities do not warrant an expectation that they will succeed in the open professions ... and those whose indolence of temperament or physical infirmities are unfit for active exertions.... The result ... is that the public service suffers both in internal efficiency and in public estimation.[104]

---

[102] HC debates, 17 February 1831, col. 625, p. 208.

[103] Northcote-Trevelyan Report on the civil service, 1854.

[104] Northcote-Trevelyan Report on the civil service, 1854, p. 4. Also *Quarterly Review*, vol. 133, July to October 1872, p. 243. For further criticism see *The Westminster Review*, January to April 1876, New Series, vol. 49, p. 467. However, there was no shortage of public officials queuing up to refute the claims in the 1854 Report. See *Quarterly Review*, vol. 108, July to October 1860, p. 577.

Movement between departments was most unusual. Each department regarded itself as a separate entity and not part of a single cohesive service.[105] The results, according to the Northcote-Trevelyan Report, were 'narrow views and departmental prejudices...[as well as] considerable inconvenience... from the want of facilities for transferring strength from an office where work is becoming slack to one in which it is increasing'.[106] It is therefore misleading to refer to a 'civil service' much before the 1860s. Trevelyan himself had been informed when he joined the Treasury in 1840 that 'there was no Civil Service but only the establishment of this or that civil office'.[107] The absence of a unified civil service meant that the Treasury was unable to establish unchallenged control over departments. Each department effectively determined its own conditions of employment and remuneration. So diverse were the arrangements that Trevelyan later observed that 'the internal arrangements and regulations of the different departments...were very imperfectly understood at the Treasury'.[108]

In the absence of a matured, unified civil service through which to operate, the Treasury's financial power in the early nineteenth century was less extensive and less complete than it is sometimes suggested. Indeed, Wright has argued that the Treasury's control over departmental expenditure was largely illusory, in the sense that it depended upon their powers of persuasion in a 'process of control' as opposed to the Treasury having any specific and enforceable 'controls'.[109] The Treasury did not have the authority simply to refuse or reduce departmental demands for money to meet increased expenditure.[110] When departments requested extra money each case was treated separately. In the early part of the nineteenth century there was little attempt on the Treasury's part to generalize its financial policies and decisions from one department to others.

Although the Treasury may not have been able to reduce or refuse departmental funding applications in a particular instance, its delaying and precise approach was designed to pressure the department into reconsidering the current application and the consequences for any future financial demands. By making the process long, difficult, and inconvenient it sought to discourage departments, reduce momentum in funding requests, and dissipate the energy of the application.[111] The Earl of Middleton, reflecting upon his time as

---

[105] Finer, 1937, p. 29; Wright, 1969, Introduction.

[106] Northcote-Trevelyan Report on the civil service, 1854, p. 8.

[107] Trevelyan to Measor, 1867, as quoted in Wright, 1969, footnote 4, p. xxiii.

[108] Sir Charles Trevelyan, 1875, in *The Nineteenth Century*, vol. 20, July to December 1886, p. 500.

[109] Wright, 1969.

[110] Royal Commission on Civil Establishment, 1887, Minutes of Evidence, Lord Welby, *British Parliamentary Papers*, First Report, vol. 19, pp. 1–9.

[111] See *Contemporary Review*, vol. 68, July to December 1895, p. 331; *The Nineteenth Century*, vol. 24, July to December 1888, p. 113.

Secretary for War, described the Treasury as 'ruthless' and the cause of 'unending struggle' in attempts to obtain extra funding.[112] Sir Robert Hamilton, Accountant General and later Permanent Secretary in the Admiralty, referred to 'perpetual clashes with the Treasury'.[113]

Seeking increases in funding over and above existing budget provisions followed an implied script, recognized by all the main players. The play consisted of several acts. At the first stage, applications for increased funding were more often than not met with requests from the Treasury for more information. The application, with suitable additional documentation, would be duly resubmitted. According to Wright, these early submissions were not always formal.[114] Prior to the closing decades of the nineteenth century the Treasury wanted to avoid a full confrontation with a department over requests for additional funding and would seek instead to arrive at an agreement through informal discussion. If these were unsuccessful the responsible minister might then discuss the position with his colleague the Chancellor of the Exchequer on a personal level. Success at this stage would depend on the relationship between the two men, the status of the department seeking the extra funding and the status of the minister. Good personal relationships between ministers and between upper levels in departmental hierarchies and the Treasury were therefore essential to the conduct of government financial business. On the rare occasions that agreement could not be reached and the matter was referred to the Cabinet, the outcome was usually dependent on the wider network of personal relationships between ministers.

Although many of the recommendations in the Northcote-Trevelyan Report took some time to be implemented, development of the civil service proceeded more positively from the late 1850s.[115] However, the prospective rise of a permanent civil service acting in support of the Executive led to renewed concern in Parliament that Treasury control of a career civil service could be used to increase Executive power, at the expense of Parliament. Fears of this kind were a contributory factor in the movement towards the

---

[112] Middleton, 1939, p. 126.

[113] Hamilton to Gladstone, 1865, quoted in Wright, 1969, p. 344.

[114] Wright, 1969.

[115] HC debates, 11 March 1862. By an Order in Council of the 21 May 1855 the government appointed the first civil service Commissioners who were given the authority to oversee conditions of appointment to government service. This was no means a universal coverage of all departments. It was not until Orders in Council of 4 June 1870 and 19 August 1871 that all candidates for the civil service were required to sit examinations set by the civil service Commissioners. It was left to the Civil Service Inquiry Commission (Playfair Commission), instituted by Gladstone in 1874, to carry further the work of Trevelyan and Northcote. Despite significant advances towards a unified civil service in the closing decades of the nineteenth century there were still frequent complaints about the parochial nature of the civil service (Select Committee on Army Estimates, 1888, Minutes of Evidence, *British Parliamentary Papers*, vol. 9, Qs. 5003–5).

introduction and extension of stronger and more formal procedures for parliamentary accountability. These were given particular prominence with the Report of the Select Committee on Public Monies in 1857, which in turn led to the establishment of the Public Accounts Committee in 1861 and the passage of the Exchequer and Audit Departments Act in 1866.

By the latter decades of the nineteenth century a constitutional bureaucracy had been firmly established and it had been accepted that the Treasury had the authority to develop general guidance on financial and accounting procedures for all departments. In the meantime, the Treasury consistently pursued every opportunity to consolidate its authority. It was determined to maintain its heavy involvement in developments taking place in the form, preparation, and audit of the public accounts. It was especially determined to protect its role and authority at all stages throughout the introduction and passage of successive audit legislation. As always, the aim was to ensure that audit remained, in effect, a subordinate arm of the Treasury.

Conclusion

In the later years of the eighteenth century, and for many years afterwards, the inadequacies in accountability and audit had become increasingly obvious as the size and complexity of public activities and expenditure increased. There was growing recognition of the need for fundamental changes in accountability between Parliament and the Executive, in the content and presentation of public sector accounts, and in the role, responsibilities, and powers of the state auditors. However, the lack of genuine appropriation accounts, with an independent and effective audit, would not be addressed and resolved until major changes were introduced in the second half of the nineteenth century.

The development of state audit in the later years of the eighteenth century and the first half of the nineteenth century was inextricably involved with the growth of the Executive, the emergence of a unified and permanent civil service, and the increasing power of the Treasury. The Treasury remained determined that the auditors should remain under their control, not only to minimize potentially awkward criticisms of Executive spending but also as an effective means of extending their financial control throughout the emerging departments of state, particularly at a time when a permanent career civil service was being established. Although the Commissioners for Examining the Public Accounts (1780–5) produced a series of penetrating reports on waste and extravagance, their successors in the Commissioners and Board of Audit were increasingly subjected by the Treasury to a more limited and passive role. The Treasury had no formal legislative backing to support its bid to secure a dominant position within the Executive and saw a subordinated statutory audit as an important element in furthering its ambitions.

Despite initial stirrings, Parliament had not yet fully recognized the importance of an independent audit as a basis for holding the Executive accountable for the funds Parliament had voted. The House of Commons was still content to leave audit and related matters largely in the hands of the Executive. Members had not sufficiently awoken to the fact that the audit was confined simply to ensuring that the imprests issued from the Exchequer to the departments had not exceeded the total amounts authorized by Parliament. They were also unaware that the auditors did not examine actual expenditure by departments. The published accounts and audit reports provided no information as to whether these imprests were fully expended or whether they had been promptly and properly used for the purposes approved by Parliament.

Delays in introducing a better framework of accountability and audit also arose from the complications of mid-eighteenthth-century parliamentary and political life where alliances and splits, coalitions, and realignments dominated government and public affairs. Significant change to long-accepted principles of public sector accountability were difficult to achieve in a flux of negotiation and party politics. Personal friendships and sometimes fierce antagonisms added to the mix, accentuating the complexity.

5

Early Victorian Reform

'These heapes of silluer will be a passing bell, calling thee to a fearfull audit.'

Thomas Drekker, *Several Sins*

Although the Exchequer and Audit Departments Act 1866 would later become the pinnacle of nineteenth-century developments in public financial account-ability and audit, it was achieved only after decades of painstaking efforts, in Parliament and outside, to overcome important shortcomings in existing arrangements, most especially the basis on which departmental accounts were prepared and the lack of independence for the Commissioners of Audit and the Board of Audit. While ever the accounts showed only the funds issued to departments from the Exchequer and gave no information on actual expenditure, it was impossible to determine whether the funds issued had been fully spent during the year on the relevant services or whether, and when, unspent amounts had been surrendered. Nor was it possible to deter-mine whether more had been spent than had been approved by Parliament or whether funds approved for one service had been spent on another. Accounts based on imprests were progressively replaced by appropriation accounts of actual expenditure incurred, compared with the spending approved in the estimates. However, the estimates were still too broadly based and expenditure too highly aggregated to provide for informed parliamentary scrutiny. Accord-ingly, examination by the Commissioners and Board of Audit was a broad and largely arithmetical check circumscribed by the restricted scope of the accounts.

Although in some departments there were from time to time more detailed examinations of departmental expenditure, this 'Detailed or Administrative Audit' was only carried out when called for by the Treasury. Examinations were directed largely towards questions of overall authority and regularity. They were conducted mainly to reinforce Treasury control rather than for parliamentary accountability. Any issues raised were submitted to the Treasury for final decision. Funding and staffing of the Board of Audit was also under Treasury control, rather than independently serving Parliament as part of the control of the Executive. Inadequate staffing of the Board of Audit, and the workload arising from the backlog of accounts that had not been cleared, contributed to long delays. The Commissioners themselves seemed to have little appetite for change. Nevertheless, their work was later fulsomely described as the:

> dividing line between the ancient and the modern. Before their work began, the clumsy hand of the Middle Ages is found still laid heavily on the financial system: before they had finished their work the enormous task had been commenced of freeing the system from its anachronistic and injurious elements. The good work continued upon the road they had mapped out until the past had little further power to harm, and the accepted standards were the needs of the present.[1]

Further reform of audit would depend upon the end of the Tory Party's long unbroken span of hegemony from the late eighteenth century to the early 1830s. It had come to be seen as the legitimate form of government, with the Whigs and others in a marginal role as the constitutional opposition. This changed dramatically with Peel's determination to repeal the Corn Laws. This split the Conservatives for over two decades and ensured that the period 1832 to 1866 became politically unstable.[2] The Tories were condemned to the opposition benches for uncharacteristically long periods or to be partners in a succession of minority governments. It was a period of ill-disciplined parties, the 'chronic evil of Executive weakness'.[3]

The fragility of successive governments meant that the legislature had the opportunity to make the responsibility of the Executive to the House of Commons a reality. The middle decades of the nineteenth century, therefore, have been referred to as the 'golden age' of responsible government; an age when the Legislature was comparatively more powerful than the Executive. Looking back over this period, Earl Grey observed with some affection that 'for a quarter of a century parliamentary Government has been established with greater purity and efficiency than it ever possessed before . . . [for] during this period innumerable measures of unequalled public importance have been adopted'.[4] Doubtful party allegiances also provided greater opportunity for a range of reformists to have an impact on government policy. As a consequence, the period 1846–66 especially was one of great social reforms in government, industry, and education. It was also during this period that

---

[1] Binney, 1958, p. 282.   [2] Hogan, 1991, p. 124.
[3] Gladstone to Lord Aberdeen, 13 March 1856, in Matthew, 1978, p. 112; Lord Salisbury, *Saturday Review*, 2 February 1861.
[4] *Edinburgh Review*, vol. 219, July 1858, p. 272.

through a succession of audit acts from 1832 the use of state audit to enhance parliamentary control over the financial affairs of the Executive began to achieve the form that has endured to the present day.

The 1832 Audit Act

Sir James Graham and Economy

Wide recognition of the serious failings of the Board of Audit meant that there were a number of people, in Parliament and outside, prepared to express their views on the need for improvement. Particularly noteworthy was Sir Henry Parnell who was a persistent critic of public accounts, arguing for simple and uniform accounting systems throughout all departments. He wanted 'proper' audits and annual reporting to Parliament.[5] Ultimately, the decisive move to introduce significant improvements in public sector audit was made by Sir James Graham, a staunch advocate of economy in public spending and the newly appointed First Lord of the Admiralty.[6] When presenting the Navy estimates for 1831 he drew attention to how 'For a series of years prior to 1831 systematic misappropriation of the separate grants made for Naval Services had from year to year taken place' and 'moneys voted for specific purposes had been systematically applied to other purposes not sanctioned by Parliament'.[7]

Graham referred to a long list of overspends and misappropriations of funds at such places as Deptford, Chatham, Woolwich, Bombay, and Leith, where 'works of great extent in the department of the naval service had been begun, completed, and paid for, without the knowledge or sanction of Parliament, or without the subject having once been brought under the notice of the House of Commons'.[8] The most outrageous example was the construction of buildings at Cremin where Parliament in 1826 had voted expenditure of £4,000 but the Victualling Board had subsequently managed to spend £229,441. This massive overspend was met by transferring surpluses from amounts voted by Parliament for other purposes. At Woolwich expenditure of £326,000 was

---

[5] HC debates, 17 February 1831, col. 625.

[6] Graham (1792–1861) was First Lord of the Admiralty 1831–4 and 1852–5, and Secretary of State for Home Affairs 1841–6. He was respected as a master of financial detail and therefore a valued member of House of Commons committees (*Dictionary of National Biography*, 1961, p. 331). He was, however, widely disliked and mistrusted (see Lord Greville to Queen Victoria, January 1849, in Ward, 1967, p. 238; Melville to Fox Maule, 30 January 1840 in Donajgrodzki, 1977, pp. 103–4). Graham's time at the Home Office was generally regarded as a failure, unlike his time at the Admiralty where his successes were widely praised, even though his manner made him many political enemies.

[7] HC debates, 25 February 1831, col. 952.   [8] HC debates, 25 February 1831, col. 950–1.

nearly double the amount originally provided for in the approved estimates. This was again met from surpluses elsewhere. At Bombay, a seventy-four gun warship costing nearly £90,000 was being built from funds provided for dockyard expansion.

Graham also disclosed that every year since 1820 the Navy had employed 1,500 to 3,000 seamen in excess of the numbers voted for by Parliament. Wages of £1.25 million for these surplus seamen had been paid from excessive funds regularly voted by Parliament based on inflated figures for purchases of timber, shipbuilding materials, and other supplies.[9] This situation had been made possible because there was only a single estimate for the funding and spending of the Navy Board, the Victualling Board, and other separate naval services that allowed surpluses and overspends to be moved freely between them. Not surprisingly, Graham argued forcibly that in the case of the Navy the existing system of attempting to safeguard appropriation simply by controlling the issues of funds from the Exchequer had clearly failed to provide effective parliamentary control and accountability.

Graham was a close friend and confidant of William Gladstone, with whom he shared a life-long obsession with economy. Graham regarded waste and extravagance as misappropriation of public funds since they were clearly not Parliament's intention when voting supply. As early as 1825 James Butler had remarked upon Graham's passion for economy and the popularity this had created for him, both within and outside the House of Commons.[10] In Parliament, Graham called for economy on many occasions.[11] Towards the end of his parliamentary career Graham reminded Roebuck that 'for two or three years before the formation of Lord Grey's Government... (particularly in 1830) I had taken a line which was considered radical on questions relating to public expenditure.... Reform and Retrenchment were the watchwords which led me to power.'[12] Lord John Russell's refusal to pledge that his government would implement a policy of stiff retrenchment was sufficient grounds for Graham to refuse the Admiralty in January 1849.[13] Graham's obsessive pursuit of economy in public spending carried over into his private life. When making his will in 1823 he followed his life's rubric by directing that his trustees should deal with his estate with 'strict economy', although he did not 'wish to enforce a niggardly system... I wish only to urge abstinence from all fruitless and unnecessary expense'.[14]

Before Graham's appointment the Navy was well known to be full of sinecures, useless duplication of offices, and centuries of clogging, accumulated

---

[9] HC debates, 25 February 1831, col. 950–4.   [10] Erickson, 1952, pp. 65, 66.
[11] HC debates: 12 February 1830; 5 April 1830, col. 1271; 14 May 1830, cols. 519, 731; 7 June 1830, cols. 279–80; 25 February 1831, cols. 953–4.
[12] Letter 4 January 1851, in Parker, 1907, vol. 1, pp. 117–18. Also HC debates, 14 May 1830.
[13] Ward, 1967, p. 238.   [14] Parker, 1907, vol. 1, p. 67.

privileges. It was notorious for its extravagance and its invulnerability to financial control. These excesses and abuses were regarded as untouchable because the Admiralty was traditionally headed by a powerful and influential Secretary of State who had ready access to all the important members of the government. Attacking the Navy's spending was seen as attacking the wellbeing of the nation itself, as well as an unacceptable intrusion into the Executive's affairs. For an island state such as England the Navy was popularly regarded as the nation's ultimate security against the 'envious plotting' of Britain's often hostile neighbours. Criticisms of excessive naval spending were countered with predictions of national vulnerability and defeat. This was usually enough to blunt all attacks and helped to perpetuate the Navy's firm place in the country's affections. So confident of their position were the supporters of the Navy that when it was suggested by Landsdowne that Graham be given the Admiralty they felt reassured that in this office 'his dangerous inclinations to economy would not have too abundant scope'.[15] Entrenched custom, however, would not be enough to protect the Navy against Graham's drive and determination.

Graham's interest in economy in the Navy had emerged very early in his crusades for frugality in government spending. In March 1830 he drew considerable attention to himself when he sought the abolition of the Treasurer of the Navy as a sinecure.[16] By the time Graham left the Admiralty in 1835 he had managed to reduce naval spending from £5,045,827 in 1832 to £4,658,000 in 1835.[17] This achievement was praised by *The Black Book of the Aristocracy* as 'a splendid example to the heads of Departments.... The energy with which Sir James Graham has proceeded to new-model the Department will leave little to desire in that branch of the public service.'[18] Popular newspapers such as *The Morning Chronicle* and *The Morning Herald* commended Graham in February 1831 for exposing the Admiralty's 'system of deception and mystification'.

Graham's primary objective of securing stringent economies in naval expenditure was not pursued in isolation. A persistent critic of the virtual absence of useful financial information being provided to Parliament and the opportunities that this created for excessive spending, he considered that the situation across departments was intolerable and could no longer be permitted to continue.[19] When it came to accountability, Graham was an early and determined advocate of improved accounts that would show the appropriation of funds approved by Parliament, with subsequent spending

---

[15] Butler, quoted in Erickson, 1952, p. 80.   [16] HC debates, 14 March 1830.
[17] Ward, 1967, p. 128.
[18] Quoted in Parker, 1907, vol. I, p. 147. Also the Duke of Bedford to Lord John Russell in Donajgrodzki, 1977, p. 105.
[19] HC debates: 30 April 1830, cols. 305, 508–9; 14 February 1832, col. 359.

examined by an effective independent audit on behalf of Parliament. He regarded accounts and audit as complementary to the pursuit of economy and efficiency. Lord Welby recognized Graham as the 'first statesman who grasped that... the only real check of expenditure is to be found in a Report to the House of Commons on that expenditure, when it had taken place, by an independent auditor'.[20] Graham was therefore instrumental in passing, as part of pent-up reforms of the new Whig government, the 1832 Audit Act.[21] At the time, and later, the reforms embodied in the Act were seen as a watershed in state audit because they introduced formal appropriation audits on behalf of Parliament. So closely was Graham identified with the 1832 Act that it was usually referred to as 'the Graham Act'.

Main Provisions of the Act

The 1832 Audit Act required the Admiralty to provide Parliament with an annual set of audited accounts that compared 'the Expenditure under the several Heads of Naval Service, as expressed in the Appropriation Act or Acts for that year'. This provision met Graham's criticism in 1831 that 'it was due to the Commons of England to let them know the exact appropriation of the money they had voted'.[22] The new Act 'would afford a means of ascertaining that a scrupulous adherence was observed of the appropriation made by Parliament'.[23] The Admiralty's report in the form of a balance sheet would also show 'what had been expended beyond the Estimates under each head or category of spending in the Estimates. The auditors should also state any discoveries of improprieties they might have made'.[24] These arrangements stripped away the secrecy that had previously hidden the handling of Navy accounts. Until Graham's reforms the Board of Audit had no part to play in the Navy's accounts. Prior to 1832 the Navy had complete control over its accounting arrangements. From 1796 all accounting had been coordinated by the Navy Board's Committee of Accounts, with day-to-day responsibility for the accounts in the hands of the Treasurer of the Navy and all the accounts audited by the Comptroller of the Navy. In 1832 accounting for the Navy Office was consolidated under the Accountant General of the Admiralty.

The 1832 Audit Act was widely praised. For the first time Parliament was now in a position to see on a regular basis that payments had been properly authorized and that expenditure had been made for the purposes approved by Parliament. The Act required the Board of Audit to see that 'the directions of parliament were obeyed... and whether the vote has been exceeded'.[25] It

---

[20] Welby to the Graham family, 27 September 1905, in Parker, 1907, vol. 1, p. 165.
[21] 2 Will. IV, c.40.   [22] HC debates, 25 March, 1831, col. 219.
[23] HC debates, 14 February 1832, col. 360.   [24] HC debates, 14 February 1832, col. 360.
[25] Committee on Miscellaneous Expenditure, 1860, Minutes of evidence, Q.520.

'converted what [had been] a nominal responsibility in the officer who brought forward the Estimates into a real responsibility'.[26] However, it was not the role of the auditors to question the merits of the expenditure;[27] they were examining only authority, not justification. As expected, opposition to the 1832 Audit Act came primarily from those closely involved in the previous discredited system, although there were also disappointments for those who supported Graham's wider ambitions.

Despite its avowed strengths, the Act was heavily criticized, notably and predictably by Navy supporters. Sir George Clerk, Treasurer to the Navy prior to Graham's taking office, condemned the new arrangements as an unnecessary complication to an otherwise straightforward system and described them as 'impracticable'.[28] Admiral Sir George Cockburn argued that the new Bill would not be any better at improving the supervision of public expenditure in the Navy and would be unable to 'secure the public service against mismanagement, or the public money against waste'. Instead, the 'cure would be worse than the disease'.[29] Predictably, all levels of the Admiralty were unyielding in their opposition to requirements for increased accountability to Parliament and any other reductions in their traditional powers of self-regulation.

When introducing the new Act in 1832 Graham had emphasized that he intended to achieve economy, efficiency, and accountability for the use of public money and an end to political appointments.[30] The Act was rightly praised for its vital contribution to improving accountability by providing for the first time the presentation to Parliament of audited appropriation accounts. However, the expenditure figures in the accounts were highly aggregated and the broad basis of presentation meant that financial disclosure of important activities was limited. This fell some way short of Graham's intention to provide information that would enable Parliament to pursue economy by subjecting expenditure to closer supervision and by challenging waste and prodigality that rebounded on the public purse, resulting in increased taxation. Though emphasized in the rhetoric, the pursuit of economy and efficiency was not directly reflected in the provisions of the Act.

A second and familiar concern was the status of the Board of Audit in the new audit environment and the nature of its examination. In the face of all the evidence, the Treasury continued to insist that the Board was an 'independent authority'. It had done so since the Board was established nearly sixty

---

[26] Select Committee on Public Monies, 1857, Minutes of Evidence, Q.2641. Sir James Graham, HC debates, 14 February 1832, col. 360. Lord Welby to the Graham family in Parker, 1907, vol. 1, p. 167.
[27] Select Committee on Public Monies, 1857, Minutes of evidence, Q.4459.
[28] HC debates, 25 February 1832, col. 958.   [29] HC debates, 6 April 1832, col. 731.
[30] HC debates, 14 February 1832, col. 129.

years before and would continue to do so until the Board was replaced thirty years later.[31] Although reports on the results of its work were now presented to Parliament with the accounts, the Board's examination was confined to the accounts as prepared and presented by the Navy. The Board was only able to examine expenditure in depth if required by the Treasury to carry out a 'Detailed and Administrative' audit. The Treasury decided when, where, and how any such work should be carried out and the results were reported directly to the Treasury for final decision. The Board's limited and largely passive view of its functions and responsibilities was all too clearly demonstrated by Commissioner of Audit Charles Macaulay when he explained to the Public Accounts Committee in 1865 that:

> The whole of our experience as appropriation auditors tends to satisfy us that we ought to have no further communication with the Executive Departments than may be necessary for the purpose of obtaining information. Whatever tends to associate us, either directly or indirectly, with the pecuniary transactions of the Government, cannot but tend to damage the credit of the reports in which we are required to submit those transactions to the judgement of Parliament.... Our functions should be neither preventive nor corrective, but simply detective. It should be no part of our business to acquit or to condemn.... We should keep all such opinions to ourselves.[32]

The introduction of the first appropriation accounts was a ground-breaking and significant event, with benefits to accountability that would in time spread throughout all departments and elsewhere in the public service. Yet, there was still a long way to go before Parliament would be presented with informative and properly audited appropriation accounts that matched Graham's original intentions. The next steps in this journey were the 1846 and 1851 Audit Acts.

The 1846 Audit Act and the 1851 Audit Act

It took fourteen years for the system of audited appropriation accounts for naval expenditure to be extended to the army and ordnance departments, by the 1846 Audit Act.[33] It then took a further five years to be extended to the Departments of Woods, Forests, and Public Works by the 1851 Audit Act.[34] Bringing army expenditure within the framework of audited appropriation accounts was the culmination of several years of improvements in War Office

---

[31] Lord Welby, Select Committee on National Expenditure, 1902, Appendix 13, p. 229.
[32] Charles Macaulay, *Observations on Appriation Audit, 1863* (Appendix to the Report of the Committee of Public Accounts, H.C. Paper No 413, 1865).
[33] 9 and 10 Vict. c.92.   [34] 14 and 15 Vict. c.42.

accounting systems under Sir Charles Trevelyan's direction at the Treasury, prompted by Graham's Act in 1832.[35]

Trevelyan was appointed to the Treasury in February 1840 where as Assistant Secretary to the Treasury he epitomized the professionalization of government that had occurred steadily since the early nineteenth century. Trevelyan provided the necessary committed civil service support to ensure that the plans of reformers such as Gladstone and Graham came to fruition. Indeed, according to MacDonagh the success of the parliamentary and financial reforms in the mid-nineteenth century in large measure can be attributed to Trevelyan who was 'profoundly disturbed' by the defects in Treasury control and in parliamentary accountability.[36] So important were Trevelyan's contributions to improved accountability that Hughes has suggested that the modern British Treasury was established as a direct result of the work of Trevelyan.[37]

Trevelyan shared with Gladstone and Graham both a passion for economy and a belief that in the absence of strong mechanisms of accountability, in particular reliable and comprehensive systems of accounting and audit, governments could not be relied upon to be wise stewards of public money. Immediately prior to the appointment of the Select Committee on Public Monies in 1857 Trevelyan agreed with Gladstone that 'the real check of simple intelligible accounts rendered at short intervals, and examined and certified by independent auditors' was the only sure way to control public expenditure.[38] Trevelyan's long tenure as the most senior civil servant in the Treasury at the time of the Select Committee on Public Monies ensured that he had the authoritative opportunity to press for the implementation of reforms that would give effect to the vision for accountability that he shared with Gladstone. As a Benthamite, a devotee of Edmund Burke, and the product of a Dissenting Church family, Trevelyan was a zealous reformer and a vigilant foe of financial excess and waste, even in the smallest of matters.[39] He epitomized Bentham's requirement that efficient government was only possible if there was 'complete popular control over public affairs, with the greatest attainable perfection of skilled agency'.[40] This, of course, would be achieved under Treasury control. Like Gladstone, Trevelyan's primary objective was to establish a powerful department of finance, aided where necessary by a 'reliable' audit.

Trevelyan was acutely aware that, as well as being, in principle, an important step in improving accountability to Parliament, the extension of

---

[35] Trevelyan to Gladstone, 8 February 1854, Additional Manuscripts 44,333.
[36] MacDonagh, 1977, pp. 204–5.   [37] Hughes, 1949, p. 54.
[38] Trevelyan to Gladstone in Hughes, 1949, pp. 54–5.   [39] Hart, 1960, pp. 95, 96, 102.
[40] Mill, 1963, p. 225.

appropriation accounts and audit to the other largest spending departments was a significant opportunity for the Treasury to increase its own authority. For the early part of the nineteenth century the Treasury had little direct influence over the War Office and the Admiralty because both had very powerful Secretaries of State. The 1846 Audit Act provided the Treasury with the means to gain some of the financial control it had been seeking. A Treasury Minute of 13 January 1846 made it clear to all concerned that the appropriation audit of army accounts under the 1846 Act would be 'conducted by the Commissioners of Audit under the superintendence of the Treasury'.[41] The 1846 Act provided for the Commissioners to examine 'accounts of Receipt and Expenditure received from the naval and military departments showing all expenditure, that is final payments not imprests, classed under the several Heads of Service as expressed in the Appropriation Act or Acts for the Year'.

Rather than marking a significant advance in accountability to Parliament, the 1846 Audit Act was a major step forward in Treasury control. The Board of Audit was in practice 'little more than the right hand of the Treasury for conducting a certain service'.[42] Treasury control of the extent, direction, and depth of the audit was a weapon in their campaign to exercise greater influence and control over departmental spending. It was a means of supporting both Treasury and general Executive powers, not an aid to the wider accountability envisaged in the 1846 Act. Controlling the recruitment, qualifications, and dismissal of Board of Audit staff ensured that the work of the Board could be heavily circumscribed by limiting its resources. Accordingly, the Treasury was characteristically unsympathetic to requests from the Board of Audit for extra staff as the extent of the Board's duties expanded into appropriation audits. Only one Board of Audit examiner was allotted by the Treasury to each department to carry out the appropriation audits required by the 1846 Act. As a consequence, observed the Committee on Public Monies in 1857, it was not possible 'for the Audit Office to have done more than continue the system in force'.[43] The Treasury's appointment of Edward Hoffray from outside the Board to the highly sought-after position of Inspector of Naval and Military Accounts in 1853 was one case in particular that stirred the resentments and jealousies of the Board's staff.[44]

The 1846 Act required the Board of Audit to transmit all audited accounts to the Treasury for final approval. In the case of any disallowances by the Board of Audit, or refusal to pass the accounts, the Treasury could send the accounts back to the departments for any corrections it thought necessary. The

[41] Select Committee on Public Monies, 1857, Appendix 2, p. 550.
[42] Committee on Miscellaneous Expenditure, 1860, quoted in HC debates, 11 March 1862, col. 1323.
[43] Appendix 2, p. 550.
[44] Trevelyan to Gladstone, 21 February 1854, Additional Manuscripts 44, 333.

accounts would then be audited again and resubmitted to the Treasury. Whenever any differences in opinion arose between the Board of Audit and a department, the Treasury had the power to override the Board of Audit and to 'determine in what Manner the Item or Items objected to shall be presented to Parliament'. Treasury authority for a transaction was all that an accountant needed to satisfy audit objections, irrespective of any of the auditor's misgivings.[45] There was no appeal from Treasury decisions; the Commissioners were unable to report to Parliament any irregularities or abuses in the public accounts or suggestions for reform. In effect, the provisions of the 1846 Act made the Treasury the ultimate auditor and, thus, reduced both the status and authority of the Board of Audit. Lord Montagu would later complain in the House of Commons that the Board was:

> merely a delusion and a sham.... The Board was laughed to scorn by the Government... The House of Commons and the people of England are deceived.... [The] powers of the Board under 9&10 Vict. c.92 are greatly weak, they cannot apply to any Secretary of State the power with which Parliament has given them; for the Secretary of State, backed by the whole power of the Treasury, only laughs at them.... [The] Board of Audit is a mere figment of Guy Fawkes. If it was intended to leave the Board in its present state, it would be better to get rid of it altogether.[46]

In the same parliamentary debate Mr Augustus Smith pointed out that the Board of Audit was deficient in powers in its dealings with the Treasury, which had 'the real control'.[47] Sir Stafford Northcote similarly suggested that in these circumstances it was understandable that 'the Members of that Board...were not satisfied with their present position...[there] were many points connected with the question of audit, on which legislation was required'.[48] However, these later criticisms by Montagu, Smith, and Northcote of Treasury powers over the Board of Audit, though cogently expressed and passionately felt, were those of a minority in Parliament.

The assistance of the Treasury was regarded by most Members as essential if Parliament was 'to exercise a beneficial influence over the money they had to vote'.[49] Speaking for the government, Peel defended the Treasury and objected to the criticisms of Montagu and Smith. He continued the standard government line by insisting that 'the Board of Audit was, in reality, an independent department'.[50] Befitting a former Chancellor of the Exchequer, Gladstone in his *Memorandum on Finance* in 1856 was also to advocate strengthening the position of the Treasury by bringing all public accounts

---

[45] Select Committee on Public Monies, 1857, Minutes of Evidence, Q.4255.
[46] HC debates, 11 March 1862, col. 1322.   [47] HC debates, 11 March 1862, col. 1347.
[48] HC debates, 11 March 1862, col. 1355.   [49] Wise, HC debates, 2 February 1860, col. 447.
[50] HC debates, 11 March 1862, col. 1356.

under its control.[51] In this way, he later wrote, he would 'complete the construction of a real department of finance'.[52]

The 1851 Audit Act required the Board of Audit to examine the accounts submitted by the Commissioners of Woods, Forests, and Land Revenues to verify that all expenditures had been made as approved by Parliament. The Board would then send the audited accounts to the Treasury to be laid before Parliament. Thus, by 1856 the Board of Audit carried out an appropriation audit in the Executive's largest departments. This broad check, however, was the full extent of the external audit of departmental expenditure. None of the 'great departments' had their accounts audited in detail by the Board; this was still the closely guarded responsibility of the departments themselves. Sir Henry Parnell was one of those who was outspoken in criticizing self-audit of their operations by departments. He argued that during such examinations 'It is inconceivable that departments will ever object to items of expenditure, however extravagant, which they themselves have authorised. . . . This absence of responsibility is highly objectionable.'[53]

Despite advances in the principle of appropriation following the 1832, 1846, and 1851 Audit Acts, the Board of Audit's appropriation audit continued to rely upon the completed accounts provided by the departments. The Board would not enquire behind these accounts once assured as to their completeness and accuracy by a department's accountants,[54] who were often hostile to further inquiries by the Board.[55] The Board was in no doubt that this situation was perpetuated by Treasury regulations 'to serve the purposes of the department itself. It . . . [was] an administrative precaution adopted in order to enable the department to keep a proper control over its own expenditure.'[56]Although the Treasury had apparently been considering a consolidating Act for some time,[57] there was no general provision that all government departments would be audited by the Board of Audit. The Treasury was entirely free to decide which accountants were to submit accounts to the Board and which accountants would be exempt. The Treasury could also change its mind at any time and withdraw accounts from audit without any explanation.[58] For example, in 1856 the audit of Commissariat accounts was transferred from

---

[51] Diary entry, 16 February 1856, in Matthew, 1978, p. 104.

[52] Diary entry, 16 February 1856, in Matthew, 1978, p. 107.

[53] Select Committee on Public Monies, 1857, Appendix 3, p. 589, 'Report on Army Accounts, 22 August 1840'.

[54] Select Committee on Miscellaneous Expenditure, 1860, Minutes of Evidence, Qs.504, 508, 510.

[55] Resistance stiffened even further after the introduction of the 1866 Audit Act (see Macaulay, 1867, p. 7).

[56] Minute from the Board of Audit to the Treasury, 30 July 1861, Audit Office 27.17.

[57] Trevelyan to Gladstone, 8 February 1854, Additional Manuscripts 44,333.

[58] Select Committee on Public Monies, 1857, Minutes of Evidence, Appendix 25.

the Board of Audit back to the War Office, to the consternation of Parliament.[59] According to Edward Romilly, Chairman of the Board of Audit:

> The circumstances which may induce the Treasury to decide in favour of sending some accounts to the Audit Office and of withholding others are of a kind that can only be known to the officers of the Treasury. . . . I am really unable to state what the circumstances are which induce the Treasury to send some accounts to us and withhold others. It rests with the Treasury; they have absolute discretion in the matter.[60]

This situation meant that for the Civil Departments there was only a partial and inconsistent coverage by the Board of Audit. This was a revelation to the members of the Select Committee on Miscellaneous Expenditure in 1860 for, as their questioning indicated, they had believed the Board examined all the public accounts.[61] No revenue departments, including the Customs Office, were required to undergo any check apart from ensuring that vouchers shown to the Board of Audit equalled the charge appearing in the accounts.[62] Even then the auditors were told to rely upon the accountants as to the correctness of the vouchers. The Department of Public Works was audited in detail, whilst the Treasury, not surprisingly perhaps, was not audited at all. Indeed, apart from the Army and the Navy, no departments headed by a Secretary of State had their accounts audited by the Board of Audit.[63] These failures in accountability were not widely recognized or realized amongst the majority of Members of Parliament, who tended to find discussion of audit matters of little interest, despite occasional anguished cries from individuals within their midst.[64] Ultimately, the audit reforms had little impact on Parliament's knowledge of the finances of departments of state. In particular, there were no parliamentary committees responsible for financial oversight of the Executive.

Select Committee on Public Monies

Sir Francis Baring, a former Chancellor of the Exchequer, had originally proposed a parliamentary committee to examine the public accounts in 1854.[65] Gladstone supported Baring's motion, which he saw as an opportunity to put

---

[59] HC debates, 24 April 1856.

[60] Committee on Miscellaneous Expenditure, 1860, Minutes of Evidence, referred to by Lord Montagu, HC debates, 11 March 1863, col. 1323.

[61] Minutes of Evidence, Qs.565, 566, 597.

[62] Committee of Public Accounts, First Report 1861, Minutes of Evidence, Qs.66–73.

[63] Select Committee on Public Monies, 1857, Proceedings, p. 508.

[64] HC debates, 24 April 1856, cols. 1453–4.

[65] Sir Charles Bowyer and Sir Henry Willoughby, later members of the Select Committee on Public Monies, both claimed the credit for suggesting this form of inquiry (HC debates, 24 April 1856, cols. 1462, 1465).

into place his far-reaching plans for reform finalized with Trevelyan while Gladstone was at the Exchequer.[66] Instead of a committee of the House, Gladstone suggested that a commission of inquiry would be better able to deal with such a 'technical and dry subject' as audit.[67] Gladstone was also aware that an inquiry conducted by the House might provide Lord Monteagle, Comptroller General of the Exchequer, with more opportunity to influence Members against Gladstone's proposed reforms.

Monteagle was a formidable and influential adversary, and with the abolition of his lucrative post at stake he had every incentive to thwart Gladstone. It was well known that Gladstone had for some time favoured the abolition of the office of Comptroller General of the Exchequer and a coincident strengthening of the arrangements for audit.[68] Monteagle was well aware of this, and when Gladstone and Trevelyan were canvassing ideas for their proposals for financial reform both foresaw that the abolition of Monteagle's post would provoke problems with the 'difficult and widely disliked Lord'.[69] They believed that Monteagle, who was 'plausible and clever',[70] would seek to embarrass the Treasury by exposing misappropriations and financial laxity during the tumult of the Crimean War, which the Treasury had not had sufficient time to correct. If the Treasury could be shown to be seriously at fault in such matters, Monteagle might use this to convince Parliament that Treasury control alone was insufficient and that the post of Comptroller General of the Exchequer should be retained as a safeguard.[71]

Monteagle was the most determined and vehement opponent of any new legislation that would diminish his authority and influence, including any substantive reform of audit.[72] As Thomas Spring-Rice he was a Member of Parliament from 1820 until 1839 and served successively from 1830 until 1839 as Secretary of the Treasury, Secretary of State for War and the Colonies, and finally Chancellor of the Exchequer from 1835–9. His career was surrounded by controversy almost from the start. As Chancellor, Spring-Rice was unpopular for his arrogance and self-seeking manner and derided for

---

[66] Select Committee on Public Monies, 1857, *Memorandum on Financial Control*, Appendix 1, p. 528.

[67] HC debates, 24 April 1856, col. 1457.

[68] Gladstone's Diary entry, 16 February 1856, in Matthew, 1978, p. 104.

[69] Trevelyan to Gladstone, 21 February 1854, Additional Manuscripts 44, 333, fol. 198.

[70] Trevelyan to Gladstone, 21 February 1854, Additional Manuscripts 44333, fol. 198.

[71] Anderson to Gladstone, 10 June 1857, Additional Manuscripts 44387, fol. 309.

[72] The Office of the Comptroller of the Exchequer was created in 1834 when the Auditor of the Receipt, Lord Greville, died. This allowed the Lower Exchequer to be reorganized by 4 Will.IV. c.15, *An Act to Regulate the Office of the Receipt of His Majesty's Exchequer at Westminster*, which abolished the offices of Auditor of the Receipt and Clerk of the Pells, the last sinecure posts of the early Exchequer. The powers and duties of these two offices were then transferred to the new office of Comptroller General of the Receipt and Issue of the Exchequer. Under the 1866 Exchequer and Audit Departments Act this post was then merged into that of the Comptroller and Auditor General.

the incompetence that eventually forced him from office.[73] The antipathy between Gladstone and Spring-Rice was well known, particularly from Gladstone's gibes in Parliament.[74] The dislike and distrust that Spring-Rice had provoked within more radical elements of his own party, and lack of support within Parliament generally, frustrated his ambition to become Speaker. In return for leaving Parliament and his removal as 'a persistent source of embarrassment and danger' he was given both his title and the 'very agreeable and well paid office' of Comptroller General of the Exchequer. This was a sinecure that he held until shortly before his death.[75] Monteagle's move to the 'peaceful and calm retreat' of the Comptrollership was bitterly resented within Parliament, especially when it was suspected that the incumbent, Sir John Newport, had been encouraged to surrender his office with the (irregular) promise of a generous pension from public funds.[76]

Baring was finally successful when, in April 1856, he moved for a 'Select Committee to inquire into the Receipt, Issue, and Audit of Public Monies in the Exchequer, the Pay Office, and the Audit Department'.[77] He envisaged that the Committee would be concerned with broader accountability issues, not the details of accounting. Nevertheless, the government opposed the motion on the grounds that the public accounting systems were more than satisfactory, that 'there was no ground whatever for supposing that our system of public audit was anything but perfectly efficient and accurate', and that the proposed Committee therefore would be a waste of time.[78] However, the dismay of Members of Parliament at the widespread and long-standing evidence of deficiencies in public accounts and audit, and a lack of trust in government assurances, were sufficient to see Baring's motion carried.[79]

The findings of the Select Committee on Public Monies of 1856–7 provided the basis for the wide-ranging improvements in audit and accountability in the 1866 Exchequer and Audit Departments Act. Lord Welby,[80] forty-five years later, described the Committee as:

---

[73] Obituary in *The Times*, 10 February 1866.

[74] Shannon (1982, p. 406) refers to Monteagle as Gladstone's 'old enemy'.

[75] Liddell, HC debates, 27 February 1840, col. 701.

[76] It had been understood when the position of Comptroller General of the Exchequer was created in 1834 that it would be without pension. However, Newport would only leave if he was given a pension. Therefore, it was obvious that Newport's resignation was being bought from public funds for blatant political purposes (HC debates, 27 February 1840 and Liddell, col. 679).

[77] HC debates, 24 April, 1856, col. 1456.   [78] HC debates, 24 April 1856, cols. 1461–6.

[79] HC debates, 24 April 1856, Williams, col. 1463, and Ellice, col. 1464.

[80] Welby entered the Treasury in 1856, was Head of the Finance Division of the Treasury from 1871 to 1885, and, as Sir Reginald Welby, was Permanent Secretary to the Treasury between 1885 and 1894. His extensive experience in government finance meant he was highly regarded and a favourite expert witness before commissions and committees of enquiry around the end of the nineteenth century.

One of the most remarkable committees both as regards to its constitution and the work it did, that I remember ... (and) as having practically decided the form in which parliamentary control over expenditure should be established. The Committee on Public Monies knocked on the head once and for all the idea that an effective control could be exercised by watching the issue of money from the Exchequer and showed that the real control of Parliament must be by ascertaining, through independent officers of its own, how the money had been spent.[81]

The Select Committee's report in August 1857, although only five pages long in which only eleven paragraphs dealt with accountability and audit, was especially influential in the development of public sector audit.[82] Contained within this document were proposals that would ultimately be used to give public sector audit the authority and constitutional credibility that it had for many years been denied by the Treasury. The strength of the Committee's proposals was underpinned by its detailed examination of witnesses, documents, and memoranda. The Committee recognized the benefits already achieved in Navy and Army accountability from the preparation of annual appropriation accounts based on actual expenditure incurred under the heads of departmental votes and recommended that this should be extended to all departments. To support the annual appropriation accounts the Committee wanted the Treasury to establish a uniform method of departmental accounting and to provide departments with continuing advice and assistance. It emphasized the need for a better and more independent audit, based on a strengthened department bringing together the Board of Audit and the Exchequer Office under a single departmental head. It recommended that the audited accounts and audit reports should be submitted annually to a Select Committee of the House of Commons created for that purpose. The Committee's report in effect adopted all of Gladstone's proposals for reform, which he had set out in his 1856 *Memorandum on Financial Control*. However, in presenting its report to Parliament the Select Committee made it clear that it was:

aware that the important and extensive changes which they have suggested cannot all be immediately carried into effect; but they believe that the continued attention of Parliament and of the Executive Government to the subject will secure, at no distant date, all the objects embraced in their recommendations.[83]

The Committee's optimism on timing was misplaced. Despite the eminence of its members and Treasury support, it took almost another ten years to bring all its recommendations into statutory effect. The only exception, which did not require legislation, was the establishment of the Public Accounts

---

[81] National Expenditure Committee, 1902, Minutes of Evidence, Q.2508.

[82] Report from the Select Committee on Public Monies 1856, Paper 279, Session 2, 1857.

[83] Committee Report, final paragraph, 18 August 1857.

Committee (PAC) in April 1861, which was converted to a Standing Committee of the House in March 1862.[84] Progress with the 1857 Select Committee's remaining recommendations was delayed for various reasons, especially when at this time the making and remaking of political coalitions made it difficult to secure consensus and effective action. The Select Committee's report was one of 'many burgeoning mid-Victorian reforms that only later came to full fruition'.[85] Much of the impetus for financial and audit reform was drained by the change of government that had occurred soon after the Committee reported. Even with a further change of government in 1859 the Committee's findings, apart from some piecemeal changes to audit, were not then implemented.

When the Select Committee invited the views of the Board of Audit on the proposals for reform the response was typically cautious. The Board's Chairman, Commissioner Edward Romilly, in his written submission and when giving evidence,[86] did not offer positive proposals for developing the nature and scope of the audit, even though he, and particularly Commissioner Charles Macaulay, made its existing narrow base quite clear and the extent to which it was subject to Treasury directions. Romilly warned that extending audit beyond a straightforward check on bookkeeping and the proper approval of expenditure would not be without its problems. Appropriation audits of the kind being recommended would require the auditors to make judgements on the legality of transactions, which would require them to suggest to the Treasury that a particular item should or should not be allowed. This would bring the auditors into direct confrontation with departments. Edward Hoffray, who had been brought into the Board by the Treasury, reinforced Romilly's concerns.

Romilly argued that the consequences of further checks on the accounts of departments of state were so profound that they would require a 'total change in our system of accountability and our existing institutions'.[87] He seemed prepared, if pressed, to accept some additional responsibilities, but certainly did not wish to take over the functions of the Comptroller General of the Exchequer. He was more forthright on the need to strengthen the Board's independence and reduce the powers of the Treasury, contending that the

---

[84] The Committee was to be nominated by the House of Commons at the start of each session under Standing Order 57. The Chairman was a member of the opposition. Originally the PAC had nine members, which was increased to 11 in March 1870, 15 in 1893, dropping to 11 members in 1933. The first PAC included Sir Francis Baring, Sir Stafford Northcote, Sir James Graham, Sir Henry Willoughby, and Richard Cobden (HC debates, 9 April 1861).

[85] Jenkins, 1996, p. 67.

[86] Paper submitted by Mr Edward Romilly dated 13 June 1857 (Appendix 2 to the Select Committee Report).

[87] Paper submitted by Mr Edward Romilly dated 13 June 1857 (Appendix 2 to the Select Committee Report), Minutes of Evidence, Q.2636.

auditors would remain at the margins of the constitution so long as they were 'subordinate officers of a subordinate department, and that they have more to hope for in their advancement in life from the chief officers of the Executive than from their own official superiors, the Commissioners of Audit'.[88]

William Gladstone and His Sacred Mission

For some time William Gladstone had had in mind far-reaching plans for strengthening accountability to Parliament with public accounts and audit, which he set out in his *Memorandum on Financial Control* in 1856.[89] At the heart of the reforms envisaged in the *Memorandum* were a common set of accounting procedures for all departments and a parliamentary finance committee that would 'assure a more simple and effectual check upon the issue and appropriation of public money'. Gladstone's conviction of the need for reform, and the lines it should take, was supported by Sir James Graham. Their shared vision was bolstered by the evidence emerging from work of the Select Committee on Public Monies. Graham praised Gladstone's *Memorandum* but cautioned him that his 'large financial scheme' could only take root if there was peace abroad and 'moderate' public expenditure at home.[90] This advice was timely. National expenditure in the ten years before the Crimean War had risen by only 8.75 per cent, but during the period 1853 to 1859, which encompassed the Crimean War, the corresponding figure was 58 per cent.[91] Between 1847 and 1851 government expenditure was £51,750,000, rising to £66,700,000 between 1852 and 1856.[92] Gladstone's proposals for stronger controls therefore came at a time when the financial burden and difficulties experienced during the Crimean War had made demands for financial restraint in government even more popular.

Gladstone's conviction of the need for reform was not primarily motivated by abstract or constitutional concepts about accountability to Parliament. Rather, the driving force, as with Graham, was his obsession with economy in public spending. He saw better information on departmental spending and an effective audit, preferably under Treasury direction, as key factors in controlling expenditure and eliminating extravagance and waste. His life-long pursuit of economy was legendary, within his family[93] and within

---

[88] Paper submitted by Mr Edward Romilly dated 13 June 1857 (Appendix 2 to the Select Committee Report), p. 52.

[89] Select Committee on Public Monies, 1857, *Memorandum on Financial Control*, Appendix 1, p. 528. Also Gladstone's Diary entry, 16 February 1856 [Matthew, 1978, p. 104].

[90] Graham to Gladstone, 6 December 1856, Additional Manuscripts, 44, 164.

[91] Shannon, 1982, p. 408.   [92] HC debates, 26 February 1866, col. 1102.

[93] Gladstone told his brother Robertson in 1859 that 'economy is the first and great article in my financial creed' (quoted in Hirst, 1931, p. 241). Buxton (1901, p. 25), who had married into

Parliament,[94] where it was carried out against all opposition, even from his government colleagues, including Prime Ministers.[95] Gladstone had the arrogant belief that his views were always right. It therefore came as a shock to him that his single-minded pursuit of economy did not always accord with the public mood at the time,[96] especially when he was not prepared to make allowances for changing circumstances that may have forced increased spending on the government and 'without any Examination of Details, to decide that Great Reductions must be made'.[97]

Soon after taking office as Chancellor of the Exchequer for the second time in 1859 Gladstone made it clear that he was unhappy with the levels and growth of government expenditure and was determined to roll back government expenditure 'to a great degree', to at least the levels of his last budget in 1853.[98] This was entirely consistent with Gladstone's strong religious beliefs and well-known Peelite crusade against profligacy in public expenditure,[99] which he saw as a 'holy war'. Gladstone believed that everything he was given was a trust from God. He reminded his wife that this placed a great obligation on everyone to turn from self and to act always with reference to the revealed will of God.[100] He stressed to the voters in his electorate that as Chancellor of the Exchequer it was particularly apposite that he should treat his authority to spend as a 'sacred obligation'.[101]

Gladstone was not alone; a number of other voices were also calling for the identification and elimination of waste. Burke's calls for economic reform had created a wave of righteous fervour in the late 1780s, the effects of which were felt for most of the next century.[102] According to one contemporary,

Gladstone's family, described Gladstone as someone whose 'passion was finance and whose dream was economy'.

[94] 'There was not a Member of the House who had more denounced prodigality than the right hon. Gentleman' (White, HC debates, 26 February 1866, cols. 1100–1).

[95] Financial retrenchment frequently brought Gladstone into conflict with his leader Lord Palmerston who supported a strong interventionist foreign policy, which required ever higher expenditures on the Navy and the Army (Palmerston to Gladstone, 19 and 22 October 1864, in Guedalla, 1928, pp. 297–300). Gladstone was not an imperialist and was therefore uneasy about increases in defence spending. Disagreement between the two men, which Gladstone sometimes aired in public and for which Palmerston reprimanded him, at one point moved Gladstone to express his regret at having joined a government 'which had extended views (on expenditure)' (Palmerston to Gladstone, 29 November 1861, and Gladstone to Palmerston, 29 April 1862, in Guedalla, 1928, pp. 197, 208).

[96] Gladstone to Palmerston, 29 November 1861, and Palmerston to Gladstone, 29 April 1862, in Guedalla, 1928, pp. 195, 200.

[97] Palmerston to Gladstone, 7 November 1864, in Guedalla, 1928, p. 311.

[98] HC debates, 10 February 1860, cols. 821–6.

[99] Gladstone to Lord John Russell, 22 July 1852, in Parker, 1907, vol. 2, p. 167; Gladstone to Palmerston, 29 November 1861, in Guedalla, 1928, p. 195; Edinburgh Review, April 1857, p. 561.

[100] Gladstone to his wife, 21 January 1844, in Magnus, 1954, p. 104.

[101] 29 November 1879, in Hirst, 1931, p. 243.

[102] Clearly seen in the appeal for retrenchment by the 1810 Committee on Public Expenditure (Fifth Report, p. 407).

'oeconomy was the word... which like the Sun, diffused its glorious spirit... over the whole kingdom'.[103] The cry was later taken up and sustained at regular intervals in Parliament in the early nineteenth century, contributing substantially to Whig popularity.[104] After the abolition of the Corn Laws the remnants of the Anti-Corn Law League had refashioned themselves in 1838 as the Financial Reform Movement and, led by Richard Cobden, sought commitments from the House in 1849 to reduce expenditure and taxes.[105] Economy appealed to Victorian financial puritanism mainly because it meant lower expenditure and reduced taxes upon which, it was claimed, the health and security of the Nation depended.[106] Public extravagance:

> meant additional taxation, which made itself felt by capitalists in lessened means of employing labour, and by the labourer in less work on the one hand and higher priced provisions on the other, as well as less education and less moral strength to meet the duties and bear the burden of life.[107]

Although Gladstone was a staunch advocate of the supremacy of Parliament, he also recognized that the Executive needed to be free to pursue its policies. Accordingly, while acknowledging the need for the state auditor to report to Parliament, he believed that 'the regular process of examination' of accounts should be 'in the hands of the Executive Government'.[108] He saw audit as having a narrow role in the firmament of government under close Treasury control, which did not extend to it becoming 'an efficient control over public expenditure'. Instead, he informed the House that the proper concern of state audit was:

> to ensure truth and accuracy in public expenditure. In point of fact, it may be called... a Board of Verification. *But it would be perfect presumption in the Board of Audit if it were for a moment to attempt to exercise a judgement as to any degree either of parsimony or of extravagance which the government might be thought to be adopting under the sanction of the House* (emphasis added).[109]

In developing their proposals for reform Gladstone and Trevelyan were assisted with the more detailed aspects by William Anderson, who had previously worked with Sir James Graham on the 1832 Audit Act. Gladstone had brought Anderson into the Treasury in December 1852 from the post of Assistant Paymaster General to become Principal Clerk of the Treasury and

---

[103] Quoted in Roseveare, 1969, p. 118.
[104] HC debates: Hume, 20 and 27 February 1829; Sir John Yorke, 13 December 1830; Sir James Graham, 29 March 1830.
[105] Northcote, 1862, pp. 118–20.
[106] Gladstone to Palmerston, 2 May 1862, in Guedalla, 1928, pp. 216, 212. Disraeli, Budget Speech, July 1856, in Northcote, 1862, p. 291; Buxton, 1888, p. ix.
[107] Candlish, HC debates, 28 June 1869, col. 628.   [108] HC debates, 9 April 1861.
[109] HC debates, 11 March 1862, col. 1350–1.

head of the Finance Department.[110] The Board of Audit was represented mainly by Commissioners Edward Romilly and Charles Macaulay. The Board's innate conservatism meant that in the early discussions their views were cautious, particularly those of Romilly, but when giving evidence to the Select Committee on Public Monies in 1856–7 their views were more positively expressed, certainly by Charles Macaulay whose personal position was then at stake.

Delays in Audit Reform and the Audit Bill

As predicted, Lord Monteagle submitted to the Select Committee in 1857 highly detailed objections to the reform proposals in a vehement and fiercely argued sixty-three-page memorandum.[111] This detailed the constitutional history and contemporary importance of his office and opposed outright virtually all the changes the Committee and the Treasury had proposed. He supported this uncompromisingly when giving evidence in person to the Committee. However, his examination went badly and he was forced on the defensive, not least because of his high-handed manner and peremptory answers to questions. For example, the Committee expressed concern that although the Exchequer Office meticulously checked Treasury requests for funding against parliamentary approvals in the Appropriation Act, they had no further interest in what happened to the funds once issued. Asked whether he considered it part of his functions to see whether the Paymaster General in any way used as approved the funds paid to him, Monteagle curtly dismissed the question: 'Certainly not. When withdrawn from the Exchequer Account, I have neither authority nor knowledge given to me by law.'[112]

The Select Committee on Public Monies was not convinced by either Monteagle's long written submission or his oral evidence. The Committee's recommendation that the Exchequer Office should be combined with the Board of Audit was eventually incorporated in the 1866 Audit Act with the creation of the new position of Comptroller General of the Receipt and Issue of Her Majesty's Exchequer and Auditor General of Public Accounts. William Anderson exulted that Monteagle was 'less successful than he expected, and the tables are somewhat turned, and he is put upon his defence'. He hoped

---

[110] Anderson was later one of the co-authors of the 1866 Audit Act and in 1867 he was promoted by letters patent to the position of Assistant Comptroller and Auditor in the newly formed Exchequer and Audit Department.

[111] Report from the Select Committee on Public Monies, 1857, Appendix 3, *Observations of Treasury Memorandum on Financial Control*.

[112] Select Committee on Public Monies, 1857, Proceedings, Question 605.

that this 'succeeds in driving a nail into the coffin of that Monster Cheat, the Exchequer'.[113]

Monteagle's extreme conservatism, though presented on grounds of high constitutional principle and historical precedent, was clearly influenced not only by his anger over what he saw as a personal attack on his position and integrity but also his concern over the abolition of his lucrative appointment under the reforms and consolidation proposed. Perhaps change was always likely to be resisted by an office that until the 1820s had persisted in accounting for transactions by notches on hazel wood tally sticks inscribed in medieval Latin (see Appendix 2). Nevertheless, despite his defeat before the Select Committee, Monteagle knew that there was a long way still to go and that whilst he remained Comptroller General reforms might be delayed. His implacable opposition therefore continued and he remained a source of continuing persistent trouble.

From the early 1860s many Members of Parliament became increasingly frustrated by delays in implementing the recommendations of the Select Committee on Public Monies. There was a major debate in the Commons on 11 March 1862 on the need to have a committee to review the estimates and to reform financial control, but especially to reform the Board of Audit. The government was repeatedly berated in and out of Parliament for its inactivity. It was accused of cynically obstructing reform that would introduce 'a system and an examination which would give the House a clear account of the way in which public money was expended'.[114] Still, others in the House were not convinced of the need for reform. Some, like Peel, acted as champions of the Treasury by disputing criticisms of the Board of Audit's independence. Following the standard Treasury line, Peel informed the House that:

> The Audit Board was, in reality, an independent department. The Commissioners held their office on a judicial tenure, their salaries were paid out of the Consolidated Fund, they were responsible to Parliament alone, and Parliament alone could remove them. With respect to the performance of their duties, they were altogether independent.[115]

Many later criticisms were about delay in reform rather than the substance of the Select Committee's 1857 Report. There were doubts also about the remit of the newly formed Public Accounts Committee (PAC). Lord Montagu questioned why the PAC's inquiries had been limited to only those accounts that

---

[113] Anderson to Gladstone, 10 June 1857, A/M 44387, fol. 309.

[114] Quote is Sir Henry Willoughby, HC debates, 20 February 1865. See also Select Committee on Miscellaneous Expenditure, 1860, Minutes of Evidence of Austin, Secretary to the Office of Works, Q.1195; Sir Francis Baring, HC debates, 21 February 1861; Lord Montagu, HC debates, 11 March 1862.

[115] HC debates, 11 March 1862.

had been audited by the Board of Audit. As the Board only audited that part of the public accounts which the Treasury permitted them to audit, this meant that the PAC's oversight, in effect, was also constrained by the actions of the Executive.[116] Other opponents of the amalgamation of the Board of Audit and the Exchequer argued that the work of the two offices was incompatible. Even two former members of the Select Committee now expressed doubts about the benefits of the proposed amalgamation. Sir George Bowyer questioned the need for amalgamation and, at the other extreme, Mr Hankey argued that the Comptrollership of the Exchequer should be abolished altogether.[117] Later, Romilly, now retired from the Board of Audit, argued before the PAC that amalgamation would lead to the Comptroller and Auditor General (C&AG) being the auditor of his own accounts and, thus, destroy any checks on behalf of Parliament that either of the offices could provide.[118]

Gladstone rejected any suggestions that a conflict of duty would arise from the amalgamation. He stressed instead what he saw as the several advantages. The status of the head of the Board of Audit would be improved, independence of the Comptrollership of the Exchequer would be enhanced and, again recognizing the priority of economy, there would be a salary saving to the state. Joining the two offices would not involve much extra work or need more staff. Procedures for issuing Exchequer bills had been greatly simplified and it did not take much time to check that issues of money from the Bank of England under Treasury warrants did not exceed the total amounts approved by Parliament.[119] Advocates of the amalgamation also argued that not only did a separate Comptroller of the Exchequer provide no worthwhile check on Executive expenditure it also weakened the opportunity for better financial control. Sir Stafford Northcote maintained that this caused 'Parliament and the country to shut their eyes to a danger that was real, and prevented them turning their attention to what was a real security . . . an efficient system of audit'.[120]

Gladstone was now within sight of the 'general re-construction . . . [of audit] upon the broad principles which the Select Committee on Public Monies had contemplated' and that were largely based on his 1856 *Memorandum*. He was determined no longer to be thwarted and to find some way around the obstacle of Monteagle's continued occupation of the Exchequer. Monteagle had been appointed 'during good behaviour', that is for life, so as to protect the independence of his office and could only be removed by an address from both Houses of Parliament, a most unlikely event given the constitutional

---

[116] HC debates, 11 March 1862. col. 1358.

[117] Sir George Bowyer and Mr Hankey, HC debates, 1 March 1866. Also Lord Belper, Lords debates, 8 June 1866, cols. 16–19; HC debates, 1 March 1866, Second Reading of the E&AD Bill.

[118] 'Memorandum to the Public Accounts Committee Inquiry' 1867, vol. 39, p. 184.

[119] HC debates, 15 June 1865, col. 286.   [120] HC debates, 1 March 1866, col. 659.

implications. However, Monteagle himself had begun to realize through correspondence with Gladstone, and by the debates in the Commons at the time of the first reading of the Exchequer and Audit Departments (E&AD) Bill, that the abolition of his position was inevitable. Also, the imminent retirement of Romilly as Chairman of the Board of Audit required an early decision on amalgamation, while the pressure to find a replacement tilted the advantage further Gladstone's way. Now in his seventies, Monteagle knew that he had little room to manoeuvre and, ever the opportunist and finding himself in the same position as his predecessor without a pension, he therefore sought to strike a bargain that would provide one. On at least two occasions he wrote to Gladstone to say he was willing to relinquish his office, on the right terms.[121] A relieved Gladstone quickly seized the opportunity to remove this last obstacle to his plans. In June 1865 he informed Parliament of Monteagle's offer to retire and at the same time proposed a pension of £500 a year.[122] Although the way was finally clear for the presentation and passage of the Exchequer and Audit Departments Act of 1866 there were further hurdles to be overcome.

Monteagle was succeeded as Comptroller General by Sir William Dunbar, a long-serving member of the Liberal Party and Gladstone's former colleague as a Treasury minister in Lord Palmerston's government. Dunbar had already been appointed Chairman of the Board of Audit in 1865 on Romilly's retirement. In professional terms, the obvious successor to Romilly had been Commissioner Charles Macaulay, the second in command, who was the acknowledged expert on the principles and practice of appropriation audit and a co-author of the 1866 Act. Macaulay, however, had been selected instead to become Assistant Comptroller and Auditor under the new arrangements. This too was destined to be a source of further trouble.

Audit was only one of the many fields in Victorian political and public life in which politically motivated appointments could take place without raising significant concern. In the negotiations to choose the successor to Monteagle and Romilly within the context of the amalgamation of the Exchequer Office and the Board of Audit under the 1866 Act, Gladstone's preferred choice was not Dunbar but Richard Cobden. Cobden had a long and distinguished record of involvement in social reform and enjoyed great respect for his brilliance as an orator and jouster in Parliament. The Executive felt that Cobden's standing and his contributions to the life of Parliament and the nation would not allow it to leave him unrewarded. Unfortunately, his outspoken ways had not endeared him to the influential and powerful. As a result he had not been

---

[121] Monteagle to Gladstone, 8 June and 28 June 1865, Additional Manuscripts 44, 406.
[122] Monteagle died aged 76, before the passage of the 1866 Act and therefore did not live to see the abolition of the post he had defended so fiercely for so long. He received a very unflattering obituary in *The Times*, 10 February 1866.

able to secure for himself a position in the Executive that came with a pension, and at that time there were no parliamentary pensions. The chosen solution was to offer Cobden the chairmanship of the Board of Audit, later to head the amalgamated Exchequer and Audit Departments from which he would then be able to retire on the pension that would accompany the position. When Gladstone offered the post to Cobden in February 1865 he did so apologetically, recognizing that the position was not 'adequate acknowledgment' of his services.[123] In the event Cobden refused the offer. He had been seriously ill for several years and died two months later in April 1865. Awarding a pension to Cobden, which would have been irregular under the terms of the 1866 Act, indicated that even Gladstone was not above using patronage when it suited his purpose, despite contradicting his strongly expressed misgivings about using gifts of public office to settle political debts.[124]

After its first reading, the Audit Bill was referred to the PAC for detailed examination. Gladstone argued that the PAC was the best forum to consider the technical reforms proposed.[125] The PAC was first appointed in April 1861, on the basis of a motion by Gladstone with a maximum of seven Members. The size progressively increased to a maximum of sixteen Members drawn from government and opposition parties, which remains the present position. The political balance of the membership reflects the overall position of government and opposition parties in the House, with the Chairman being a leading member of the main opposition party, often an ex-minister with Treasury experience. The Committee can raise any issues it wishes on the accounts coming before it and has full powers to call for persons, papers, and records. However, by convention it avoids calling ministers or becoming involved in policy or party political issues and directs its questions to the Accounting Officers of the audited departments.[126]

The PAC initially focused on the key proposal that the system of appropriation audit applied since 1846 to expenditure by the Army and the Navy should be strengthened, confirmed as being carried out on behalf of Parliament, and extended to all the Civil Departments, including the Treasury and the revenue departments. When the PAC turned to the issue of audit independence, Sir William Dunbar and Charles Macaulay stressed that the C&AG should be responsible to Parliament, and to Parliament alone, and that no authority should be able to influence the C&AG's judgement when it came to the practices of audit.[127] However, it was already clear that Gladstone did not envisage a fully independent state audit. In Parliament he had strongly

---

[123] Gladstone to Cobden, 10 February 1865, Additional Manuscripts 44, 535, fol. 14.

[124] See Gladstone in Hughes, 1942, p. 59; Graham to Gladstone, 4 January 1854, Parker, 1907, vol. 2, pp. 212–13.

[125] HC debates, 9 February 1866, col. 275.   [126] See also Flegmann, 1986.

[127] PAC Special Report, 1866, Qs.182, 183.

criticized Lord Montagu's suggestion that the Board of Audit should be an office of Parliament and answerable only to Parliament. 'It can scarcely be seriously intended', he mocked, 'that such Executive functions, which can only be exercised by a Department fully cognisant of facts and official precedents [that is the Treasury] should be transferred to a Committee of the House of Commons.'[128]

Conclusion

Introducing a better framework of accountability and audit continued to be impeded by the complications of mid-eighteenth-century parliamentary and political life, where alliances and splits, coalitions, and realignments dominated government and public affairs. Significant changes to long-accepted procedures were difficult to achieve in a flux of negotiation and party politics. Personal friendships and sometimes fierce antagonisms added to the mix and accentuated the complexity but also proved decisive in delivering major reforms. Most important was the conviction and commitment of William Gladstone and Sir James Graham, with their supporters in Parliament and in the Treasury, which saw that the introduction of a robust framework of appropriation accounts, audit, and reporting would be required to provide the control and accountability needed to match the increasing scale and complexity of government expenditure that was rapidly becoming a feature of Victorian public life. There was wide agreement that in these circumstances it was essential to establish a reformed and strengthened audit department, even though there were uncertainties about its role and remit on matters of economy. Most significantly, there remained the fundamental issue of whether an independent audit was to serve Parliament in holding the Executive to account or whether it was a means for the Executive to control expenditure by individual departments.

[128] HC debates, 11 March 1862.

6

The 1866 Audit Act and the Modern State

'The Exchequer and Audit Department...another Gladstonian creation when the Grand Old Man was at the Exchequer in the mid-1880s and was a master planter of sturdy oaks.'

Peter Hennessy, *Whitehall* (1990)

By the later decades of the nineteenth century a constitutional bureaucracy had been firmly established and it had been accepted that the Treasury had the authority to develop general guides on financial and accounting procedures for all departments. The Treasury continued to pursue every opportunity to consolidate its position. In particular, it was determined to maintain its close involvement in developments taking place in the form, preparation, and audit of the public accounts. It was therefore especially concerned to protect its role and authority at all stages throughout the introduction and operation of the Exchequer and Audit Departments Act (1866 Audit Act). The Bill for the new legislation was drafted by Mr Childers and Mr Anderson of the Treasury, together with Mr Macaulay of the Board of Audit. According to Childers,[1] whose father was the Chancellor of the Exchequer at the time, the passing of the 1866 Audit Act 'established once and for all the active and living control of the House of Commons over public expenditure, and it is an efficient guarantee for the maintenance of order in the financial administration of the State'. Gladstone referred to the 1866 Audit Act as 'closing the circle of [financial] control',[2] while a Treasury minute of 20 March 1876 noted that the 1866 Audit Act ushered in a 'revolution in public accounts'.[3] MacDonagh suggests the Act was the capstone to mid-nineteenth-century government financial and political reforms.[4]

When Gladstone, as Chancellor of the Exchequer, presented the Bill to the House he made it clear that the primary purpose of the legislation was to

---

[1] Childers and Childers, 1901, p. 129.   [2] Einzig, 1959, preface.
[3] Cited in the Report of the Public Accounts Committee, 1876, p. 140.
[4] MacDonagh, 1977, p. 205.

eliminate the inconsistencies of the existing audit and introduce a more coherent and uniform system. He pointed out that:

> Some of the expenditure was audited by the Audit Board...some of it by the Treasury, which was quite wrong, for the Treasury was a department for controlling, and not auditing, the expenditure...and a good deal of it was not audited at all. The Government proposed to substitute for that threefold irregular and anomalous method of proceeding a uniform method by which the whole of the expenditure should be audited by...the Audit Board.[5]

The Bill gave effect to all the recommendations of the report of the Select Committee on Public Monies. It required the preparation of annual appropriation accounts for all departmental supply grants, based on the strict cash basis of sums that had actually come into course of payment during the financial year. It required the Treasury to introduce a revised framework of accounts and accounting systems. The audit sanctioned by the 1866 Audit Act was one exclusively concerned with accounting procedures, regularity, legality, and accuracy. Section 32 of the Act stated that the:

> Comptroller and Auditor-General shall call attention to every Case in which it may appear to him that a Grant has been exceeded, or that Money received by a Department...has not been applied or accounted for according to the Directions of Parliament, or that a Sum Charged against a grant is not supported by Proof of Payment, or that a Payment...was...not properly chargeable against the Grant.

The 1866 Audit Act merged the Audit and Exchequer Offices under one single head, the Comptroller and Auditor General (C&AG), with powers to carry out annual audits of the appropriation accounts and other accounts on behalf of the House of Commons, and to report the results. In these and other provisions the Act would establish the framework for establishing stronger accountability by departmental Accounting Officers. It would also revise the controls over the issue and accounting for public funds, with the C&AG exercising direct control over the drawing down of funds from the Exchequer. The Act, despite its title, therefore went well beyond the work of the new Exchequer and Audit Department (E&AD). Although directed at the heart of improving parliamentary accountability it was only a starting point; the task of carrying forward and giving full effect to its provisions rested on the inter-related responsibilities of the C&AG, the Public Accounts Committee (PAC), the Treasury, and the Accounting Officers in the spending departments. The fulfilment of these responsibilities according to the Act would depend on the nature of the independence allowed the C&AG.

---

[5] HC debates, 9 February 1866.

Independence of the Comptroller and Auditor General

The need to ensure the independence of the C&AG was a fundamental element in the discussions leading up to the 1866 Act. The importance of securing the right safeguards was heightened by the lack of independence of the Board of Audit. Curiously Romilly, now retired from the Board of Audit and who had for several years chaired a collegiate system that had proved woefully inadequate in protecting the independence of the Board of Audit, also now urged those examining the Bill to consider carefully the importance of the C&AG's independence, particularly if it were to be an individual appointment. He was apprehensive that, without full and clear legislative authority, devolving all audit responsibility to one person would 'be destructive to the independence and usefulness of the department'.[6] He considered that a board would be more likely to guarantee the honesty of the auditors than if the House had to rely on the conscience of one individual. Romilly argued that, given the difficulty of guaranteeing personal independence, it was hard to believe that the C&AG would be immune from pressures exerted by the Executive. He questioned whether it is 'human nature or consistent with political experience that a government should not exert itself to prevent any questionable transaction . . . from being submitted to the criticism of the House of Commons?'[7] More convincingly, Charles Macaulay argued that a more important threat to audit independence arose from the provisions in the Bill giving the Treasury powers to direct the audit. He urged instead that:

> the only authority that ought to limit the examination . . . is the authority on behalf of which the account is audited. If the Treasury were to exercise that power, then the Appropriation Audit, instead of being a check on the Government on behalf of Parliament will become whatever the Treasury might choose to make it.[8]

Treasury witnesses nevertheless maintained that the intention of the legislation was indeed that the audit should be on behalf of Parliament.[9] To support this assurance the Treasury pointed out that they had been working on a Bill for audit reform for some time that provided for direct access for the auditor to Parliament.[10] However, the stillborn Bill referred to by the Treasury was more a means of consolidating existing audit legislation than

---

[6] Romilly to Disraeli, *British Parliamentary Papers*, vol. 34, 1867, p. 183.
[7] Correspondence on the Subject of the E&AD Act 1866, HC 97 of 1867, p. 26.
[8] PAC, Special Report, 1866, Q.287.
[9] William Anderson, PAC, Special Report, 1866, Qs.227, 228.
[10] Treasury Minute, 23 November 1858, in Select Committee on Miscellaneous Expenditure, 1860, p. 175.

an attempt to introduce far-reaching reform. Nor did it contemplate any reduction of Treasury influence over the activities of the Board of Audit. Instead, by continuing to allow the Treasury to withdraw or exclude an account from examination by the Board it confirmed the intention of the Executive to maintain its domination over the range and nature of audit examinations.

The 1866 Audit Act provided the usual formal measures to protect independence for the new post of C&AG, under his full title of 'Comptroller General of the Receipt and Issue of Her Majesty's Exchequer and Auditor General of Public Accounts'. Appointed by the Queen by letters patent, the C&AG could only be removed by the Queen following an Order of both Houses of Parliament. His independence from possible financial pressures from the Executive was protected by provisions covering his salary and pension. As with a High Court judge, these were to be borne by the Consolidated Fund and were not therefore subject to annual supply procedures. The C&AG was also regarded *de facto* as an officer of the House of Commons, though this was not formally confirmed until the National Audit Act 1983. The 1866 Act provided that the work of the C&AG and his new department was to be carried out on behalf of the House of Commons and his reports presented to the House of Commons. His responsibilities, in principle, were therefore directed firmly towards Parliament and parliamentary accountability, not the Executive. Lord Welby assured the Committee on National Expenditure in 1902 that these provisions made the C&AG 'absolutely independent of the Executive Government'.[11]

The core of audit independence, then as now, did not lie in statutory provisions on the appointment and status of the C&AG. These provisions were likely to be directly called upon only in exceptional circumstances and as a last resort. They were important as a sign of independence: they were not a guarantee. The key issue was to establish independence in the day-to-day conduct of the audit, in the actions and decisions taken, in the results set out in the C&AG's reports and how these were followed up. Although the 1866 Act was directed primarily towards accountability to Parliament it was also important that the audit should wherever possible provide 'added value' to the bodies being audited and to the Treasury. The Treasury welcomed the benefits of the C&AG's audit to their own oversight of departmental spending. When Lord Selby, former Permanent Secretary to the Treasury, was extolling

---

[11] Committee on National Expenditure, 1902, Appendix 13, p. 230. A Treasury Minute of 1879 had referred in virtually identical terms to the Auditor General as 'a parliamentary officer altogether independent of the Executive Government'.

the benefits of the 1866 Act to the Committee on National Expenditure in 1902 he emphasized that:

> the new system has taken away, and rightly, the unlimited discretion which the Treasury had formerly. It has done more; for whilst it has subjected the Treasury to a very needful control it has at the same time enabled the Treasury better to discharge its responsibility for the maintenance of financial order, because the Treasury learns much now from the Reports of the Auditor which it never would have learned under the old system.

Though the spending departments and their Accounting Officers recognized the benefits from the results of the C&AG's examinations of their accounts, they did not welcome the public criticisms. Nor did they welcome the additional authority given to the Treasury. References to Treasury powers of direction, in one form or another, were contained in s.27, s.29, s.30, and s.33 of the Act. Section 27 re-emphasized that the appropriation accounts were to be examined 'on behalf of the House of Commons' and set out the main objectives of the audit. It also added that the Treasury could require the C&AG to examine expenditure to ascertain whether it complied with Treasury authority and report to the Treasury accordingly. Despite the apparent control that this gave the Treasury, there is no evidence about the frequency, extent, or circumstances of any specific examination of this kind being called for by the Treasury. When asked to clarify their approach in such matters, the Treasury confirmed to the PAC that:

> it was beyond any part of... [the Treasury's] function to control the ordinary expenditure placed under the charge of the several departments, within the limits of the sums set forth under the subheads of the several grants of Parliament, and that it is only in exceptional cases that the special sanction of the Treasury should be held to be necessary.[12]

The provisions of s.27 were specifically confined to expenditure requiring Treasury authority; it did not extend to the much wider range of other aspects of accounting and regularity, including statutory requirements, which were subject to the C&AG's normal examination. Other issues involving the need for Treasury authority were recognized as matters for the C&AG's judgement and discretion. Very often the C&AG would have common cause with the Treasury in examining matters further and, thus, this was not a restrictive condition that threatened the independence of the C&AG. If there were unwelcome features in any Treasury requirement that could not be resolved,

---

[12] Treasury Minute, April 1868. Appendix to PAC Report, HC 252, 13 December 1868.

later experience would show that the C&AG could always call on the support of the PAC. Section 31 of the Act provided that where audit objections could not be resolved with departments, the Treasury was finally responsible for deciding how the matter should be shown in the accounts. It would then be normal audit practice for the auditors to decide whether their concerns were sufficiently material to qualify their opinion and/or to raise the issue in their report.

The provisions in s.29 and s.30 were concerned with the degree of reliance the C&AG was expected, or allowed, to place on departmental examinations of their own accounts. Section 29 and the related Schedule B applied to Army and Navy expenditure and provided that the C&AG, after satisfying himself that the departments themselves had thoroughly checked, certified, and passed the vouchers supporting the account, '*may* (emphasis added) admit the same as satisfactory evidence of payment in support of the charges to which they may relate'. In other words, the C&AG did not have to carry out a detailed examination unless he thought it necessary. Although the Act was clearly worded in permissive, and not prescriptive terms, it was widely interpreted as entirely excluding the C&AG from any detailed examination of transactions, unless specifically required to do so by the Treasury and even then only in such manner as 'the Treasury may think fit to prescribe'. Thus, the C&AG was expected to certify the correctness of by far the two largest appropriation accounts, the Navy and the Army, without being free to carry out any independent detailed examination of expenditure. This would effectively prevent examination of matters of appropriation, regularity, and propriety called for under the Act. Even more confusing, s.30 reversed the position for the Civil Departments where the interpretation was that the C&AG was expected to examine all transactions and could only rely on internal examination and certification if the Treasury agreed.

This potentially unsatisfactory situation was quickly the subject of concern, criticism, and subsequent remedial action. Objections were quickly raised by the PAC, which in 1868 and 1869 recommended that the C&AG should be able to examine detailed Army and Navy expenditure, particularly to provide assurances on matters of regularity and propriety. This issue was specifically and deliberately pursued in the House in 1876 on a Motion by J. Holms MP, who pointed out that:

> the principle involved [the right of the C&AG to determine the extent of examination on all accounts, including detailed examination where appropriate] was not one upon which there was any controversy. On the contrary, the principle was admitted by financial authorities on both sides of the House as well as by financial authorities outside the House. . . . It was clear from both speeches made at the time and from the terms of the Act itself, that such an arrangement [for the Army and Navy accounts] was only tentative; that a larger application of the principle was

contemplated; and that it was intended to extend the system of examination by the Comptroller and Auditor General to the Army and Navy Accounts.[13]

In response the Chancellor of the Exchequer, Sir Stafford Northcote, who had served on the PAC when the E&AD Bill was being considered, fully accepted the points raised. He explained that the provisions of the 1866 Act had been drafted so as to recognize what was at that time the greater strength of internal examination of the Army and the Navy and that more reliance could therefore be placed upon the results of their examinations as compared to that in the Civil Departments. However, he also confirmed that 'Now that the very great advantages of the kind of control and audit exercised by the Comptroller and Auditor General had been ascertained [on the Civil Departments]... the same test should be applied as far as possible to the Military Departments.'[14] E&AD staff numbers were increased by around one-third to deal with the additional work arising from more detailed examination. With the barrier to in-depth scrutiny of appropriation accounts removed, there followed a range of C&AG reports on such matters as: excess votes; exercise of virement; unusual transactions requiring Treasury authority; securing new audits and access rights; special payments of all kinds; and various issues of misappropriation, regularity, and propriety.

The emphasis on the constitutional importance of the appropriation of voted funds was not confined to the UK. In the United States it was similarly recognized in Congress's approval of budget provisions. There were also similar manoeuvres to find a way round controls when things went wrong and approved spending was exceeded. Some came from unexpected quarters. In 1861 Mary Lincoln, the wife of President Abraham Lincoln, was given an appropriation of $20,000 to purchase curtains, carpets, and other items to refurbish a run-down White House, but her extravagant spending produced bills of more than $7,000 over the approved figure. Some of this she managed to conceal by having the White House gardener inflate his expense accounts to provide additional funds. As the bills mounted she finally had to disclose the overspend to her husband. 'Honest Abe', at a time of financial crisis, angrily refused to seek additional public funds to be spent on what he described as 'flub dubs for that damned old house', and was prepared to meet the overspend from his own pocket. Nevertheless, Mary Lincoln privately sought the advice of a powerful friend who then enlisted a helpful Congressman to arrange for the excess to be hidden in a complex list of military appropriations.[15]

---

[13] Hansard 16 June 1876, vol. 229, cc 2001–5.
[14] Hansard 16 June 1876, vol. 229, cc 2008–10.
[15] Goodwin, 2013, pp. 401–2.

Departmental Accounting Officers

The role of modern departmental Accounting Officers arose from the decep-
tively simple provision in s.22 of the 1866 Act that the duty placed on
departments to prepare and submit appropriation accounts 'shall be con-
strued as including any public officer or officers to whom that duty may be
assigned by the Treasury'. In 1872, after the PAC had criticized the lack of any
fixed principle to guide who should sign and render the appropriation
accounts,[16] the Treasury decided that there should be a more uniform basis
of appointment under the term 'Accounting Officer'. A Treasury Minute of
14 August 1872 therefore provided that:

> It cannot be doubted that the officer entrusted with the duty should occupy a
> sufficient standing to enable him not only to exercise a direct supervision and
> control over the persons executing the detailed business of account and book-
> keeping, but also to influence the working of his department in all those respects
> which affect the methods of its receipts or expenditures. He must also be qualified
> to represent his department before the parliamentary Committee of Public
> Accounts. . . . These conditions are satisfied in the Permanent Chiefs of the various
> departments.
>
> My Lords are therefore prepared to lay down the rule that, in the exercise of the
> powers conferred upon them by the Exchequer and Audit Act, they will nominate,
> whenever it is practicable, the Permanent Heads of Departments to render the
> Appropriation Accounts of grants for the services under their control.[17]

The inclusion of 'whenever it is practicable' weakened the strong line the
Treasury had originally intended and encouraged strong objections by depart-
ments. After sixteen months of protracted discussions, the Treasury conceded
a significant number of appointments at lower levels.[18] In a Treasury Minute
dated 20 December 1873, the Treasury set out the full list of approved
Accounting Officer appointments. This conspicuously excluded the War
Office, the Admiralty, the Foreign Office, the Colonial Office, Customs, Inland
Revenue, and the Home Office. Also excluded were the Treasury and the
Exchequer and Audit Department. Irrespective of the level of appointment,
an Accounting Officer's responsibilities were not limited to what appeared in
the accounts. Responsibilities for financial administration extended to matters
of regularity, propriety, and the proper conduct of public business. Like the
medieval sheriff, the Accounting Officer was expected to promote stewardship
and good husbandry in the resources put in his charge.

---

[16] PAC Second Report, 1872, HC 198.
[17] Appendix to PAC First Report 1873, HC 110, p. 78.
[18] Appendix to PAC Report 1874, HC 242, p. 125.

Although a key feature of parliamentary accountability had been set in place, the level of appointment and the responsibilities of Accounting Officers would be the subject of recurring examination, dispute, and amendment for more than 100 years. The Treasury, with Cabinet support, however, was able to push through further reforms in the early 1920s, which were a major factor in making it standard practice to appoint the Permanent Head of a department as Accounting Officer. The responsibilities of Accounting Officers were progressively clarified and consolidated over the twenty-five years following the 1866 Act. Later, as the provisions of the Act came fully into effect, the C&AG's strengthened audit, with the firm support of the PAC, made Accounting Officers increasingly accountable across a wider range of business.

Individual cases highlighted and helped to clarify particular aspects of an Accounting Officer's responsibilities. For example, PAC examination of reports on irregular payments at the South Kensington Museums (1872), the Post Office Telegraph Account (1877), and the Dundrum criminal lunatic asylum (1879) led the Treasury in 1883 to confirm the Accounting Officer's personal financial liability for improper or irregular expenditure, and to issue guidance on what Accounting Officers should do if instructed to make a payment with which they did not agree.[19] Provided they stated their objections in writing, and the political head of their department then instructed them in writing to make the payment, they would be discharged of any further responsibility. Some of the service chiefs in the Army and Navy, who wanted to retain ultimate military authority over the Accounting Officer, attempted to overturn this ruling but were finally silenced in 1904–5. The agreed procedure on such 'protests' applied only to improper or irregular transactions, where Accounting Officers were seen as 'outposts of the Treasury' and, more particularly, where their personal liability was at stake. In practice, however, personal financial liability was from the outset a token rather than a realistic prospect. Only in two cases does it seem to have been seriously considered, the Dundrum criminal lunatic asylum case,[20] and the Post Office Telegraph case,[21] before being waived. This issue periodically emerged and re-emerged, until it was generally accepted that it signified an Accounting Officer's personal responsibility on matters of financial propriety and regularity, not any associated financial penalty.

As the E&AD audit ranged more widely, Accounting Officers would be increasingly questioned on issues of waste, extravagance, and other aspects of economy and efficiency. By 1902, when giving evidence before the Select Committee on National Expenditure, it was fully accepted by the Treasury and

---

[19] Treasury Circular 21070/82, October 1883.

[20] PAC Report 1882, HC 269, p. 33.

[21] PAC Report 1876; Treasury Minute,13 March 1877.

the major spending departments that Accounting Officers were responsible not only for formal aspects of appropriation accounting but also for all matters related to financial management and control, including the economy and efficiency of administration. It followed that the exercise of those responsibilities was necessarily open to examination by the C&AG and the PAC. This position, however, had only been arrived at after successive C&AGs and their staff had faced and overcome strong objections by spending departments.

After its brief period of dominance in the middle decades of the nineteenth century, in the later years of the century Parliament was no longer the supreme power. The Executive was in the ascendancy and government became 'party government' based upon an 'electoral dictatorship'. The significance of the political changes that had occurred in the nineteenth century were underlined by Mills' conclusion in *The English Constitution* that 'an observer who looks at the living reality [of the constitution] will wonder at the contrast to the paper description'. As a principal servant of Parliament in holding the Executive to account, and in that role a frequent critic of Executive spending, this shift in constitutional power put the C&AG in a difficult position, particularly in a period of significant change in his own powers and responsibilities.

Early Challenges

Accounting Practices

Although the need for reform had been widely accepted, the new accounting procedures and revised form of accounts required under the 1866 Act took several years to be fully introduced. In the early years following the 1866 Act the C&AG, the PAC, and the Treasury spent a great deal of time considering the revised forms of appropriation and other accounts, and clarifying the nature and scope of the audit. The Act came into force in April 1867, yet by mid-1869 the accounts of most of the major departments, including the two great departments of state, and largest spenders, the Army and the Navy, had not yet conformed to the Act.[22] Of the 163 votes for the civil service, twenty-four had been passed by the auditors, eighty-eight were either incomplete or incorrect, and for fifty-one nothing at all had been presented for audit. Senior departments of state such as the Colonial Office, the Foreign Office, and even the Treasury, had submitted neither accounts nor a statement.[23] Many of the accounts contained serious errors and were submitted beyond the date

---

[22] The C&AG was still complaining in 1891 about the Army dragging its heels in providing information.

[23] HC debates, 28 June 1869, cc. 626–8.

specified in the 1866 Act. Gladstone blamed these early deficiencies on the difficulties of completing accounts, which in some cases had to come from the far corners of the Empire, and the lengthy process of implementing new accounting systems to enable departments to prepare appropriation accounts to a standard sufficient for them to be presented for audit.[24] Although compliance with audit requirements gradually improved, towards the end of his term in office Sir William Dunbar was still fighting battles with departments, with varying success, for better access to accounts and supporting information.[25] The Treasury supported Dunbar in some of these exchanges because it was concerned that departments were not following accounting procedures that it had laid down.

To give effect to recommendations on improving accounting systems and forms of account, s.23 of the 1866 Act directed that 'a plan of Account Books and Accounts, adapted to the requirements of each service, should be designed under the superintendence of the Treasury'. It also empowered Her Majesty, by Order in Council, to prescribe the manner in which each Department should keep its Accounts. In 1866 the Treasury appointed a Committee for this purpose and in 1867 this was converted to a Commission of Public Accounts. Ambiguity in departments as to the role of the Commission with regard to their own responsibilities was one of the causes of accounting irregularities at the South Kensington Museums. The result was that the PAC's Second Report of 1872 recommended that the functions of the Commission should be more clearly defined.[26] The Treasury agreed, and in January 1873 an Order in Council replaced the Commission with two 'Treasury Officers of Accounts' to be responsible for the maintenance, development, revision, and inspection of the system of accounts, and to provide continuing advice to departments. This was a demanding task. Many of the existing accounting systems were unable to provide the more detailed and timely information required by the appropriation accounts, requiring fresh forms of account and account books to be devised. In one department the accounts had to be recast from 1853 to obtain a reliable opening balance. It was 1873 before the manner in which departments should keep their accounts was formally prescribed, and it took several years after that before complete accounts of all supply votes had been prepared and audited.

The senior of the two Treasury Officers of Accounts was expected to exercise only general superintendence of the work, with involvement only in more serious issues. This responsibility was allocated ex officio to a senior Treasury official who represented the Treasury before the PAC but whose main duties lay elsewhere. The second position required 'an officer with a thorough and

[24] HC debates, 28 June 1869, cc. 629, 631.   [25] Dunbar to Gladstone, 24 March 1886.
[26] HC 198, p. 128.

technical knowledge of accounts'. It was established as a separate appointment within the Treasury, at enhanced pay. The first person appointed, Richard Mills, the Treasury Accountant, was the obvious choice because of his technical knowledge and his close involvement with all aspects of accounting developments both before and after the 1866 Act. He served as Treasury Officer of Accounts for sixteen years and then became Assistant Comptroller and Auditor, and later C&AG.

The difficulties in making departments provide the accounts and information needed for audit were nothing new and, despite Gladstone's excuses, were not wholly attributable to the new accounting systems and revised forms of account being introduced. The Board of Audit had over the years encountered similar problems with recalcitrant departments, with the result that it had frequently expressed concern to the Treasury about the extent and nature of the resistance they encountered and the Board's lack of any power to deal with it, particularly with the senior departments.[27] In commenting on the 1866 Act, both Romilly and Macaulay warned from hard previous experience that there would be difficulties and delays ahead. Relationships would be particularly difficult with the large departments of state, which had always been accustomed to minimal levels of interference in what they regarded as their internal affairs.

There were also some later concerns over s.33 of the 1866 Act. Although the Act focused on the audit of the appropriation accounts, s.33 provided the Treasury with the authority to direct the C&AG to examine other accounts relating, directly or not, to the receipt or expenditure of public funds. This ongoing power to direct the C&AG to audit certain accounts, and to determine the nature of the examination to be carried out, has been criticized as a potential threat to the C&AG's independence. In practice, it provided a means to ensure that as an increasingly diverse range of bodies became involved in and around public spending programmes their accounts were progressively brought under the C&AG's audit and, therefore, within parliamentary accountability, without needing fresh legislation. It guarded against some accounts being overlooked, a feature welcomed by the PAC. There is no evidence that s.33 was intended, or was ever used, to require the C&AG to audit accounts that he considered were not appropriate to his position and responsibilities. Nor was it used to direct that any audit should be carried out in ways that prevented or inhibited the exercise of the C&AG's professional judgement. Implementation of s.33 was not decided upon by the Treasury in isolation. The accounts concerned were discussed and agreed with the C&AG in advance, including any extra demands on E&AD resources. The Treasury

---

[27] Letter 30 July 1861, Audit Office 27.17.

was also required in each case to lay a Minute before Parliament for approval. The prospect of a determined Treasury seeking to impose an inappropriate or unwelcome task on an unwilling C&AG was always unlikely and there is no evidence that it was ever contemplated. Had it been attempted, the C&AG would have had recourse to the PAC and its robust support.

By far the largest and most important of the accounts audited under s.33 of the Act were the Revenue Accounts of the three main revenue departments; Customs and Excise, Inland Revenue, and the Post Office. Expenditure on salaries, wages, and other administrative costs was shown in their respective appropriation accounts and audited accordingly by the C&AG. The assessment and collection of revenue from taxes, duties, and levies by these departments, and other receivers of money payable by law into the Exchequer, were accounted for in separate Revenue Accounts also audited by the C&AG. The audit was directed towards establishing that adequate systems, regulations, and procedures were in place and working satisfactorily. The E&AD did not audit in detail the confidential affairs of individual taxpayers or the correctness of their tax calculations. Individual taxpayer assessments were examined essentially to test the operation of systems and controls and to identify broader issues that might need further scrutiny.[28]

Staffing and Asserting Independence

Another perceived risk to the C&AG's independence was Treasury control over E&AD staffing and budgets. The Department remained within the civil service and the staff were civil servants, which meant that the E&AD was subject to the same controls on numbers and terms and conditions as other departments. The Treasury therefore appointed the staff and determined numbers and pay scales, but there is no evidence that the Treasury used its powers over staffing to shackle the Department's examinations. Instead, E&AD staff and budgets increased substantially to meet the rising demands of the work, with the result that in the forty years after the 1866 Act staff numbers almost doubled. The C&AG also had full power to make rules for the conduct of the internal business of the Department and to promote, suspend, or dismiss staff. As noted earlier, Edward Romilly had stressed to the Select Committee on Public Monies that auditors should be able to look to the C&AG, not to the Treasury, for advancement in their careers. This safeguard

---

[28] Section 33 of the 1866 Act was effectively replaced by s.3 of the Exchequer and Audit Departments Act 1921. Section 2 of the Act also provided separately for the audit of the revenue accounts, free from any residual power of Treasury direction.

was provided by the 1866 Act.[29] A related issue was the status and qualifications of staff and the basis of recruitment.

At the outset, the E&AD was largely staffed by officers transferred from the Board of Audit who were experienced in the examination of appropriation and other accounts. However, the new responsibilities and powers of the C&AG would mean changes in the work that would be expected from E&AD staff. The report by the 1854 Northcote-Trevelyan commission of inquiry into the civil service had recommended that the existing system of appointment to the civil service by nomination by a Member of Parliament followed by selection should be replaced, with appointments instead being based upon open competitive examination. This breakthrough has been described as introducing 'a test of talent, not family connection or the influence of land or fortune... and transformed British Government from a grazing ground of aristocratic patronage into a true meritocracy'.[30] Recruitment, however, was still in a period of flux because the new arrangements were not universally welcomed and took some time to be introduced across departments.

C&AG Dunbar and the Assistant Comptroller and Auditor Sir William Anderson, both traditionalists, were amongst those who personally favoured the previous system of patronage. They regarded 'moral fitness' as a key requirement for E&AD staff and saw an auditor's special position of trust as 'shewing integrity to be more desirable than a high standard of education'.[31] Nevertheless, the E&AD was one of the first departments to have staff selected by open examination under the new arrangements.[32] This brought in grammar school candidates at sixth form level as middle-rank Executive Class officers. This same level of recruitment was by far the most common across the majority of departments, including the finance and accounts staff that E&AD auditors dealt with in day-to-day examinations.

Dunbar and his senior staff were alert to any attempts by the Treasury to interfere in recruitment of E&AD staff, especially the potential impact that this might have on the quality of staff appointed.[33] This concern was not

---

[29] 'Real independence is... tied to the autonomy of its internal administration and particularly to the methods of staff recruitment and promotion' ('Cours des Comptes and the Control of Public Finance', quoted in Normanton, 1966, p. 300). When the Audit Act was revised in 1921 the C&AG was allowed to appoint staff but it still required ultimate Treasury approval. Essentially this remained the position until budgets and staffing were removed entirely from Treasury control under the National Audit Act 1983.

[30] Schama, 2003, p. 233.

[31] Quoted in an analysis of E&AD papers on establishments and staffing by Mr R. A. Hoblyn, Keeper of Manuscript Records, dated 11 February 1888.

[32] Dunbar to Gladstone, 6 February 1873, Additional Manuscripts 44, 437.

[33] For example, in 1873 the E&AD complained to the Treasury that their examiners at the War Office 'should not be unduly weakened as to position relatively to other Departments'. Lowering the status of E&AD staff would make their already difficult tasks of 'criticism and judgement' even more onerous (Internal letter from Nicholas to C&AG, March 1873, Audit Office 27.16).

confined to new entrants. At one point the Treasury insisted that the Department should accept a number of redundant staff from other departments but Dunbar strongly and persistently objected to their fitness for audit work, even though he was well aware that the power of appointment rested ultimately with the Treasury. Amongst some departments there was an unwarranted perception that E&AD staff were of inferior status and insufficiently qualified, to the extent that the audit was adversely affected and undermined the position of the C&AG. In practice, their results demonstrated that their examinations were not inhibited by any differences in class or status between them and those they were auditing, certainly not by any feelings of inferiority. Eminent social scientist William Mackenzie has pointed out that:

> an office thus constituted [E&AD] was in Victorian times a formidable instrument. Very able lower middle class boys were available at 16 or 18. The organisation of the office gave them great independence, and this had social force behind it. These officials were not the same sort of persons as generals or admirals or Clubland civil servants. But the Commons lent them power and prestige and they were not reluctant to use them.[34]

Out in the field, departments were always sensitive to audit criticisms. Matters raised during the audit that could not be resolved quickly were frequently passed up the line to more senior departmental staff who might be expected to use the authority of their position to intimidate auditors. E&AD auditors, however, were expected not to be intimidated when pursuing their enquiries and discussing their findings with more senior staff. The conclusions reached and the need for any further E&AD action would be determined by the weight of audit evidence and the materiality and nature of the amounts involved, not the status of the departmental officers concerned. Auditors in the field could also be confident that well-founded criticisms would be supported by senior E&AD staff and, if necessary, the C&AG.

The results of audits earned widespread praise from the PAC, from the House of Commons, and from informed commentators. However, there was a lingering perception that when particularly difficult or sensitive matters arose during audit the C&AG's independence could be questioned because the majority of C&AGs had previously served in the Treasury. Lord Welby, who as Sir Reginald Welby had been Permanent Secretary to the Treasury between 1885 and 1894 after a long Treasury career, assured the Committee on National Expenditure in 1902 that, however it might appear, there was no question of any threat to the C&AG's independence arising from previous service in the Treasury. He emphasized that the C&AG was 'absolutely independent of the

---

[34] W. Mackenzie, Foreword to Normanton, 1966. Professor Mackenzie was Normanton's sponsor and mentor in the research for his book.

Executive Government' and 'when once...he is appointed he is so independent that no undue weight may be given to that objection'.[35]

It has been claimed that rather than the Treasury having an obvious presence in audit with explicit Treasury directives, its influence over the actions and decisions of the C&AG has been far more subtle but nonetheless certain. Robert Lowe, Gladstone's Chancellor of the Exchequer in 1873, noted that Treasury training was a means of socialization and cultural indoctrination that created 'a sort of freemasonry among men which is not easy to describe, but which everybody feels'.[36] From the end of the eighteenth century officials from the Treasury were also sent out increasingly to 'colonize' departments, including a few to the Board of Audit.[37] This was criticized as creating a powerful network of personal relationships and diffusing a reverence for the authority and methods of the Treasury throughout departments. The popular press added its voice to this criticism by claiming that:

> For years it has been the constant policy of Sir Reginald Welby and the Treasury Ring of permanent officials to use their utmost endeavours to the end that the principal posts in all the Departments in any way affiliated to the Treasury shall be filled by Treasury Clerks or Private Secretaries—the object being that, no matter what Party may happen to be in office, the Ring, working through its various offshoots, may still continue to wield the real power.[38]

There was also a perception that C&AG's were in some way subordinate to the Treasury because their reports were presented formally to Parliament by the Treasury. The PAC in 1870 were of the opinion that 'the C&AG would have a higher and more independent position in the eye of the several Departments of State if his reports were presented directly by him to the House'. The C&AG's audit was statutorily carried out 'on behalf of the House of Commons' and the reports were prepared for the information of, and submitted to, the House of Commons. It was only by a quirk of procedure that at the final, formal stage this was done through the medium of the Treasury for the audit reports had to accompany the appropriation accounts, which the Act required were to be presented by the Treasury. The Treasury, however, had no power to

---

[35] Committee on National Expenditure, 1902, Appendix 13, pp. 230–1. A Treasury Minute of 1879 had referred in similar terms to the Auditor General as 'a parliamentary officer altogether independent of the Executive Government'.

[36] Quoted in Roseveare, 1969, p. 178.

[37] At the Board of Audit, J. Martin-Leake, a Treasury official, was appointed to the new Board in 1785 (Roseveare, 1969, p. 123). In 1853 Treasury official Edward Hoffray was also appointed to an important post in the Board. A succession of ex-Treasury C&AGs led to the conclusion that the Treasury 'has been adept at filling top positions in state audit from within its own ranks' (Roseveare, 1969, p. 174). More widely, the rise of an integrated civil service under Treasury control in the nineteenth century gave it access to most of the higher positions in the civil service, and this became a particularly fertile field of Treasury patronage throughout departments and elsewhere in the public sector.

[38] *Vanity Fair*, 2 June 1888.

withhold, amend, qualify, comment upon, or delay the C&AG's reports. The Treasury, in effect, was a postman.[39] The issue of C&AG and E&AD independence would re-emerge, particularly in the 1980s as part of a wider examination of the C&AG's role.

The First C&AGs

The first C&AG, Sir William Dunbar, 7th Baron Mochrum, came from a long line of Scottish aristocrats, with an ancestor who fell at Flodden in 1513.[40] A long-standing member of the Liberal Party and a close associate of Gladstone, he had been a minister in Lord Palmerston's government and had spent from 1859–65 as a Lord of the Treasury. Dunbar quickly showed that by background and temperament he was well equipped to defend his powers and independence, which he did vigorously throughout his record twenty-two-year tenure as C&AG. In doing so he established a high public profile for his new department.

Throughout Dunbar's tenure reports on losses, waste, and extravagance were increasingly appearing alongside those on misappropriations. Criticizing instances of spending that involved loss to the public purse was becoming increasingly accepted as the legitimate concern of the public sector auditor. So well received were these disclosures that *The Star* suggested that in their absence the E&AD might as well be abolished.[41] For the newly constituted C&AG to come across instances of waste and extravagance and to do nothing about it offended the core principles of the Liberal financial creed embodied in Gladstonian government.[42] Given Dunbar's long political and personal association with Gladstone, the encouragement that he gave his officers to criticize waste and extravagance was not entirely surprising.

Gladstone was in frequent communication with Dunbar. Indeed, it was during Gladstone's second long period as Chancellor of the Exchequer, prior to Dunbar's appointment as C&AG, that Dunbar had been promoted from his position as a Lord of the Treasury to Chairman of the Commissioners for

---

[39] PAC First Report, 1870, HC 301, para. 26. The requirement that all C&AG's reports, including those on value for money, had to be appended to the annual appropriation accounts later became a potent source of delay and lack of immediacy, particularly when dealing with major value-for-money reports from the 1950s onwards. This was finally dealt with in the 1983 National Audit Act.

[40] Dunbar was not the only aristocrat in the early days of the Department. One of the inspectors of audit, C. A. de Valmer, succeeded to a French family title and re-emerged in the establishment list as Charles Auguste, Vicomte de Valmer.

[41] *The Star*, 7 March 1888; also *St James Gazette*, 27 February 1888.

[42] Committee on National Expenditure (1902), Minutes of Evidence, Welby, Q. 2522; Roseveare, 1969, p. 200.

Auditing the Public Accounts.[43] Gladstone therefore had a staunch ally in place as Comptroller and Auditor General for the first twenty years of the 1866 Audit Act, a critical time for Gladstone to embed his reforms.

Although comments on waste, extravagance, and losses came to be recognized as part of the responsibilities of the C&AG, Dunbar was well aware that he was not to make specific recommendations for improvements in departmental management, nor did he have the authority to force the Executive to remedy the deficiencies that his office might bring to light.[44] To do so was seen as interfering with the rights of the Executive to do the job as it saw fit, and thereby weaken the accountability of the Executive to Parliament.[45] Certainly, as Gladstone stipulated, the public sector auditor was never to question the merits of government policy. Raising instances of losses and extravagance was to be strictly limited to the actual spending and not the reasons for, or merits of, the spending as approved by Parliament—a concern still being voiced over 100 years later in the early days of performance auditing.[46]

One of Dunbar's earliest battles was very much internal. He had been prepared to become C&AG by previously being installed in 1865 as Chairman of the Board of Audit and, on Lord Mouteagle's retirement, as Comptroller General of the Exchequer. One of his fellow Commissioners, Charles Macaulay, was similarly positioned to be appointed by letters patent under the 1866 Act as Assistant Comptroller and Auditor (AC&A).[47] However, less than a month after the Act came into force a heated dispute arose between Dunbar and Macaulay over the relationship between their two posts. Macaulay's anger was based not only on what he saw as an unacceptable reduction in the powers he had expected to exercise under the new arrangements but also what he saw as the devious way in which matters had been finalized. He believed that originally the government had intended that the AC&A would have powers coordinate with those of the C&AG. He maintained that early drafts of the Act provided that both posts would have powers under letters

---

[43] Before taking up the senior civil service post of Comptroller and Auditor-General, Dunbar had firstly to resign from Parliament. According to Wright (1969), this was not an unusual occurrence in nineteenth-century England. A move from Parliament to the employment of the government was often accompanied with a generous pension, something not yet available to unpaid Members of Parliament.

[44] Public Accounts Committee Special Report, 1866, Q.174.

[45] For comments on the need for executive freedom see the Select Committee on Public Monies 1857, Minutes of Evidence, Q.2636.

[46] HC debates, 11 March 1862, col. 1350–1; *National Audit Act of 1983*.

[47] As there was also a Secretary of the Department at senior level, it was not clear what particular purposes the Assistant Comptroller post was intended to serve, other than to provide further high-level support to the C&AG. The post did, however, become the normal stepping-stone to becoming C&AG, before renewed doubts about its value, highlighted by the disruptive personality of the incumbent, led to its abolition under the Exchequer and Audit Departments Act 1921.

patent that would guarantee their separate independence and importance. Macaulay was accustomed to the more collegiate working of the Board of Audit and he had envisaged the C&AG being responsible for the 'executive' functions of the office and, recognizing that Macaulay was an experienced auditor and an expert in the field, the AC&A being responsible for the 'judicial' or reporting functions. Instead, the final version of the Act provided that the AC&A was to exercise powers only in the absence of the C&AG, and even then he would not be able to sign the audit reports to Parliament. Macaulay pointed out that denying the AC&A any independent authority to report to Parliament meant that should he at any time come to conclusions different from those of the C&AG he could, despite his apparent powers, be silenced as a mere subordinate. Macaulay argued that in this situation:

> the Assistant Auditor had been placed in an entirely false and untenable position; that his dignified titles on one side, and his utter powerlessness on the other, represented a ridiculous contrast and could lead to nothing but irritation and embarrassment.[48]

Macaulay was also furious that both he and the Board of Audit had been deceived during the passage of the Bill through Parliament. He roundly disputed the claims of Dunbar and William Anderson of the Treasury, one of the co-authors of the Act, that the Board of Audit had been involved in all stages of the drafting of the Bill, and that the Board had 'acquiesced' in the final arrangements.[49] Macaulay stressed that any involvement he had with the Treasury in the finalizing of the Act had been in a private capacity outside his official association with the Board of Audit. Apart from his personal involvement:

> At no time has the Board expressed any opinion on the subject of any provision of the Bill. If by 'acquiescence' is meant that the Board did nothing to oppose or obstruct the Bill, this is true. But the Board have not been in the habit of volunteering opinions on public questions which had not been officially referred to them; and as the provisions of the Bill never were referred to them ... they never expressed any opinion on the subject at all.[50]

These arguments were aired in increasingly acrimonious public correspondence. When Dunbar made it abundantly clear that he alone would be firmly in command, Macaulay declined the appointment as AC&A.[51] He was promptly replaced by the ever-present William Anderson from the Treasury, who was fated, however, to serve for many years as AC&A without becoming C&AG

---

[48] Confidential letter to the Treasury, 29 April 1867.
[49] Dunbar to the Treasury, 14 December 1866, *British Parliamentary Papers*, 1867, vol. 39, p. 169; Anderson, Evidence before Special PAC Inquiry, 1866, Q.6, p. 523.
[50] Confidential letter to the Treasury, 29 April 1867.
[51] Macaulay to the Secretary to the Treasury, 16 June 1866, in *British Parliamentary Papers*, 1867, vol. 39, pp. 163–5.

because Dunbar clung to office well into his seventies. When there was no sign of him retiring, efforts began behind the scenes to secure Dunbar's resignation. Reports started to appear in the press to the effect that Dunbar was now seldom in his office, that his grasp of his responsibilities was failing, and that the work of the Department was largely being conducted by the AC&A, Sir Charles Ryan.[52]

As Dunbar neared retirement he complained to Gladstone that all heads of the Exchequer since the Restoration had been rewarded with appointment as a Privy Councillor, to which he was the only exception. Anxious for a peerage, he nevertheless sensed that, given the difficulties he had caused the Executive, it would not help his case to appeal for recognition of the value of the work of his Office and his leadership. He therefore reminded Gladstone that of ninety peerages granted in the past thirty years only three had been Scottish—and he referred to his family's distinguished history.[53] He also added that 'Decorations and similar honourable...distinctions have during the last twenty years been conferred without stint on official men serving in the Public Departments but they have always stopped short of the Head of this Department.'[54] Gladstone replied somewhat unenthusiastically that the government was not at present considering new peerages but when it did Dunbar would be considered.[55]

When Dunbar heard in 1886 that new peerages were to be considered he again wrote to Gladstone reiterating the grounds that he considered qualified him for state honours and reminding Gladstone of his previous correspondence and assurances. This time he also played the party political card. At a time of political crisis for Gladstone in 1885, Dunbar had written to him assuring him that he could count on 'your political friends outside the walls of Parliament'.[56] As well as hoping to rely on past favours, Dunbar again emphasized his close association with Gladstone within the Liberal Party, which he boasted he had supported for forty-five years.[57] Still no peerage emerged. Dunbar finally resigned in May 1888 on grounds of ill health and, still unennobled, died in December 1889. On his retirement *The Standard* newspaper described him as 'a financial officer who has introduced a real

---

[52] It was suggested in the press that Dunbar's retirement was engineered by a campaign by high government officials whom he had offended in the 'zealous' pursuit of his duties. *The Observer* on 26 February 1888 reported that Dunbar was to retire. The following day *The Standard* announced that *The Observer*'s report had been premature and unauthorized. On the same day the *St James Gazette* criticized the announcement of 26 February as a mischievous attempt to remove Dunbar—not an innocent mistake.

[53] Dunbar to Gladstone, 15 June 1884, Additional Manuscripts 44,498.

[54] Dunbar to Gladstone, 17 July 1884, Additional Manuscripts 44,491, fol. 315.

[55] Gladstone to Dunbar, 18 August 1884, Additional Manuscripts 44,499, fol. 32.

[56] Correspondence, 25 April 1885, Additional Manuscripts 44,490, fol. 146.

[57] Dunbar to Gladstone 15 June 1886, Additional Manuscripts 44,498, fol. 23.

system of audit and check into the...public service...such as had never previously existed in this country'.

Sir Charles Ryan, Dunbar's successor, first made his name in the Treasury and, thus, was often portrayed as an ex-Treasury man. His first civil service appointment, aged twenty, was as a junior examiner in the Audit Office, although he served there for only a year before moving to the Treasury for the next fourteen years. He returned in 1865 as Secretary to the Audit Office and then to the Exchequer and Audit Department. He became Assistant Comptroller and Auditor on Sir William Anderson's retirement and then served as C&AG from 1888 to 1896. In all, he served a total of thirty years in the Department.[58] During his time at the Treasury, Ryan served as Private Secretary to the two giants of Victorian politics, Disraeli and Gladstone, and was fond of comparing their different styles:

> Mr Disraeli had no liking for hard work and spared himself as much as possible. He spared his private secretaries also, under the belief that they disliked hard work as much as he did, and he was always most considerate to them. Mr Gladstone, on the other hand, was a glutton for work and thought that his secretaries must love it as much as he did. He did not spare them, though he was always appreciative of their work.[59]

Ryan's double achievement of being a Private Secretary to Disraeli and Gladstone was later surpassed by that of C&AG Sir David Pitblado who served as a Private Secretary to three Prime Ministers: Attlee, Churchill, and Eden. Ryan was succeeded in 1896 by Sir Richard Mills, who had been AC&A since 1888 after his sixteen-year tenure as Treasury Officer of Accounts. They were the first two of the high proportion of C&AGs who had at one period in their career served in the Treasury.[60] Mills had spent thirteen years as Treasury Accountant before his sixteen years as Treasury Officer of Accounts. For more than 100 years he was the only specialist accountant to have become C&AG, most of whom have been classicists or, more recently, economists. Under C&AGs Ryan and Mills many reports still dealt with questions of appropriation, accounting, regularity, and related matters, across a range of departments. Some of these reports, though mundane in themselves, offered intriguing glimpses of events in far-flung outposts of the Empire. These included reports on expenditure for: stores and Nile boats for the relief of

---

[58] *The Star* described Ryan as 'a skilled financier, a rigorous worker and qualified to the tips of his fingers' (3 May 1888).

[59] Quoted in Ryan's obituary in *The Times*, 22 November 1920.

[60] Of the 17 C&AGs up to 2010, eleven spent a significant part of their career in the Treasury. These were Sir Charles Ryan, Sir Richard Mills, Sir John Kempe, Sir Malcolm Ramsay, Sir Gilbert Upcott, Sir Edmund Compton, Sir Bruce Fraser, Sir David Pitblado, Sir Douglas Henley, Sir Gordon Downey, and Timothy Burr. Four of them, Richard Mills, Bruce Fraser, Douglas Henley, and Timothy Burr, also served as Treasury Officer of Accounts.

General Gordon at Khartoum; the China expedition to protect British interests during the Boxer rebellion; punitive expeditions in Africa; sanctions against renegade army officers who took part in the Jameson Raid into the Transvaal; ransoms for Britons captured by Turkish bandits; and the relief of distressed British sailors overseas.

Introduction of Value-for-Money Audits

The audit provisions of the 1866 Audit Act were directed solely towards the formal examination and certification of the appropriation and other accounts. The Act made no mention of examinations of economy and efficiency. Gladstone had already made it clear that, like Sir James Graham before him, he saw audit examinations as a valuable aid in identifying individual examples of waste and extravagance, but he wanted such examinations to be carried out on behalf of the Executive, not Parliament, and within Treasury control. He did not wish to see auditors exercising an independent right to pursue or to report the results of such examinations directly to Parliament. Nevertheless, the early C&AGs quickly and progressively introduced examinations of this kind, using to the full their detailed appropriation account access to departmental files and other documents. During Dunbar's time the first foundations were laid for examinations of losses, waste, extravagance, excesses, unnecessary advances to contractors, and other unusual or questionable transactions that would gradually lead into the value-for-money examinations that would later become a significant part of the E&AD's work. Although the 1866 Act provided no mandate for such examinations they were from the outset firmly and enthusiastically encouraged and supported by the PAC. Initially, the reports on losses, waste, and related matters were treated essentially as matters of appropriation and accounting, or involved issues that required Treasury authority, but towards the end of Dunbar's period in office the words 'extravagance', 'economy', and 'efficiency' were increasingly included in his reports.

In terms of accountability, criticizing losses, waste, and extravagance was a natural extension of appropriation audit, if only on the grounds that, as Sir James Graham had argued at the time of the 1832 Audit Act, the sums involved were not properly chargeable against approved grants because they could not be regarded as proper expenditure on services for which Parliament had intended to provide when voting supply. This was recognized by the requirement that losses and other adjustments needed Treasury approval and were noted in separate statements appended to the appropriation accounts. Similarly, the rules requiring open competitive tenders when placing contracts were designed not only to ensure propriety in the conduct of public business but also to promote economy from lower prices. It would also have been against the Victorian ethic, as well as the Gladstonian creed, to identify examples of waste and extravagance during audit and not bring them to Parliament's attention.

Another significant improvement under Dunbar was the extension of E&AD audit into more detailed examinations of departmental stores accounts. Following C&AG criticisms of stores accounting in the Stationery Office in 1881–2, a series of PAC Reports from 1881 to 1886 reflected increasing concern over standards of stores accounting in departments generally, and particularly in the Army and the Navy. The Committee concluded that internal examination of stores accounts by staff of the departments did not provide the assurances that Parliament required and that there should also be independent external examinations by the C&AG.[61] After a long period of gestation, the Treasury finally agreed and, after further discussions with the C&AG, new arrangements were introduced that significantly extended the audit.[62] Statutory authority for the C&AG's audit of stores accounts, however, was not given until the Exchequer and Audit Departments Act 1921.

Though welcomed by the PAC, Parliament, and the press, the C&AG's early ventures into questioning economy and efficiency in administration initially provoked protests from departments, particularly the War Office. Ironically, a turning point in recognizing the C&AG's rights to carry out such examinations arose from a direct challenge by the War Office. An ostensibly trivial enquiry into the purchase of medal ribbons was ill-advisedly chosen by the War Office as a test case to challenge the C&AG's powers of examination under the 1866 Act. After the Army had cancelled a contract to buy medal ribbons at fourteen shillings and replaced it with a contract at twenty shillings, the C&AG asked for an explanation why there had been a loss of public money for which there did not appear to have been any real necessity. The War Office flatly refused to answer, on the grounds that 'the Exchequer and Audit Departments Act does not empower the Comptroller and Auditor General to enter upon matters of administration'. This rather foolish refusal opened the door to wider-ranging examinations of value for money. The PAC fully supported the C&AG, pointing out that: 'If, in the course of his audit, the C&AG becomes aware of facts which appear to him to indicate an improper expenditure or waste of public money, it is his duty to call the attention of Parliament to them.' The Committee also chided the War Office by noting that 'it may often happen that a few words of explanation may save

---

[61] PAC Third Report, 1881, HC 350, para. 13; Second Report, 1883, HC 187, para. 12, Second Report, 1884, paras 128–31; Second Report, 1886, HC 169, para. 70.

[62] Treasury Minute 17540/86, 15 November 1886.

much time and labour'.[63] In a landmark response the Treasury Minute endorsed this view:

> recognising the importance of situations where audit tranches on matters of administration.... My Lords think it important that the Comptroller and Auditor General should have great freedom in drawing his reports to Parliament. He may draw attention to any circumstance that comes to his knowledge in the course of audit, and point out its financial bearing.... It is impossible to deny that it is always his right, and will often be his duty, to take this step, but it is equally obvious that the occasion and manner of such report must be matters of discretion... A fortiori, when, as in the cases actually discussed before the Committee of this Session, there is an apparent financial inconsistency in the actions of the department itself, the Comptroller and Auditor General appears to be more than justified in raising a query on the point.[64]

Persistent to the end, the War Office, again unwisely, sought to exploit a perceived weakness in the Treasury Minute when in 1912 they refused as a matter of administration to respond to the C&AG's questions on purchases of horses at prices that were considerably higher than those known to be available elsewhere. By that time, however, the C&AG's powers to raise such value for money matters were generally accepted, which forced the War Office's Accounting Officer to admit to the PAC that there were no reasons of public policy why an explanation should not have been given. The PAC and the Treasury again firmly supported the C&AG, not only on the substantive criticisms in his report but also on the challenge to his powers. The War Office then backed down, subject only to asking for some minor adjustments on how exchanges on such matters should in future be handled.[65]

The growth of value-for-money audit therefore originated from modest beginnings. Reports on such small-scale subjects as medal ribbons, purchases of horses, competitive tenders, contract delays, and unexplained cost increases were harbingers of today's large-scale investigations into military procurement and capital projects of all kinds. Criticisms of extravagant dinners by the Lighthouse Commissioners, prompting gleeful newspaper lists of expensive wines and cigars,[66] would in time be followed by examinations of the reasonableness of administrative costs of all kinds. Though such early reports could be seen as trivial in themselves they were the basis for establishing the C&AG's rights to examine value for money that would in later years develop into major reports on wide-ranging aspects of departmental expenditure. The Treasury and

---

[63] PAC Second Report, 1888, paras 71 and 72, and War Office letter dated 31 May 1887, printed at p. 208 of Army Appropriation Account, 1886–7, HC 39/1888.

[64] Treasury Minute, 10 January 1889, responding to PAC Second Report, 1888. Printed in full in Epitome of Public Accounts Committee Reports, 1857–1937, pp. 207–8.

[65] PAC Third Report, 1912, HC 156. Treasury Minute, 10 December 1912.

[66] Quoted in *The Star* newspaper.

the spending departments quickly recognized the unwelcome prospect that such examinations, though small to start with, could develop into an established and acknowledged part of the C&AG's powers. They knew that such developments would be supported by the PAC, welcomed by the House of Commons, and applauded by the public and the press.[67] These fears lay at the heart of the fierce opposition received by the early C&AG's reports.

There was also a growing number of reports aimed directly at issues of economy, rather than emerging from examinations of appropriation and regularity. When such reports involved the War Office, which they often did, the response was always unpredictable, and sometimes hostile. In 1892, when questioning unexplained variations in Yeomanry staff numbers, the C&AG delicately suggested 'he would be glad, in view of the financial considerations involved, to be furnished with any observations on the subject which the Secretary of State may desire to offer'. In reply he was bluntly told that 'the subject is one of administration, on which Mr Secretary Stanhope must decline in any way to recognise the right of the C&AG to invite his observations'. The PAC regretted the War Office's attitude and discourtesy, and reminded them of the C&AG's rights of enquiry into matters of economy, established in the medal ribbons case and others quoted above. It also warned them that it regarded this as a serious matter, which it expected to be pursued further and reported again if the C&AG was not satisfied. The Treasury also agreed that 'the C&AG was justified in commenting on a matter of such financial importance'.[68]

Also in 1892, the PAC and the Treasury again combined to support the C&AG against the War Office when a fraud on building works would have been discovered earlier, or in part prevented, had E&AD warnings not been disregarded. They both pointed out:

> the advantages which Departments might often derive from greater alacrity in attending to points raised by the Comptroller and Auditor General. The assistance afforded by a thorough system of audit deserves a welcome which it does not always receive from those who are responsible for administration.[69]

In a later case, the War Office readily accepted a C&AG suggestion, made in the interest of possible economy, that it should widen competitive tendering for purchases of medicines by approaching contractors already supplying medicines to the Navy.[70] Elsewhere, E&AD audit of heavy expenditure in the ordnance factories and the Navy dockyards pursued questions of economy

---

[67] *The Star* suggested that in the absence of a concern for waste the Audit Office might as well be abolished (7 March 1888; also *St James Gazette*, 27 February 1888).

[68] PAC Second Report, 1892, HC 180, para. 28 and Treasury Minute, 5 November 1892.

[69] PAC Second Report, 1892, HC 180, para. 39. Treasury Minute, 5 November 1892.

[70] PAC Second Report, 1893, HC 255, paras 4–6.

and efficiency by comparing costs of construction for similar activities in different establishments and, where possible, between those establishments and private contractors. Individual areas examined included excessive use of overtime, variations in piecework rates, and other controls over wages. The PAC and the Treasury again supported the C&AG in extending his audit in these ways.[71] Stores examinations, particularly in the Army and the Navy, increasingly questioned a wide range of activities, including criticisms of the lack of competitive tendering, high prices, delays and penalties, inadequate controls over receipts and issues, prevention of waste, losses of all kinds, potential frauds, illegalities and irregularities, and weaknesses in stocktaking.

Reports of this kind throughout the 1880s, and increasingly in the 1890s, aroused considerable public interest and were keenly followed up by the PAC.[72] Many of the more significant examinations seem to have been primarily the responsibility of Mr D. C. Richmond, who served for four years as AC&A under Sir Richard Mills before succeeding him as C&AG in 1900. In evidence before the Committee on National Expenditure in 1902, Richmond made it very clear where he stood:

> I think it is my duty to report anything which in my judgement...concerns the House of Commons to know....I do not feel myself debarred from calling attention to anything which has occurred in the course of my audit during the year which indicates loss or waste....I have to act with great care and discretion. It is not for me to criticise administrative action...but if I find the result of administrative action has been a loss or wastefulness of public money, then I think it is not going beyond my duty of reporting as an officer of the House of Commons if I call attention to matters of that kind, even though the account itself would not disclose the facts.

Richmond's most prominent success came as a result of E&AD examinations of stores expenditure in the South African War of 1899–1902, particularly in drawing attention to what became known as the 'dual system' of stores contracts.[73] Large surplus stocks in South Africa at the close of the war were being sold at very low prices to local contractors whilst the same or similar supplies were being repurchased from them at much higher prices. Richmond's reports culminated in the appointment in 1905 of a Royal Commission under Lord Justice Farwell to hold an investigation into war stores in South Africa. The Commission commended Richmond for his 'vigilance and pertinacity' without which, they stated, most of the transactions they investigated would never have come to light.[74]

The E&AD also had a non-professional interest in the conduct of the South African War. In 1859 the Audit Office had the unique distinction of being the

---

[71] PAC First Report 1896, HC 227, para. 10. Treasury Minute, 16 November 1896.
[72] Epitome of Public Accounts Reports, Vol. 1.   [73] Funnell, 2005.
[74] PAC Third Report, 1905, HC248. Royal Commission on War Stores in South Africa (Cmnd 3127, presented in 1906, particularly paras 181–7). PAC Fourth Report, 1906, HC 352.

only national audit office ever to found an army regiment, The Prince of Wales' Own Civil Service Rifles. The Audit Office Company subsequently played an important part in all the regiment's many activities, military and social. The Prince of Wales was Honorary Colonel-in-Chief of the regiment and his participation in its activities attracted some 500 official supporters entitled to wear the elaborate uniform, 'but of a more advanced age than one is accustomed to seeing in the ranks'. Many were prominent members of Victorian public life, in society, politics, science, literature and the arts. Sir Richard Mills, during his time at the Treasury and as C&AG, served in the regiment for thirty-five years, rose to become Colonel-in-Chief, and set up the regimental headquarters in the Audit Office at Somerset House. South Africa saw the regiment's first wartime activity when it marched on Pretoria and fought at Diamond Hill. It later fought in France, Turkey, and Egypt in the First World War before being disbanded in 1921.[75]

Richmond retired in 1904 and in the first 140 years of the 1866 Act was the only C&AG not to receive a knighthood. Richmond's family believe that the reason for denying him a knighthood was the unwelcome reaction to his reports in powerful official circles.[76] Except for Sir William Dunbar, who had an inherited title, all C&AGs either had a knighthood before their appointment or received one during their period in office. Possibly to avoid a like-minded successor, Richmond had been followed as C&AG in 1905 by Sir John Kempe, aged fifty-eight, who had been brought in at the end of a distinguished career in the Treasury and Customs and Excise to serve a few months as AC&A before becoming C&AG. During this time the Department was largely run by Mr (later Sir) Henry Gibson, who had become AC&A in 1905 at the relatively early age of forty-five, after a twenty-year financial career in the War Office. Gibson's energy and success as the driving force in the Department throughout his period as AC&A from 1905–11 cemented his reputation and earned the high opinion of the PAC. It was suggested that Gibson's achievements had forestalled a possible Treasury wish to have 'one of their own' to replace Kempe as C&AG. Gibson was C&AG from 1911–21, when he retired early due to ill health.

The Welfare State

Major welfare reforms in the early twentieth-century presented the E&AD with an array of new challenges and responsibilities, in both nature and

---

[75] *The History of the Prince of Wales' Own Civil Service Rifles*, 2002.
[76] Confirmed by one of Richmond's great-granddaughters in conversation with C&AG Sir Douglas Henley.

scope. A significant early concern with Old Age Pensions was the appropriate depth and coverage of the C&AG's examination. It was accepted from the outset that the appropriation accounts themselves should be subject to a test examination only, with the C&AG's certification audit being able to rely largely on prior examination by approved departmental officers. However, on the question of the action to be taken when pensions were found to have been awarded wrongly, the PAC was deeply concerned over what they saw as a constitutional as well as an accountability issue. They reported that:

> A question of grave importance has been raised by the contention of the Treasury that because (the local committees appointed under the Act) were the final judges whether the conditions of a claim justify the grant of a pension, neither the Accounting Officer for the Vote, nor the Comptroller and Auditor General, nor your Committee, can recommend for disallowance any pension made under an Old Age Pension award. Your Committee are of the opinion that this contention cannot be allowed to prevail; for they see no evidence in the Old Age Pension Act that Parliament either intended to or did in fact repeal or render nugatory any part of the Exchequer and Audit Departments Act 1866, and so deprive itself of the right of scrutinizing to the full the propriety of any payment made out of sums granted by Parliament.[77]

After reiterating these objections, the PAC set out four principles designed to challenge the Treasury contention on disallowance. Though the Treasury made some carefully worded assurances on some general aspects of accountability, it would not give way on the central issue of disallowance. The Treasury insisted, based on law officers' lengthy opinion, that the Old Age Pension Act 1908 provided quite clearly that only the local committees had final responsibility for pension awards and any remedies to deal with incorrect awards. No other parties had any powers to recommend disallowance.[78] The PAC tried twice to pursue the issue, but faced again with the same legal advice they decided, very reluctantly, not to press matters further.[79]

The difficulties that could arise on the regularity of detailed pension awards were later illustrated with war pensions. These were paid by the Ministry of Pensions under Royal Warrant. In 1918 the Accounting Officer of the Ministry and the C&AG drew attention to 'an increasing tendency on the part of the Ministry of Pensions to interpret the terms of the Royal Warrant in a strained and unnatural sense to the extent which involves improper expenditure of public money'. Typical cases were put to the PAC, in some of which the Minister had overruled the Accounting Officer's protest that the awards were irregular and required Treasury sanction. In other cases the C&AG had

[77] PAC Third Report, 1909, HC 126, paras 20–9.
[78] Treasury Minute, 10 June 1909.
[79] PAC Fifth Report, 1909, HC284, paras 20–2 and PAC Second Report, 1911, HC 110, para. 20.

endorsed the Accounting Officer's concerns and referred the awards to the Treasury, who also regarded them as not covered by the terms of the Warrant. The PAC took evidence from the Parliamentary Secretary to the Ministry who explained the policy of the Minister and claimed that he must be allowed a very wide discretion as interpreter of the Warrant. The PAC, however, were clearly of the opinion that some of the awards were *ultra vires*. As regards the Minister's powers of interpretation, the Committee emphatically asserted, as its predecessors had done on several occasions involving other awards, that any action taken under a Royal Warrant 'should be in accordance with the simple and ordinary meaning of the language . . . , any discretionary interpretation should not be opposed to but in harmony with the natural meaning, intention and purpose of the Warrant'.[80] Otherwise, Treasury approval should be obtained.

In a coded rebuke to the Minister, the Committee emphasized that 'it is of the utmost importance in the interest of the taxpayer that the very heavy expenditure on war pensions should be administered under all proper and necessary safeguards'.[81] The Committee's views on all aspects of the affair were firmly shared by the Treasury. Despite pledges that the Minister had given to the Treasury, he continued to argue on the principles as he saw them; the moral obligations of government to the servicemen involved and proposals to recover awards wrongly made. Correspondence continued for some months, with the Treasury clearly angered by the Ministry's persistence. In the end, the Treasury refused to give way.[82] The PAC returned to the subject the following year. By then, matters had been put on a proper footing, the C&AG had reported that the arrangements made were working satisfactorily, and the PAC expressed its satisfaction with the result.[83]

A recurring issue on all pension payments was the need to check continuing entitlement, often over many years and for pensioners living abroad. However, there was no uniform or systematic method of personal identification in force in the various departments involved and pensions were continuing to be paid long after the pensioner had died, sometimes for decades. These issues had been raised in 1913 and when fraudulent payments were still being reported in 1921, with 3.5 million pensioners on the books of the Ministry of Pensions, the PAC obtained assurances from the Treasury that measures were being introduced across departments to check on matters affecting continuing eligibility, such as death or remarriage, and to prosecute offenders and recover improper payments.

Complications also arose on the audit of the National Insurance accounts, prepared by the National Health Insurance Commissions and the Board of

---

[80] PAC Report, 1918, HC100, para. 77. [81] PAC Report, 1918, HC100, para. 77.
[82] Treasury Minute, 11 September 1918. [83] PAC Second Report, 1919, HC 145. para. 42.

Trade. Before the universal scheme introduced by the 1911 Act, there were various insurance schemes administered by Approved Societies and Insurance Committees, and these were brought under the new statutory arrangements. The accounts of these bodies, which were the basis for the government's 25 per cent contribution to the National Insurance Fund, were audited by the newly created National Insurance Audit Department. The C&AG had agreed, based on a precedent from local government grants, that he would not himself examine the results of that audit and that he would rely on certificates of expenditure from the National Insurance Department auditor in support of his own examination of voted funds. The PAC did not seem to be fully convinced by these arm's-length arrangements, noting that 'as the new scheme, involving very large expenditure of public money, is more or less in the experimental stage, the working of the financial machinery should be carefully watched'.[84]

The PAC was right to be cautious. In 1916 the C&AG reported that Approved Societies and Insurance Committees had incurred considerable expenditure on benefits and administrative expenses that could not be certified by the National Insurance Audit Department as being in accordance with the Act and the relevant regulations. No record of any of these transactions had yet appeared in the accounts either of the National Health Insurance Funds or of the several Votes. Arrangements, however, had since been made, including legislation, for proper disclosure of these irregular payments and to minimize the impact on public funds. Powers of surcharge against individual members of the societies and committees were being strengthened, again by amending legislation. However, there had also been serious delays of up to two and a half years in submission of some accounts, affecting the audit by both the National Insurance Audit Department and the C&AG. The PAC wanted 'severe action to be taken, including withholding advances of funds and other necessary measures; and they propose to watch the results in future years'.[85] They did so in 1917 and 1919 and were satisfied with the further steps taken.

Colonial Audit

In self-funding colonies the audit was carried out by local audit offices reporting to their own governments, but expenditure in Crown Colonies receiving substantial grants-in-aid from the Exchequer was subject to audit on behalf the UK government. Originally the responsibility of the Commissioners for

---

[84] PAC Report, 1915, HC 249, paras 15–16. [85] PAC First Report, 1916, HC 83, paras 13–21.

West India Accounts and the Commissioners for Colonial Accounts, this audit was statutorily transferred in 1832 to the Commissioners of Audit. The intention was then to make the C&AG responsible for the audit under s.33 of the 1866 Act, but the Treasury forgot to present the necessary Treasury Minute to Parliament. As a result the audit of Crown Colony accounts was largely suspended from 1867–8 until 1876–7, although partial examinations identified serious omissions, inaccuracies, and delays in the accounts being submitted. The Treasury in 1879 issued revised instructions on the preparation and submission of revised forms of accounts and other financial returns, but the position on staffing and funding the audit remained anomalous.[86]

There then followed a variety of different arrangements for the staffing, funding, organization, and operational responsibilities for the work carried out by the E&AD and the Colonial Audit Branch of the Colonial Office. In 1910 a new Colonial Audit Department was established at the Colonial Office and the PAC agreed that in his own audit of the appropriation accounts the C&AG could accept the certificate of the head of the new department as evidence of the proper application of the grants-in-aid within the colonies, subject to any supplementary examination the C&AG might decide was necessary. The Treasury agreed,[87] and in 1912 the PAC was informed that the new arrangements at both the Colonial Office and E&AD were working satisfactorily.[88]

Expenses of Members of Parliament

Throughout the history of the C&AG's audit there have often been aspects that have a tendency to reappear. One of these involved MPs expenses. In 1912 MPs were paid a salary of £400 a year, but the Treasury had agreed that a standard amount of 25 per cent should be deducted when calculating a Member's liability for income tax, on the grounds that it could be regarded as an allowance for expenses. The Treasury had acted without legal authority and without taking legal advice. Its explanation was that a standard allowance 'obviated administrative difficulties in dealing with claims for abatement submitted by Members, such claims presenting questions of complexity to the officials in the Paymaster-General's office, who act as Commissioners of Income Tax in respect of public salaries . . . and from whose decisions there seems to be no appeal'.[89] This was an apparent delicate way of suggesting that

---

[86] PAC First Report, 1878, HC 83. Treasury Minute, 25 September 1878.
[87] PAC Third Report, 1910, HC 144, paras 20–1. Treasury Minute 11 December 1910.
[88] PAC Second Report, 1912, HC 119.
[89] PAC Second Report, 1913, HC179 and Treasury Minutes, 7 January and 2 February 1913.

it was not for mere officials to question and give final rulings on the financial affairs of MPs. (A culture of deference was also a factor in the public outcry over the expenses of MPs a hundred years later). Though the scheme was known to have the personal support of the Chancellor of the Exchequer, C&AG Sir Henry Gibson was determined to pursue the issue. He pointed out that the £400 was clearly voted as salary and he doubted whether a standard allowance, without proof of actual expenditure 'wholly, exclusively and necessarily' incurred in the performance of parliamentary duties, could be regarded as satisfying the income tax legislation. PAC members themselves were clearly in a difficult position, but in its report the Committee did not accept that the Treasury had the discretionary power claimed and recommended that if the allowance were to continue it should be given statutory authority. The Treasury conceded and the position was regularized in the Finance Act 1913.

Conclusion

As well as building lasting monuments in bricks, steel, and glass the Victorians built lasting monuments in public administration and finance. At the beginning of the Victorian age, control and accountability for public expenditure was incomplete and uncertain: by its end a robust framework of appropriation, audit, and reporting was firmly in place. In 1820 public sector audit lacked independence and operated within narrow traditional limits: by 1901 it had been consolidated into one organization with established independence and wide and growing responsibilities. The centrepiece of nineteenth-century developments in public financial accountability was the Exchequer and Audit Departments Act 1866. The 1866 Act was overwhelmingly a reforming Act, in both its immediate and longer-term effects. Lord Welby, when giving evidence to the National Expenditure Committee in 1902, reminded the Committee that:

> the Act of 1866 was a reform of the greatest administrative importance. It is possible that it was unpopular at first because no one likes control. The unpopularity had passed before I left the service, and I doubt whether any public servant worth his salt would wish a return to the old system. The new system has converted the nominal control of Parliament into a real control. I cannot say how much the Comptroller and Auditor General's reports conduce to the maintenance of financial order, and enforce a very salutary restraint on Ministers and Civil Servants alike.[90]

[90] HC 387, 1902, Appendix No. 13.

From around 1905 the general pattern of the C&AG's audit was to a large extent a continuing process of consolidation and steady improvement, rather than innovation, building on the advances and achievements following the 1866 Act. Many of the C&AG and PAC reports explored familiar territory, not least because there were continuing failings and lessons yet to be learned. The focus was still primarily on Army and Navy expenditure on contracts and stores and on works and buildings, both civil and military. There were also reports on various certification issues on the three main revenue departments, on diplomatic services, and on a range of other departments. Increasing attention was also directed towards spending on new social programmes and the different audit challenges to be addressed, for example with the passage of the Old Age Pensions Act 1908 and the National Insurance Act 1911.

At the request of the PAC, C&AG Sir Henry Gibson in 1916 prepared a memorandum to celebrate 'Fifty Years of the 1866 Act', which was then presented to both Houses of Parliament.[91] He listed key developments and measures introduced during those fifty years, including strengthening and extending the scope and coverage of the audit, and paving the way for a more efficient certification audit based on systems and tests rather than a detailed and narrow scrutiny of vouchers. Audit had been carried increasingly into the operations of manufacturing and trading accounts, particularly the Navy dockyards and the ordnance factories. Stores and contracts audit had been significantly extended while the different audit needs of the revenue departments had been brought fully on board. Examinations of economy and efficiency had grown with reports on 'uneconomical' activities, 'waste of public money', and 'manifestly bad bargains'. Examinations now pursued 'the merits of expenditure without criticising the policy which determines it'. Forms of account and departmental accounting, financial control, and reporting systems had been significantly improved. These were not successes of the E&AD alone: the PAC, the Treasury, and the audited departments had played crucially important parts.

When planning the 1866 Act Gladstone had envisaged that the E&AD should be led by a 'safe' C&AG as the junior member in a 'partnership' with the Treasury directed towards strengthening Treasury control of departmental spending. The C&AG should have no powers to report independently on economy and efficiency. Instead, what was planned as a partnership between the C&AG and the Treasury to serve Executive control emerged as a partnership between the C&AG and the PAC to serve parliamentary accountability.

---

[91] Cmnd 8337 of 1916.

7

Audit, Accountability, and the Impact of the Two World Wars

'The sinews of war are unlimited money.'

Cicero, *Fifth Phillipic*, ch. 5

Wars have always provided challenges to parliamentary financial control, accountability, and audit. Heavy military expenditures present stronger demands and continuing pressures. Normal standards, procedures, and financial controls are inevitably reduced or suspended to reflect challenging wartime circumstances, unforeseen emergencies, and military priorities. These cast a shadow before them and leave a difficult post-war legacy. Wartime operations can also stimulate fresh thinking and indicate new methods of working aimed at greater economy and efficiency, in audit as well as in departments.

The impact of the First and Second World Wars on accountability was at three levels: parliamentary funding; controls over the conduct of departmental business; and the scope and depth of audit. During the First World War the estimates and supplementary estimates presented gave only limited information for MPs to consider proposed expenditure. This was partly for security reasons and also because of difficulties in forecasting levels of expenditure at such uncertain times and apportioning them over different votes. There were many token estimates, and timetables for approving estimates were shortened. There were also reductions in the disclosure of expenditure in some appropriation accounts where, again on security grounds, figures for separate votes were grouped together and presented in abstract terms only. More generally, at least in the early years, the climate of opinion in the House of Commons, anxious to show support for the war, was not conducive to close questioning of the government's financial proposals.

First World War

Treasury Control of Departments

Some of the Treasury's powers increased during the First World War while others were reduced or relaxed. The main extension to Treasury powers followed from the introduction of Votes of Credit. With major funds for wartime expenditure now being under the control of the Treasury, it played a key part in decisions on allocating funds between different wartime needs, based on the demands of the fighting services and other priorities and emergency requirements. In normal times these appropriations would have been the responsibility of Parliament. As part of these arrangements, emergency inter-departmental committees were set up with the Admiralty, and later the Ministry of Munitions, to enable the Treasury to keep in close touch with funding needs and to exercise necessary control but without creating undue delay to the work. Similar arrangements were considered impracticable for the War Office. Thus, prior Treasury sanction was not required for expenditure 'certified to be vitally necessary to the public interest and to have been incurred under such conditions of urgency that it could not be submitted to the Treasury beforehand'.[1] Certificates of Urgency were signed by the War Office's Financial Secretary on the authority of the Secretary of State. Though occasionally the War Office was committed to expenditure before the Certificate of Urgency was obtained, 'the Financial Secretary speedily made it clear that he would refuse to give the necessary certificate unless he was asked before the expenditure was incurred'.[2]

For some smaller bodies, Treasury officials were appointed to serve on their finance committees in order to be kept informed about spending plans as they were being formulated and to be in a position to stop or moderate them. The PAC was concerned that these Treasury officials could in time become 'quasi-departmental' and less independent, but the Committee was reassured by the Treasury that this would not happen. More generally, Treasury controls were reduced or relaxed to give departments wider powers on such matters as writing off of losses and overpayments, special and unusual payments, waiver of outstanding debts, freedom from competitive tendering for smaller non-urgent contracts, and straightforward cases of vote allocation and virement.

The most significant reduction in Parliament's wartime control over funding was the use of Votes of Credit. These granted the Treasury large annual lump sums to be spent as the government decided, without prior parliamentary approval, on urgent and unforeseen measures directly needed for the war

---

[1] Treasury Minute of 8 December 1914, para. 11. Certificates under this provision were to be submitted to the C&AG with the relevant accounts.
[2] PAC Second Report, 1916, HC 115, paras 23–4.

effort. The exigencies of war precluded the preparation and submission of detailed estimates. Votes of Credit were mainly used to fund expenditure on the fighting services but also for such matters as protection of food supplies and other essential services, and for emergency needs. The initial Vote of Credit at the outbreak of war was £100 million, after which subsequent increases brought the total for 1914–15 to £362 million. Further annual amounts were provided throughout the War. For 1915–16 and subsequent years these covered the total expenditure of the Navy, the Army, and the Ministry of Munitions, with only token estimates presented to Parliament. Votes of Credit were not intended to be used to meet excess expenditure on services already provided for in estimates and supplementary estimates, but this distinction was not always maintained. Amounts used from Votes of Credit were subsequently shown either in the relevant appropriation accounts or as a direct charge to the Vote of Credit. Details of the arrangements for allocating and accounting for sums drawn down from the Vote of Credit were set out in extensive Treasury Minutes.[3]

The House of Commons had always reluctantly accepted Votes of Credit as a necessary evil in exceptional circumstances. However, whilst recognizing the continuing demands of wartime operations, the House of Commons had by 1917 become increasingly uneasy about the curtailments and constraints on its traditional powers. These concerns were fuelled by burgeoning levels of expenditure, taxation, and debt, and the number of new services and organizations that Votes of Credit were being used to fund. Resentment about these issues emerged clearly in the debate in Parliament in July 1917 on a motion to appoint a new Select Committee on National Expenditure.[4] In 1917 the PAC produced a special report on 'Estimates and Treasury Control in Wartime Conditions' and, although there were some specific areas of concern, the broad picture presented was that: 'During the year under review the accounting by Departments and the work of the Comptroller and Auditor General have been carried out in face of abnormal difficulties caused by the war, and they have, on the whole, been satisfactorily overcome.' Looking forward, however, the Committee believed that:

> Whatever may have been the necessity for Vote of Credit procedure in the early stages of the war, the time has now arrived when Estimates more approaching those in force in normal times should be presented to Parliament, not merely for the fighting services, but also, where practicable, for the new services now charged direct to the Vote of Credit.

---

[3] Treasury Minutes, 20 August 1914 and 22 November 1915. PAC Second Report, 1916, HC 115 paras 68–72.
[4] Hansard, 6 July 1917, vol. 95, cc 1493–569.

The Treasury responded by explaining at some length in a Treasury Minute the continuing need for Votes of Credit, at the same time agreeing to provide, where possible, further information on the main services for which it was expected to be used and to extend the presentation of token estimates for the new departments being created. Predictably, and with barely suppressed irritation, the Minute did not accept the PAC's criticisms of Treasury control.[5]

Controls on Contracts

The largest single area of concern about reductions in controls over the conduct of departmental business was the placing and pricing of contracts. The accepted principle was that government contracts should wherever possible be placed on the basis of fixed-price competitive contracts from a range of suitable suppliers. Although departments paid lip-service to the principle it was often difficult to persuade them to follow it consistently in practice. Sometimes this was due to pressures of other work, sometimes to lack of effort to find different suppliers, and sometimes for more complex technical reasons. For example, the War Office and the Admiralty, which together incurred by far the heaviest contract expenditure, frequently asserted that special in-service requirements and priorities meant that only a strictly limited number of companies, or sometimes only one, had the skills, experience, and production capacity to meet demanding specifications and timescales and to ensure continuity of supply. They also argued that companies would not invest in new manufacturing facilities to improve efficiency without guarantees, or near guarantees, of a share in future work. Subsequent contracts, placed by negotiation and not competitive tendering, were often claimed to be necessary.

In matters of pricing, it was thought unreasonable to expect contractors to quote firm prices at the outset of a contract when specifications or timescales were not finalized and would inevitably be subject to frequent change during a time of great uncertainty, when new demands emerged often unexpectedly and with great urgency. The preferred alternative of pricing contracts on a cost-plus-percentage profit basis was regarded as being in the government's interest as well as that of contractors, even though this brought its own uncertainties and difficulties in verifying contractors' costs and establishing an acceptable profit based on return on capital employed. These arguments, which were sometimes difficult to dismiss in normal circumstances, were even more difficult to challenge under wartime priorities and pressures. As a result, in the lead-up to 1914, and increasingly during the war, many of the largest

---

[5] PAC Report, 1917, HC 123. Treasury Minute, 1 November 1917.

contracts, particularly for Army and Navy procurement, were placed on a non-competitive cost-plus-percentage profit basis. Nevertheless, the C&AG continued to produce reports on the larger or more questionable contracts for examination and report by the PAC. The reports focused mainly on action being taken to secure fair and reasonable prices, rather than seeking to maintain the principle of competitive tendering. Increasingly it seemed to have been accepted that, certainly as the war progressed, emergency needs meant that on large military procurement contracts this was largely impracticable. Some large civil projects were also affected, for example the £2 million building programme under the Housing Act 1914.[6] Even in areas where there was still some competition there were concerns over the risk of company 'rings' conspiring to fix prices to obtain excess profits.

Early in the First World War the Admiralty's arrangements for checking contractors' prices were less than satisfactory, particularly for ship repairs, new ships, and munitions. For example, a lack of dockyard capacity meant that urgent ship repairs were increasingly placed with private yards, even though they had previously been found to be much more expensive. Instructions were issued that tenders should be obtained if time permitted, but otherwise officers 'should make the most advantageous terms they could with any competent firm'.[7] There were provisions allowing technical officers to inspect some areas of contractors' costs, but whilst the PAC accepted that these provided some safeguards against extravagance they concluded that 'more specific powers should have been taken to secure due economy'.[8] Ships were sometimes being ordered and construction started before prices were agreed. Where broadly similar ships had been built before, in the dockyards or privately, an approximation could be made as to the cost.

With munitions, the Admiralty had no data as to the actual cost of supplies such as shells and guns. Their usual method of purchase was to invite tenders from their existing suppliers and to determine the reasonableness of prices solely on the basis of previous prices and the opinions of their professional officers. In contrast, the Ministry of Munitions had instituted a system of actual costing of shells and other supplies and, coupled with the powers conferred by the Munitions Act and regulations under the Defence of the Realm Act, the Ministry had been able to secure substantial reductions in prices as compared with those paid in the early stages of the war, irrespective of the increased cost of labour and material. Although the Admiralty had recently introduced a system of placing orders for shells, leaving the price to

---

[6] PAC First Report, 1916, HC 88, paras 5–6.
[7] PAC Second Report, 1916, HC 115, paras 7–11.
[8] PAC Second Report, 1916, HC 115, paras 7–11.

be settled later, and employing skilled accountants to investigate the firms' books, the PAC report:

> greatly regretted that no such system seems to have been adopted before the War, in order to break down rings which were known to exist among contractors, and that even now, with the experience of the Ministry of Munitions, the system is but slowly being introduced; so that prices paid by the Admiralty for shell and other supplies show no such reduction from the rates ruling just after the commencement of the War, as has been effected by the Ministry of Munitions.[9]

For army supplies, the War Office at the outbreak of war at once resorted to direct negotiation with contractors, appointing expert agents to shop around and buy from stock, or negotiate deals directly with the manufacturers. This procedure, however, was soon found to be unsatisfactory. The government were taking nearly as much as some industries could produce, and in some cases wanted far more, which meant that all the goods offered had to be accepted irrespective of prices. In June 1915 the War Office started to require manufacturers to justify their quoted prices by giving statements of the cost of manufacture and negotiating price reductions where possible. Further developments culminated in February 1916 in an amendment to the Defence of the Realm regulations, which gave the government power, in the last resort, to requisition the output of any factory in the country and to pay for that output at a fair agreed price. Contractors had to show that their prices were reasonable by disclosing their costs of manufacture and satisfying expert departmental advisers. This also had the effect of breaking up and preventing combinations of manufacturers against the government.[10]

In the absence of competitive tendering, cost-plus-percentage profit contracts were increasingly seen as the most effective basis for settling fair and reasonable prices under wartime conditions. When the PAC returned to the subject in 1917 and 1918 they commented favourably on the cost-accounting expertise of the War Office that had enabled them to secure substantial economies by reducing contractors' prices. The Committee also referred to the considerable advances in the powers now available to the War Office, Admiralty, Ministry of Munitions, and the Food Controller to examine contractors' books and fix prices on actual costs of production. It emphasized that the exercise of powers of detailed investigation not only helped to reduce prices but also brought home to manufacturers the demands this placed on their own conduct of business and helped to secure economies in their production processes. The PAC thought these arrangements 'a development that would be widely welcomed on both sides' and 'were likely to have large and

---

[9] PAC Second Report, 1916, HC 115, para. 11.
[10] PAC Second Report, 1916, HC 115, para. 28.

far-reaching effect in the future...[and] trusted that these powers will be retained on return to normal conditions'.[11] As a result, cost-plus contracts, with their benefits and uncertainties, would continue to be a dominant feature of government purchasing through to the Second World War and for many years afterwards. These and the many other changes to normal processes demanded by the unpredictable demands of war presented the C&AG with many urgent challenges.

Wartime Audit

The extent and the nature of the C&AG's audit throughout the First World War was greatly affected by the vast increase in all kinds of expenditure, not only on the fighting services but also on supporting activities and more widely throughout the economy. New and less experienced bodies were increasingly involved, with greater risks. Departments too were having to cope with officers leaving for active service, to be replaced with temporary and less skilled staff. Expenditure was also being incurred worldwide, often in operational circumstances that made accurate record keeping and accounting difficult to maintain. This led to some serious delays in the submission of accounts to parent departments. Not surprisingly, the needs of accounting and audit were not uppermost in the minds of those engaged in dangerous and more demanding duties. Indeed, enforced changes in the process of funding departments had a major impact on audit. The C&AG's loss of experienced staff for active military service greatly accentuated these difficulties.

Even on a test audit basis the coverage of audits grew increasingly thin, though it was always officially held to be sufficient to discharge the C&AG's statutory responsibilities for the certification of appropriation and regularity. To some extent the demands on audits were reduced because it was no longer necessary to scrutinize the large number of detailed matters where the need for Treasury authority had been removed. Reports on value for money tended to deal with broader and more important issues of weaknesses in systems and controls over major areas of expenditure, rather than individual cases of waste and extravagance. Consciously or not, it seems to have been recognized that Whitehall and Parliament would regard reporting individual failings in economy as being of secondary importance when pursuing wartime priorities. The care taken by the C&AG to maintain the right balance in wartime examinations was made clear in an exchange at the PAC in 1919 when the Ministry of Munitions confirmed that:

> There had been no undue pressure either by the Treasury or the Comptroller and Auditor General of excessive or minute audit in cases where financial interests

[11] PAC Report, 1917, HC 123.

did not justify it. Further, he has been careful to draw attention to improvements or reforms in financial and accounting procedures where they have been effected.[12]

The PAC agreed that there had been no unfairness in the C&AG's reports and was satisfied that he had exercised his statutory powers with due discretion.[13] Cooperation occasionally worked both ways. In the report referred to above, the PAC welcomed the fact that the Ministry had agreed to a request from the C&AG that his officers should be associated with the Ministry's own accountants in an examination of confidential documents and accounts of a company seeking reinstatement of profits on a Ministry contract. The Committee emphasized that they regarded it 'as of paramount importance that the Comptroller and Auditor General should have access to all documents substantiating payments out of public funds so that he may satisfy himself as to the propriety of the payments'.[14] The C&AG's wartime work had also been praised by Members of Parliament in a debate in the House of Commons in 1917, during which some members took the opportunity to criticize the long delays between expenditure being incurred and reports to Parliament on findings, criticisms, and action taken.[15] The timetable for audit, presentation of a C&AG report, the associated PAC hearing and report, and the subsequent Treasury Minute could take up to two years to complete. Such delays would not be fully resolved until the provisions of the National Audit Act 1983 were enacted.

Peace and Restoration of Parliamentary Control

Appointment of Accounting Officers

One of the immediate post-war priorities was to restore parliamentary control over expenditure, including determined moves to return to normal peacetime estimates and supply procedures. During the war these had largely been set aside, or reduced to token measures, to give the government greater freedom in the use of lump sum Votes of Credit to fund urgent needs and overriding military priorities. Measures to review and update the arrangements for parliamentary accountability and audit began again in 1919. These were driven by the Cabinet's determination to secure strong central oversight of departmental spending to bring under control the spiralling

---

[12] PAC Third Report, 1919, HC 223, paras 5–6.
[13] PAC Third Report, 1919, HC 223, paras 5–6.
[14] PAC Third Report, 1919, HC 223, para. 27.
[15] Hansard, 6 July 1917, vol. 95, cc 1493–569.

expenditure of the war years and to reduce the 'mushroom ministries' that had appeared. From 1919 onwards there was therefore a determined programme to re-establish traditional Treasury controls and to pursue stringent economies across the public sector.[16] These included slashing cuts of more than 25 per cent in civil service numbers that were to come from the swing of the 'Geddes Axe'.[17]

The comprehensive programme of reorganization, reform, and modernization was made the direct responsibility of the determined and forceful Sir Warren Fisher who had in 1919, at the age of only thirty-nine, been made Permanent Secretary of a rejuvenated Treasury, which was poised to return to a position of power following the recommendations of the Bradbury Report in 1919.[18] Coincidentally in America, President Warren Harding was pushing through a broadly similar programme to cut government spending by 40 per cent. His Budget and Accounting Act 1921 set up a Bureau of the Budget specifically to subject budget authorizations to central scrutiny and control, and established the General Accounting Office to pursue greater economy and efficiency.

The concern for economy in the immediate post-war years made it a key aim that financial considerations should be taken fully into account from the outset when preparing departmental programmes and budgets.[19] Here the status and responsibilities of the Principal Finance Officer should have been an important safeguard. However, the Baldwin Council had noted that 'in many Civil Departments the Principal Finance Officer ranks only as one of a number of Assistant Secretaries' and emphasized that 'the relation between the Chief Finance Officer and his permanent head requires very careful adjustment'.[20] The Council's report, with some amendments suggested by Fisher, received general Cabinet approval in February 1920, and new arrangements to establish the basic structure of financial accountability were promulgated in

---

[16] For fuller analyses of the genesis and carrying through of this programme, and the longer-term effects, see *Civil Service Reorganisation, 1919–22*, (Published RIPA); and Hennessy, 1990, pp. 69–75.

[17] Sir Eric Geddes was one of the businessmen brought in by Lloyd George during the war to help boost munitions production. He became a minister in the post-war coalition government. In February 1922 he was given the role of securing sweeping cuts in departmental budgets, and this was the main reason why civil service numbers fell from nearly 400,000 in 1919 to less than 300,000 by 1926.

[18] Sir John Bradbury was one of the triumvirate of Permanent Secretaries at the Treasury during the war. One of the main recommendations of his *Inquiry into the Organisation and Staffing of Government Offices* in 1919 was that the Treasury should be reorganized on functional lines under one Permanent Secretary, which took effect in 1919.

[19] The Treasury felt it had been bypassed too often on this point, and in December 1919 one of its men was placed in the Cabinet Office to vet departmental proposals when they were submitted for Cabinet approval.

[20] The Baldwin Council was a group of departmental Chief Finance Officers appointed in 1919 to discuss financial reform and administrative economies, under the chairmanship of the Financial Secretary to the Treasury, Stanley Baldwin.

Treasury Circular 'Control of Expenditure' dated 12 March 1920. An extensive review of the historical background of the choice of Accounting Officers and the detailed discussions leading up to the revisions proposed by Sir Warren Fisher was included in the PAC's Fourth Report in 1920.[21]

Although the Cabinet had accepted in principle that in the service departments the permanent head should be the Accounting Officer, neither the Cabinet decision nor the Treasury Circular said specifically who should be the Accounting Officer in the civil departments. Fisher became increasingly convinced that, for all departments, proper accountability and concern for finance would only come if responsibility for expenditure—and responsibility for policy and administration giving rise to that expenditure—were combined at the top level. Adopting a broad interpretation of his Cabinet authority, Fisher therefore resurrected the Treasury's original 1872 proposal that in all departments the Permanent Heads should be appointed as the Accounting Officers. In doing so, his primary focus was to ensure that clear emphasis was given to economy.

Fisher told the PAC, when discussing his proposals with them in 1920 and 1921, that he was 'very anxious indeed that it should not be open to any permanent head to say "Please, Sir, it wasn't me". Pin it on him in the last resort and you have got him as an ally for economy.'[22] This view was strongly supported by C&AG Sir Henry Gibson, who thought the Accounting Officer proposals 'admirable' and, accordingly, had written to Fisher expressing his full support. Gibson also believed that 'The most important function of the Accounting Officer nowadays is the striving after economy. You want the biggest guns for the purpose and that is the permanent head of the department, whereas the present type of man that fills the post in the offices you are dealing with does not, with one or two exceptions, carry sufficient weight.'[23] Once again, Fisher's proposal provoked predictable objections from a number of departments, but this time the Treasury was determined and finally won the argument.

Surprisingly, the proposal to upgrade the status of Accounting Officers did not have an entirely smooth passage through the PAC. The Committee wanted further consideration given to the position in the large civil departments where they foresaw difficulties because of the extra load on busy Permanent Heads, particularly in getting to grips with detailed questions of accounting and regularity.[24] Fisher, however, meanwhile had embarked on detailed personal discussions with the Permanent Heads and by the time he

---

[21] PAC Fourth Report, 1920, HC 281, paras 9–45. Treasury Minute, 1 February 1921.

[22] PAC Third Report, 1920, HC 152, para. 12; and PAC Fourth Report, 1920, HC 281, paras 9–45. Treasury Minute, 1 February 1921.

[23] Letter of Gibson to Fisher, 2 February 1921.

[24] PAC Third Report, 1921, HC 212, paras 9–18.

appeared again before the PAC his determination and powers of persuasion had brought almost all the departments sufficiently close to his views for the proposal to proceed. Fisher's forcefulness was illustrated by the complaint of Sir Lewis Selby-Bigge, Permanent Secretary at the Board of Education 1911–25, an opponent of Fisher's proposals, who at the end of their discussions rather plaintively remarked: 'I doubt whether Fisher will mention my views to the PAC, or give me an opportunity of stating them.'[25] He was right, for Fisher did neither.

Despite the C&AG's firmly expressed support for Fisher's proposals, they were strongly criticized in an extraordinary outburst at the PAC by the Assistant Comptroller and Auditor, Roland Wilkins.[26] In front of the Committee he argued fiercely with Fisher that it was far better for the Accounting Officer to be one of the senior financial accountants in a department, since only they had the necessary technical training and, therefore, possessed the professional knowledge and experience. Wilkins then moved into even more dangerous territory by challenging whether Fisher had the Cabinet's authority for his proposals, implying that Fisher had misled the PAC when presenting the proposals to them. This potentially self-destructive attack pitched Wilkins into a highly confrontational battle at a level he could not possibly win.

Fisher was known to be scathing about the practice of taking 'gilded youths' as soon as they had emerged from the examination mill of the Civil Service Commission. 'If you do that', he said, 'then they get to work and take their little pens in their infant hands and they write away little criticisms of every sort and kind, very clever ones no doubt, but there is no training for constructive work, or work that would get them any practical experience.'[27] Wilkins fitted Fisher's comments perfectly. He was widely regarded as being 'pedantic to the point of eccentricity', and was later said to be the model for 'Mr Pro Hac', an archetypal 'stuffy' civil servant in the novels of Arnold Bennett. Such characteristics were anathema to the modernizing Warren Fisher and Wilkins had been moved to the position of Assistant Comptroller and Auditor from the post of Senior Treasury Officer of Accounts shortly after Fisher became Permanent Secretary.

Wilkins later paid the price for his actions when the abolition of the post of Assistant Comptroller and Auditor was raised in the discussions leading up to the Exchequer and Audit Departments Act 1921. As to be expected, he argued strongly for the post to be retained, essentially on the grounds that it offered the C&AG access to an 'intellectual and social' pedigree that Wilkins believed was lacking in the rest of the staff. Gibson, however, flatly rejected this outdated and superior view and expressed every confidence in the advice

---

[25] Letter of Selby-Bigge to Masterson-Smith, 5 July 1921, quoted in O'Halpin, 1969, pp. 54, 66.
[26] O'Halpin, 1969, pp. 51–2.   [27] Hennessy, 1990, pp. 70–1.

and support he already received from the Secretary of the E&AD and the senior staff. Wilkins lost the argument and the post was abolished by the 1921 Act. To avoid having Wilkins back in the Treasury, Fisher tried first to have him sidelined as Librarian of the House of Lords. When this failed Fisher had him moved to an obscure backwater as Assistant Paymaster General, where he stayed for the remaining eleven years of his career. It was ironic that Gibson's views on the limited value of the post of Assistant Comptroller and Auditor should be a key factor in its abolition. It was in that post that Gibson himself, under the lacklustre Sir John Kempe, had largely run the Department and become C&AG.

In 1925 the PAC finally accepted that: 'As a general rule the larger Civil Departments should be brought into line by the appointment of the Permanent Head of those Departments as the Accounting Officer.'[28] Resolution of this last lingering uncertainty was warmly welcomed by the new C&AG, Sir Malcolm Ramsay, who had moved from the Treasury to succeed Gibson in 1921, and had quickly been made the E&AD Accounting Officer. Ramsay wrote to Fisher: 'I am extremely glad that the Committee have now adopted the view which you and I have throughout held, and the road, I trust, is now perfectly clear.'[29] The new Accounting Officer arrangements that were confirmed in a Treasury circular of 1 January 1926 were still not implemented by some departments until well into the 1930s. The most notable was the Foreign Office, even though the unsatisfactory position there had been strongly criticized by the PAC as far back as 1920.[30] The long-awaited agreement that had now been achieved still left a number of related matters unresolved.

At the time of the 1872 discussions about Accounting Officers, and again in the 1920s exchanges, the Treasury gave an assurance that all Accounting Officers would receive a formal letter setting out their responsibilities. However, this was not done on any consistent basis. It was not until the PAC in 1937 reminded the Treasury about this promise that matters were put on the agreed footing. Another more substantial point arose on what should happen if an Accounting Officer was overruled on matters significantly affecting their responsibilities. As already noted, virtually from the outset it had been agreed that if the Accounting Officer was being overruled on a matter of regularity or propriety of expenditure, where his personal liability was potentially involved, then to protect his position he should have the instruction formally confirmed in writing and the matter should be reported to the Treasury and the C&AG. It had never been clearly set out what should happen if the matter were one of economical administration or other aspects of value for money.

[28] PAC Second Report, 1925, HC 196, paras 6–7.
[29] Letter of Ramsay to Fisher, 9 May 1925.
[30] PAC Third Report, 1920, HC 182, para. 22. Treasury Minute, 1 December 1920.

When the Permanent Head became the Accounting Officer the position was complicated; the person doing the overruling would then be a minister, thus adding a political dimension. Fisher himself was untypically ambiguous on this point. Overwhelmingly, the broad position adopted was that value for money was not a 'protest' matter.

The issue was raised again when the content of the Accounting Officer appointment letter was re-examined in 1952 at the instigation of Sir Edward Bridges, the Permanent Secretary of the Treasury, in consultation with a dozen or more Permanent Secretaries of the major departments and C&AG Sir Frank Tribe. The procedures for formal 'protests' on matters of regularity and propriety were quickly confirmed and discussion then centred on the handling of questions of economy and efficiency. The Treasury's original draft letter was designed to re-emphasize an Accounting Officer's responsibilities in these areas, and some Accounting Officers were doubtful about what action they should take if their views and advice on such matters were being overruled by ministers. The Treasury then proposed that in important cases of this kind Accounting Officers should be able to ask for a formal direction from ministers, broadly in line with the 'protest' procedures. There was some support for this but the overwhelming view was that this was taking matters too far beyond the accepted relationships between senior officials and ministers on policy decisions. The idea of a formal ministerial direction on matters of economy and efficiency was therefore dropped and the position adopted that in the event of the minister adhering to his or her decision the situation should be defended by the Accounting Officer who, if pressed further, could then refer to the policy ruling of the minister.[31] However, the uncertainties would not go away.

Things were brought to a head in 1973–4 when the Department of Trade and Industry made substantial grants under the Industry Act 1972 in attempts to rescue/resurrect three failing businesses: Kearney, Trecker Marwin Ltd; Meriden Motorcycle Company; and Scottish Daily News. All three were favoured projects of the Industry Minister, Anthony Wedgewood Benn, yet all quickly failed. Faced with what they regarded as a largely foreseeable waste of public funds, some PAC members asked the Accounting Officer, Sir Peter Carey, whether he had lodged a 'protest' against the expenditure but had been overruled. Sir Peter pointed out that the grants were within the provisions of the Industry Act and, with the support of the Treasury, made it clear that the expenditure involved value for money, not regularity, and did not therefore fall within the scope of the formal 'protest' procedures. On the wider question of the advisability of the grants, he was not prepared to disclose his

---

[31] These discussions were summarized twenty-five years later in an unpublished review of the relevant Treasury papers by Mr C. J. Carey, Treasury Officer of Accounts.

department's advice to the Minister. He suggested that if members wished to pursue the matter further they should direct their questions to Mr Benn. However, the long-standing convention was that the Committee did not call for ministers to appear and the issue was not pressed.

Although the Treasury continued to provide periodic advice to Accounting Officers, changes in the conduct of business and in relationships meant that the distinction between ministerial involvement in matters of regularity and propriety and in matters of value for money came under increasing strain. From 1990 a system of 'ministerial directions' was therefore introduced to protect Accounting Officers whose views and advice on important issues of value for money were being overruled by ministers.

Restoring Financial Control

In the 1920s early PAC post-war reports illustrated a number of specific areas where departmental controls had suffered during the War. For example, the C&AG's examination of the 1917–18 aerodrome construction accounts had disclosed such serious failings in the system of financial control and accounting that he had reported the situation immediately to the Treasury, and suggested that an independent body should be appointed to carry out a special inquiry. To examine these matters in detail, the Treasury set up a small expert committee whose report in August 1918 confirmed a catalogue of grave defects and recommended a series of remedial measures. The Accounting Officer later assured the PAC that almost all of these recommendations had been put into effect and that the overall position had greatly improved. The PAC noted that an important contributory factor to the failings was the inability of the Accounting Officer to ensure adequate control of expenditure as a result of gaps and uncertainties in his responsibilities, arising from the peculiar nature of the organization of the Air Ministry. The Treasury Minute fully supported the PAC's view of the seriousness of the matters disclosed, including the importance of clear Accounting Officer responsibilities.[32]

There were also difficulties with various trading accounts that had been set up during the war and financed from the Vote of Credit. These covered such matters as the supply and control of general food supplies and a wide range of raw materials connected with war services. Other accounts dealt with normal services such as the development of agriculture and fisheries, farm settlements, and the National Stud. Although the C&AG was not responsible for auditing and certifying the accounts, his report on the 1918–19 Vote of Credit appropriation accounts drew attention to wide variations between

---

[32] PAC Third Report, 1919, HC 223, paras 44–9.Treasury Minute, 2 February 1920.

departments on the form of trading accounts and on accounting practices adopted for the inclusion and treatment of non-cash entries. Accountabilities between the individual bodies administering the services and the parent departments were not clear, and the Accounting Officer did not sign the accounts. Confronted with these ongoing deficiencies in the public accounts, the PAC was pleased to learn that: 'The Exchequer and Audit Department and the Treasury, working together, will attempt, during the next twelve months, to co-ordinate the various accounts kept throughout the public service, with a view to a reasonable measure of uniformity.'[33]

The PAC also suggested that one volume should be prepared for the information of Parliament, showing comprehensively the trading accounts of all departments. The Committee added, innocently or mischievously, that if the Treasury Officers of Accounts had insufficient time to devote to the question 'it might be worth considering whether they should be afforded the assistance of an outside chartered accountant'. The Treasury did not seem too concerned over the need to introduce greater uniformity, when its pursuit of post-war economy and reductions in civil service numbers meant that one of the priorities was to close down the various bodies administering these wartime services as soon as possible.[34]

In the PAC's examination of progress in 1919 a volume of trading accounts for the majority of the wartime schemes for the period to 31 March 1919 was disclosed to have been unsatisfactory and that the C&AG did not report on it. However, for the first time a volume had subsequently been published containing all departmental trading accounts and balance sheets, for both wartime services and normal services, together with a report by the C&AG. The accounts covered various periods up to 31 March 1920, in some cases from the beginning of the war. The PAC noted that the Treasury had done its best to secure uniformity in the form of accounts by issuing instructions to departments during 1921. As a result, the accounts on the whole had been presented in a comparable form, although there were still variations in accounting practices. The PAC expected these difficulties to be resolved because they regarded 'the institution and business-like compilation of these trading accounts as of the greatest importance in affording an effective instrument to bring about economies'.

The PAC noted in its 1919 report that in many cases the accounts had still not been signed by the Accounting Officers and though the accounts had been reported on by the C&AG there was no statutory enactment imposing this duty upon him nor did they bear his certificate. The PAC was fully aware that this issue had already been dealt with in the new Bill to amend the

[33] PAC Third Report, 1920, HC 182, paras 1–6. Treasury Minute, 1 December 1920.
[34] PAC Third Report, 1920, HC 182, paras 1–6. Treasury Minute, 1 December 1920.

Exchequer and Audit Departments Act, which would require the C&AG to certify and report on all trading and manufacturing accounts to the House of Commons. The Treasury Minute confirmed that the accounts would in future be signed by the Accounting Officers and submitted to and audited by the C&AG under the provisions of what had by then become the Exchequer and Audit Departments Act 1921.[35]

In this post-war period the PAC also reviewed the wider constitutional issue of the Treasury's exercise of the power of virement, which allowed it to authorize underspending on one area of a department's business to cover overspending on another, thus avoiding the need to seek a supplementary estimate or incur an excess vote. Virement was a long-standing area of concern that had been examined on many occasions by the PAC, and discussed in Parliament. It provided the government with flexibility but also infringed the House of Common's prerogatives on voting supply by anticipating the approval that would only later be sought in a subsequent Appropriation Act. The wider use of virement during the war was understandable, given the difficulties in estimating the scale and timing of expenditure, but in 1921 the PAC questioned whether it was still being used under proper control now that many of those difficulties has passed. Listing only a few of many instances of virement in the 1919–20 accounts, involving several millions of pounds, the PAC pointed out that:

> it is mainly by the exercise of this power of virement that expenditure not specially provided for in the Votes of the House of Commons can be incurred with impunity in anticipation of parliamentary sanction.... We think it right to call attention to the fact that large sums are thus applied, subject to Treasury sanction, to purposes not expressly authorized by the parliamentary grants.... We view with some alarm the recent extension of this practice, and we are of the opinion that the time has come when the Treasury should more jealously restrict the exercise of this power.... As part of the process of re-establishing parliamentary control over expenditure, a stricter interpretation should be given to the [previous] rules.[36]

The Treasury strongly defended its use of virement and disputed some of the specific examples quoted by the PAC. Nevertheless, it added a cautiously worded assurance that:

> My Lords in the exercise of the power of virement will bear in mind the views expressed by the Committee, with which they are largely in agreement.... My Lords anticipate a progressive return to normal conditions in the accuracy of estimating and a consequent diminution of the need for virement.[37]

---

[35] PAC Third Report, 1921, HC 212, paras 39–44. Treasury Minute, 24 November 1921.
[36] PAC Third Report 1921, HC 212, paras 1–8.
[37] Treasury Minute, 24 November 1921.

The post-war return to more traditional controls over appropriation and regularity meant that a number of the C&AG's reports in this period revisited well-known criticisms of failings in accounting, in compliance with rules and regulations, and the need for Treasury authority. There were also reports on losses that arose as a result of continuing post-war difficulties. For example, the abrupt drop in the demand for military supplies following the armistice left the ordnance factory at Woolwich with excess capacity and faced with having to put large numbers of employees out of work. This was addressed by breaking the normal rules and building 100 locomotive engines without any purchasers in sight. Other orders were taken on fixed prices that did not cover their costs, financing this work by the irregular use of funds voted by Parliament for other purposes. Ultimately, this 'experiment in commercial manufacture' incurred an Excess Vote of more than £1 million. The Navy also incurred losses of £70,000 on a scheme to lend surplus trawlers and drifters to the Ministry of Agriculture to be used on an ill-fated 'profit sharing' fishing operation to provide employment to ex-service fishermen. This too involved the irregular use of funds voted for other purposes, as did several programmes in other departments.

On the basis of a report by the C&AG, the PAC also reported in 1922 on a loss on exchange of over £3 million because 'British troops in Bulgaria had been able, by use of the official machinery of exchange and unauthorized traffic in canteen stores, to make large profits for themselves, the official rate of exchange departing widely from the market rate.' This was not the first time that servicemen overseas had manipulated differences in exchange rates to their personal advantage. The PAC wanted steps to be taken 'to prevent such abuses by revising the official rates at shorter intervals, by limiting the right of the individual to transfer money home through official channels, or by some other means. In future it should not be possible for the official rate of exchange to be used as a source of profit at the cost of the State.' The Treasury confirmed that steps had been taken to prevent such abuses in future.[38] Phoenix-like, it would arise again in similar circumstances in 1945.

In 1923, following a review of the PAC's terms of reference, the Committee took the opportunity to review the whole range of accounts coming before it. The most striking feature to emerge was the tendency in recent years towards the creation of special funds to finance new forms of government activity, particularly in relation to agriculture, unemployment, and assistance to Special Areas. With these adding to the PAC's work as well as that of the C&AG, the Committee was anxious to ensure that the preparation of accounts in these new bodies was carried out to a high standard. The Committee also turned its

---

[38] PAC Third Report, 1922, HC 167, para. 71, Treasury Minute, 18 November 1922.

attention to the need for the C&AG to be appointed as the auditor of certain trust funds and welcomed Treasury confirmation that this would be done under the powers of s.3 of the Exchequer and Audit Departments Act 1921.[39]

Exchequer and Audit Departments Act 1921

Key Reforms

A strong and effective audit by the C&AG was a key element in the government's determination after the war to re-establish financial control and accountability across the public sector as a whole. Strengthening and clarifying the responsibilities of Accounting Officers, including the pursuit of economy, needed to be accompanied by examinations and reports on how those responsibilities had been discharged in practice. It had already been recognized that there was a clear need for a post-war review of the work and staffing of the E&AD, as had been suggested in the C&AG's 1916 Memorandum and supported by the PAC. The government, the PAC, and the C&AG were united in the view that a new Act to bring the legislation up to date would improve the efficiency of audit and tighten up accountability by making specific provision for measures that had been periodically introduced to meet changing circumstances after the main scope and direction of the work was laid down in the 1866 Audit Act. Based on the June 1921 report of the special Treasury committee appointed to recommend modifications to the 1866 Audit Act,[40] the Exchequer and Audit Departments Act 1921 became law in August 1921 but would operate with the continuing provisions of the 1866 legislation. The key features of the Act are outlined below with reference to the main sections of the Act.

Section 1. The principal concern identified in the Treasury committee's report was the 'literal and inelastic' requirement in s.27 of the 1866 Act that the C&AG should carry out a complete and detailed examination of the vouchers or proofs of payment supporting the charges in the appropriation accounts, except for the accounts in Schedule B to the Act, that is Army and Navy accounts, where the C&AG could carry out a test examination based on evidence of satisfactory checks by the departments themselves. A test examination had in practice been relied on for many years for all accounts, particularly during the period 1914–18 as a result of greatly increased wartime expenditures combined with staff shortages. The 1866 requirements, and related requirements of the Army and Navy Audit Act 1889, were repealed by s.1 of the 1921 Act, which gave the C&AG discretion to certify the accounts on the basis of a test examination, provided he was satisfied with the examination already carried out by the departments concerned.

[39] PAC Report, 1935, HC 99.   [40] Cmnd 1383 of 1921.

The appropriation accounts for 1920–21 were the first to be presented under the new legislation, with a new form of C&AG's certificate to reflect the fact that the accounts were now being certified as correct, without qualification, on the basis of a test examination only. The C&AG, however, assured the PAC that there had been no departure from the practice of recent years and that he contemplated no relaxation in the scope of his audit.[41]

Section 2. The revenue accounts of the Inland Revenue, Customs and Excise, the Post Office, and other receivers of money payable by law into the Exchequer were examined and reported upon by the C&AG under s.33 of the 1866 Act. Section 2 of the 1921 Act provided fresh authority for this work in broadly similar terms and with the same systems-based objectives as before. More particularly, the transfer of authority from s.33 of the 1866 Act removed any Treasury power to prescribe regulations for the C&AG's conduct of the work, while s.2 of the 1921 Act made it clear that the examination should be carried out as the C&AG believed appropriate.

A complication emerged that concerned the C&AG's ability to examine some Inland Revenue tax assessments. Assessments for weekly wage earners were made by the Commissioners of Inland Revenue and all documents, therefore, were open to inspection by the C&AG. The documents relating to all other assessments of income tax, however, were the property of the General and Special Commissioners of Income Tax and were therefore confidential under the Income Tax Acts and were not open to inspection by the C&AG. This severely limited the C&AG's ability fully to discharge his responsibilities under the 1921 Act. Although the Royal Commission on Income Tax had recommended in 1920 that this anomaly should be removed by transferring the property in such assessments to the Inland Revenue, legislation introduced to deal with the problem was abandoned. The PAC's criticism of the situation was fully endorsed by the Treasury, who could only promise to put forward legislation on the subject 'when opportunity offers'.[42]

Section 3. The valuable provision of s.33 of the 1866 Audit Act, which gave the Treasury powers to direct the C&AG to audit the accounts of a range of bodies, mainly those dependent upon grants and other assistance from public funds, was replaced by a similar provision in s.3 of the 1921 Act. A Treasury Minute then reinforced this by reviewing the several types of account covered by s.3 of the new Act and certain other provisions, clarifying the broad nature of the C&AG's examination in terms that clearly indicated that the Treasury was content to leave detailed audit matters to the C&AG's discretion. The Minute also removed the audit of all grant-in-aid accounts from the scope of s.3.[43] Over time, the use of s.3 powers diminished and access to many bodies was instead secured by agreement.

---

[41] PAC Third Report, 1922, HC167.
[42] PAC Report, 1923, para. 2. Treasury Minute, 1 November, 1923.
[43] Treasury Minute, 1 January 1923. Appended to PAC Report, 1923, HC 125.

Section 4. This section provided overdue statutory authority for the C&AG's long-standing and successful examinations and reports on departmental store and stock accounts.

Section 5. As already noted, the PAC had developed a close interest in the production and audit of trading and other accounts for the 'commercial' activities of departments and had pressed for these to be put on a consistent statutory basis. Section 5 of the 1921 Act widened the range of accounts to be certified and reported upon by the C&AG to include 'the income and expenditure of any shipbuilding, manufacturing, trading or commercial services conducted by departments, together with such balance sheets and statements of profits and loss and such particulars of costs as the Treasury may require'. This brought the dockyard and ordnance factory accounts within the provisions of the 1921 Act instead of the Army and Navy Audit Act 1889. The 1921 Act also provided the same rights of access for examinations of trading accounts as were provided for appropriation accounts under the 1866 Act.

The PAC returned to the subject of trading accounts in 1924 when the Committee's report continued its support for these accounts, whilst recognizing the differences in operational priorities between commercial enterprises pursuing profits and public sector bodies serving the community. The report outlined some of the intricacies of accrual accounting for the benefit of the wider parliamentary audience and pointed out a continuing lack of conformity in the forms of account, particularly for wartime services. Overall, however, their report concluded that the more recent accounts had been prepared on a uniform and coherent plan.[44]

An important omission from the 1921 Act was the continued absence of any mention of examinations of economy or efficiency. Although these had become an established and accepted part of the E&AD's work, supported by the PAC, they were still regarded by some as an area where the C&AG was expected to proceed cautiously and with due discretion, rather than as a firm and unequivocal right or duty supported by statutory powers. Over the coming years the C&AG would nevertheless be able to carry out value-for-money examinations despite these uncertainties, which would not be finally resolved until the National Audit Act 1983.

Appointment of Professionally Qualified Audit Staff

The work of the E&AD clearly needed to be of a high standard in the new era of accountability and financial control being introduced under the Fisher reforms and to implement the provisions of the 1921 Act. Well-trained staff, therefore, were essential. One of the more important domestic measures

---

[44] PAC Second Report, 1924, HC 138, paras 48–55.

introduced during Gibson's period as C&AG, and one of his lasting legacies, was his decision in 1917 to commission a review of staff training. The review was carried out by a small committee led by John Tenney, one of the Directors of Audit. It was prompted by serious concerns over two cases where the conduct of the audit was found to be unsatisfactory. The Tenney Committee's reports in 1917 and 1918 dealt with the lessons learned in these particular cases and what needed to be done to update audit guidance, clarify the responsibilities of the different audit grades, and revise the classification of accounts.

A more fundamental issue identified by Tenney was the need to improve staff training at all levels on a more systematic and professional basis. The existing civil service approach of 'Sitting beside Nellie', where officers learned on the job by working alongside more experienced staff, would no longer suffice, for a variety of reasons. A significant number of permanent but relatively inexperienced officers were returning from war service and new entrants were also being recruited to replace temporary wartime staff. With audit moving increasingly away from detailed checking to a more analytical and broader-based scrutiny and test examination, a wider knowledge of accounting principles and practice was required. The development and examination of new forms of account, including the growth of trading and manufacturing accounts, required a greater understanding of commercial accounting and cost accounting. The continuing move towards expanding the range and depth of value-for-money examinations also required further investment in development and training.

After considering the training arrangements in a number of bodies in the public and private sector, including the Institute of Chartered Accountants, the Tenney Committee's fourth report in October 1918 recommended that a more demanding system of professional training should be compulsorily required for all new entrants, with voluntary arrangements for some existing staff. These should be centred on a specially commissioned series of lectures at the London School of Economics (LSE). This external three-year course was to be supported by a revised scheme for moving staff around on jobs with appropriate training opportunities. New assessment and promotion procedures meant that staff could only progress up the pay scales if they passed the required examinations. C&AG Gibson approved virtually all the Tenney Committee recommendations in May 1919 and 'Ten gentlemen of the Office, some newly returned from the War duly attended the London School of Economics for the first series of lectures at a fee of half a guinea a term.'

The LSE since the early 1900s had established a key role in the education of military officers in the practices of business.[45] Between 1907 and 1914, each

---

[45] Funnell, 2006.

year thirty students in the latter part of their careers were selected to begin their twenty-week course in October, finishing in the following March. The students were most often officers of the rank of captain and above, selected from line commands and most of the administrative departments, with the Army Service Corps providing each year the largest number of students.[46] Other departments which were eligible to provide students included the Royal Artillery, Royal Engineers, Infantry, Medical Corps, Ordnance Corps and the Indian Army.[47] The students were instructed by eminent experts in their fields who were drawn from business, the universities, and government. Richard Haldane was a frequent lecturer and Sir Charles Harris and Colonel Grimwood of the Finance Department at the War Office, who had been implacable critics of Army accounting systems,[48] took an active interest in the success of the Army class, with Harris appearing often as a guest lecturer.[49]

A follow-up review of the LSE classes for E&AD staff concluded that the new system had been less successful than expected. This was partly because the exceptional intake of some eighty new Assistant Auditors between July 1919 and January 1921 had overwhelmed the arrangements for allocating staff to the work of the Department. Also, the external lectures were heavily directed towards commercial and private sector circumstances and left large areas of the Department's parliamentary work barely covered, for example on regularity audit and examinations of stores and contracts. Proposals to second staff for training to other suitable departments had also proved impracticable. Although a Staff Training Board had been set up it was never put into operation.

The review committee recommended that the external lectures at the LSE should be revised and continued but should be supplemented by a range of internal lectures on areas directly relevant to the Department's work, including public sector accounts and constitutional and parliamentary issues. Arrangements for allocating staff to suitable training posts were revised and a special training officer appointed. This remained the basis of post-entrant training into the 1960s, with the lectures at the LSE having been transferred in the 1950s to the City of London College. By the 1970s the required training for new entrants had become a full professional qualification under the Chartered Institute of Public Finance and Accountancy. In the 1990s this was switched to qualification under the Institute of Chartered Accountants.

---

[46] Gilbert, 1961, p. 21; Dahrendorf, 1995, p. 89; Amery, 1909, p. 620; Advisory Board, 1911, p. 3, and 1912, p. 3; LSE Archives, File 232/B; 'B' 1907, p. 673.

[47] Badcock, 1926, p. 104, Badcock, 1925.

[48] Harris, 1911, pp. 65, 67; Harris, 1931, p. 314; Committee to Consider Decentralisation of War Office Business (Brodrick Committee) 1898, Questions 484–7, p. 21.

[49] Letter from Lawrence Dicksee to LSE, 14 June 1919, LSE Archives, File 232/C and 232/D; Grimwood, 1919.

Trial Introduction of Accrual Accounts

Cost accounts for the manufacturing activities of the ordnance factories and the Navy dockyards had been prepared on an accruals basis for many years and audited by the C&AG under the Army and Navy Audit Act of 1889. In 1919 it was decided that, as a trial, a departmental appropriation account prepared on the traditional cash basis should be replaced with a new form of account prepared on an accruals basis. The Army estimates for 1919–20 had therefore been presented to Parliament in a new form 'so as to show the cost of each branch of the service, each hospital and generally each main object for which expenditure is incurred, as would be done in a commercial business'.[50] The choice of the Army appropriation account for the trial was clearly ambitious, given that it was by far the largest and most complex set of accounts. At the same time, the War Office's work during the war had confirmed that it could call upon also the largest number of experienced accountants and cost accountants. More particularly, the choice reflected the strong and enthusiastic belief of Sir Charles Harris, Joint Secretary of the War Office, in the virtues of accrual accounts in his career-long pursuit of economy in Army expenditure. Harris was appointed Joint Secretary to the War Office for the last four years of his service, which coincided with the period of the trial. This seems to have been a special one-off appointment in 1920 to serve alongside Sir Herbert Creedy, the existing Secretary. On Harris's retirement in 1924 the post reverted to the single occupancy of Creedy and was also renamed as Permanent Under-Secretary of State for War.

An initial suggestion for introducing accrual accounts had been made, almost in passing, in the House of Commons debate in 1917 on the need to strengthen post-war parliamentary accountability. The idea was then considered by the Select Committee of National Expenditure in 1918, which in their Seventh Report on the form of public accounts supported the progressive introduction of a new format. Introduction of accrual accounting on a trial basis in the difficult post-war conditions meant that in the first year the new system fell well short of what had been promised.[51] In 1921 the PAC took evidence from the War Office and the Treasury on the merits of the new system and the advisability of extending it to other departments. The War Office contended that 'the new system, even in its limited application, had been of considerable value in improving financial control and effecting economies'. Although the War Office accepted that there had been heavy costs, approximately £400,000, to recruit additional staff to form an entirely new Corps of Military Accountants, they hoped to reduce this in later years.

---

[50] PAC Third Report, 1921, HC 212, para. 17.   [51] Funnell, 2006.

The Treasury, however, 'were not fully satisfied as to the merits of the new system, and would regard with some apprehension the probable large cost in its general extension to other departments, especially before further experience had been gained of the merits as applied to the Army'. The PAC agreed that it would be wise to await fuller experience of the results obtained from the trial scheme.[52] The PAC returned to the issue in 1923.

The PAC's 1923 inquiry examined in detail the benefits obtained from the additional information provided under the new accrual accounting system and the cost comparisons it afforded between different establishments, at home and abroad. Although the Committee noted the War Office's continuing confidence in the new system of accounting, they pointed out that the account for the year 1921–2, though a considerable advance upon its two predecessors, was in many respects incomplete and imperfect and was still in the transition stage. There were great difficulties in arriving at proper valuations of assets, with major overstatements having to be corrected. These and many other defects in the accounts detracted from its value as an accurate record and as a basis for reliable comparisons of performance. The PAC contrasted the subjectivity and scope for variation in arrangement and presentation in income and expenditure accounts with the certainty available from accounts prepared on a cash basis. With reference to the benefits of the change, the PAC found that 'it was at present impossible to arrive at any figure which will show even in a general way what administrative economies have been effected by the new system, the operation of which has been obscured by the drastic reductions which have been effected in the Army by general measures of economy'. The PAC concluded that 'it must inevitably be many years before it will be possible effectively to compare Army accounts under the new system over a period of years'. They noted that a high-level War Office committee was now considering 'how far the new form of account was likely to be useful and with what degree of elaboration it should be kept'. The related Treasury Minute confirmed that they hoped soon to receive that committee's report.[53]

In October 1923 the War Office Committee recommended continuance of the new accounts,[54] 'subject to an investigation as to the possibility of improvements and simplification with a view to economy in its working'.[55] Two further committees were then set up to pursue these matters further. The PAC looked at the position again in 1924, with progress still uncertain and final decisions remaining outstanding.[56] A year after Sir Charles Harris retired,

---

[52] PAC Third Report, 1921, HC 212, paras 17–23. Treasury Minute, 24 November 1921.
[53] PAC Report, 1923, HC 125, paras 65–71. Treasury Minute, 1 November 1923.
[54] Cmnd 2073.   [55] Cmnd 2073.   [56] PAC Second Report, 1924, HC 138, paras 26–34.

the Army Council in 1925 reversed the previous War Office advocacy for accrual accounts and submitted to the PAC 'a proposal to abandon the system of Army accounting which has been in partial operation for the last six years, and to revert to Estimates and Accounts similar in form to those of other departments, prepared on a cash basis'. The proposal was the result of the Army Council's unanimous decision that 'the economies effected, or likely to be effected, by the new system when developed do not justify its cost'.

The PAC exhaustively reviewed the aims of the new accounting system, the progress made in introducing it and the results achieved. The Committee took evidence from witnesses, including, most unusually, the Secretary of State for War, over six separate sessions from July until December 1925, based on memoranda submitted by the War Office, the Treasury Officers of Account, the C&AG, and Sir Charles Harris. From the evidence given it appeared that, in addition to the high costs and delays, the technical difficulties with the reliability of information provided by the trial accrual accounting system, and the subjectivity of important figures, there were continuing problems with persuading operational staff of the value of the benefits promised. In contrast to the enthusiasm of the accountants, operational staff did not seem convinced that the new system provided information useful to their work. Sir Charles Harris had rather sorrowfully told the Committee in 1923, some three years after the project started, that:

> This is the sort of information we can lay before the administrative authorities; if the administrative authorities will tell us how far this is useful it may be that we can usefully expand it in some directions and it may be that we can considerably simplify it in others.... My idea all through has been only to elaborate any feature of the system to the extent to which it showed that it paid its way and was worthwhile.[57]

Determined to the last, and now free in a private capacity to speak against the Army Council's decision to abandon the scheme, Sir Charles Harris, together with General Sir Herbert Lawrence, Chairman of the War Office Committee that had recommended in 1923 that the trial of accrual accounting should continue, told the PAC that they personally held to the view that if it were developed 'the machine would ultimately become a potent instrument for economy'. They did acknowledge that this would require a complete, and extremely expensive, change in the Army's administrative system from the War Office downwards. The Army Council, in contrast, was satisfied that any such advantages could not be secured without changes that 'could not in the circumstances be at all commensurate with the cost of the machinery'.[58]

---

[57] Evidence to PAC 1923 (Q. 5938).
[58] PAC Second Report, 1925, HC 196, paras 50–68. Treasury Minute, 1 January 1926.

The PAC and the Treasury agreed, with the Treasury emphasizing particularly that:

> The expense of preparing such accounts must be regarded as a factor in deciding in what cases they should be kept. My Lords do not think the Committee would desire that such accounts should be maintained for particular services, if the cost of producing them were excessive as compared with a reasonable estimate of the value of the benefits likely to accrue from their preparation.[59]

A more formal difficulty was that initial proposals for the trial scheme seem to have assumed that the new form of account was a statutorily acceptable substitute for the annual appropriation accounts required to be produced under the 1866 Audit Act. However, in the C&AG's report on the 1919–20 accounts, the first in the new form, he concluded that it was doubtful that the accounts could be regarded as appropriation accounts because they were not confined to cash receipts and expenditure actually incurred in the year concerned, as the 1866 Audit Act required. Given the uncertainty over the statutory requirements, and his own responsibilities, he had therefore certified only the cash transactions.[60] The position on the later accounts does not seem to have been satisfactorily resolved and the C&AG continued to certify the cash items only until the trial was abandoned. Arguments about the advantages and disadvantages, and uncertainties, of accrual accounting continued intermittently until the introduction of across-the-board departmental resource accounts in 2000.

An unwelcome and embarrassing development for the PAC in 1934 was the realization that, because the terms of the Standing Order under which it was appointed in 1862 referred only to appropriation accounts, there were doubts whether it had the necessary powers to examine the large numbers of other accounts it had examined on many occasions in the intervening seventy years. Some of these accounts were relatively small but others involved substantial expenditure. Although the C&AG had clear powers to examine the accounts, and they had been properly laid before Parliament, the Committee's own powers of examination, formally interpreted, were open to question. The PAC also revealed that over the last twenty-five years a significant number of other accounts had been added to the list of bodies where its powers of examination were questionable, and that the numbers were growing. The Committee said it was confident that the House of Commons would accept that until then its examination had been carried out under the usual practice of giving Select Committees wide powers to interpret their terms of reference as they saw fit. Now, in view of the number and importance of the accounts involved, the Committee asked for its Standing Order to be amended to give

---

[59] PAC Second Report, 1925, HC 196, paras 50–68. Treasury Minute, 1 January 1926.
[60] PAC Third Report, 1921, HC 212, para. 104.

greater flexibility to its powers of examination by providing for it to examine 'such other accounts laid before Parliament as the Committee may think fit'. Standing Order 148 was amended accordingly in November 1934.[61]

The Second World War and C&AG Audit

Threats to Effective Audit

The late 1930s marked the start of what would become seismic changes in the size, range, and delivery of government spending programmes. These, in turn, would have significant and challenging implications for the scale, nature, objectives, and priorities of the C&AG's audit and the demands placed on the commitment, skills, and experience of E&AD staff. In some respects, wartime audit would also raise issues that were similar to those that had arisen with the First World War, particularly in regard to contracts. Most especially, the huge differences in scale and complexity of public sector spending and operations in a time of war meant that the C&AG's audit would be under great strain in meeting the demands and challenges to be faced, not only during the war but in dealing with continuing post-war difficulties.

Reliance on a test examination had from the late nineteenth century become in practice an increasing part of the C&AG's certification audit, particularly on larger accounts and those based on a large number of individual small payments such as pay and pensions. A test audit was essentially a pragmatic response to the growth in the scale and range of public expenditure, the impact on the C&AG's workload, and his limited resources. Only much later would it be recognized that, in conjunction with examinations of the strength of systems and controls, assessments of materiality and risk, the use of statistical and other sampling methods, and the extent of internal audit, a test examination was a more efficient and informative basis for the audit. After the 1921 Act gave formal statutory power for the C&AG's work to be conducted on the basis of a test audit this had been the dominant practice throughout the 1920s and 1930s. Yet, even this would come under increasing strain from the outset of the Second World War.

Loss of experienced auditors recruited into the armed services and shortages of new recruits meant that reductions in staffing could only partly be filled by employing older and temporary staff. The reductions in E&AD resources and the impact on audit coverage became a source of continuing concern to the C&AG and the PAC. In 1942 the PAC reported that the C&AG had confirmed that:

> In view of the extent of the field to be covered it has been necessary for him to use to the fullest possible extent, and with a liberal interpretation, the powers which

---

[61] PAC Special Report, 1934, HC 97.

the Exchequer and Audit Departments Act 1921 gives him to dispense with a detailed audit, having regard to the nature of the departmental examination.... His audit is now very largely of a test nature, and he thought that its relaxation has been carried out to the utmost limits.... But he was prepared to say with confidence that he would be able to bring to notice, if necessary, any cases of importance or in which serious questions of controversy arise.[62]

At the same meeting the Treasury told the Committee that manpower constraints meant that the aim within departments was 'a maximum of administrative simplicity'. The Treasury emphasized that although departments had since 1941 dropped or modified their own controls as far as could be done safely, further 'simplification' might become necessary 'in the light of current demands upon manpower'. The Treasury accepted the risks that might have to be taken, and added that:

While the estimation of the degree of risk involved in suggestions for the reduction of internal checks must necessarily be a matter for the Accounting Departments, My Lords will be very ready to consult with Departments in the matter; and if it be agreed that a particular degree of risk ought to be taken, having regard to the general manpower situation and to the staff which will be saved, My Lords will, of course, share the responsibility for the decision.

In this situation, and given pressing manpower priorities, there was not much more that the PAC could realistically do other than express the rather pious hope 'that the standard of audit should be maintained'. Nevertheless, the Committee recognized that 'it may be necessary to review these processes, that is departmental financial controls, from time to time in the light of current demands upon manpower'. These reservations were soon confirmed when in 1943, at the request of the government, the PAC inquired especially into the question of a possible reduction in the level of the C&AG's audit and in E&AD staff numbers. The Committee's conclusion and committed support of the C&AG were clear and uncompromising. The report warned that:

Any further reduction in staff would require a substantial suspension of his statutory functions. Your Committee consider that the introduction of legislation to suspend or curtail this statutory audit would be most undesirable. They feel that the continuance of the independent audit of the Comptroller and Auditor General, and of its examination on its basis of the accounts by the Committee on behalf of Parliament, is an important element in the maintenance of public confidence in the financial administration and efficiency of Departments.[63]

While noting the PAC's inability 'to recommend any reduction in numbers at present' the Treasury had 'no doubt that, as the Committee anticipate, the

---

[62] PAC Second Report, 1942, HC 127, paras 2–4. Treasury Minute, 3 February 1943.
[63] PAC Report, 1943, HC 116, paras 1–2. Treasury Minute, 12 February 1944.

Comptroller and Auditor General will keep the position under constant review'. Though matters were formally left open, this exchange seems to have stopped the possibility of any subsequent Treasury attempt to impose staffing reductions. However, it ruled out any increases, despite the vastly increased complexity, scope, and size of the C&AG's responsibilities during the war. The continuing reductions in departmental checks, problems in securing timely and reliable information on heavy expenditure overseas, increasing difficulties in verifying figures for contract pricing, and the widening range of corporations and other bodies supplying expenditure figures for inclusion in departmental accounts, meant that E&AD examinations had increasingly to deal with financial information that was lacking, limited, or late. Nevertheless, although audit standards had for some time already been relaxed 'to the utmost limit', in the absence of any significant criticisms it appeared that they were sufficiently flexible to accommodate these extra demands.

The need to maintain minimum audit standards in a time of war was obviously more significant for certification audits, which were a statutory responsibility of the C&AG, than value for money examinations—which were not. With certification audits there were changes during the war that, in contrast to problems elsewhere, provided some help towards the C&AG's ability to meet certification responsibilities. As in the First World War, there was extensive reliance on Votes of Credit without detailed estimates and supplementary estimates, and appropriation accounts were presented on a broad aggregated basis with limited detail. Some detailed information previously published as audited supplements to the accounts was also discontinued on security grounds. A valuable reduction in audit work also followed from the decision that in wartime circumstances the dockyard production accounts and many departmental trading accounts should no longer be regarded as official accounts to be certified by the C&AG, though simpler versions continued to be prepared for administrative reasons.[64] These reductions in certification responsibilities made only a relatively modest contribution towards easing staffing pressures.

Audit of Expenditure Overseas

The extended overseas dimension to the C&AG's work added appreciably to wartime difficulties. Although the bulk of wartime expenditure could be audited satisfactorily from accounts and supporting information available in the UK, arrangements had to be made for an acceptable audit of expenditure incurred abroad that could only be examined locally. This was done by setting

---

[64] PAC Report, 1943, HC 116, paras 60–2. The publication and presentation of trading accounts, certified by the C&AG, was resumed progressively from 1946–7.

up posts overseas, by sending out staff from the UK for local audits, and by relying on arrangements agreed with other audit bodies. For example, purchases of war stores in the United States were made by various Commissions representing the UK departments concerned. The Commissions had their own accounts sections and their expenditure was audited locally by representatives of the C&AG. In Canada, the Canadian Department of Munitions and Supplies purchased supplies as agents of the UK while the Canadian accounts were rendered to, and audited by, the Canadian Auditor General on behalf of the UK departments, with copies of his reports sent to the C&AG. Being able to rely on the Canadian Auditor General's detailed examination enabled the C&AG to direct his local examination mainly to general systems and controls, contract procedures, and capital assistance and agency schemes. In their report on these arrangements the PAC noted that, in both countries, contract procedures followed as far as possible the same general lines as in the UK and that the Accounting Officers of the UK departments concerned had expressed satisfaction with the arrangements.

A significant amount of overseas expenditure was passed through the United Kingdom Commercial Corporation, which had been set up in 1940 as an independent commercial agency with capital subscribed by the Treasury for the purpose of promoting trade with certain neutral countries, chiefly in the Balkans. From this modest original purpose, the Corporation and its subsidiary companies undertook certain pre-emptive and other special purchases at the instance of the government. Later these activities assumed a wider scope and extended to many parts of the world, particularly in connection with supplies in the Middle East and organizing supplies to Allied countries. Very large sums were issued to the Corporation and its subsidiaries out of monies provided by Parliament, with the directors granted wide discretionary powers in the management of these funds. The funds were issued from the bulk Votes of Credit and were not therefore identified to Parliament at the time of approval. The Corporation accounts were audited by a firm of professional accountants appointed with the approval of the Treasury.

In 1943 the PAC concluded that 'it was inadmissible that expenditure of the nature and magnitude now being incurred, wholly financed from public funds, should be entirely exempt from control and examination on behalf of Parliament'.[65] The Treasury then reviewed the position and furnished the Committee with further confidential particulars of the organization and work of the Corporation and its subsidiaries. As a result, it was agreed that the C&AG would be furnished with audited copies of the accounts of the Corporation and its subsidiaries and would be granted access to their books.

---

[65] PAC Report, 1943, HC 116, paras 68–9.

For future appearances before the PAC, the Treasury Accounting Officer would be accompanied by the Corporation Chairman and other members of the Board as necessary 'to enable the Committee to have a full explanation of the details of the transactions undertaken by the Corporation with the public funds at their disposal'.[66] In 1944 the C&AG submitted a memorandum to the PAC on the generally satisfactory results of his examination of the Corporation's books.

In British-occupied territory in Germany and Austria local expenditure was handled by Army Paymasters acting on behalf of all services, with civilian Command Secretaries responsible for financial and contract matters. The latter sent internally audited accounts and supporting vouchers monthly to the War Office, where they were subject to test audit by E&AD staff. This audit was supplemented by a programme of local audit visits to the countries concerned. The long period of occupation in Germany meant that these arrangements lasted well into the 1950s. In Berlin, joint audit arrangements were introduced to reflect the tri-partite Allied occupation. In light of his inquiries the C&AG was able to inform the PAC that examinations by the UK representative under these arrangements were in effect the same as those that would have been carried out by his own officers. They therefore provided an acceptable level of audit and accountability for the UK funds involved.

It was in Germany that audit history once again demonstrated its capacity to repeat itself when substantial losses were incurred after servicemen and civilians serving in Germany took advantage of artificially high fixed exchange rates, together with illicit sales of goods to the civilian population, to make large personal profits that were then sent back to the UK using official channels. Virtually the same situation had arisen in Bulgaria after the First World War, where losses to the UK of £3 million were involved. This time the failure to learn the lesson resulted in losses of more than £59 million. There were also suspicions of similar manipulations and unrecorded losses elsewhere. These problems arose from the substantial amounts of German marks accumulated by servicemen from currency speculation and from selling to the civilian population large quantities of goods that were in short supply.

Excessive prices were charged for cigarettes, tobacco, alcohol, and other attractive commodities, which the servicemen themselves could buy cheaply from army canteens and other outlets. The German marks obtained could then be laundered by buying sterling postal orders at the official fixed exchange rate of forty German marks to the £, which were then sent back to the UK. Alternatively, marks could be exchanged for sterling, at the same favourable rate, at the port of embarkation for personnel returning to the UK permanently or on leave. The scale of the transactions involved can be gauged

[66] PAC Report, 1943, HC 116, paras 68–9.

by the amount of surplus marks returned to Army Paymasters in these ways, which considerably exceeded the total issues of servicemen's pay. The position was complicated by the decision by the Allied authorities to maintain German currency as legal tender and by a variety of mutual aid arrangements with other Allied forces.

The PAC emphasized in its 1943 report that the losses recorded in the accounts were not paper losses and that the actual sterling losses of over £59 million had fallen on the British taxpayer. After reviewing the situation at some length, and despite concerns over the circumstances and scale of the losses, the Committee recognized the difficulties involved and settled on a balanced final conclusion that:

> The War Office and the local Army authorities faced a very real problem ... the maintenance of a high standard of discipline in a victorious army occupying enemy territory is notoriously difficult. ... But we are satisfied that the loss could have been reduced if preventive measures had been taken earlier, and we have referred to the omission to take precautions which in the light of subsequent events appear to have been necessary.[67]

Audit of Contracts for Supplies and Services

As in the First World War, the main focus of C&AG and PAC reports was contracts for supplies and services, especially for military procurement and other essential supplies. The overwhelming reliance on non-competitive contracts placed with selected companies meant there were unavoidable difficulties in agreeing fair and reasonable prices based on reliable and verifiable costings and acceptable profit levels. Wartime priorities and the overwhelming need to maintain the production capacity of the main defence contractors to ensure continuity of supply meant that for military procurement and other essential supplies non-competitive contracts effectively became normal practice.

As early as 1939 the C&AG had reported significant departures from the pre-war rule that non-competitive contracts over a certain monetary limit required ministerial approval. In 1942 the PAC accepted a Treasury proposal that the existing rule should be abandoned for the duration of the war and to leave it to the service and supply departments to decide whether to dispense with competition, based on their own internal arrangements. Still, in their report, the PAC sought to retain similar controls to those that were being formally abolished. The report warned that:

> While we are of the opinion that the established rule worked well in peace-time, we accept the view that it cannot be applied with advantage under war conditions.

---

[67] PAC Second Report, 1946–7, HC 115, paras 8–45.

We therefore raise no objection to the new arrangements, on the understanding that it will be for the responsible Accounting Officers to satisfy themselves that the arrangements, though they may be flexible, ensure that, where a real exercise of judgement (which should normally be in advance of the placing of the contract) is required, this is done by sufficiently high authority and, in large and important cases, by Ministers.[68]

The main emphasis then turned to contract pricing. Here the perennial problem of cost-plus-percentage profit contracts was to establish reliable estimates of costs at a sufficiently early stage of production to agree prices that provided contractors with an incentive to be efficient. Second World War conditions made this much more difficult than in 1914–18, for a variety of reasons. In some more traditional areas of construction, such as shipbuilding, pre-war costs and prices provided some guidance, at least in the early stages of the war, but elsewhere new models, new designs, more complex technical specifications, higher volumes, and tight delivery schedules were creating new problems. Industrial capacity amongst the large contractors experienced in military procurement was proving insufficient to meet increased demands on the timescales required. Work was therefore being placed with less experienced manufacturers who were not necessarily equipped with the reliable production and costing systems that were needed by defence department examiners when seeking to negotiate fair and reasonable prices. Sometimes the firms' inexperience of departmental costing requirements made them reluctant to provide relevant data promptly, even when it was available. Many of these manufacturers were subcontractors to the larger firms, which further complicated price investigations. The C&AG rarely had direct access to contractors' books and records and the E&AD's own examination had to rely on reliable and timely information on costing and related matters obtained by the defence departments.

Reports by the C&AG and the PAC on these and related matters continued throughout the war. Notwithstanding the criticisms made, and recognizing the possible impact on public confidence, reports were careful to recognize the difficulties the departments faced and the special circumstances in which they were operating. Reports, understandably, were also reticent on issues of security and confidentiality. The strongest criticisms came, as so often before, on failures in financial oversight and inadequate technical investigations by the Admiralty, leading to excess profits on warship construction and ship repairs, including large fraudulent claims.[69] The Admiralty was also criticized in a number of other reports on contract performance.

---

[68] PAC Second Report, 1942, HC127, paras 10–11.
[69] PAC Report, 1943, HC116, paras 12–20.

Although the main focus of the C&AG and the PAC was on direct military procurement, there were also concerns over accountability for purchases and control of essential materials, mainly iron and steel but also timber, food, and other supplies. These matters were not handled directly by the departments involved but, under their authority and supervision, by control boards drawn from the industries concerned. In some cases the arrangements provided for the control of production, in others for the purchase of imported supplies and sometimes only for the use of raw materials. From the early days of the Second World War these arrangements were characterized by complicated provisions on funding, pricing, build-up of reserves, and price stabilization. Control accounts were to be kept in accordance with best commercial practice, the intention being that trading accounts audited by private firms of accountants would be presented at some time. These never materialized, as a result of the general discontinuation of trading accounts in 1943. The C&AG had no direct rights of access or inspection of these control boards but, on the basis of available departmental information, he produced several reports for further examination by the PAC.

Particular attention was given by the C&AG and the PAC to the fixed prices agreed for iron and steel. Many of these were based on pre-war contracts that had not been subject to departmental cost investigations. There was also evidence of price rings operating amongst contractors. The PAC in 1941 reviewed the statutory control arrangements introduced in 1939 and the price-fixing operations of the Iron and Steel Control, whose staff were paid by the Iron and Steel Federation, which represented the industry as a whole and which also appointed the accountants advising on prices. Departments in general accepted the Federation's prices without further cost investigation. Given the potential conflicts of interest, the C&AG reported that:

> No investigation on behalf of the Minister of pre-war or current costs had been brought to his [the C&AG's] notice...he had recently received summaries of weighted average costs, but no written reports of the investigating or the advisory accountant had been furnished to him. In the absence of knowledge of the basis on which the costs were founded or the details from which they were built up he was not in a position to express any opinion on the adequacy of the current arrangements for determining prices.[70]

Faced with this uncertainty, the PAC:

> regretted that the results of their examination have not given them sufficient information on which to base any conclusions regarding the price-fixing arrangements in the iron and steel industry. . . . Your Committee must rely largely on facts reported by the Comptroller and Auditor General and he has not yet been able to

---

[70] PAC Report, 1941, HC 105, paras 43–4.

give any assistance. They were therefore glad to be assured that the Ministry are prepared to ensure him access to all information on which the control and contract prices are based.[71]

After allowing time for the new arrangements to be embedded, the PAC returned to the subject in 1943,[72] relying on a full report by the C&AG on the controls implemented. These were based on fixing uniform prices for different products, irrespective of individual firms' costs of production, with the aim of maintaining essential production capacity in firms where costs were higher than in more efficient firms. The use of centrally determined control prices meant that there were no cost investigations of individual contracts. Consequently, there were varying results for different firms according to their efficiency or other circumstances; some made losses while others made very large profits. A complicated system of cross-subsidy, using a central prices fund, involved grants being made to those firms incurring losses to maintain pre-war variations in profitability between the different sections of the industry. Despite these efforts, some firms continued to make large profits. The PAC accepted the various reasons advanced for acquiescing in these unusual and costly arrangements, in part recognizing the peculiar wartime circumstances but also that the arrangements involved questions of the government's wider industrial policy. The Committee carefully concluded that:

> Your Committee see no reason to question in principle the wisdom of the Ministry's policy of maintaining uniform prices in the various sections of the industry, and not attempting any detailed control of particular firms and their profits.... Your Committee note that it is considered necessary to keep the high cost producers in being and, whilst accepting this as a war-time measure, they trust that every effort is made to ensure that the high costs are not due to any avoidable inefficiency on the part of the firms concerned.... With the trading results available to the Comptroller and Auditor General, he is in a position to inform Parliament how the arrangement is working.[73]

The C&AG's reports enabled the PAC to return to the subject in 1950–1 and 1951–2. By then, however, the government was no longer the predominant purchaser of iron and steel products and the Treasury was prepared to challenge directly the right of the C&AG, and the PAC, to continue to question the reasonableness of prices paid by government departments under common pricing arrangements involving private consumers. The Treasury maintained that the ministerial price-fixing powers brought with them a duty to protect private consumers and, therefore:

> for the Committee to assess and possibly criticize the reasonableness of prices paid by Government Departments for goods for which the Government was not the

---

[71] PAC Report, 1941, HC 105, paras 43–4.   [72] PAC Report, 1943, HC 116, paras 52–7.
[73] PAC Report, 1943, HC 116, para. 57.

predominant purchaser could not fail to call in question the reasonableness of prices paid by the consumers as a body; and that any such investigation of those prices would give an unfair advantage to Government Departments as against private consumers. It was the Treasury's view that, in the absence of arrangements authorised by Parliament which would provide specifically for a review of the manner in which the Minister exercised his statutory functions on behalf of the community, the presumption must remain that the prices paid by Government Departments were reasonable and could be accepted as such without special investigation.... They were not prepared, unless directed by Parliament, to make available to the Comptroller and Auditor General data which had been obtained for a purpose other than judging the fairness of prices for Government purchases.[74]

On other areas of procurement, a series of C&AG reports indicated that the risk that some firms would make excess profits was greatest in the early stages of the war when reliable information on costs was at its lowest. Companies, particularly those working on departmental contracts for the first time, were sometimes reluctant to cooperate with departmental pricing examinations. The position was made more difficult by shortcomings in departmental expertise in some of the industries concerned. Although some of the excess profits were recouped in subsequent negotiations and repricing, settlement and recovery could take a long time. Following individual reports by the C&AG, the PAC in 1942 expressed concern over lengthy negotiations on a number of contracts.[75] In quick response, the Treasury in October 1942 published a Command Paper listing the individual contractors involved and the progress being made towards final settlements.[76] The PAC was also concerned over fears that 'in the absence of settlements satisfactory to the contractors, production or delivery might be unfavourably affected'. However, it concluded: 'As a result of full inquiry into the cases now in question, Your Committee are glad to state that they are satisfied generally that, whatever disputes may have occurred in the course of negotiations, there was in fact in no case any restriction of production or failure to deliver the articles required.'[77]

During these lengthy negotiations the contractors examined were united in their view that departmental efforts to bring contract prices closely into line with current costs were unnecessary, on the grounds that any extra profit accruing to contractors would be addressed by Excess Profits Tax. This suggestion was dismissed by the Treasury and the Inland Revenue with a lengthy note submitted to the PAC. In summary, this comprehensively dismissed the

---

[74] PAC Third Report, 1951–2, HC 253, paras 99–100. Treasury Minute, 18 November 1952.
[75] PAC First Report 1942, HC104, paras 1–30.
[76] Cmnd 6398, October 1942. Epitome of PAC Reports 1938–69, pp. 49–52.
[77] PAC First Report 1942, HC104, para. 3.

idea on the grounds that: 'It is the business of the State in dispensing the taxpayer's money to avoid extravagance and waste.'[78] In the light of further information given in evidence, the PAC was satisfied that 'in the interests of economical production, the effect of taxation should not be brought into the reckoning in fixing contract prices and that the policy of "fair and reasonable" prices should be maintained'.[79]

Conclusion

There were many similarities in the demands placed on accountability before, during, and after both the First and Second World Wars. The latter, however, involved substantially higher expenditures, a greater variety of pressures and priorities, and a more extensive overseas dimension. Contracts for military procurement and purchases of essential raw materials dominated the audit, with recurring examinations of contract pricing and related matters. There were familiar difficulties in securing reliable information on costs and capital employed, and extensive negotiations on excessive profits. Criticisms in the C&AG's reports, and those of the PAC, were nevertheless tempered with recognition of the operational difficulties and priorities facing the spending departments.

Although Parliament was prepared during wartime to accept reductions in its constitutional powers and simplifying supply procedures, the end of hostilities brought early pressure to restore normal controls. Parliament and the Executive shared financial concerns over burgeoning levels of debt, the need to reduce the number of new bodies that had been set up to deal with wartime tasks, unsupportable levels of public expenditure, and worldwide economic difficulties. The Treasury, with the full support of the C&AG and the PAC, was determined to re-establish its controls over departmental spending, with renewed emphasis on economy under revised arrangements for holding Permanent Secretaries to account.

In both wars, wartime circumstances and the loss of staff to military service stretched to the limit the extent of the C&AG's certification audit of departmental appropriation accounts and the accounts of other bodies. At the same time, continuing high levels of departmental expenditure, particularly during and after the Second World War, brought increasing pressure from the PAC to direct attention to examinations of economy and efficiency, which became

---

[78] PAC First Report 1942, HC104, para. 3 and Epitome of PAC Reports 1938–69, p. 44.
[79] PAC First Report 1942, HC104, para. 6.

the most prominent aspect of the Department's work. Dealing with the twin priorities of certification audit and examinations of value for money, though carried through successfully for many years, meant that less attention was paid to longer-term operational and management issues within the E&AD, and the strategic planning that would be needed as the public sector moved into a period of increasing change.

8

Post-War Strengths and Challenges

'The Comptroller and Auditor General's effectiveness largely depends on the fact that his reports are considered and followed through by the Committee; the Committee's effectiveness on the fact that they have his reports as a starting point.'

Rt Hon John Boyd-Carpenter, MP, Chairman of
the Public Accounts Committee 1964–70

The Exchequer and Audit Department (E&AD) emerged from the Second World War with an impressive record on the financial and regularity audit of accounts and on examinations and reports on economy and efficiency. The challenge for the E&AD in the post-war period was how best to deal with the major expansion of government programmes and very large increases in expenditure in post-war Britain under successive governments. Continuing high levels of military procurement, the introduction of the National Health Service (NHS), extended programmes in pensions, welfare and social services, housing, and industrial and infrastructure rebuilding added significantly to the E&AD's responsibilities on both certification of accounts and value-for-money examinations. The resulting pressures on the Department's available resources, already stretched from the war, required an early response to improve numbers, deployment, training, and experience as staff returned from the armed forces to replace temporary staff recruited during the war.

Although the Exchequer and Audit Departments Acts of 1866 and 1921 had provided the statutory authority for E&AD audit for more than eighty years, the existing statutes would continue to provide the necessary legislative framework until later developments made it important to supplement them with the additional provisions of the 1983 National Audit Act. Throughout the E&AD's post-war work the constitutional and statutory safeguards on the appointment, status, salary, and removal of the Comptroller and Auditor General (C&AG) under the 1866 Audit Act would continue to protect not only the C&AG's personal position but also his operational independence and, by extension, that of E&AD staff. The authority and impact of audit was similarly ensured by statutory powers to present and have published reports to Parliament on the results of the audits, followed by examination and a report by the Public Accounts Committee (PAC). More generally, the E&AD remained highly regarded within Parliament and enjoyed strong press support as the 'public spending watchdog', particularly when reporting the results of individual value-for-money examinations.

Redrawing the Lines

Throughout the war, and during the early post-war years, the Treasury, the C&AG, and the PAC were fully aware that financial controls on many areas of public expenditure had been reduced or relaxed to an extent that was acceptable only because of wartime circumstances and priorities. As these faded, it was recognized that it was essential to restore the controls necessary for the special nature and demands of public expenditure, the large and complex spending programmes being introduced, and the extensive legislative and regulatory framework within which many of these were set. More general issues of accountability were also being raised. With the war over there were growing concerns to re-establish full parliamentary control over supply and to restore more traditional accountabilities.

Redrawing the lines of accountability did not mean simply returning to pre-war arrangements. There were lessons to be learned from the flexibilities required during the war. It was important to avoid overprescription, highly detailed and intrusive regulation, and undue centralization. At the same time, it was widely accepted that the conduct of public business required a high level of care, accuracy, consistency, and probity, and that it had to comply with detailed statutory requirements. Spending public funds and delivering public services inevitably involved accountabilities that went well beyond those of the private sector. In this situation, the priority was directed towards restoring accepted civil service standards. More fundamental changes in objectives, culture, and management that would require major changes, driven from the top, would not come for at least another thirty years.

A priority for the PAC—indeed they 'felt it was their duty'—was to ascertain whether Treasury control was now as effective as it had been. Thus, in 1951 the PAC took detailed evidence from Sir Edward Bridges, Permanent Secretary of the Treasury, on a lengthy memorandum by the Treasury referring to the arrangements agreed in the early 1920s setting out the position on Treasury and departmental responsibilities as then accepted.[1] The areas covered in the

---

[1] PAC Fourth Report, 1950–1, HC 241, and Treasury Minute, 29 November 1951.

Treasury memorandum included: the development of the Accounting Officer's functions; the respective responsibilities of departments and the Treasury; the formulation and submission of financial proposals; execution and administration; and, finally, audit and reporting.[2] From the PAC and C&AG point of view, the key elements of the memorandum and the evidence given by the Treasury were reiteration and clarification of the responsibility of departmental Accounting Officers and their relationship with the Treasury. To some extent the memorandum drew together previous clarifications but it did usefully reconfirm that Accounting Officers were accountable to the PAC, and thus subject to examination by the C&AG for not only matters of accounting and regularity but also for 'more fundamental responsibilities', which the memorandum identified as:

> the responsibility for securing 'economy' in the widest sense. . . . An Accounting Officer, although he is personally responsible for the efficient conduct of his Department, could not be held financially liable for the results of a failure to secure economy in the same way as in theory, and indeed on extreme occasions in practice, he is held for failure to secure regularity. . . . Although questions of policy, as being ultimately the responsibility of the Government, fall outside the scope of the Public Accounts Committee, *the methods by which Government policy have been carried out are very much the Committee's concern.*[3] (emphasis added)

The memorandum referred later to the Accounting Officers' responsibility for the 'economy and efficiency' of their department's conduct of projects and delivery of services. Significantly, it took matters further by making it clear that they were also accountable 'if by reason of unforeseen difficulties the expenditure of the money has not produced the results that were expected'.[4] In practice, therefore, the Accounting Officer was accountable for effectiveness. At the same session the PAC also examined the increasing number of miscellaneous bodies supported by grants-in-aid, with heavy expenditure not fully accountable to Parliament. Again, they were helped in their examination by a memorandum prepared by the Treasury.[5] The memorandum confined itself to general matters of principle without going into specific cases, an approach that was also adopted in the PAC report. The Committee, however, did recommend that 'the books and accounts of all bodies which receive the greater part of their income from public funds should be open to inspection by

---

[2] *Memorandum by the Treasury on the Responsibilities of Accounting Officers and the scope of Departmental and Treasury Responsibility.* Epitome of PAC Reports, 1938–69, pp. 189–95.

[3] *Memorandum by the Treasury on the Responsibilities of Accounting Officers and the scope of Departmental and Treasury Responsibility.* Epitome of PAC Reports, 1938–69, pp. 189–95, para. 3.

[4] *Memorandum by the Treasury on the Responsibilities of Accounting Officers and the scope of Departmental and Treasury Responsibility.* Epitome of PAC Reports, 1938–69, pp. 189–95, para. 28.

[5] *Memorandum by the Treasury on the Financial Control of Grant-Aided Bodies.* Epitome of PAC Reports, 1938–69, pp. 196–7.

the Comptroller and Auditor General so that he may, if necessary, report on them to Parliament'. The Treasury Minute cautiously agreed that this should 'normally' be the case, and that 'they will seek to ensure that this becomes the general practice for the future'. Efforts to reform accountability notably excluded the universities and the BBC, both large spenders whose comparative lack of accountability had long been the subject of reports by the C&AG and the PAC.

The PAC's Fourth Report of Session 1950–1 was one of the most important of the early post-war years. It signalled the end of the reduced accountabilities and relaxed financial controls acceptable in the special circumstances of war and, as normal procedures were progressively re-established, the need to return to tighter arrangements for accounting, regularity, and value for money. It provided the basis for the accountability and audit necessary for the continuing heavy expenditure throughout the 1950s, 1960s, and beyond. Although the Treasury memorandum was directed primarily at clarifying the respective responsibilities and relationships of the Treasury and departments, there were also valuable lessons for E&AD audit and important matters for later PAC examination.

A significant post-war issue was whether the C&AG should become the appointed auditor of the nationalized industries and other public corporations being established by the Labour government under Clause 4 of their constitution, which committed the government to 'common ownership of the means of production, distribution and exchange'. However, the appointment of the C&AG for nationalized industries was not pursued, mainly on the grounds of practicality but also on a point of principle. The C&AG at the time, Sir Frank Tribe, was not in favour of taking on this additional heavy task, given the pressures the E&AD already faced in dealing with post-war staffing problems and likely further demands. He was also concerned whether he could provide enough staff with the necessary level of commercial auditing expertise, which he felt could be provided far more readily by the larger accountancy firms. There was also a more constitutional point that the C&AG's audit and reports were strongly associated with accountability to Parliament and detailed follow-up by the PAC, which were not consistent with the deliberate distancing of the corporations from government intervention and detailed parliamentary oversight, nor with maintaining their commercial freedom of action.

Although value-for-money audits had a higher public profile, the strength of the C&AG's certification audit of annual accounts, including the examination of regularity, propriety, and the proper conduct of public business, was equally important, both professionally and constitutionally. Under the Exchequer and Audit Departments Acts, other statutes, and by agreement, the C&AG was the statutory auditor of the appropriation, revenue, stores, and trading accounts of all government departments and the annual accounts of a large number of other public sector bodies. Increasingly, post-war expansion in government spending programmes would extend the audit to cover expenditure and revenue amounting to hundreds of billions spread across a large number of separate accounts. Elsewhere, the E&AD's international status was confirmed by its position as the appointed auditor of some of the largest United Nations agencies. The Department held more appointments than any other country's national audit office, all of which had been obtained and retained in the face of strong competition.

Value-for-Money Examinations

Before and during the Second World War the E&AD had established a prominent role and public presence in examinations of value for money. These were based on long-established, although non-statutory, rights to conduct a wide range of value-for-money examinations in departments and other bodies subject to the C&AG's audit or inspection. They reflected experience and skills developed from the successful conduct of examinations over many years. The Department was one of the first public sector audit bodies to carry out value-for-money audits. In the high-spending post-war era, value-for-money examinations became a priority, with reports on the results becoming the principal means to promote the Department's work. During the 1950s and 1960s more than 1,000 major reports were presented to Parliament and followed up by the PAC.

There were a number of recurring themes and areas of criticism, including limited competitive tendering on contracts, or sometimes none at all, particularly on large defence projects. This continued to be defended on the grounds that there were only a few companies with the specialist skills and experience to meet demanding technical specifications, and/or had the production capacity to meet the volumes and timescales required. With many contracts on a cost-plus profit basis there was little or no incentive to minimize costs and this could even make higher costs more profitable to contractors. In some cases full-scale production was started before designs and specifications were sufficiently advanced for reliable estimates of costs to be prepared, with frequent amendments jeopardizing approved costs and timescales. Applications for revised Treasury approval might not be submitted until expenditure was close to current authority levels, with large commitments still outstanding. Some projects proved technically too ambitious, and failure to meet planned in-service performance as well as increased costs could lead to production numbers being cut back. Some schemes failed to reach completion and had to be abandoned and the costs written off.

Cost-plus contracts also presented difficulties in establishing actual costs incurred and settling reasonable profit margins. Contract prices were negotiated with contractors in the light of technical estimates of prime cost prepared by Ministry officers and estimates or reports by the Ministry's accountants in regard to overhead charges and prices paid for any earlier deliveries. Profit rates were assessed as a percentage of capital employed. There was no equality of information and no access to contractors' books and records. The C&AG was able to examine the information available in Ministry files, but did not have direct access to contractors. After prices were negotiated in the early stage of contracts there were frequently further exchanges and renegotiations as development and construction advanced and manufacturing experience increased. Wider questions also emerged on the appropriate sharing of the risks that were inevitably involved in such contracts, and how to achieve the right balance between the assurances required by government that prices were fair and reasonable and maintaining incentives to contractors to pursue greater efficiency. These complex issues had been matters of continuing departmental, Treasury, and E&AD concern over many years, and had featured in a succession of C&AG and PAC reports.

The uncertainties on price fixing, and the resulting risks to public funds, were well illustrated in the multi-million-pound Bloodhound guided missile contracts placed by the Ministry of Aviation with Ferranti Ltd from the early 1950s, with an in-service date of 1958. Special circumstances meant that on this occasion there was more detailed information available on costs and, particularly, on the allocation and apportionment of overhead costs amongst the different factories and subcontractors involved. From this information, E&AD examination identified questionable costs and high overhead charges amounting to several million pounds. Following PAC reports in 1963–4 and 1964–5,[6] a wide-ranging special investigation by Sir John Lang confirmed that Ferranti had made large excess profits.[7] The company subsequently agreed to refund £4.25 million. The Minister of Aviation acknowledged in the House of Commons that securing this refund was the direct result of the vigilance of the C&AG's officers.[8] Similarly, excess profits made on contracts with Bristol Siddeley Engines for the overhaul of aero engines involved refunds of £5.4 million on work done over almost ten years.[9] These two cases, and others, resulted in extensive changes in price fixing on all cost-plus contracts,

[6] PAC Second Report, 1963–4, and PAC Third Report, 1964–5, HC 265, paras 28–32. Treasury Minute, 17 November 1965.
[7] Cmnd 2428 dated July 1964, and Cmnd 2581 dated February 1965.
[8] HC Debate 28 July 1964, c 1233.
[9] PAC Second Special Report, 1966–7, HC 571, paras 1–7. Treasury Minute, 8 November 1967.

stronger controls in Ministry procedures, and the introduction of a Review Board to establish fair and reasonable profit rates.

C&AG and PAC reports exposed numerous projects with a succession of major increases in the costs on which they were originally approved, long delays in completion, and failures to meet original operational specifications. Though these were predominantly in defence procurement, the list extended to large building and civil engineering projects. Reports on defence procurement included: cost overruns and poor performance on army combat vehicles, armament, and other projects; development and production of the TSR-2, Swift, and other combat aircraft; the Blue Streak guided missile and other weapons systems; warship construction; and excessive provisioning of stores and equipment. On non-military projects there were reports on: hospital building; road construction; scientific development; industrial reconstruction; and regional development programmes. Reports on civil aviation identified problems with the Comet and Concorde aircraft and instrument landing systems. There were also reports on individual science projects such as the construction of the Jodrell Bank space telescope. On current expenditure, there were reports on health service areas such as hospital running costs, pharmaceutical pricing, and the remuneration of doctors, dentists, chemists, and opticians. There were criticisms of agricultural subsidies for fertilizers, milk, cereals, and livestock production. Examinations of research and development involved the research councils, universities and the Atomic Energy Authority. Other diverse areas of activity included the trading operations of the Crown agents, support for international development, and overseas aid.

Rights of Access and Inspection

The C&AG's examinations are critically dependent on rights to secure extensive access to books of account, files, documents, and all other information and explanations considered necessary to conduct a successful audit. The 1866 Audit Act fully safeguarded these rights for certification audits and they had been extended in practice to cover examinations as they progressed towards value-for-money issues. Pressure over many years had also secured rights of access and inspection for hundreds of other bodies in and around the public sector for whom the C&AG was not the appointed auditor but which received grants, grants-in-aid, and other support and assistance from public funds.

A significant achievement in the 1960s was securing the C&AG's rights of access and inspection to the books and records of the University Grants Committee and those of all universities. This had been strongly resisted for many years as part of a recurring debate on how best to reconcile the conflicting demands of public funding and protecting university independence and essential academic freedoms. There had been continuing PAC concerns since the 1930s over weaknesses in accountability and audit of grants-in-aid, particularly in those cases where grants were made towards continuing operations of the bodies concerned, rather than one-off grants for particular situations. Concerns over limited accountability for grants-in-aid, including those for universities, re-emerged in 1948 but the PAC at that time stated that, in view of difficulties outlined by the Treasury, 'they understand the rather special latitude afforded to the University Grants Committee'.[10] In 1950, however, the PAC expressed concern that grants-in-aid to universities had risen from £1.68 million in 1932–3 to £9.775 million in 1947–8 and had then increased steeply each year to an estimated £23.284 million in 1950–1. The Committee noted once again that expenditure by universities from grants-in-aid was not accounted for to the C&AG and reminded the Treasury of the previous PAC's hope that the:

Treasury would consider whether, without impairing the independence of the universities, any further means could be adopted to inform Parliament more precisely how the grant-in-aid proposed in the Estimate is to be spent and to assure Parliament that grants made to the universities are wisely used.

In response, the Treasury promised that a very close review was planned which would examine in considerable detail the question of possible extravagance. The Committee:

trusted that in the forthcoming review the Treasury will consider carefully with the University Grants Committee and the university authorities whether there are any means by which fuller information may be made available to enable future Committees of Public Accounts to judge whether they can give Parliament an assurance that the grants are administered with due regard to economy.[11]

The PAC in the following years continued to question individual aspects of university expenditure, based on the C&AG's examinations of the limited information available in the books and records of the Department of Education and Science, and information obtained at the C&AG's request from the University Grants Committee. Reports included such matters as the need for more comparative analyses of variations between universities' recurrent expenditure in similar areas, and concerns over lack of progress in reviews of standards and cost limits for capital expenditure on academic buildings and

---

[10] PAC Third Report, 1948–9, HC233, para. 18.
[11] PAC Fourth Report, 1950, HC138, paras 36–40. Treasury Minute, 4 January 1951.

student accommodation. In examining these matters the PAC criticized the time being taken to improve systems as promised and emphasized that a greater sense of urgency was required.[12]

Parliamentary accountability for university expenditure was later referred to in the recommendations of the 1963 Robbins Committee report on Higher Education.[13] The Robbins Committee recommended major expansion in all areas of higher education, including universities, involving increases in funding from an estimated £219 million in 1962–3 (including £129 million for universities) to between £506 million and £742 million in 1980–1.[14] The report recognized that such major increases in public funding might require a greater element of public accountability in broad policy areas. The Committee emphasized that they 'yield to no one in our condemnation of extravagance in the use of public money'. Nevertheless, it recommended that, irrespective of any changes in ministerial responsibility:

> the present policy on accountability should continue. We recommend, further, that as more institutions at present within the scope of parliamentary audit acquire autonomous status in accordance with our recommendations and come under the aegis of the Grants Commission, the same immunity should be extended to them ... *with the same measure of freedom from accountability.*[15] (emphasis added)

In effect, Robbins wanted major increases in public money for universities, existing and prospective, while rejecting any extension of public accountability for spending that money. Against this background, the PAC in 1966 began a series of special sessions to re-examine university accountability, focused particularly on the question of rights of access and inspection by the C&AG. This was based on a closely argued submission by C&AG Sir Bruce Fraser, particularly well qualified as a former Permanent Secretary at the Department of Education. The Committee took evidence from the Department of Education and Science, the University Grants Committee, Vice-Chancellors from a number of universities, and the C&AG. In response to concerns by some witnesses that the C&AG's audit could put academic freedom at risk, directly or indirectly, the C&AG explained in detail how examinations would be planned to avoid trespassing on academic issues and other aspects of university policy. He also pointed out that his examinations already dealt with important artistic, scientific, and medical freedoms in bodies such as the Arts

---

[12] PAC Third Report, 1964–5, HC 265, paras 68–84. There were also reports on university expenditure in 1951–2, 1952–3, 1956–7, 1960–1, and 1962–3.
[13] Cmnd 2154, published October 1963.
[14] Cmnd 2154, published October 1963, paras 604 and 616.
[15] Cmnd 2154, published October 1963, paras 754–5.

Council, research institutes, and hospitals, without adverse effects. In presenting its report the PAC confirmed that the task before it was to:

see whether the proper demand of Parliament for assurance that public funds are spent by the universities with due regard to economy and efficiency can be reconciled with the proper demand of the universities that academic freedom be preserved: and to consider whether the present arrangements achieve the best possible balance between these two demands.

From the outset the Committee was:

in no doubt that the present arrangements constitute an exception, of rapidly growing magnitude, to the normal requirements of Parliament, and the onus thus lies on those who would propose that the exception should continue...Your Committee would feel bound to regard as prima facie unsatisfactory any arrangements which do not provide Parliament with such an assurance, which is indeed an important element in Parliament's control over the Executive and thus of high constitutional significance.[16]

The PAC's report recommended that the C&AG should be given access to the books and records of the University Grants Committee and of all universities. This time opposition had fallen sufficiently for the Secretary of State for Education and Science to announce in the House of Commons on 26 July 1967 that the government accepted the recommendation and that it had been made a condition of grant that such access would apply from 1 January 1968.[17] Three E&AD teams then began a programme to visit every university over the next four years. This work produced several reports to Parliament, mainly on capital projects, and raised other issues with the University Grants Committee and the Department of Education and Science. By far the largest number of matters pursued were resolved in discussions with the universities concerned and in management letters sent after each visit. At the end of this initial programme it was acknowledged that the C&AG's examinations and the matters raised had not adversely affected academic freedoms. As well as securing improved parliamentary accountability and audit in a large and important field of public expenditure, the exchanges on university funding provided another telling example of how determination and persistence by the C&AG and the PAC, sometimes over several years, could achieve significant improvements in initially unpromising situations and in the face of strong and vocal opposition.

E&AD Audit Relationships

A particular strength over many years had been the close and effective partnership with the PAC that had from the outset been a feature of the E&AD's

---

[16] PAC Special Report, 1966–7, HC 290, paras 7–9.
[17] PAC Special Report, 1966–7, HC 290, para. 2. Treasury Minute, 8 November 1967.

work. Like all good partnerships this had benefits for both sides. The symbiosis was acknowledged by John Boyd-Carpenter, Chairman of the PAC 1964–70, when he told the House of Commons: 'The C&AG's effectiveness largely depends on the fact that his reports are considered and followed through by the Committee; the Committee's effectiveness on the fact that they have his reports as a starting point.'[18] From long experience of Whitehall and Parliament, Professor Peter Hennessy noted that 'the key to the PAC's pre-eminence was and remains the formidable backup provided by the Exchequer & Audit Department'.[19] The four-pronged approach, which included a critical C&AG report, followed by detailed questioning of the Accounting Officer before the PAC, a subsequent report to the House of Commons by the PAC as its most powerful Select Committee, and a required government response in a Treasury Minute, ensured that the Westminster system of parliamentary financial accountability provided the model for many other countries.

Relationships with the PAC went well beyond the information in the C&AG's published reports. Though technically the C&AG and his staff appeared as witnesses, before every PAC hearing there was a detailed E&AD briefing of the Chairman and members of the PAC on factors underlying the reports, with suggested lines of questioning. Arming the Committee in this way was necessary because the normal timetable allowed only two hours to question well-prepared Accounting Officers on each report. Members also had limited time to prepare because of other parliamentary, political, and constituency duties. To ensure that the best use was made of the available time, on some more complex reports the Accounting Officers could also be given some broad indication by the E&AD of areas the Committee might wish to explore in more detail, to enable relevant information to be at hand rather than having to be produced later. Clearly this had to be handled carefully; members were very jealous of any suggestion that the hearing was stage-managed and that they were being deprived of the element of surprise. Drafts of the Committee's own reports, taking into account the evidence given by the Accounting Officer, were also prepared within the E&AD immediately after each hearing and submitted for approval by the Committee. Briefing was also provided on the government's response in the subsequent Treasury Minute, which could again be followed up by the Committee to monitor whether effective action had been taken.

Relationships with audited departments were more uncertain, given the inevitable wariness between auditors and the audited. On matters arising from the financial and regularity audit of accounts, relationships were

---

[18] Stated in one of the annual debates reviewing the main features of the PAC's reports in the previous Session.
[19] Hennessy, 1990, p. 332.

generally cordial and straightforward. Here, the C&AG's permanent position as the statutory appointed auditor contributed to continuity of relationships and encouraged the development of longer-term knowledge and understanding on both sides. This was helped by the policy of allocating auditors to specific departmental audits for several years at a time. With value-for-money matters, Accounting Officers and their senior finance staff recognized—and in principle supported—the importance of the Department's role and its place in the framework of public accountability. Nevertheless, relationships could become strained on individual value-for-money examinations, particularly when departments faced a critical public report with the result that their Accounting Officer would be more vulnerable when appearing before the PAC. C&AG Sir Douglas Henley noted how: 'Departments to some extent acquiesced on the devil-you-know philosophy. They understood the rules of the game and played by them.'[20] One of the 'rules' that departments valued in particular was the E&AD procedure of sending advance 'Reference Sheets' notifying them of intended criticisms and giving them the opportunity to respond on facts, balance, and fairness of presentation before moving to the formal report. Some of the more commercially minded non-departmental bodies made it very clear that they preferred the potentially more comfortable regime of private sector auditors, without value-for-money examinations, public reports of criticisms, and examinations by the PAC.

Relationships with the Treasury were generally cordial and supportive, though for obvious reasons deliberately short of a partnership. The view that the E&AD acted as 'an outpost of the Treasury' had long disappeared. In constitutional terms they were on opposite sides, with the Treasury aligned with departments and the Executive, and the C&AG with the House of Commons and the PAC. The C&AG's reports and the examination of Accounting Officers before the PAC provided the arena where conflicts were discussed and, hopefully, resolved. Despite the difficulties that could arise, the C&AG and the Treasury shared common cause on the need for strong controls on the proper conduct of public business in all areas of public spending. On matters involving the form and content of appropriation and other accounts there was always close liaison.

Emerging Concerns

Whilst acknowledging the E&AD's many strengths, there were a number of areas in the structure of the Department, its management and operations, that

---

[20] Sir Douglas Henley, *Unpublished memorandum* (February 1996), para. 4.

needed re-examination. By the late 1960s it was becoming clear that there were aspects that needed to be reviewed, not only to bring matters up to date but also to reflect changes emerging in the delivery of government services across a wide range of spending programmes. Increasingly, responsibilities and accountabilities were being devolved to a variety of second-tier non-departmental agencies or private sector bodies, with varying experience in the proper conduct of public business. Within departments, higher-level control was being relaxed, with encouragement to push day-to-day decisions and management further down the line. This changing and more challenging audit environment, together with existing strains being identified within the E&AD itself, made it essential to re-examine the management and conduct of all aspects of the Department's work, to identify where it would need to develop in both the shorter and longer term. The future would inevitably mean higher expectations, more demanding standards, potential threats, and new opportunities. It was also important to retain the best of what was already being done.

Some emerging concerns were the result of matters wholly or largely outside the E&AD's control. A key area was budgets, staffing, and pay. Although the C&AG was operationally independent, the E&AD remained a normal civil service department and in these areas was therefore subject to annual Treasury and civil service controls on budgets and staffing. In practice, post-war constraints on funding and on manpower meant that in some areas the Department's resources had not kept pace with massive increases in the number of accounts to be examined, and in the scale and complexity of the expenditure and operations involved. Sometimes staff numbers were even below approved complements. The Department's inherent concern for economy had to some extent created a difficulty for itself, making it reluctant to press sufficiently strongly to secure the necessary increases in staff numbers.[21]

Another difficulty was the absence of a central headquarters building where the majority of the staff could be brought together in order to encourage greater coordination, flexibility, and efficiency in the use of available manpower. Audit House, the existing cramped and antiquated headquarters, accommodated only the C&AG and his senior advisers, some of the Directorate, and central administrative staff. The rest of the Department was spread across dozens of different locations in London and the provinces. Most of the directors were separated from their divisions, and staff were sometimes in small sections located a long way from their responsible line managers.

---

[21] Older staff fondly remembered C&AG Sir Frank Tribe's insistence on using the tram, rather than an official car, to travel from Audit House at Blackfriars along the Embankment to the House of Commons for meetings of the PAC.

A Departmental Staff Side review in 1970 noted that a Chief Auditor's visit to some far-flung sections could involve a round trip of more than 1,000 miles.

There were also matters needing attention that were wholly or largely within the Department's control. Attitudes could be inward looking and, in some respects, complacent. More needed to be done to improve working relationships with the audited departments: a determination to maintain operational independence could be taken too far. The need for earlier and better communication was perhaps greatest on the initiation and conduct of larger value-for-money examinations. There was no central planning of content and delivery of an overall programme for value-for-money examinations nor central control or monitoring over progress, timing, and costs. These were regarded as matters for the audit divisions concerned, where great store was set on the individual initiative of the responsible auditors. There were no centrally agreed strategic plans for future development, nor arrangements for regular and systematic senior management consideration of wider issues or priorities, including emerging opportunities or threats.

Although the C&AG personally signed almost all the certified accounts, and gave final approval for all subjects to be included in the reports, the main operational decisions on almost all matters on both financial and value-for-money examinations were made within the audit divisions, led by the Directors of Audit. Only occasionally did the C&AG take direct personal charge on important issues. Douglas Henley noted on his arrival as C&AG in January 1976 that the:

> C&AG was not expected to concern himself with the technicalities of the audit but to concentrate on external relations with Accounting Officers and the PAC. The ten Directors were the 'barons' of the Department. They ran their own audit divisions, covering all the government departments and other public bodies audited by the C&AG, and they ran them according to long-established oral traditions, largely unencumbered by written methodology or other prescriptive material. It was most unusual for the Directors or any other group to meet collectively.[22]

A further concern was the absence of any uniform system for recording staff time and costs. There was no reliable way of establishing the cost of individual financial or value-for-money examinations, preparing budgets, setting timetables, or controlling the resources used. With financial audit there were doubts about consistency of standards across the wide range of certified accounts. There were no centrally approved procedures for planning, monitoring, and review of the work completed. Divisions were free to adopt different approaches. The results of the work were scrutinized at different levels within

---

[22] Sir Douglas Henley, *Unpublished memorandum* (February 1996), paras 14 and 16.

the responsible audit divisions but there were no arrangements for independent review and quality control. This was in sharp contrast to the best professional practice increasingly being adopted in the larger private sector accountancy firms. The absence of standard documentation meant that the audit overall was not demonstrably being conducted to the highest modern standards. Given the Department's status and responsibilities, this uncertainty was unsatisfactory and could not be allowed to continue.

Although value-for-money examinations had developed originally from the financial and regularity audit of the annual appropriation accounts, certification audit was no longer a sufficient platform for exploring the more substantial opportunities offered by examinations aimed directly at the management, delivery, costs, and timescales of large departmental spending programmes and projects. Auditors were increasingly allocated either to certification audit or to examinations of economy and efficiency. Though specialization was not as complete as it would later become, staff worked in different teams to carry out the two kinds of audit using essentially similar detailed examinations of vouchers, files, contract papers, and other records. Hennessy noted how the 'old E&AD tradition of meticulous filleting of the files continues, conducted by a battalion of relentlessly tidy-minded accountants...fashioning ammunition to place in the hands of MPs on the Public Accounts Committee'.[23] This 'document based' and 'bottom up' approach had important benefits by providing hard practical evidence of weaknesses and failures in control that were difficult for audited bodies to refute. *The Times* newspaper pointed out that: 'The most devastating type of parliamentary inquiry is that which forces ministers to justify particular expenditure in a precise location at a specific time.'[24] This 'smoking gun' approach provided valuable material for the PAC when questioning well-briefed Accounting Officers defending carefully prepared positions.

Despite the many individual successes achieved, there was a growing need to re-examine audit objectives, to review the range and depth of examinations, to develop stronger and more consistent audit methodologies, and to bring new skills to bear on individual examinations. It was also important to increase examinations of effectiveness. E&AD reports mainly concentrated on economy and efficiency, and largely left untouched specific examinations of the degree to which programmes and services had met their objectives. To some extent this was making the best use of available resources. Examinations of economy and efficiency had proved to have a high likelihood of success based on firm evidence, whereas the results of examinations of effectiveness were more conjectural because outcomes were often less clear-cut. However, it

---

[23] Hennessy, 1990, p. 332.   [24] *The Times*, Editorial, 27 April 2002.

would be increasingly recognized that examinations aimed directly at effectiveness were the natural, indeed inevitable, extension of the existing work. They would provide valuable opportunities to improve accountability on larger programmes as well as offering enticing professional challenges.

One of the ways forward on all value-for-money work was to adopt a more 'top-down' and 'systems-based' approach, planned on the basis of assessments of materiality and risk, and concentrating on the objectives, systems, management, performance, and achievements of larger and more complex departmental programmes and services. This would move the audit forward into more significant examinations of economy and efficiency, and onwards towards examinations of effectiveness. Carried through successfully, examinations and reports of this kind would increase the relevance and impact of the E&AD's work and its contribution to parliamentary and public accountability. It would also help to reduce the occasions when, as acknowledged even by one of the staunchest supporters of both the Department and the PAC, 'The Committee sometimes concentrated on minnow-matters instead of sharks and whales.'[25] New types of examinations would have to be introduced progressively and would run alongside rather than replace the existing well-tried range of examinations. It would be vital to maintain the emphasis on hard evidence and, where necessary, the critical edge. Despite the need to be more thorough and systematic, it would also be important for the methodology to remain flexible and avoid overprescription and rigidity.

A strong emphasis on the initiative and flair of individual auditors pursuing their own chosen lines of inquiry had always been regarded as important for producing good value-for-money material and providing job satisfaction. If value-for-money work were to become wider-ranging, more complex, and demanding, it was essential not only to preserve individual initiative and flair but also to have early senior management involvement in the selection, objectives, overall design, and direction of studies, not only within divisions but across the Department as a whole. A team approach would also be needed for larger or more complex examinations. Developing value-for-money examinations in these ways would require better planning and new skills, and would take time to achieve. The Department would need to revise its approach, develop new methods, and strengthen its own control and management procedures. Specialist support would increasingly be needed in a variety of non-audit disciplines, particularly in economics and statistics and other forms of quantitative analysis. This would require some inward secondments and broadening the scope of the Department's internal training.

[25] Hennessy, 1990, p. 332.

Considerable efforts would also be needed to build up a better dialogue with audited bodies in planning and carrying through examinations and assessing results. Audited bodies frequently saw E&AD examinations and reports as largely inquisitorial and, by concentrating on mistakes, designed essentially to provide 'red meat' for the PAC. Sometimes the audited bodies did not regard the work as fair and balanced because they did not consider that it gave sufficient weight to the wider circumstances of the programmes and projects concerned, or to the practical pressures that departments faced. They often claimed that the reports depended mainly on hindsight and did not add any fresh insight or analysis. They pointed out that some examinations consisted largely of uncovering and repeating information already set out in their own files. This response failed to recognize that the purpose of E&AD examinations and reports was not to tell audited bodies things they already knew or should have known, but to provide independent information, analysis, and advice to Parliament and the PAC.

Outside the E&AD's control were the delays in presentation and publication of the C&AG's annual reports. Reports, even those dealing wholly with value-for-money issues, could only be presented alongside publication of the certified annual appropriation or other accounts of the departments and other audited bodies. Invariably this caused delays in the clearance of reports at the busiest time of the year. As the accounts were not normally published until some nine months or more after the end of the financial year, this could be up to twenty-one months after the relevant expenditure was incurred. It could then take several weeks before the matters in the report were examined by the PAC. There could be further delays until the PAC's own reports were published and the government response issued in a subsequent Treasury Minute. This lengthy process reduced immediacy and impact. Burying the C&AG's reports within the massive volumes of the published appropriation accounts also gave the reports a low public profile, particularly as it was not the Department's practice to issue press notices or other briefings. The drafting style of the reports accentuated the problem.

Audit reports were generally brief, factual, dry, and rather flat. This was partly because they were published formally with the accounts and partly to assist in clearing the facts and ensuring completeness, balance, and fairness of the reports with the audited bodies. Drafting also sought to avoid upstaging the PAC or anticipating the Committee's own examination. The approach was to summarize the facts as briefly as possible and let them speak for themselves, rather than pointing up key issues by explicit analysis, comment, conclusions, or recommendations. The reports tended to concentrate on things that had gone wrong, without going on to identify why they went wrong, what could and should have been done to prevent or minimize problems, and how systems and controls could be strengthened for the future. Messages were implicit or heavily coded. With some reports this worked well, but the rather stiff and pedestrian presentation reduced their wider appeal and impact. The Department to some extent relied on the opportunity when drafting the PAC's own reports to revisit the original report and develop the criticisms, provide more insight, and introduce conclusions and recommendations.

In the mid-1960s there was a setback in the highly favourable external perception of the Department and its work with the publication of the results of Normanton's research in the early 1960s comparing the responsibilities of the national audit offices of ten Western European countries and the General Accounting Office of the United States.[26] He praised several aspects of E&AD's work over the years but also made some familiar points about limitations in the C&AG's remit compared to the position on state spending elsewhere, for example on nationalized industries and public corporations, local government, and other parts of the public sector. Importantly, however, it did not examine the position in any of the larger Commonwealth countries such as Canada, Australia, and New Zealand, where the constitutional and parliamentary arrangements and accountabilities would have provided more valid comparisons with the E&AD and the results of its work. Nevertheless, on the narrow point of formal trappings and status Normanton contrived to make the sweeping assertion that E&AD staff had status and careers that were 'unquestionably and demonstrably the lowest in any major country in the Western world'. This assertion was repeated word for word by Garrett and Sheldon in their November 1973 Fabian Society tract on administrative reform.[27] Although Garrett and Sheldon criticized restrictions on the C&AG's audit remit and some aspects of value-for-money examinations that were not supported by the facts, they concluded that: 'Over the years in pursuing evidence of waste and extravagance...[the C&AG]...has rendered valuable service.' They also wanted more examinations of effectiveness, and criticized the lack of systems of accountability for performance within departments. They supported the view that: 'The Exchequer and Audit Department should be totally independent of the Treasury and the Civil Service Department.'

Conclusion

After the Second World War the public sector environment was rapidly changing and there were potentially serious dangers in not responding to these

---

[26] Normanton, 1966.
[27] J. Garrett and R. Sheldon, *Administrative Reform: The Next Step*, (Fabian Tract 426, November 1973), p. 11.

changes. Continued failure by the E&AD to adapt and evolve might well in practice have adversely affected its standing or even its survival.[28] The post-war E&AD established a strong reputation as the public spending watchdog as a result of the C&AG's major reports on value-for-money examinations, and was highly regarded within Parliament and both nationally and internationally. The audit of appropriation and other accounts, though less heralded, was seen by departments and other bodies as providing valuable support to their own responsibilities, although they were less enthusiastic when attention turned to value-for-money reports pursued by the PAC. There was also close liaison with the Treasury on matters of common concern, such as the form of accounts and rights of E&AD access. There was a particularly strong relationship with the PAC that was briefed extensively on every report coming before it.

With appropriation audit more steps were necessary to ensure a consistent standard of audit across the E&AD, based on better methodology and with lessons to be learned from developments in the larger private sector firms. On value for money there was a need for greater direction of examinations towards systems and controls on larger programmes and projects, using a 'top-down' and 'systems-based' approach but without losing the proven benefits of hard, well documented evidence. Costs and timescales for all audits needed closer control. It was important to increase the earlier involvement of senior management in the selection and conduct of larger examinations, and to develop a more corporate approach to the work of the Department as a whole. This would require stronger central oversight of annual programmes of work and better strategic planning to identify future challenges, opportunities, and priorities.

Within the E&AD there were different views on the extent and the priority for change, particularly amongst more senior staff. Given the Department's established status and reputation, some considered that only relatively modest changes would be required as part of normal development. By the late 1960s there was a growing recognition that changes were necessary. Public sector audit offices, however long and distinguished their pedigree, are not immune from Darwinian imperatives. In a changing and more demanding world the key issue was not the Department's successful past or even its successful present: the important question was whether it was fully equipped for a successful future.

---

[28] A similar example of fundamental change in the responsibilities and remit of a public sector audit office occurred with the New Zealand Auditor General's Office in the 1990s. A new 'contestability' regime required a large proportion of the Office's existing financial audits to be put out to tender in competition with private sector firms. As a result some 40 per cent of audits by fees value moved to the private sector.

9

Audit in the Time of the New Public Management

'Change is not made without inconvenience, even from worse to better.'

Samuel Johnson, *Dictionary of the English Language*, preface

In the late 1960s governments began a revolution in public sector management, widely referred to as the New Public Management (NPM), that sought to change management philosophies, objectives, and systems in the departments and other public bodies that the Comptroller and Auditor General (C&AG) audited. These developments in public sector management meant that the Exchequer and Audit Department (E&AD) would need to re-examine its own planning and operational procedures to ensure that these took full account of changes being introduced in the management and delivery of departmental programmes. This would be especially important when planning and carrying out examinations of economy, efficiency, and effectiveness. The E&AD would have to recognize and work in a manner consistent with the aims and practices of new management regimes, whilst remaining independent and free to draw attention to weaknesses in financial control and performance as new arrangements were introduced. From the late 1960s onwards this became an important challenge facing the E&AD as departments and other bodies began a fundamental reappraisal of their methods of management and delivery of programmes, projects, and services. At the same time, the E&AD was re-examining its own objectives, structure, and methods. Securing fundamental changes in departmental financial management and control would prove to be a long process. It would require far-reaching changes in civil service culture and structure at both senior and lower levels, new management systems, and strong and persistent political will.

Fulton Report

High-level financial controls over departmental spending programmes were introduced in the early 1960s under the system of Public Expenditure Surveys following from the investigations of the Plowden Committee in 1959–61. Despite these improvements, there remained concerns over the nature and effectiveness of management within departments. There were widespread views outside the civil service, including some in Parliament, that management of programmes and projects was given insufficient priority at senior levels. It was argued that Permanent Secretaries and other senior civil servants saw their primary responsibility as providing policy advice to ministers, handling matters relevant to ministers' responsibilities to Parliament, keeping ministers well briefed on emerging issues and generally protecting them against unexpected demands and difficulties. There was little internal enthusiasm or support for changes that would take senior staff away from the rarefied and glamorous atmosphere of policy adviser, a role in which they excelled, and turn them into managers, a role in which they had not been seen to excel or to which they were attracted. At lower levels, departmental systems and controls were seen as being inadequate for effective management. There was a concentration on inputs not outputs, and on bureaucratic process rather than results. There was a perceived fear of failure and an aversion to risk. More generally, there was a lack of the regular information and analysis that were essential for effective management of large, complex, long-term programmes and projects.

Continuing concerns over the quality of public service management in the 1960s were taken sufficiently seriously for the Estimates Select Committee to recommend in 1965 that they should be the subject of a wide-ranging further inquiry.[1] Accordingly, in February 1966 Prime Minister Harold Wilson informed the House of Commons that a committee of inquiry chaired by Lord Fulton, Vice Chancellor of the University of Sussex, would be set up with broad terms of reference 'to examine the structure, recruitment and management, including training, of the Home Civil Service and to make recommendations'.[2] Some believed that the primary concern of the Fulton Committee should be the adequacy of the Whitehall machine to cope with the increasing workload that modern circumstances required it to bear.

The structure of the British civil service had altered little since the reforms that followed the Northcote-Trevelyan Report of 1854. Although British society and the scale and nature of government activity had been completely transformed in the intervening century this had not been matched by changes

---

[1] Sixth Report from the Estimates Committee, 1964–5, 'Recruitment in the Civil Service'.
[2] HC Debates, 8 February 1966, col. 210.

in the civil service. Metcalfe and Richards observed that 'conventional forms of public organization are ill equipped to deal with the problems facing them; innovation in public administration has not kept pace with the increasing scale, scope and complexity of modern government'.[3] It was argued that identifying the nature, extent, and causes of this fundamental problem was the essential first step before attempting to recommend second-order solutions involving structure, recruitment, management, and training. This was the sort of radical inquiry that seemed to have been envisaged by the Estimates Committee. However, when announcing the establishment of the Fulton Committee, the Prime Minister made it clear that it would not deal with such 'machinery of government' questions. In explaining this pre-emptive move he emphasized that any consequential changes that might be considered in the civil service:

> does not imply any intention to alter the basic relationship between Ministers and civil servants . . . Civil servants, however eminent, remain the confidential advisers of Ministers, who alone are answerable to Parliament for policy; and we do not envisage any change in this fundamental feature of our parliamentary system of democracy.

The Fulton Report, presented to Parliament in June 1968,[4] acknowledged the civil service's many strengths but also identified six main respects in which the Committee thought the civil service was inadequate for the most efficient discharge of the present and prospective responsibilities of government. The Committee concluded that the civil service was still too much based on the philosophy of the 'amateur/generalist/all rounder', most evidently in the dominant administrative class. The proliferation of classes of appointment, many with separate pay and career structures, seriously impeded its work. Scientists, engineers, and other specialists were frequently given neither the full responsibilities and opportunities nor the authority they needed to carry out their duties. Particularly contentious was the accusation that too few civil servants were skilled managers. The result, it was alleged, was a civil service that was isolated from the community it was meant to serve. To tackle these issues the Committee made twenty-two separate recommendations. Initially these had only a limited impact, for the vision propounded by the Report was not matched by the specific changes introduced.

Only three proposals were quickly accepted: the creation of a Civil Service Department to take over the Treasury's personnel role in structure, recruitment, and career planning; the establishment of a Civil Service College to strengthen training, particularly in management; and the consolidation of the

---

[3] Metcalf and Richards, 1987, p. 3.
[4] Cmnd 3638, June 1968, *The Civil Service: Report of the Committee 1966–68.*

administrative, executive, and clerical classes into a more unified structure. Even these changes had their determined opponents. On consolidation of the three largest civil service classes, for example, it was clear that genuine unification would not be secured simply by the removal of labels. Instead, it would require significant changes in culture, attitudes, recruitment, career planning, and operational relationships. The support of the civil service trade unions would be essential, not only on emerging issues of principle but also in continuing negotiations on the detailed fabric of personnel changes, including pay, pensions, conditions of service, and promotion. Fulton's vision of bringing 1,400 separate scientific, engineering, and other professional grades within this framework was frustrated by the opposition of the Institute of Professional Civil Servants, which saw little benefit to its members.[5] Changes arising directly from Fulton were regarded as modest or marginal when compared to its declared ambitions.

There were various reasons why Fulton's confronting aims were not matched by achievements. From the outset there were widely different views within the Cabinet, and more generally within the government, on the acceptability of, and priorities between, the large number of changes proposed and the timing for their introduction. These differing views were even more evident and fiercely held and debated within Whitehall, where political considerations linked with the prospect of a general election encouraged caution. As the UK's economic prospects became increasingly uncertain, at a time of rising world oil prices, longer-term matters such as civil service reform became far less urgent than government efforts to tackle growing economic pressures by cutting the high levels of public expenditure resulting from previous social and economic policies.[6] Frustration over delay and lack of progress undermined determination and commitment, which led to a loss of momentum. This created openings for Fulton's opponents and allowed the return of civil service scepticism and inherent inertia. In many areas it became business as usual.

Change following Fulton was hesitant, with only marginal modifications in departmental practices and little improvement in the roles performed by, and expectations placed upon, civil servants. Departments were not reorganized or equipped to take on a modern management role. Financial controls, information systems and associated skills were still directed towards narrow fiduciary concerns and not geared towards management performance.[7] Some researchers

---

[5] Integration or exchange between professional and administrative grades was never really seen as realistic by Whitehall, not least because except in special cases it would essentially be a one-way traffic: scientists could become administrators but administrators could not become scientists.

[6] Between 1960 and 1976 public sector expenditure rose from 41.1% of GNP to 58.5% (Wright, 1977, p. 146).

[7] Harrison, 1989, pp. 150–1 and p. 171.

argued that a major impediment to sustained reform was a habitual 'disbelief system' amongst civil servants, derived from a long-held perception that most changes called for by their political masters would ultimately prove to be superficial and transient. The proposed changes were seen as designed to serve ends that owed more to political expediency than visions of a better civil service. As a result, the history of civil service reform was strewn with short-lived measures that withered because they were not the result of a long-term perspective and clear commitment. It was difficult for civil servants to take seriously political encouragement for a strategic approach to their work when much of their time was spent in responding to short-term crises.[8]

The wording of the Fulton Report encouraged resistance. It had been care-fully drafted and redrafted to accommodate widely different views between members of the Committee so that it could be presented on a unanimous basis. However, from the first chapter the Report was certain to elicit deter-mined opposition and resentment with the use of provocative words such as 'amateur' and 'generalist' to criticize the abilities of senior civil servants and the administrative class as a whole. Nothing could be more calculated to offend and alienate those who would be mainly responsible for implementing its proposals. The criticism of 'amateurism' was strongly rejected in a formal note of reservation by Committee member Lord Simey, former Professor of Social Science at Liverpool University, on the grounds that it was 'unfair' and 'failed to recognise many achievements'. He dismissed the need for 'revolu-tionary change' and argued for 'the evolution of what is basically the present system'. He concluded that: 'We have in the existing Civil Service an asset it would be utterly foolish to discard.'[9]

Some of Fulton's proposals also gave rise to concerns in the lower classes of the civil service, which greatly valued the existing system of safe and steady advancement based largely on seniority with annual increments in pay within defined pay scales. This meant that they could not be expected to give enthu-siastic support to proposals for 'major changes in promotion procedures, including a movement to advancement on the basis of ability and pay deter-mined by individual annual reviews of performance'.[10] Proposals that grades should be determined on the basis of job evaluation and that changes should be made in pensions and for the replacement of 'established' status by new terms of appointment meant a culture change just as threatening as that worrying those at senior levels.

A particular aspect of Fulton's proposals to improve departmental manage-ment that, had they been implemented, would have been directly relevant to the C&AG's audit was the recommendation that: 'In the interests of efficiency,

---

[8] Metcalf and Richards, 1987, pp. 18–19.   [9] Fulton Report, pp. 101–3.
[10] Fulton Report, ch. 6.

the principles of accountable management should be applied to the organisation of the work of departments. This means the clear allocation of responsibility and authority to accountable units with defined objectives.'[11] This proposal was seen as reflecting mainly the views of Committee member Norman Hunt and his management consultant adviser John Garrett, later a Labour MP. It would in turn have required the introduction of management information systems involving the setting of performance goals and the collection of data to measure performance and achievement against those goals. Information of this kind would have been especially valuable in the C&AG's examinations of efficiency and effectiveness. These and related issues would re-emerge in the PAC's 1980 examination of the role of the C&AG, and also in connection with the introduction of resource accounts in 2000. Similarly, Fulton's suggestion of further inquiries into the desirability of 'hiving off' activities to non-departmental organizations would return, in strengthened form, from the 1980s onwards, again with major implications for audit and accountability.

Reorganization of Central Government

In 1970 the new Conservative government under Prime Minister Edward Heath published the White Paper 'The Reorganisation of Central Government'.[12] This initiative was the direct result of the Prime Minister's deep personal interest in the machinery of government, on which he had worked intensively while in opposition. The White Paper concluded that the main problem was 'the weakness that has shown itself in the apparatus of policy formulation and in the quality of many government decisions over the last 25 years'.[13] Accordingly, the White Paper sought to tackle the persistent problem of ministerial overload, by reducing the time spent on day-to-day business and on dealing with short-term crises. The Cabinet would then have more time to address strategic policy issues, supported by improved information and analysis from a new policy unit in the Cabinet Office. From previous experience as a Chief Whip, and as a minister, Heath believed that the lack of strategic thinking was a critical failure of the previous Conservative governments of Sir Anthony Eden, Harold Macmillan, and Sir Alec Douglas-Home.[14] Despite these concerns, the White Paper still concluded that 'public administration and management in central government has stood up to these strains'.

The changes proposed in the White Paper were mainly structural rather than functional, and were intended to streamline and sharpen the conduct of high-level business, particularly in the Cabinet. There were mergers to

[11] Fulton Report, p. 105.   [12] Cmnd 4506, HMSO 1970.   [13] Cmnd 4506, p. 6.
[14] Hennessy, 2000, pp. 337–40.

create fewer and larger ministries, while some executive responsibilities were transferred to separate agencies. The largest of these were the transfer of management of the government estate to a new Property Services Agency and making military procurement the responsibility of a new Procurement Executive. Although these measures met the aim of improving focus and discussion in the Cabinet, by reducing its size from over twenty to eighteen, the creation of much larger departments with more wide-ranging responsibilities would in some respects accentuate the difficulties of effective management. The White Paper did not address the widely perceived weaknesses in day-to-day departmental management. It did not consider measures to tackle such issues as the shortage of skilled managers and the lack of effective information and control systems to support more accountable management, particularly for large, complex, and long-term programmes. Nor did it address the underlying issues of civil service culture and inertia that were a barrier to change.

Promoting good government and better policy decisions by a radical improvement in the information available to ministers was pursued by the creation of a multi-disciplinary Central Policy Review Staff (CPRS) based in the Cabinet Office. Although under the supervision of the Prime Minister, the CPRS was at the disposal of the government as a whole, working for ministers collectively. The White Paper stated that the purpose of the CPRS was:

> to enable Ministers to take better policy decisions by assisting them to work out the implications of their basic strategy in terms of policies in specific areas, to establish the relative priorities to be given to the different sections of their programme as a whole, to identify those areas of policy in which new choices can be exercised and to ensure that the underlying implications of alternative courses of action are fully analysed and considered.[15]

The CPRS would also have an analytical role in the annual public expenditure survey cycle, and would be responsible for ensuring that the Cabinet and its committees worked from agreed sets of data. Under the new Labour government from 1974 the CPRS' oversight of government overall strategy became increasingly intermittent and mostly concerned with discrete and often unrelated topics. The CPRS was created to provide analysis and advice to a government seeking to direct policies and events: it was less useful to a government having to introduce policies in reaction to events, driven by economic and other pressures, on both the domestic and international fronts. Competitors also emerged. The establishment of a separate Policy Unit within 10 Downing Street provided the Prime Minister with an alternative source of advice and other minsters began to appoint their own policy advisers. The new priorities

---

[15] Hennessy, 2000, pp. 14–15.

and the distinctive style of the Conservative government elected in 1979 under Margaret Thatcher eventually saw the CPRS disbanded in 1983.

New Management Techniques

The nature of the civil service and its complex responsibilities meant that sustained improvements in departmental management would require more than the introduction of fashionable new management theories. Nevertheless, there were experiments in the 1960s and 1970s with a series of public management initiatives centred on rational decision-making techniques. For example, Programme Planning and Budgeting Systems (PPBS) were introduced to extend government planning horizons beyond the customary twelve months. These involved service-wide reforms aimed at integrating budgeting and planning throughout the public sector, thereby improving coordination and control. Despite the great expectations that accompanied its borrowing from the USA, PPBS proved only of limited success and it was not long before it ran into the same trouble as it did later in the USA. In Britain, the problems of PPBS stemmed from its implementation in a form that did not recognize sufficiently the complications and interdependencies that characterized the British public sector.[16] Also, PPBS was too broad in approach and insufficiently tailored to specific departmental needs.[17]

PPBS was followed in the 1970s by Programme Analysis and Review (PAR), another US import. PAR was designed to assist ministers to coordinate, control, and manage the tasks of their departments. Whereas PPBS had been concerned with budgets, time frames, costs, and outturn of programmes at government level, PAR was aimed at the consideration of objectives and the evaluation and review of individual departmental programmes. Although PAR was conducted principally within departments, this was done under the watchful eye of the central coordinating departments, mainly the Central Policy Review Staff in the Cabinet Office. It was envisaged that about twelve departmental programmes would be selected each year for review by a committee of ministers, Treasury officials and the department concerned. An initial flurry of activity provided PAR with some early successes but within a few years it began to lose momentum or, as one senior civil servant expressed it, 'was run into the sand'.[18] The economic problems of the 1970s all but destroyed PAR.[19]

---

[16] Tomkins (1987, pp. 24–5) argued that PPBS failed in Britain mainly because it was based on unrealistic political, analytical, and social assumptions.

[17] Jenkins and Gray, 1987, p. 6.

[18] Sir Ian Bancroft, 1981, quoted in Jenkins and Gray, 1987, p. 1.

[19] Jenkins and Gray (1987, p. 6) attributed the failure of both PPBS and PAR to technical, organizational, and political constraints. Often the necessary information to carry out the

The deepening economic plight of Britain from the mid-1970s heightened concerns not only for improved management but also the need for greater accountability for the performance of the public sector and the role of the Treasury in promoting efficiency and effectiveness. More than one parliamentary committee criticized the seeming inability of the Treasury to improve matters. The Select Committee on Expenditure in 1975 noted that: 'The Treasury's present methods of controlling public expenditure are inadequate in the sense that money can be spent on a scale which was not contemplated when the relevant policies were decided upon.'[20] In addition, it was very difficult for interested parties to find out what departments had achieved and how far the results achieved had met their objectives. For example, PAR was regarded as an internal government exercise and neither the subjects of the reviews nor the results were made public.[21] There was neither the information nor the procedures in place to assess whether departments and other public sector bodies were using their resources efficiently and effectively.[22] It was clear to the Select Committee on Procedure in 1978 that 'the present financial procedures of the House are inadequate for exercising control over public expenditure and ensuring that money is effectively spent'.[23] These concerns were supported by the Select Committee on Expenditure 1977–8 which, perhaps optimistically, envisaged an 'ideal' system of public sector accounting that would meet traditional needs of financial stewardship and provide information on the efficiency and effectiveness of management performance. Such information, they found, 'barely existed'.[24]

These increasing concerns from the 1970s onwards about weaknesses in departmental management and the lack of systematic accountability for the efficiency and effectiveness of performance prompted parallel developments to strengthen and extend the C&AG's audit. The need to prepare for a more challenging audit environment had already been recognized within the E&AD. As well as preparing for the professional requirements of wider-ranging and more technical audit examinations there would also be demands from potential changes in relationships, not only with departments but also with

---

planning and evaluation of policy was scarce or non-existent, skilled personnel were often not available, departments and central organizations were not well structured for these new demands, and departmental and party politics provided few incentives. Wearied and sceptical public servants who had lived through other reforms were not sufficiently convinced that the changes were anything other than superficial or had the full support of the Executive. When ministerial interest waned it was easy for departmental interest also to drop. For more on PAR see Jenkins and Gray, 1987, pp. 105–13.

[20] Quoted in Wright, 1977, p. 143.
[21] Treasury and Civil Service Committee, 1982, Third Report.
[22] Harrison, 1989, p. 146.
[23] Select Committee on Procedures, 1977–8, First Report, vol. 1.
[24] Select Committee on Expenditure 1977–8, Fourteenth Report, para. 21.

the other bodies that would emerge from various changes in the ways that programmes and services would in future be delivered.

The movement towards the introduction of more formal management disciplines throughout departments, at all levels, was therefore entirely consistent with, and helpful to, the E&AD's own reappraisal of the range and depth of its examinations of economy, efficiency, and effectiveness. A 'top down' and systems-based approach to such examinations fitted well with movements towards departmental regimes that established clear and quantified operational and financial objectives for major spending programmes, projects and services, and communication of these to all staff. There was an associated need to establish management control and information systems to collect relevant data and the introduction of reviews of progress and emerging results. A revised managerial emphasis in all aspects of departmental operations widened the opportunities for more penetrating audit examinations, particularly in areas of effectiveness in meeting programme and policy objectives.

Reform of the E&AD

Impetus for Change

The growth in delivery of public programmes and services through agencies and other non-departmental bodies and contracting out to the private sector, would change operating philosophies and methods across important parts of the public sector. Some of the bodies taking on new responsibilities would not necessarily be fully aware of the special requirements surrounding probity and propriety in the proper conduct of public business. There would be new financial regimes and accountabilities.[25] The E&AD, accordingly, would need new approaches, new methods, and new skills to conduct its audits effectively, to maintain its standing with departments and Parliament, and to remain in the front rank of public sector audit.

The arrival of Sir Douglas Henley as C&AG in January 1976 marked the beginning of significant reform of the E&AD. Like many of his predecessors he came from the Treasury and, therefore, he had some knowledge of the role and style of the E&AD and some more direct experience of its work from his time as Treasury Officer of Accounts (1959–62). From this outside perspective he

---

[25] For example, it became essential to distinguish clearly between the responsibilities and accountabilities of the main departmental Accounting Officers and the heads of the second- and third-tier agencies and other bodies being set up. The Treasury therefore issued specific guidance on the appointment of lower-level Accounting Officers, the sorts of issues on which they were to be directly answerable to the PAC, and the continuing responsibilities of the main departmental Accounting Officers.

saw the E&AD, not exactly flatteringly, as 'a worthy organisation, filling a long established and carefully delineated role by the application of traditional, virtually sacrosanct, methods verging on the arcane'.[26] This perception ensured that he came armed with 'a fairly strong conviction' that changes were necessary, although he wisely decided that: 'For the time being, however, it was necessary to acquire a fuller understanding of the Department's work, attitudes and beliefs.'[27]

During Henley's first two years as C&AG he undertook wide discussions within the E&AD, with overseas audit offices, and other parties in the UK. By the end of 1977 Henley was convinced that the time was right to move decisively forward and that the best way to begin the process of change was to have a full-scale management review of all aspects of the Department's work, organization, and its management. A management review had a number of advantages. Importantly, initiating the review within the Department pre-empted any attempted imposition of an examination from outside, thereby putting control of the review and management of the nature, extent, and timing of subsequent changes firmly in the C&AG's hands. The involvement of both the Treasury and the Civil Service Department in the review, though without any prior commitment as to the outcome, gave added credibility to the independence of the exercise and helped to provide support for subsequent action.

Management Review

The Management Review started in January 1978, with broad terms of reference: 'To consider the objectives, working methods, management structure and staffing of the Department in order to ensure the most efficient and effective discharge of the Department's current responsibilities.' The examination concentrated on current responsibilities because this was the priority area and contained enough important matters to occupy fully the time available. Although the review deliberately did not deal with the broad issues that had already been raised in connection with the possible legislative widening of the C&AG's role and responsibilities, the work done to ensure a professionally well-armed Department was to provide important benefits when legislated changes were enacted.

The steering committee in overall control of the review was chaired by Douglas Henley. Members were drawn from the E&AD, the Treasury, the Civil Service Department, the Accounting Officer of a major spending department, the Government Accounting Service and a senior partner from the private

---

[26] Sir Douglas Henley, *Unpublished memorandum* (February 1996) para. 4.
[27] Sir Douglas Henley, *Unpublished memorandum* (February 1996), para. 7.

accounting practice Coopers and Lybrand.[28] The detailed examination was carried out by a review team whose membership was broadly similar to that of the steering committee.[29] The first stage of the review was a wide-ranging preliminary survey to determine the main areas to be covered in detailed examination and the key issues to be pursued. This identified five further studies. Two of these dealt with the professional conduct of the audit, one with planning, monitoring, and review, and the other with audit procedures. The third covered manpower planning, staffing, and training. The fourth study examined relationships with departments and other audited bodies, the Treasury, the Civil Service Department, and the PAC. The final study examined the organization and structure of the audit divisions, the provision of central services, and the role and structure of senior management. These five studies were completed and the results and recommendations reported to the steering committee over the following seven months.

During their enquiries the review team interviewed a large number of E&AD staff at all levels. Many supported the aims of the review and the prospects for change, though understandably reserving their position on individual recommendations that might emerge. Others, particularly amongst older and more senior staff, were more sceptical or suspicious of the aims of the review. They were not convinced that what they regarded as essentially a private sector-based model was best suited to the Department's public service role and special circumstances. Some regarded the criticisms of present practices and the arguments for early and significant change as pessimistic and alarmist. There were also fears that the close-knit culture of the Department would be eroded by the adoption of what was seen as an over-regimented approach. Some also saw the extensive changes suggested as somehow denigrating the Department's substantial achievements, past and present.

There were discussions with the Accounting Officers and senior finance staff in many departments and other organizations. The Accounting Officers fully supported the importance of the C&AG's role and the emphasis of the work of the Department on parliamentary accountability. At the same time, throughout the interviews there was a sense of growing doubt whether the Department was able to meet new expectations from the direction in which the public sector was developing, or that its approach and methods sufficiently reflected modern

---

[28] The Departmental members were John Cheetham (Secretary), Paul Billett and Don Smith (Deputy Secretaries), and Gerald Debenham (Director of Establishments and Accounts). The outside members were John Anson (Treasury), Richard Wilding (Civil Service Department), Sir Peter Baldwin (Permanent Secretary, Department of Transport), Sir Kenneth Sharp (Head of the Government Accountancy Service), and Lord Roger Chorley (Coopers & Lybrand partner).

[29] The review team was led by Director of Audit David Dewar. The other Departmental members were John Higgins, Toni Lovett, and John Pearce. The remaining members were Nick Gurney (Civil Service Department), David Jamieson (Civil Service Department), Andrew Winckler (Treasury), Michael Lawrence (Price Waterhouse partner) and Bruce Picking (Arthur Andersen partner).

needs. These reservations were almost entirely concerned with value-for-money work, sharpened by concerns about the aggressive attitudes sometimes displayed by the PAC. In contrast, the Accounting Officers drew considerable reassurance and comfort from the E&AD's certification audit in regard to their own responsibilities.

Extending the compass of the review, the review team spoke to staff of the national audit offices of Australia, Canada, the Federal Republic of Germany, the Netherlands, New Zealand, and the USA. There were discussions with a former Chairman and the current Chairman of the PAC and with the Chief Secretary to the Treasury, Joel Barnett, who later became PAC Chairman, who was strongly supportive of the E&AD. Views were also obtained from the District Audit Service and from bodies representative of the accountancy profession. Amongst all those consulted there was broad and unequivocal support for a review of this kind. The steering committee's final report in December 1978 reviewed the overall results of the team's examination in each of the areas studied and made thirty recommendations. The recommendations emphasized that there must be the ability:

- To ensure that the financial and regularity audit of accounts matched the best professional standards and practices, whilst continuing to meet the special demands of parliamentary accountability. Though directed primarily at measures to underpin the certification audit, the intention was also to move towards a more systematic and systems-based approach to wider-ranging value-for-money examinations.

- To extend and strengthen relationships with audited organizations and with the Treasury, without prejudicing audit independence. This should include the discussion of broad audit plans and consultation on specific issues as they arose. This was especially directed towards the proposed extension of value-for-money examinations, including effectiveness. This approach was later endorsed by the PAC.[30] Establishing closer relations with the audit profession generally would also help to make the E&AD more outward-looking and more accessible.

- To revise systems for manpower planning, staffing, career management and training, and to broaden expertise and experience by inward and outward secondments. Here the aim was to develop the right resources and use them where they were most needed, both on existing work and on new kinds of examinations.

- To retain broadly the present divisional structure and allocation of work, whilst introducing greater use of audit teams and more flexibility in the

---

[30] PAC, 1979, Second Special Report, Appendix 1, 'Report of the Steering Committee'.

handling of work by divisional management. A number of other developments were to be kept under review. However, the existing arrangements had a number of advantages and there was no obviously better alternative and, given the other changes being proposed, it was the wrong time to risk unnecessary disruption.

- To establish a Senior Management Group, with an enlarged membership and supported by a new central division for policy and planning and other central services. The aims were several: to provide coherent top-level management under the direct control of the C&AG and his senior staff; to address strategic and longer-term issues; to establish objectives and priorities for agreed programmes of work across the Department as a whole; to direct efforts and resources to key areas of materiality and risk; and to improve communication up and down the line on a regular and systematic basis.

The steering committee noted that they had concentrated on major issues and had deliberately formulated their recommendations in quite general terms to indicate the more important directions in which the Department should move. They emphasized that given the C&AG's special status and independence it was for him to decide on the extent, manner, and timing for the implementation of their suggestions. This formal caveat was in practice hardly necessary given Douglas Henley's firm commitment to the need for change and his close involvement in discussions of the detailed recommendations. A significant number of recommendations had already been adopted whilst the review team's work was still ongoing and before the final report was issued. Eventually all the proposed changes were implemented.

The Management Review was not an entirely open-minded exercise. Douglas Henley and the E&AD members of the review team went into it with a strong commitment to change and a list of the issues and improvements they wanted to see emerge, which were fully reflected in the final report. In contrast, those on the steering committee and the non-EAD members of the review team had to be convinced. All members recognized that implementing the agreed recommendations, and other developments flowing from them, could take several years. It would require careful planning and management to maintain the Department's existing commitments whilst modifying and strengthening present practices and, most importantly, retaining the best of what was already being done.

Throughout the review the steering committee had become well aware that there were mixed views amongst the staff about the advisability of introducing changes of the nature and extent being proposed, and the impact on the E&AD's established approach and methods. The steering committee emphasized that 'it will be most important to secure the full cooperation of the staff during implementation and this will require a clear exposition and full understanding of the objectives'.[31] The first stage in this process, in itself an innovation, was for the C&AG to address a meeting of all staff in the suitably evangelical setting of Church House, Westminster.

The Management Review, though directed primarily at strengthening the E&AD's planning and management systems, was also a stimulus to the developments taking place in professional skills and in the scope, nature, and depth of both certification and value-for-money examinations. Taken together, these changes would in turn prove valuable in forestalling potential threats from the election in 1979 of the Conservative government under Margaret Thatcher and the dramatic changes to the public sector that it had promised. Given the new government's well-known *animus* towards the public sector and preference for private sector alternatives there was also the possibility that this could affect the C&AG's dominant position in public sector audit with the transfer of some or all of his responsibilities elsewhere, including commercial auditors. Any opportunity to take over part of the Department's client list would have been an extremely tempting prospect for the larger private sector accountancy firms who were already being prepared to make substantial inroads into local government audit. In the event, the C&AG's position remained unchanged.

The 1979 Conservative government had from the outset a deep distrust of the attitudes and management skills of the civil service and an ideological conviction that many public services needed fundamental re-examination to determine whether they should still be provided by the state or could be provided at less cost or more efficiently by other means, most especially the private sector. The Prime Minister's mind-set towards the work of 'overprivileged' senior civil servants has been portrayed as a belief that 'We have several friends in the private sector who could do the job in a morning with one hand tied behind their back.'[32] Understandably this was not well received by those being maligned.[33] Unlike some of the attempts at management reform over the previous decade, the reforms of the 1980s were to prove robust and effective, primarily because they were driven forward by Thatcher's strong political backing and a conviction that certain reforms, on ideological or practical grounds, were essential and must succeed.

There were three components in the changes introduced. First, the government's fundamental political crusade was based on the professed need to 'roll back the boundaries of the state' and cut public expenditure by dispensing with activities and services that, on financial or ideological grounds, they

---

[31] Steering Committee Report, ch. 1, para. 13.   [32] Hennessy, 1990, p. 633.

[33] After their retirement, Sir Ian Bancroft (former Head of the Civil Service) and Sir John Herbecq (former Permanent Secretary at the Treasury) wrote a joint letter to *The Times* to distance themselves fully from the Prime Minister's views disparaging the civil service.

considered the state should no longer provide. Second, where activities and services were to remain a state responsibility, operational management and delivery should be transferred as far as possible to non-departmental agencies or contracted out to the private sector. Finally, where matters were to remain wholly within government, there should be a drive to improve management at all levels and to introduce systems of accountable management and other management philosophies and techniques, including those used in the best of the private sector.[34] Those fundamental and essential functions that the state was committed to retaining had to be managed economically, efficiently, and effectively, as a trust placed upon the government by those dependent on its services and by the wider tax-paying public. This time, rather than relying on recommendations from high-level committees of 'The Great and the Good', stimulating change would be made the particular responsibility of Sir Derek Rayner (later Lord Rayner), who had been brought in by Mrs Thatcher from Marks & Spencer, a firm highly regarded for its efficient conduct of business, to become her Efficiency Adviser from 1979 to 1983.

Raynerism

Rayner pursued change by targeted scrutinies of selected areas of departmental management for detailed investigation and to report findings. The challenge was to promote radical changes in civil service financial management, in both the shorter and longer term. The work of Rayner and his staff, both during and after his period as Efficiency Adviser, was a determined drive to reduce paperwork and bureaucracy with a programme of more than 300 scrutinies of specific departmental policies, activities, or functions. This would provide the means to identify savings and scope for greater efficiency and effectiveness, and to propose solutions and necessary action in the pursuit of 'lasting reforms' for the conduct of public sector business. A small but carefully chosen team supported Rayner in the selection and management of scrutinies, with the scrutinies themselves carried out not by outside management consultants but deliberately by civil servant 'insiders', mainly from the departments themselves.[35]

---

[34] Tomkins, 1987, p. 64; Helseltine, 1980, in Pollitt, 1986, p. 159. A belief in the remedies of management accounting was reflected in the information system developed for Michael Heseltine in the Department of the Environment in the early 1970s, usually referred to as MINIS or Ministerial Information System. MINIS sought to bring ministers into the management structure of their department and to give them more information on what was happening (see Harrison, 1989, p. 154 and also Metcalf and Richards, 1987, pp. 1, 24.) Some influential voices, however, saw the idea of 'ministers-as-managers' as 'nonsense' and not what they were there to do. Certainly, systems such as MINIS were not met with wider enthusiasm and did not long survive Heseltine's departure.

[35] 'The reasoning behind the scrutiny programme is that Ministers and their officials are better equipped than anyone else to examine the use of the resources for which they are responsible.

The scrutinies were planned to take sixty to ninety days to complete, with the final recommendations staying within the department and communicated to the relevant minister. They were bottom-up approaches to improvement carried out within individual departments, unlike PAR and PPBS that were run from the centre. The scrutinies did not attempt to generate a 'grand scheme' for improvement. Instead, they sought to generate smaller-scale improvements quickly, in areas that had been identified by the departments themselves. Rayner believed that reform would be successful if it was marginal, incremental, and internally generated, not foisted on departments from outside agencies. The mandate of the scrutiny teams was to bring new thinking to the management and delivery of the activities and services concerned, generate fresh ideas, and identify radical alternatives to improve management and performance. Naturally these were not always welcome, with the result that some suggestions were not fully implemented while some more radical ideas were abandoned when met with strong public opposition. A particular example of the latter was the widely criticized proposal to secure savings by changing the arrangements for payments of pensions and child benefits. In the first four years to 1983 the first 130 scrutinies were estimated to have produced savings of £170 million, and economies from abolishing 16,000 posts a year. A further £39 million in once-and-for-all savings and another £104 million worth of possible savings were identified. In just over eight years the estimated savings had risen to over £1 billion, with continuing economies estimated at another £325 million having been implemented.[36]

The Prime Minister was a close friend and admirer of Sir Derek Rayner and a strong supporter of the scrutiny programme, the management philosophy it espoused, and the changes in civil service management it was seeking to achieve. Her enthusiasm strongly underlined the priority that civil servants were expected to give to the programme and helped to maintain momentum. However, in an insightful study of the early Thatcher civil service reforms, Metcalf and Richards have pointed out that strong political support has never in itself been enough for successful reforms. It cannot guarantee success in the face of a culture entrenched in present methods and antithetical to management change:

> Winning the attention of those at the top is only the first stage of implementation. Later stages depend on the capabilities and commitment of civil servants at several levels. . . . As so often happens, cultural lag means that the ruling ideas appropriate

---

The scrutinies, therefore, rely heavily on self-examination. The main elements are the application of a fresh mind to the policy, function or activity studied; the interaction of that mind with the minds of those who are expert in the function or activity; the supervision of the Minister accountable to Parliament for its management and the resources it consumes; and the contribution of an outside agency in the shape of my office and me.' *The Scrutiny Programme: A Note of Guidance by Sir Derek Rayner*, p. 3. (Quoted in Hennessy, 1990, p. 597).

[36] Hennessy, 1990, pp. 598–9.

to an earlier age persist and continue to exert an influence on administrative behaviour and organisational structure long after the conditions in which they developed have disappeared.[37]

The narrow focus of individual scrutinies was recognized in the PAC's description of them as 'a radical self-examination of a specific policy, activity or function, to enable identification of ways the work could be carried out more efficiently and effectively and at less cost'.[38] Looking ahead towards wider issues, Sir Robyn Ibbs, Rayner's successor, who had been brought in from Imperial Chemical Industries, told the PAC that he did not envisage that the scrutinies would be a permanent fixture of government. Rather, they would cease when public sector managers became like their private sector counterparts and believed that 'getting the most from the available resources, from delivering value for money, doing the right thing by the customer, is the one thing which keeps them in business...and anything which can help (this) they will spring to'.[39]

The Rayner scrutinies had a political attraction in that they were commissioned internally, thereby allowing the reports to be treated as internal management documents and not required to be published or submitted to Parliament. They were available, however, to the C&AG under his normal access rights. In 1986 C&AG Sir Gordon Downey presented a report on the results of a National Audit Office (NAO) review of a selection of some 20 per cent of scrutiny reports from 1979–83, the action taken, and the results achieved.[40] In some respects he was 'doing a Rayner on Rayner'.[41] The report, which was generally favourable, was essentially an interim review of a pioneering programme. After providing a number of suggestions for improvement the overall conclusion was to endorse 'the continuing usefulness of the scrutiny process as a high level management technique to improve value for money'.

Although the Rayner scrutinies epitomized the sort of fresh thinking that identified changes in detailed aspects of management and performance, they were not a sufficient basis for generating service-wide change. For this the Thatcher government turned to the Financial Management Initiative.

The Financial Management Initiative

After four years of Rayner scrutinies the government embarked on the Financial Management Initiative (FMI) in May 1982. The programme was directed

---

[37] Metcalf and Richards, 1987, pp. 15–16.   [38] PAC Report, 1985–6, para. 1.
[39] PAC Report, 1985–6, Minutes of Evidence, Q.2148.
[40] C&AG Report, 1986, *The Rayner Scrutiny Programmes 1979–1983*.
[41] Hennessy, 1990, p. 599.

by the Financial Management Unit in the Treasury and the Management and Personnel Office of the Cabinet Office. As a prelude to the FMI, a government White Paper called upon departments to establish 'where practicable, performance indicators and output measures...which can be used to assess success in achievement of objectives.... [The] questions departments will address is where is the money going and what are we getting for it.'[42]

The FMI differed from the Rayner scrutinies not so much in aims but in the time horizon over which those aims would be achieved. Whereas the Rayner scrutinies were quick, hard-hitting efforts, the FMI's efficiency strategy was to get departments to improve management on a wider front, rather than focus on individual problem areas.[43] Managers would be expected to develop a clear view of their objectives and the ability to measure performance against these objectives.[44] Responsibilities for performance would be clearly designated and authority for meeting specified aims would be devolved to line managers. To support the process, information systems would be introduced to assist them in monitoring progress towards meeting these aims. By such means the FMI would seek to generate a cultural change in management attitudes in departments.

It has been recognized that in terms of management systems the FMI led to noticeable improvements in departmental management. Some commentators have been more critical and suggested that it encouraged the pursuit of efficiency, primarily on the basis of measured inputs, to some extent at the expense of effectiveness. Also, the emphasis on management techniques borrowed from the private sector was accused of giving insufficient weight to maintaining key elements of civil service ethos and values, such as probity and propriety and a professional commitment to public service. Doubts of this kind were present at different levels within the civil service as well as outside. On the fundamental issue of changing the management culture within departments, Harrison, for example, saw Raynerism and the FMI as having made little difference in the culture of public sector management between 1979 and 1989.[45] He argued that, although the text-book management techniques being introduced by the FMI were producing results, there were continuing areas of concern to which methodology alone was not a sufficient answer.

In 1985–6 C&AG Gordon Downey initiated an investigation, as he had done with Rayner, of the impact of the FMI in twelve government departments. The NAO's examination noted that 'real progress was being made in the development of suitable systems' but found that the FMI had not convinced middle and lower management about the benefits of the new

[42] Cmnd 8616, 1982.   [43] Metcalf and Richards, 1987, p. 187.
[44] Tomkins, 1987, p. 29.   [45] Harrison, 1989, p. 157.

arrangements. Their reservations appeared to reflect mainly the limited extent of their power, as they saw it, to control many of the costs for which they were nevertheless held accountable in their budgets. Downey pointed out that:

> If the FMI is to succeed at these levels, it is essential that managers should feel personally responsible for achieving targets which contribute to Ministers' overall objectives. To this end, managers should, within the limits inescapably imposed by the ultimate responsibility of Ministers and by the maintenance of common standards across the Civil Service, be aware of their full costs and be given as much personal responsibility as possible, with powers closely matched.[46]

In a climate of 'responsibility without power' there was a risk that, in the mind of managers, failure avoidance and risk aversion would assume priority over operational success. There was still the perennial question of the lack of any public sector equivalent to the private sector incentive that good management and performance was essential to staying in business. Many saw these factors as lying at the heart of the civil service's management malaise.

Next Steps

The momentum in the Sisyphean task of changing civil service management culture was maintained with the Next Steps programme started in 1988. This adopted what turned out to be a more radical, and ultimately more successful, approach. Taking standard management objectives and techniques and applying them as a whole to departments with many different functions, and which were organized on a largely unitary and centralized basis, tended to dissipate impact and momentum. There were many functions where a 'one size fits all approach' failed to convince and take hold. Instead, drawing together wider lessons leading to lasting reforms would need to be pursued by structural changes, which involved transferring selected functions from the departmental mainstream into separate executive agencies. These would not be subject to detailed departmental and Treasury controls and, with wider operational freedoms and flexibilities allowed to managers, it was envisaged that an improved management culture could more readily be introduced and sustained. Building improved management would involve the sort of machinery of government changes that had previously been denied from Fulton onwards.

Controversy surrounded these revolutionary elements of Next Steps, which became the subject of intense political and Whitehall debate. It was made clear from the outset that changes in structure and responsibilities would not extend to the central government functions of the Treasury and the Cabinet

---

[46] C&AG, 1982, *The Financial Management Initiative*, pp. 1, 10–11.

Office, with their high policy and political content. Elsewhere, the enthusiasm and growing momentum of Next Steps meant that progress with transferring department functions was quicker and more extensive than many observers had originally expected. In what was clearly an interim review on progress, completed by the NAO in May 1989, C&AG Sir John Bourn, who had succeeded Gordon Downey in 1987, concluded that: 'Generally the National Audit Office consider that the [Next Steps] Project Team have carried out their role in relation to the launching of the Next Steps initiative in an energetic, well-organised and effective way.'[47]

The NAO report listed the thirty-seven executive agencies scheduled to be separated from a department by May 1989. These included trading bodies such as the Stationery Office and regulatory bodies such as the Vehicle Inspectorate, Driver and Vehicle Licensing, the Planning Inspectorate, and the Patent Office. In addition there were information services such as the Central Statistical Office, the Central Office of Information, and the Meteorological Office, and a large number of scientific and research establishments. A miscellaneous range of bodies were covered in such areas as social security, employment and resettlement services, recruitment and training, historic buildings, and royal palaces and parks. Total staff posts involved was nearly 175,000.

The increasing number of departmental functions being transferred to agencies and other authorities did not mean any reduction in accountability to Parliament. The C&AG remained the appointed auditor of their accounts, which were published and presented to Parliament. In addition, he was also able to carry out a full range of value-for-money examinations. The audit of agencies added to the NAO's certification audit workload and value-for-money examinations had to tread the sometimes shadowy line in practice between the responsibilities of departmental Accounting Officers and those of agency Accounting Officers, even though the Treasury and departments had taken great care to clarify accountability relationships in formal appointment letters to agency heads. Moreover, agencies could not be audited as if they were mini-departments subject to traditional constraints and operating methods. To do so would fail to recognize the fundamental purposes of the transfer of functions and be contrary to the more flexible ways in which it was intended that they should operate. In judging performance, the agencies could reasonably be expected to meet high management standards, based on appropriate systems of objective setting, and performance monitoring and reporting.

Importantly, agency staff were not necessarily those who had dealt with the same functions and services in departments, with the agencies recruiting staff at all levels from a variety of outside sources. Operating as public bodies

[47] C&AG, 1989, *The Next Steps Initiative*, pp. 13–14.

engaged in public business and spending public funds, agencies with less experienced staff would need to take special care to maintain established standards for the proper conduct of public sector business, including such ethical matters as probity, propriety, and equity. As the functions of many agencies were directly concerned with the delivery of services to public 'customers', NAO reports on how well those services were managed, and the results achieved, would inevitably have a wider public and parliamentary resonance and a high profile. Against this background, and in view of the growth in the number and diversity of agencies and in the public expenditure incurred, the NAO would be involved in a substantial programme of agency examinations in subsequent years.[48]

Wide-ranging programmes to improve public sector management were also under way in countries other than the UK. These developments were similarly being kept under review by the national audit offices concerned, though using different approaches. In Australia, for example, a more proactive position was adopted with the staff of the Auditor General who were sent out at an early stage to tackle poor civil service management by identifying weaknesses and areas in need of improvement so as to provide valuable information to support subsequent management reforms. In the UK, and in Canada, the introduction of management reforms was seen as essentially an Executive responsibility, which meant that audit examinations tended to follow events to establish whether government measures for reform were working effectively, rather than risk becoming entangled in changes whilst they were being formulated and before they had been given the opportunity to produce reliable results. Developments in audit could not sensibly be considered in isolation from the numerous reforms upon which the respective governments had embarked.

Further Developments in Audit

The changes introduced in the E&AD, and later the NAO, which were prompted by new management initiatives in the late 1970s, were to run through into the 1980s and well beyond. It became not just a process of working through a list of specific developments but embarking on a regime of virtually continuous change in all aspects of the management and conduct of the work. Embracing change proved to be an invaluable ally in adapting

---

[48] Hennessy (1990, pp. 589–627) provides a detailed analysis of the genesis and objectives of Raynerism, its operational philosophies and methods, staffing, personalities, achievements and impacts both short and long term, and its continuing influence alongside Next Steps, the Financial Management Initiative, and the work of the Efficiency Unit.

attitudes, approach, and methods to meet the significant developments that were by that time taking place in the organization and delivery of public programmes and services.

Changing the objectives, content, and conduct of audit work followed a different pattern for certification audit than it did for value-for-money audit. With certification audit it was not a question of seeking to extend or expand audit responsibilities, rather it was to specify those responsibilities more clearly and to discharge them more efficiently and more consistently with the latest professional standards. Developments encompassed: systems-based examination; closer analyses of materiality and risk; improved procedures for planning, monitoring, review, and quality control; better documentation; greater use of statistical and other sampling methods; wider use of computerized techniques, and greater reliance on internal audit. Although similar practices in private sector accountancy were well documented, it was not simply a matter of following established private sector models. Arrangements had to be developed and adapted specifically to meet the audit's public sector role and the unique features of its responsibilities. For example, care was needed to maintain the necessary high level of regularity audit and to tailor the work to the varied pattern of bodies and forms of account being audited. Programmes and procedures had to be revised, standard documentation created, and audit manuals rewritten. Being effective in response to the need for change meant that care was needed in order to avoid sliding into the excessive prescription and over-documentation that had afflicted similar developments in the private sector.

On value-for-money examinations the aim was more radical and the consequences of poor practice in a transformed public sector landscape more obvious. There were no readily available models in the public or private sectors for changes that were essentially breaking new ground. The broad directions in which developments should move had been identified before and during the 1978 Management Review, resulting in new survey and planning procedures being introduced. A further in-house review of value for money in 1981 made a number of more specific recommendations.[49] Progress depended on working these through into practical effect in individual studies.

The initial group of newer studies had varying degrees of success. Two of these were across-the-board studies involving the examination of a single subject in several departments, one of which was a successful examination of the professional standards of departmental internal audit and the other a review of the quality of departmental investment appraisal for capital projects. A difficulty with across-the-board examinations was deciding on the right

---

[49] *Review of Value for Money* (Internal NAO report, December 1981).

departmental Accounting Officer to appear before the PAC. A third study, which examined the system of cash limits for controlling departmental expenditure, drew heavily on Douglas Henley's knowledge in developing and running the system whilst at the Treasury. Two further studies on export credits guarantees and on the Central Office of Information encouraged a number of improvements in procedures and controls but did not proceed to a full report.

One of the boldest attempts by the Thatcher government to reconstruct the public sector was the sale of council houses. This was the subject of a report initiated and prepared personally by Douglas Henley, based on views he had reached whilst at the Treasury. It had two main risks. The first was that the more penetrating the report the more likely it would be seen as raising questions on an important issue of government policy, the area generally accepted as falling outside the C&AG's audit. The more immediate threat was that it dealt with a controversial and high-profile subject that was intensely party political and inevitably put severe strains on the bi-partisan approach that was an important factor in the efficient working and effectiveness of the PAC. Consequently, the Committee decided to pass on the report for possible examination by another Select Committee and in the end it was not pursued. These events provided a valuable lesson: as well as proceeding on the intellectual merits of a proposed examination, it was also important to look ahead and weigh the party-political and PAC dimensions.

Some of the new examinations were carried out by a Special Studies Unit that had been set up to lead value-for-money development. The Unit comprised a small group of E&AD staff together with two secondees; an economist, Norman Glass, and an operational researcher, Keith Aldred. Despite some innovative work the Unit did not produce the sort of impact and recognition that had been expected, mainly because the Unit, with just six members, was too small to complete sufficient study reports quickly enough to generate momentum. The Unit was also carrying out examinations within audited bodies that remained in all other respects the responsibility of line audit divisions, which were keen to embark on newer kinds of studies themselves.

The vast majority of the changes in the E&AD's work were initiated, developed, and successfully implemented by existing E&AD staff, rather than by employing large numbers of outside consultants. Advice and assistance was provided by two audit managers who were employed briefly from the private sector accounting firms Arthur Young McClelland Moore and Arthur Andersen. These were followed by other specialists on short-term contracts to provide economic, statistical, and other advice. To gain access to departmental perspectives there were also secondments from Whitehall for limited periods at directorate and senior management level. Thus, rather than building up a large specialist in-house capability, the approach deliberately adopted was to contract in specific work from specialist advisers as required for individual studies. Bringing in outside advisers was also done in full consultation with the audited bodies in order to minimize friction with their own experts.

A prominent appointment from outside the Department was Douglas Henley's decision to bring in Philip Cousins, a former colleague from the Treasury, as his second-in-command when John Cheetham retired as Secretary of the E&AD in 1979. Douglas Henley wanted 'an experienced Whitehall administrator, with a wide financial background, an understanding of the forward path for the E&AD, and a commitment to it'.[50] As the Secretary was traditionally appointed from within the Department, to balance the normal appointment of the C&AG from outside, this caused a good deal of concern within the Department and some formal protests. However, working first alongside Douglas Henley and then his successor Gordon Downey, and distanced from the Department's previous approach, Philip Cousins' incisive style made a significant contribution to the important developments taking place.

Developing the E&AD's external standing was also pursued by taking a more positive role in the work of the accountancy profession, in both the public and private sectors. Douglas Henley was elected to the council of the Chartered Institute of Public Finance and Accountancy (CIPFA) and senior members of the Department joined the Auditing Practices Committee and other committees of the Consultative Council of Accountancy Bodies. In 2008 Caroline Mawhood, one of the Assistant Auditors General, became President of the CIPFA Council. There was also a widening circle of professional contacts between members of the Department at all levels and private sector accountancy firms and other organizations. Associations with other national audit offices were strengthened, both individually and through the Contact Committee of European Auditors, the Commonwealth Auditors General, and the International Organisation of Supreme Audit Institutions (INTOSAI). A growing number of visits and exchanges or secondments of staff were made with other countries, mainly within the Commonwealth and from Europe but also more widely, for example with Japan, China, and Chile. These contacts with people from different disciplines and professional backgrounds helped broaden thinking, enlarge horizons, and generate ideas.

Douglas Henley was succeeded as C&AG in 1981 by Gordon Downey. Less volatile and demonstrative than his predecessor, Gordon Downey's quiet leadership and wholehearted commitment to the developments needed to meet the challenges and opportunities facing the Department ensured that the changeover did not slow the momentum for change. His determined and methodical approach successfully established department-wide structures,

---

[50] Sir Douglas Henley, *Unpublished memorandum* (1996) para. 33.

teamwork, and management systems, with careful attention to the motivation, commitment, and training of staff.

Many of the changes that were set in place following the Management Review, though important and far-reaching, were essentially concerned with strengthening the E&AD's internal operations and management systems in order to meet its existing responsibilities. They were not directly linked with the possible widening of the C&AG's role, responsibilities, and powers, which were pursued by a series of parliamentary committees from 1976–7 until 1981–2,[51] starting with the Eleventh Report from the Expenditure Committee, Session 1976–7.[52] The Committee's main recommendations would have involved an extensive enlargement of the C&AG's field of operations and fundamental changes in the relationship with the Executive and Parliament. Similar recommendations were contained in the First Report from the Select Committee on Procedure, Session 1977–8.[53] Further consideration was given to these matters in 1979 when the PAC reported on the status and functions of the C&AG. The position was again reviewed in a government Green Paper in 1980, for which the PAC took evidence and produced a further report in 1981. Running through these discussions was a distinct Executive reluctance to widen the C&AG's responsibilities and powers, reflecting an instinctive preference for accountability to be exercised more discreetly through reports to departmental management and the relevant minister, rather than announced in independent public reports to Parliament with strong follow up by the PAC.

There were three main sets of issues facing the various committees examining the future of public sector audit. The first was the extent of the C&AG's remit across the public sector outside central government. Most especially, whether the C&AG should carry out examinations in the nationalized industries, other public corporations, and whether there should be a role in the audit of local authorities. This was also related to the widening circle of second- and third-tier bodies being established to decentralize the management and delivery of government programmes and the growing involvement of the private sector. The second concern was whether statutory changes were needed in order to strengthen the C&AG's powers to conduct value-for-money examinations of wider kinds, including examinations of effectiveness

---

[51] Expenditure Committee, 1977–8, Fourteenth Report, 'Financial Accountability to Parliament', HC 661; Select Committee on Procedure, First Report 1977–8, HC, Sessional paper 588, Volumes 1, 2, 3; Expenditure Committee, Session 1976–7, Eleventh Report HC 535, 7; Committee of Public Accounts, 1978–9, 'Functions of the Comptroller and Auditor General', Minutes of Evidence, 2 April, Sessional Paper 330; Committee of Public Accounts, Session 1978–9, Second Special Report, 'The Work of the Committee of Public Accounts and the Status and Functions of the Comptroller and Auditor General'; Green Paper, 1980, Cmnd 7845, presented by the Chancellor of the Exchequer: 'The Role of the Auditor General'; Committee of Public Accounts, 1981, First Special Report, 'The Role of the Comptroller and Auditor General', Vols. 1–3.
[52] HC 535 of 1976–7 and HC 318 of 1977–8.   [53] HC 588 of 1977–8.

that could bring matters closer to policy issues. The third matter was whether the C&AG's constitutional status and powers needed to be revised to ensure financial and operational independence in these changing circumstances. There had over many years been suggestions that previous service in White-hall could be a risk to C&AG's independence when contentious issues arose.

C&AGs, the Treasury, and Audit Reform

From the earliest days following the 1866 Act some commentators thought that a C&AG with previous service in the Treasury would inevitably be inhibited in reporting matters unwelcome to the Executive.[54] In 1906 these 'ex-Treasury man' concerns were raised in the House of Commons by Prime Minister Sir Henry Campbell-Bannerman. After he confirmed that 'The appointments [of the C&AG] have for some time past been in the nature of selections by the Treasury from amongst permanent Civil Servants', he then sought to reassure the House that 'the selection for any future appointment will be made by the Prime Minister for the time being who will, I am confident, use his best endeavours to secure the services of the person who happens to be most suitable for discharging the duties of this important post.'[55]

Other Westminster-style parliaments such as Australia and New Zealand had also had a number of Auditors General appointed from Treasury backgrounds. Nevertheless, some members of the PAC were not convinced by previous assurances on the matter given over the years by Lord Welby and others. In 1979, when taking evidence from C&AG Douglas Henley, individual members of the PAC continued to press him on the details of his appointment, despite his repeated personal assurances on his independence. He was clearly angered by the persistent refusal to accept his word and described the views being expressed as 'an insult' and 'absurd'. In stark contrast to the conciliatory terms normally employed by a Permanent Secretary when responding to questions from members of a parliamentary select committee, he added that 'People hold that view because they do not know the Office, do not understand how it works, and probably have not studied adequately the work of the Committee.'[56]

Successive PACs for over 100 years had enjoyed the closest connections with the work and character of all C&AGs and were therefore in the best

---

[54] This criticism was not directed at the first two C&AGs, Ryan and Mills, because they were the obvious choices given their long experience of accounts and audit, and their close involvement with the formulation of the 1866 Act and the details of its introduction.

[55] Hansard, 20 December 1906, vol. 167, c. 1696.

[56] PAC, Second Special Report, 1979, Minutes of Evidence, Questions 1481, 1482, 1477, 1487. Always volatile, Henley's response was perhaps understandable given that his personal integrity and independence was being challenged, and particularly as his own track record of criticizing the Treasury was clear from his reports.

position to judge their independence. Seeking to communicate conclusively their absolute confidence in the personal and professional integrity of present and past C&AGs, it was stated very firmly that: 'We do not believe there is any foundation for the suggestion that the former career of a Comptroller and Auditor General in Whitehall detracts from his ability to make independent judgements as Comptroller and Auditor General.'[57] The PAC's strong vote of confidence in the integrity and professionalism of the C&AG recognized that it had long been standard practice for the Prime Minister to discuss proposed appointments with the Chairman of the Committee. Later, the formal agreement of the PAC Chairman to the appointment was made a statutory requirement under the National Audit Act 1983.

It had also been argued at various times that the E&AD should be headed by a C&AG who was a professionally qualified accountant, or at least had extensive audit experience. Others at senior levels, such as Sir Anthony Rawlinson, Second Permanent Secretary at the Treasury, argued: 'It is a detailed knowledge of the workings of Whitehall which is most essential to the highest audit office and not the technicalities of state audit.'[58] This was also Henley's view based on his experience as C&AG. Clearly a high level of audit expertise could be a considerable benefit but experience had shown that it was not essential in the context of the public sector where the C&AG's role is not personally to audit the accounts, for which he depends on a department of experienced officers. The C&AG manages a national audit office with wide and growing responsibilities in a challenging and changing public sector. In these circumstances, there is a strong argument that a solid knowledge of the workings of Whitehall is more valuable due to the way in which it can help to identify opportunities for major investigations and to avoid pitfalls. The benefits of interchange at senior levels between audit and government is recognized in other national audit offices, notably the French Cour des Comptes.

From time to time there have been suggestions from outside the E&AD that the absence of any promotion to C&AG from within the Department could have an adverse effect on careers and motivation and be resented by the staff. On the contrary, few staff regarded it as significant, nor did it contribute to any lack of motivation or commitment. A C&AG with extensive outside experience, supported by experienced senior staff within the Department whose professional audit advice was always sought and welcomed, was recognized within E&AD as a strong and effective combination. There was also an established career and promotion framework for all staff to every other senior post.

The Expenditure and Procedure Committees also resurrected concerns over Treasury control over the numbers, appointment, and conditions of service of

---

[57] PAC, Second Special Report, 1979, para. 14.   [58] PAC, 1980, Minutes of Evidence, Q.29.

E&AD staff. The Procedure Committee in 1979 recommended that audit staff should be paid from a separate vote of the House of Commons, which the Committee envisaged would make them servants of the House and therefore more independent. Significantly, the Procedure Committee saw one of the benefits of making the staff servants of the House as opening the way for committees of the House to call directly for assistance from the C&AG. Sir Douglas Henley responded to the Procedure Committee's suggestions by pointing out that under the existing conditions his ability to carry out audits on behalf of Parliament, but without being at its specific direction or its servant, ensured that his independence from the Executive as well as from the Legislature was both apparent and real.[59] He was therefore opposed to any changes that brought him further under parliamentary control. On most of the issues raised by the Procedure and Expenditure Committees the PAC was, in general, sympathetic to the views of the C&AG, realizing immediately that the prospect of the C&AG's involvement with other committees of Parliament was a threat to its own primacy in dealing with the C&AG's reports.

The PAC was also worried that the effect of making the C&AG an investigative arm of Parliament, instead of maintaining the present audit function, would seriously undermine independence, not enhance it as the Procedure Committee seemed to believe. Requiring the C&AG to respond to the requests of parliamentary committees would also mean that the core audit work of the Department could suffer.[60] It might also lead to confusion amongst auditees about the functions the auditors were performing. When E&AD officers carry out a statutory audit they are entitled under the legislation to have all reasonable access to accounts and relevant departmental documents and records, but when they are acting as consultants to parliamentary committees their access rights could be much reduced.[61]

The PAC decided not to make specific recommendations on the C&AG's role in its 1979 report and reserved judgement until the new Conservative government issued the Green Paper it had announced was being prepared on the various matters raised by the PAC and the other Select Committees.[62] The Green Paper issued in 1980 (Cmnd.7845), which was written by the Treasury, confirmed that the government recognized that there should be changes in the C&AG's role and responsibilities but did not believe that these should go as far as had been proposed. For example, it continued to maintain that the C&AG should not become the appointed auditor of the nationalized industries and should not be made an officer of the House of Commons. Significantly,

---

[59] Procedure Committee, 1979, Minutes of Evidence, 12 February.

[60] PAC, 1979, Second Special Report, para. 15.

[61] PAC, 1979, Second Special Report, para. 20.

[62] Green Papers are consultation documents produced by the government to widen debate and seek views on issues where, for example, new legislation is being considered.

in response to the long-standing criticisms of Treasury control over E&AD staff numbers and conditions of service, the government was prepared to consider alternatives to the current E&AD funding arrangements.[63] More generally, it was accepted that there should be a minimum of Treasury direction in the work of the C&AG.

The Green Paper also signalled an important step forward by confirming that, as well as continuing to examine the efficiency and economy of public expenditure, the C&AG should 'in appropriate cases ... investigate the effectiveness of programmes and projects in meeting established policy goals'. This reflected the Treasury's awareness of growing concerns from the mid-1970s that, given the massive sums and long timescales involved, there was a serious lack of parliamentary accountability for the management and outcome of government spending programmes. Criticisms had focused on three key aspects: the lack of published measures on policy and programme objectives; inadequate information and analysis of performance in meeting those objectives; and, as the E&AD had already recognized, the need for more direct audits of effectiveness to carry forward the existing examinations of economy and efficiency. The cautious wording of the Green Paper confirmed the Treasury's continuing concern that audit was not to trespass on policy issues. This caution was later addressed in the drafting of the National Audit Act 1983.

The PAC responded to the Green Paper by conducting its own inquiry in 1981. The evidence confirmed that the changes outlined in the Green Paper did not go far enough for the PAC or for some of its witnesses. One of the most vocal witnesses, with particularly strong views, was once again John Garrett, who had lost his parliamentary seat in the 1979 victory of the Thatcher government and had returned to being a management consultant specializing in the public sector.[64] As a well-known critic of both the Treasury and the C&AG he repeated some of his now familiar criticisms before the PAC. For example, in direct contrast to the PAC's own view only two years before, he continued to maintain that the close association between the C&AG and the Treasury had undermined the substance and confused the appearance of the C&AG's independence. He insisted, again without providing firm evidence, that this relationship had deprived the C&AG of both the motivation and the ability to improve the accountability of the Executive to Parliament. Historically, he believed that Gladstone had intended that the C&AG should be an officer of the House of Commons but that this had been subverted along the way.[65]

---

[63] Cmnd 7845, para. 64.
[64] Garrett was a member of the Fabian Society and in 1972 had published a text *The Management of Government*.
[65] PAC, 1981, Appendix IV, p. 9.

From his time as an adviser to the Fulton Committee, Garrett had been also a persistent advocate of the need for better accountability for departmental performance. He wanted public sector accounts that showed quantified objectives for departmental programmes and published measures of achievements, validated by the C&AG. His frustration over the lack of direct examinations of effectiveness by the C&AG had previously led him to announce in Parliament: 'Over the past 100 years Honourable Members have eulogised our system of state audit. . . . It does a very useful job within its limitations, but these limitations are now so scandalously great that they constitute a major constitutional weakness.'[66] Garrett argued in his evidence to the PAC in 1981 that, under the influence of Treasury directions, public sector accounts continued to be obfuscatory, uninformative, and useless for management planning and control.[67] He concluded that there was certainly nothing in the appropriation accounts that could be used to judge the efficiency or the effectiveness of departments in administrating major expenditure programmes.

The subsequent PAC report did not accept the limitations on audit coverage suggested by the government. It recommended instead that the C&AG be given access to the accounts of all bodies that were substantially supported by public sector funds, including the nationalized industries.[68] In welcoming the Green Paper's acceptance of possible new funding arrangements for the E&AD, the PAC envisaged that this should be carried forward by the formation of an autonomous non-departmental audit office funded by a separate vote by the House of Commons. To oversee this new office, to be called the National Audit Office, and the new financing arrangements, the PAC advocated the creation of a Public Accounts Commission from the House of Commons, which would take the place of the Treasury and the Civil Service Department in setting budgets, appointing audit staff, and determining their conditions of employment.[69] The Commission would be Parliament's means of ensuring the provision of the resources and the freedom necessary for the discharge of the C&AG's responsibilities, free from Executive control, and the ability to extend and strengthen the accountability of all public sector agencies. The PAC's overwhelming conclusion following its 1981 examination of the government's Green Paper was that:

> present legislation is out of date and does not reflect the nature of the audit at present carried out by the Comptroller and Auditor General. More importantly, it is essential to make statutory provision for a framework of public audit in this country sufficient to ensure accountability to Parliament for the wider range of public expenditure now and in the future.[70]

---

[66] HC debates, 9 December 1976.   [67] PAC, 1981, Appendix IV, p. 9.
[68] PAC 1981, para. 8.10.   [69] PAC 1981, para. 8.14.   [70] PAC 1981, para. 8.1.

Despite the strength of the PAC's recommendations, the government in July 1981 excluded any general extension of the C&AG's mandate to agencies other than those covered by existing legislation. They considered the existing legislation sufficient to deal with any desirable changes. Audit reform was certainly not one of the government's priorities. Nevertheless, the C&AG's possible audit involvement with nationalized industries, local authorities, and areas of wider access in the public and private sectors remained an issue of continuing debate. With nationalized industries and other public corporations, the suggestion was that the C&AG might carry out examinations of value for money and other aspects of financial management, but it was no longer proposed that the C&AG should become the appointed external auditor of their accounts. The latter had been rejected by the then C&AG Sir Frank Tribe when the nationalized industries were being set up in the late 1940s, mainly because of the extra staffing that would be required and the need for commercial auditing experience. The main reasons advanced for justifying C&AG access were: the need for better parliamentary accountability for a significant part of the public sector; the ultimate dependence of the public corporations on Exchequer credit; Treasury control of their borrowing powers; and, in some cases, the potential need for substantial subsidies from the taxpayer. The government countered with the less than convincing argument that there was some accountability to Parliament by means other than audit by the C&AG, that there could also be investigations by the Monopolies and Mergers Commission. Ironically, the C&AG was later able to carry out a very successful series of examinations and reports into privatization of nationalized industries because these had a direct impact on public funds.

Timing and the government's own agenda for change were also barriers to any agreement that the audit of local government should be brought under the C&AG. Whatever the merits of the arguments for or against such involvement, by the early 1980s the government itself was urgently introducing a range of measures to hold down local authority expenditure and reduce the high levels of support grants from central funds. The responsible Minister, Michael Heseltine, decided that one of these measures should be to replace the District Audit Service with a new and more powerful Audit Commission, with extended powers to examine and report on value for money and efficiency.[71] This was done in the Local Government Finance Act 1982. In this situation, with a new audit regime being established and developing its work, there was no need to involve the C&AG, other than to cooperate with the Commission in various areas of joint interest. Under the legislation the C&AG was appointed as the Commission's auditor and was able to report to the PAC on its work.

[71] Thatcher, 1993, p. 643.

Conclusion

From the mid-1970s the E&AD embarked upon a major programme to revise audit methodology on both certification audit and value-for-money examinations, to improve training, strengthen controls on budgets, introduce better planning for annual programmes of work across the Department as a whole, and identify challenges and opportunities in the longer term. These were given added impetus following the recommendations of the 1978 Management Review. Opportunities were also taken to establish a more consultative relationship with departments and other audited bodies, and to extend the E&AD's contacts with professional bodies, both nationally and internationally.

A major influence on the E&AD's work was the series of initiatives to improve management across government departments, including the introduction of a growing range of non-departmental bodies to deal with functions and services that were no longer the direct responsibility of departments. Changes in management objectives and style, greater delegation of decision making, and wider freedoms meant that the E&AD would need to respond constructively to the cultural and operational changes involved, while maintaining the emphasis on the special requirements inherent in the proper conduct of public business and the use of public funds.

The expectation that the C&AG should be empowered 'to follow public money wherever it goes', though well-intentioned, was too simplistic to provide a clear way forward when so many different bodies and circumstances were increasingly involved. It would have brought together a wide range of organizations, at home and overseas, in the public and private sector, with different objectives and operating frameworks and with a variety of relationships with central government. There were in practice many different forms of public money, generally undefined but including direct grants or grants in aid, reliance on Exchequer credit, various kinds of guarantees, and other forms of explicit or implicit support. As a result it was not clear how far auditors should be expected to go in their investigations, whether it would extend to companies involved in providing supplies and services under government contracts of different types, and when 'public money' stopped being 'public money' as it filtered downwards in these varying circumstances. Nor was it clear what practical benefits there would be from an unfettered extension of the C&AG's existing fields of examination, given that the E&AD had over the years established rights of access and inspection by agreement with many of these bodies, particularly the larger and more important ones.

As the field of audit extended there was growing concern over the need for independent assurances on broader issues of propriety and the proper conduct of public business, particularly in organizations where such issues were not necessarily familiar and well-recognized. An important step to clarify public money for the purposes of accountability and audit, including the C&AG's access, would later be taken in the report 'Holding to Account' in February 2001 by Lord Sharman of Redlynch. These and other emerging issues could not be resolved by negotiation and agreement. Instead, it was becoming increasingly clear that only new legislation would provide a way forward and clarify matters in the interests of both the E&AD and departments and other bodies subject to its audit. There was already acceptance within government that the time had come to free the C&AG from Treasury controls on E&AD staffing and budgets, and to provide statutory authority for a widening range of economy, efficiency, and effectiveness examinations. The challenges and opportunities to be faced in the 1980s and for the foreseeable future could not be dealt with satisfactorily under legislation framed in 1866 and 1921. This was the genesis of the National Audit Act 1983.

10

The National Audit Office

'Cease to dwell on days gone by, and to brood over past history. Here and now I will do a new thing. This moment it will break i' the bud.'

Isaiah, 43:18–19, New English Bible

By the early 1980s it was recognized that the original provisions in the 1866 and 1921 Audit Acts needed to be re-examined and brought up to date. Any new legislation would supplement the 1866 and 1921 Audit Acts rather than replace them. The earlier legislation remained the statutory authority for what was still the Comptroller and Auditor General's (C&AG) largest area of responsibility—the financial and regularity audit of departmental appropriation accounts, revenue, and stores accounts. The aims of the National Audit Act 1983 were ambitious.[1] The 1983 Act provided vital statutory support for the changes taking place in the responsibilities and work of the C&AG and the major developments to come in the next two decades and beyond. It had an impact well beyond its length by being carefully drafted to address the specific issues identified to carry through the changes that had been taking place following the Management Review.

The developments in the management and conduct of the C&AG's work before and after the 1983 Act, together with the changes taking place in the wider public environment, raised concerns about maintaining the balance between National Audit Office (NAO) priorities, those of the Public Accounts Committee (PAC), and the expectations and concerns of departments and other audited bodies. There were also concerns about a growing political dimension in some of the fields that the NAO was examining. Further, the consequences of

---

[1] The full title was 'An Act to strengthen parliamentary control and supervision of expenditure of public money by making new provision for the appointment and status of the Comptroller and Auditor General, establishing a Public Accounts Commission and a National Audit Office and making new provision for promoting economy, efficiency and effectiveness in the use of such money by government departments and other authorities and bodies; to amend or repeal certain provisions of the Exchequer and Audit Departments Acts 1866 and 1921; and for connected purposes.'

devolution of financial and audit responsibilities to Scotland and Wales would need to be examined, as would implications of the abolition of the Audit Commission and the adoption of a completely different basis for the preparation of departmental accounts. Subsequent legislation revising the position and powers of the C&AG and the structure of the NAO would also introduce fundamental changes.

Initiating Reform

Although the Thatcher government had demonstrated no enthusiasm for audit reform and was not prepared to give the required legislation any priority in their already full legislative programme, the PAC and other parliamentary committees were not prepared to let the matter rest. In 1982 the influential Treasury and Civil Service Committee added its voice to the need for reform, warning that:

> Without the creation of a National Audit Office under ultimate parliamentary control . . . as the Public Accounts Committee propose, neither Parliament nor the country has adequate machinery independent of the executive with which to point out where inefficiencies in the executive lie so that they can be remedied. An audit largely controlled and influenced by the Treasury . . . is not sufficient for this purpose.[2]

Pressure for change was also growing from the expanding range and depth of the C&AG's audit from the late 1970s and further expected developments. In particular, it was becoming increasingly apparent that the time had come to put on a statutory basis the C&AG's authority to conduct value-for-money examinations. Developing more penetrating examinations into wider areas of economy and efficiency and, particularly, effectiveness, would inevitably put severe strains on the broad consensus between the E&AD, the Treasury, and departments about the boundaries of value-for-money examinations. Legislation would help to meet these concerns by clarifying responsibilities and rights, both for auditors and auditees. It was important, however, that any statutory provisions should provide clear authority for the C&AG to examine all of the 'three E's' of economy, efficiency, and effectiveness. In particular, it should not allow the spectre of questioning policy to inhibit in-depth examinations of effectiveness.

Irrespective of the increasing acceptance of the need for audit reform, the Conservative government's other legislative commitments meant that there was no realistic prospect that any priority would be given to these reforms.

---

[2] Treasury and Civil Service Committee, 1982, Third Report.

This changed with the success of Norman St John-Stevas, MP, in the annual ballot for Private Members Bills. Editor of the collected works of Walter Bagehot and 'historian, parliamentarian, constitutionalist and, in the best sense, showman',[3] Norman St John-Stevas was a long-standing advocate of stronger parliamentary accountability. As Leader of the House of Commons at the beginning of the first Thatcher administration he persuaded a sceptical Cabinet to take the landmark decision to set up the system of departmental select committees, announced in June 1979. Now returned to the back benches by 'the Blessed Margaret', his own wry Catholic term for the Prime Minister, he had secured a high place in the 1982 ballot for Private Members Bills and decided to introduce a measure to revise and strengthen the C&AG's role and powers. Not only did this reflect his interest in parliamentary accountability and in constitutional and historical developments, it also met the criteria for the type of Private Members Bill that experience showed had the best chance of passing through into statute. It was not controversial or party political but instead sought to amend current legislation in specific ways as a result of experience in the working of that legislation. Accordingly, it was unlikely to face government objection and could even gain its support. Senior E&AD staff worked closely at all stages with Norman St John-Stevas and the parliamentary draftsmen on the content and drafting of the Bill and were also available to provide continuing advice, including briefing on amendments and other matters arising in House of Commons debate as the Bill passed through the various legislative stages.

The Parliamentary Control of Expenditure (Reform) Bill was given its Second Reading in Standing Committee on 28 January 1983.[4] Aspects of the Bill had already been discussed with the Treasury during drafting, and the sponsors of the Bill had accepted some compromises, for example by limiting the scope for following public money. The Second Reading debate was dominated by arguments for and against powers for the C&AG to carry out examinations in the nationalized industries and public corporations. As already noted, the strength of the government's opposition had been made clear in its 1980 Green Paper and repeated in exchanges with the PAC and other Select Committees. Cabinet papers prepared for the Second Reading debate confirmed that the government remained completely opposed to extending C&AG examinations in these areas.[5] The responses from the Chief Secretary to the Treasury, Leon Brittan, made it clear that excluding the C&AG from examinations in the nationalized industries and public corporations was a non-negotiable condition on government support for any new legislation.

---

[3] Hennessy, 1990, p. 330.   [4] HC Debate, 28 January 1983, cc.1149–214.
[5] Memorandum by the Chancellor of the Exchequer, dated 17 January 1983, discussed at Cabinet on 19 January 1983.

On more general rights of access, the government was prepared to accept movement towards extending the field of audit but not to the extent proposed in the Bill. The government was not prepared to give the C&AG statutory rights of access to private companies and contractors receiving substantial public funds. The government, however, was prepared to accept statutory provisions giving the C&AG wider rights of access to other bodies mainly supported by public funds. Supporters of the Bill recognized that a general statutory right would clearly be stronger than the existing basis of agreements mainly negotiated case by case.

In contrast to the government's refusal to accept the proposals for the widest-ranging extensions to the C&AG's access rights, it was fully prepared to enhance the C&AG's operational independence by removing Treasury control of NAO funding, staff numbers, and conditions of service. The government was determined that with this greater freedom there should be a provision in the Act to ensure that the C&AG had 'complete discretion in the discharge of his functions'. Neither the PAC nor any other parliamentary body should have the power to direct the C&AG's work or require the C&AG to carry out particular examinations. Although it was right for the PAC to be involved in general discussions of the C&AG's planned programme of examinations, final decisions on individual examinations would remain entirely a matter for the C&AG. The C&AG would be made an officer of the House of Commons, not its servant subject to its direction, and would continue to report to the House of Commons rather than the PAC. If the government could not have a greater say in the work of the C&AG then neither would others, not even Parliament or its Select Committees. The Chief Secretary confirmed that the government would only accept 'a genuine independence and not the substitution of the direction of one body for that of another'.[6] Experience would show that it could be difficult to hold this purist line when faced with a PAC with determined views on priorities for value-for-money examinations, particularly when a high-profile issue emerged and the PAC wanted an early report.

There was also significant disagreement on procedures for choosing the C&AG. The Bill proposed that to recognize the C&AG's independence from government the appointee should be decided by the Chairman of the PAC and then approved by a vote of the House. The government pointed out, however, that such a procedure would be unconstitutional. The Crown appointment of the C&AG involved an address to the monarch, which meant that the provision of appropriate advice to the Crown was constitutionally a government responsibility.[7] The C&AG's special powers of access

[6] HC Debate, 28 January 1983, c.1182.   [7] HC Debate, 28 January 1983, c.1182.

meant that the choice of C&AG was also a matter of government concern on practical grounds. The Chief Secretary reminded Parliament that:

> Whatever the unique rights of access the C&AG has, the Government also have not a unique but a legitimate and strong interest in the appointment of the C&AG.... The Government's interest is that the C&AG has access to the papers of the Government's Departments...that include some highly sensitive papers...(and means)...that the Government has a substantial, although not exclusive, interest in his appointment.[8]

The government later accepted a statutory provision that strengthened the interests of the House of Commons in the appointment of the C&AG by replacing the informal consultation that had taken place for many years with a statutory requirement for the agreement of the Chairman of the PAC with the choice of C&AG.

The government did not oppose the Bill on its Second Reading. It recognized that there was a momentum for change that was in its interest to manage rather than oppose. The sponsors of the Bill also recognized that, given the reality that Private Members Bills were ultimately dependent on government support, there would need to be compromises for securing many of the improvements in accountability that they had set out to achieve. They too could see from the debate and other discussions that there were opportunities to negotiate valuable advances. On both sides, therefore, there was agreement to move forward to the committee stage, where residual difficulties with the Bill, now the National Audit Bill, could hopefully be resolved in detailed clause-by-clause discussion. So it proved, and the new National Audit Act was passed in 1983.

National Audit Act 1983

The Act provided that the C&AG was to be appointed by a motion to the House of Commons made by the Prime Minister, acting with the agreement of the Chairman of the PAC. This both formalized and strengthened the previous arrangements for appointment, which were based on informal discussions with the PAC Chairman. The 1983 Act also reaffirmed previous safeguards on salary, pension, and removal of the C&AG that were designed to underpin independence. It was finally and formally confirmed that the C&AG was an Officer of the House of Commons, which had previously, but wrongly, been assumed to be the position.

---

[8] HC Debate, 28 January 1983, c.1182.

The 1983 Act gave the C&AG wide-ranging powers to carry out examinations of the economy, efficiency and, notably, effectiveness with which resources had been used by bodies for which the C&AG was the appointed auditor.[9] The powers extended to bodies where there were rights of access and inspection by statute or by agreement and to other bodies mainly supported by public funds where the C&AG had 'reasonable cause to believe that any authority or body . . . has in any of its financial years received more than half its income from public funds'.[10] This was a standing authority; it did not require agreement case-by-case. This provision was later modified with the passage of the Government Resources and Accounts Act 2000. Recognizing concerns that effectiveness audit could come close to policy areas, the 1983 Act specifically provided that in all such examinations the C&AG was not 'entitled to question the merits of policy objectives'.[11] This was a carefully drafted provision, suggested by the E&AD, which was designed to alleviate Treasury and departmental concerns without significantly inhibiting the NAO's examinations.

Independence was significantly strengthened by taking the C&AG's budget and staffing from Treasury control, thus removing any lingering doubts that Treasury control of the purse strings could be used to control or influence the C&AG's audit. In future the budget was to be approved directly by the House of Commons after consideration by a new committee, the Public Accounts Commission (TPAC). The Chairman of the PAC was a member of the TPAC and was thus able to advise and reassure the Commission on the merits of the C&AG's operational proposals and the resources needed to carry them out. The staff of the NAO ceased to be civil servants and their numbers, grades, and salaries were to be determined by the C&AG, although having general regard to civil service terms. This provided welcome flexibility to recruit and retain the best staff.[12] The 1983 Act also removed the Treasury's power to direct the C&AG's audit on certain accounts. This power, originally under s.33 of the 1866 Act and then s.3 of the 1921 Act, had lingered from the Treasury's previous dominance over the Commissioners of Audit and was overdue for removal. Though much criticized over the years as in principle undermining the C&AG's independence, it had not inhibited audit criticism. Less satisfactory was a rather convoluted provision to give statutory rights of access and inspection to bodies where the C&AG was not the appointed auditor. This

---

[9] National Audit Act 1983, s.6(1).   [10] National Audit Act 1983, s.7(1).

[11] National Audit Act 1983, s.6(2) and 7(2).

[12] The C&AG's powers on budgets and staffing under the 1983 Act were at that time significantly greater than those of other Commonwealth audit offices still subject to Treasury constraints. The benefits of the staffing and budget provisions of the 1983 Act were later relied upon when some of those audit offices were pressing for comparable freedoms in their own legislation (see Australian Auditor General John Taylor in a presentation and accompanying paper in *Department of the Senate, Papers on Parliament Nr7* (March 1990).

provision was in some respects narrower and less flexible than the 'by agreement' basis on which such rights had previously been negotiated. Later some access rights came under challenge.

Assessments of effectiveness would involve examining a number of stages in the implementation of a policy, including whether:

- departments had set clear policy objectives for a programme or project that were expressed in terms that made it possible to measure performance and achievement;
- policy objectives had been translated into lower-level management objectives and communicated to and understood by those at working level;
- responsibilities were clearly allocated;
- relevant policy instruments had been introduced as the tools to carry forward the work;
- systems were in place for regular monitoring and review of progress, including timescales and costs;
- prompt action had been taken to deal with emerging problems;
- there had been unintended consequences; and
- activities and decisions of bodies such as local authorities, charities, and other bodies in the public or private sectors could impact upon, or be affected by, the government's programme.

Existing examinations directed at expenditure that was uneconomic, inefficient, wasteful, extravagant, irregular, or fraudulent already involved aspects of effectiveness. The boundary lines between these types of examinations and examinations of effectiveness are sometimes blurred with differences being matters of degree or even timing. Audit experience showed that in practice it was not particularly difficult to carry out penetrating examinations where policy issues were involved and to raise important questions and criticisms without crossing the final line of 'questioning the merits of policy objectives'.[13]

Although the statutory provision on effectiveness set limits on ventures into policy areas, and had to be handled carefully because of Treasury and departmental sensitivities, the broad terms used meant that there was generous scope for wide-ranging interpretation. The areas deemed acceptable for effectiveness examinations were referred to in statements and assurances on the operation of the statutory provisions given when the Bill was being discussed in Standing Committee. The views expressed demonstrated common ground between the sponsors of the Bill and the government on the main issues. It

[13] Dewar, 1991, pp. 95–102. See also articles by Sharkansky and Geist in the same publication.

was agreed that the C&AG could not say that the policy objectives set were wrong, nor attempt to specify what they should be. It was not, however, questioning the merits of policy to examine whether defined policy objectives had been set, to seek clarification of those objectives where necessary, and to examine the success of policy instruments introduced to implement those objectives. Effectiveness audit was therefore concerned with the extent to which a body, project, or programme achieved its stated objectives, not the merits or desirability of those objectives. Subject to these limitations, the PAC could be relied upon to support extending relevant audit coverage and depth. In some respects a more important danger was that some policy objectives could be very close to party politics, and the NAO's examinations and audit reports could, depending on the sensitivity of the programme or project involved, need to be careful not to threaten the PAC's bi-partisan approach.

The powers of effectiveness examination in the 1983 Act were significantly stronger than those in contemporary statutes for the national audit offices in some other countries. For example, in Canada the 1977 Auditor General Act limited the Auditor General to reporting on the adequacy of procedures in departments to measure and report on the effectiveness of programmes. There was no power to carry out direct examinations of actual results achieved. It was implicit in the Canadian Act that the government had primary responsibility to measure and report on the effectiveness of its programmes. In Australia the limitations went even further. Amending legislation in 1979 provided powers for examinations of efficiency but entirely excluded the Auditor General from considering issues of effectiveness in achieving programme objectives. Again this reflected concerns that external examinations of this kind would bring audit too close to policy issues, which were regarded as matters entirely for government. In time, some of these limitations would be eased by amending legislation. In a modern democracy in an increasingly complex world it was unrealistic to expect otherwise; the effectiveness of government spending and the need for it to be audited independently on behalf of Parliament are universal concerns.

The impact of all value-for-money examinations was significantly enhanced by s. 9(1) of the 1983 Act, which provided that reports on the results could be presented to Parliament throughout the year as examinations were completed, and not just with the annual accounts. This apparently simple provision was in practice a major stimulus to improving not only the timeliness and accessibility of reports but also, as lessons were learnt, did a great deal to improve the scope, quality, and penetration of the developing range of value-for-money examinations. Considerable efforts were made to improve drafting, readability, and impact as the reports were to become the single most important public demonstration of the NAO's work. More generally, the requirements flowing from a demanding programme of publishing around fifty major reports a year made a significant contribution to the new management and operational culture and the sense of priorities developing in the Office.

The National Audit Act undoubtedly introduced valuable changes in the C&AG's powers and fostered and underpinned important advances in the conduct of the audit. Some observers, however, have mistakenly seen it as the starting point for significant value-for-money examinations, or even the main reason for the C&AG's pre-eminent position in UK public sector audit. As established previously, modern value-for-money audit developed gradually over many years; it was not the product of a single event. Although the 1983 Act was building on foundations previously laid, it nevertheless strengthened the framework for further development by generating improved resources and clearing impediments to the NAO's work.

In a long overdue, early move to assist the NAO's future progress, the Public Accounts Commission approved funding for a new headquarters building. After considering various options it was decided to acquire the former Imperial Airways terminal in Buckingham Palace Road, Victoria, and refurbish it to meet the Office's specific requirements. The new headquarters was opened by Bernard Weatherill, Speaker of the House of Commons, in 1986. Although cohesion and style depend on people not places, the new building was an important factor in reinforcing the Office's corporate identity. More specifically, the provision of enhanced computer facilities, improved information systems, better central services, and easier communication and liaison within and between the audit divisions made a vital contribution to the wide-ranging changes being introduced and the efficiency with which they were pursued.

With audit staff no longer being civil servants, they were required to enter into fresh contracts of employment where relaxing the constraints of standard civil service pay scales and conditions of service permitted greater flexibility and incentives, with scope for a wider range of recruitment at more senior levels. A major departure from previous arrangements was the introduction of a weighted system of performance-related pay, with staff in the same grade able to earn significantly different salaries. This was based on a stringent system of job-by-job and annual assessments of individual staff performance.

The overall operational management of the Office was the responsibility of the Senior Management Group, chaired by the C&AG and including the Deputy C&AG and the four Assistant Auditors General (AAG). One AAG was responsible for human resources, staff training, finance and budgets, central planning, and common services. Each of the others headed a unit comprising a number of line audit divisions headed by Directors of Audit responsible for auditing specified departments and related bodies. The divisions were responsible for both financial accounts and the related regularity audits and value-for-money examinations. Increasingly, staff tended to specialize in one type of audit, given the growing requirements of compliance with detailed financial accounting standards and the widening scope and demands of value-for-money examinations. In time, specialization became standard practice.

To increase its own accountability, the Office started to publish annual reports on key features of its work and performance during the year. These included information on staffing and other costs, on progress and results on financial and regularity audits, and on the annual programme of fifty reports presented to Parliament on value-for-money examinations, as well as lower-level matters cleared directly with departments. The reports showed that estimated savings from efficiency gains and other benefits from the Office's work had increased steadily.

Treasury Response to Reform

The Treasury had been generally supportive of the provisions of the National Audit Bill as introduced by Norman St John-Stevas, though in return for government support it had sought changes in some of the specific provisions. The Treasury did not object to giving up its budgetary control of funding and staff numbers with a department as small and specialized as the NAO. There was the added advantage that the staff would no longer be included in civil servant numbers. The Treasury was also pleased to lose the little-used, but often criticized, powers they had under the 1921 Audit Act to issue directions to the C&AG on a miscellaneous range of accounts. It welcomed the clarification proposed on the role and status of the C&AG and their relationship with Parliament, and supported the statutory involvement of the Chairman of the PAC in the appointment of the C&AG, which strengthened what for many years had already happened informally.

Whilst recognizing that interpretation of the statutory provisions could ultimately be a matter for the courts, the Treasury issued a range of guidance to departments on these and other issues. The guidance included a degree of caution and some reservations on Treasury and departmental positions. A good deal of the guidance was directed towards how departments should handle examinations touching on policy issues, and how to respond to examinations in a variety of second- and third-tier bodies below main departmental level that received grants and other support from public funds. Although the prospect of examinations of effectiveness had initially caused concern within the Treasury and departments, in practice there were only isolated problems and disagreements. This was partly due to agreement in Standing Committee on the basic approach to be taken, and the NAO being careful to avoid potential difficulties and sensitivities when setting the scope and conduct of examinations and reporting the results.

One of the issues that did emerge as the provisions of the 1983 Act were implemented was the need to take into account potential conflicts between policy objectives. In a modern, complex society, expenditure programmes may have a range of objectives, some stated and some implicit or corollary. Some may involve different financial impacts on, or other disadvantages to, different groups affected. Others bring in more general factors. For example, a 1988 NAO examination of road safety pointed out that although the regulations for the use of seat belts applied at the time only to front-seat passengers, accident statistics disclosed serious risks also to rear-seat passengers not required to use seat belts. Clearly this did not question the merits of the primary policy objective of improving road safety. Still, the Department of Transport objected on behalf of their minister, who regarded any reference to the absence of requirements for wearing rear seat belts, and the attendant risks, as questioning a second-order policy objective of 'preserving individual freedom of choice'. The immediate issue was resolved by changes in drafting and regulations were later altered to make the wearing of seat belts compulsory for all passengers. In any non-totalitarian state a balance will often need to be struck between policy objectives directed primarily towards financial and operational outcomes and those involving more general, but important, factors in and around such 'soft' areas as personal freedoms, choice, and civil liberties. It is the responsibility of government to decide the most acceptable approach in reconciling potential conflicts between policy objectives, and it is the job of the auditor to recognize the complexities in the planning, conduct, and reporting of examinations.

Maintaining and Extending Audit Access

By the 1990s the provisions in the 1983 Act to protect the C&AG's rights of access and inspection to publicly funded bodies where he was not the appointed auditor were coming under increasing strain. Pressures were coming from two directions: first, to maintain in full the rights already in existence and, second, to ensure that similar rights were secured for the diverse range of new bodies involved in the growing disengagement and dispersal of departmental functions, including developments in such areas as contracting out. Different forms of support and partnership were in some cases blurring what constituted 'public' funds and resources.

Throughout the 1990s there was continuing departmental concern over the widening range and penetration of the C&AG's examinations and reports, particularly on economy, efficiency, and effectiveness. These were moving into programmes, projects, and issues that were close to the heart of key departmental operations and were raising important criticisms. Changes in the relationships between departments and some of the bodies they sup-ported, and in the status, responsibilities, objectives, and management of the bodies themselves, were being used by the Treasury or departments to question whether it was still appropriate to accept the full scope of examin-ations envisaged under previous access agreements, with some attempts to withdraw existing rights of access. Different types of organizations, in both the public and private sector, were becoming involved in spending pro-grammes and with varied relationships with the relevant departments. There were questions about whether the C&AG should be the appointed auditor of some of these bodies, or what degree of audit access was appropriate in these varying circumstances. This in turn brought further complications where bodies or their subsidiaries were operating under the Companies Acts, where the C&AG was not at that time eligible to audit.

Examinations were regarded by some Accounting Officers and Principal Finance Officers as pushing beyond what they and the Treasury had originally expected to be the boundaries of the NAO's statutory remit under the 1983 Act. The spectre of the NAO questioning policy was again being raised as departments found that NAO reports were able to focus on and identify significant areas and issues. In particular, they did not like the higher press profile of the reports nor, most especially, the enthusiastic and, at times, aggressive PAC follow-up. It was known that such issues became at times a regular item for anguished discussion at the weekly meetings of Accounting Officers.[14]

The NAO initiated a number of measures to tackle these emerging worries and to allay Treasury and departmental concerns. Regular meetings were held between NAO senior management and groups of Principal Finance Officers from the larger departments, together with the Treasury. These were designed not only to respond to emerging departmental concerns but also to give early warning of developments in the NAO's work and to obtain departmental views. Meetings were also held with individual Accounting Officers and their finance staff to discuss the forward programme of work in their area, including the rationale underlying the scope, content, and timing of proposed examinations. Further discussions at the outset of individual studies explained the objectives and methods of the main stages of the work, and issues and findings were cleared periodically as the examination progressed. Throughout these different levels of discussion a careful line had to be drawn between responding positively to departmental concerns, suggestions, and counter-proposals, and maintaining the NAO's independence and freedom of action.

---

[14] Private conversation with an Accounting Officer.

There could be no question of seeking departmental approval for the NAO's programme of work, or the nature, scale, or content of individual examinations and the content of the resulting reports.

A more specific departmental worry was how far and in what detail they were expected to 'agree' the C&AG's reports before publication. For many years departments had been asked to confirm that E&AD reports were 'a fair summary of the relevant facts'. This had caused few difficulties since these reports were generally brief and factual, and contained little overt analysis or conclusions. The position was much more complicated with the newer style of C&AG's reports, which dealt with wider-ranging and more complex subjects. The reports also analysed issues where evidence and findings could be less clear-cut and where there was scope for different interpretations or conclusions. The PAC had always expected Accounting Officers to have fully agreed the reports with the C&AG in order to avoid significant and time-wasting disputes over wording when the Committee was attempting to complete its examination within a normal two-hour session. Departments felt, however, also with some justification, that it was unrealistic to expect them to agree to virtually every detail of the different kinds of reports now being produced. These concerns were highlighted by the 'Hancock' affair.

When appearing before the PAC in 1986 Sir David Hancock, Permanent Secretary at the Department of Education, mentioned at an early stage in the proceedings that he did not accept a particular passage in the C&AG's report. He was immediately challenged by PAC Chairman Robert Sheldon on whether he had or had not agreed the report when it was being prepared. Hancock maintained that the passage concerned was expressing the view of C&AG Sir Gordon Downey and was not therefore something that the Accounting Officer was required to comment upon or correct. Irritated by what he saw as an evasion and a suspicion that Hancock was 'playing to the Whitehall gallery', Sheldon immediately suspended the session and instructed Hancock and Downey to clarify the position in a further paper to the Committee. An agreed joint note was submitted to the Committee at a subsequent session and the examination of the report was completed without further trouble. The exchanges at the PAC, and the Committee's insistence that Accounting Officers should not question the accuracy of the C&AG's reports when giving evidence, meant that departments immediately began to look even harder at the detailed wording of draft reports being cleared with the NAO. The resulting delays in clearance were to become a significant problem, with some complex reports taking many weeks to clear. Despite these difficulties, clearance nevertheless remained an important contribution to making reports better by considering legitimate departmental views, not only on accuracy and completeness but also on fairness and balance in presentation.

Responding to New Demands

Sharman Report

The 2001 report 'Holding to Account' by Lord Sharman of Redlynch reviewed a range of issues on audit and accountability for central government. The report recommended the need to pursue strong systems of internal control in departments, to ensure well-resourced and independent internal audit, and to introduce formally constituted audit committees with independent outside members. The report also emphasized the importance of continuing to improve risk management, with more research needed into the benefits of incentives and rewards. There were recommendations to encourage innovation and change and to foster 'joined up' working within and between departments. The report also commended the move towards regular performance reporting by departments, with the external validation of key published data to assure Parliament and the public that published information was reliable.

Sharman recommended that, as a matter of principle, the C&AG should be appointed the auditor, on behalf of Parliament, of all non-departmental public bodies. The provisions of the Government Resources and Accounts Act 2000 were to be used to allow this to happen as existing audit contracts expired. Consideration should also be given to removing the then present obstacles to the ability of the C&AG to be appointed as an auditor under the Companies Act. This would significantly widen the range of publicly funded bodies, or bodies supported by departments in other ways, where the C&AG would then be eligible to be the appointed auditor. The necessary legislation was later provided in the Companies Act 2006. However, it has taken time for a significant number of bodies to be brought within the C&AG's audit. The Sharman Report saw strong grounds for formalizing many of the C&AG's rights of access and inspection, which were based on negotiated agreements or convention. Access should be made statutory in appropriate cases, using existing legislation. The Report also recommended that the C&AG should have statutory rights of access to bodies such as grant recipients, registered social landlords, train operating companies, and private finance initiative contractors. Possibly the most controversial recommendation was that, unless there were strong arguments to the contrary, the C&AG should also be given rights of access to the BBC.

Recognizing the importance of making the most of audit activity, the Report suggested that public auditors should be involved in government-wide reviews, with further development of high-level overview reports by the NAO and the PAC to draw lessons from reports on similar subjects. (A similar issue was previously raised in the US.[15]) The Report further suggested that the

---

[15] Concerns on the need for more across-the-board examinations were being voiced by the US General Accounting Office (now the Government Accountability Office) in the early 1980s.

NAO should publicize its findings in a wide range of ways in addition to its published reports. The C&AG should also be provided with the resources to brief other Select Committees annually on significant financial issues, without in any way undermining the key relationship between the NAO and the PAC. In this same context the government subsequently invited the C&AG to validate departmental data systems used in reporting on performance against Public Service Agreement targets, as a further step towards improving parliamentary accountability.

The recommendations of the Sharman Report made a valuable contribution not only to stronger departmental financial controls but also to continuing developments in the C&AG's role and remit. The emphasis on relationships with departments and other audited bodies, and on closer involvement with the private sector accountancy and audit profession, sought to strengthen the contributions of the C&AG at a time of great change for the accountability of governments. The government accepted nearly all the recommendations of the report in May 2002.

Environmental Auditing

Sharman also referred to the strong interest of the Environment Select Committee in having the C&AG carry out a programme of environmental audits, with the reports being considered by that Committee rather than by the PAC. From the late 1980s to the early 1990s there had been a deliberate movement into NAO examination of environmental issues. Fifteen reports were produced, supported by discussion papers and other material linked with participation in outside 'green' conferences.[16] However, environmental auditing was then less actively pursued. Sharman noted that the suggestion that subsequent environmental audit reports might be pursued by the Environmental Select Committee rather than the PAC represented a potential clash of interest between the two Select Committees. Coincidentally, a more flexible attitude was emerging that would in time lead to closer and more regular NAO relationships with Select Committees other than the PAC. The appointment of a new PAC Chairman in 2001 led to a more relaxed view on the respective

The GAO had recognized a similar gap in its own work and had begun a programme of examinations under the heading of 'General Management Reviews'. Such work was pursued separately from, but supplemented, the GAO's ongoing program reviews. Assessing the benefits of this work, Charles Bowsher, head of the GAO stated that:

> The General Management Reviews are challenging the GAO to think more broadly about the systemic barriers to government management improvement. The more narrow program reviews were not conducive to assessing agency general management and generally did not stimulate efforts within the GAO to look for cross-cutting management issues and common lessons learned. (Bowsher, 1991, p. 368)

[16] See Dewar, 1991.

boundary lines, a change that was actively supported by both the Public Accounts Commission and the House Liaison Committee. Greater flexibility later resulted in the introduction of arrangements for the NAO to provide expert advice to the Environmental Audit Select Committee as part of an extensive programme of work on their behalf, including seconding staff and preparing research and briefing papers. Similar advice and assistance was subsequently provided to the Select Committee on Energy and Climate Change. In the period 2003–14 the NAO produced eighty-two environmental audit reports, including related briefings, compared with twenty-eight reports in the period 1993–2002.[17]

Reporting Practices

Though the contents of final reports to the House of Commons were statutorily matters for the C&AG, it had always been recognized that discussion of drafts with departments helped to ensure that final reports were complete, accurate, fair, and balanced. Having reports cleared in this way also helped more efficient examinations of Accounting Officers by the PAC. In this process it had always been important to strike a balance between responding to legitimate views by departments and avoiding delays that put reporting deadlines at risk and disrupted plans for a steady flow of reports to Parliament. In more recent years the need for prompt clearance has increased, partly because of the increasing pace of business but also with the growing concern of the PAC to ensure immediacy and impact in their examinations, including the ability to respond quickly to emerging and high-profile events. To achieve this, a broader and less detailed clearance process has been progressively introduced, with timing a priority and any significant unresolved matters being dealt with as necessary during PAC examination. As a result, the average clearance time for reports approved for publication was reduced in 2013–14 to seven weeks. Overall examination times were also reduced, with 74 per cent of reports being delivered within nine months of the commencement of examinations, and 35 per cent within six months.[18]

Relationship with Departments

Throughout the transformation of the public sector the implications for audit and accountability meant that the E&AD and then the NAO had from the outset maintained a close interest in the fundamental changes in

---

[17] Details of environmental audits worldwide, analysed by country, are collected and published by the INTOSAI Working Group on Environmental Auditing, of which the UK is a member.
[18] NAO 2013–14 Annual Accounts and Report, HC 170, Session 2014–15, 9 June 2014.

management objectives, operating methods, and financial control and information systems being introduced in departments, agencies, and other bodies. Over time, as part of the NAO's agreed improvement mandate, liaison with departments and other bodies on a range of aspects of financial management has developed into a more direct provision of advocacy, advice, and assistance, particularly on questions of accountability. By 2015 the NAO had been engaged for many years on this continuing programme of improvement support, as confirmed in its annual Strategy Reviews and with separate funding within its approved budgets. In 2013–14 the NAO produced twenty reports on the results of this work, together with a further eighty-five good practice guides and seventeen reports on data systems. This responsive policy and more direct involvement with departments was carefully managed so as to avoid prejudicing audit independence.

As delivery of departmental programmes and services was increasingly devolved from the centre to second- and third-tier bodies, and particularly to the private sector, under a variety of contractual and non-contractual arrangements, the C&AG's rights of access and inspection and reporting had also been progressively reviewed and extended, either by agreement or by legislation. With these changes there have been recurring suggestions that those rights of access should be further extended to give the C&AG a general right to 'follow public money wherever it goes'.

'Following Public Money'

It has always been accepted that there is a point where 'public' money could no longer reasonably be regarded as public and the C&AG's rights of access would not apply. The difficulty has been to decide clearly where that point should be, given the different circumstances and arrangements under which funds are distributed and expenditure incurred. The position was complicated by the lack of a mutually accepted definition of what constitutes public money. Sometimes public funds were intermingled with private funds or funds provided by other donors and the line of C&AG audit access was therefore blurred. In this situation the risk of potential objections was addressed by NAO assurances that the purpose of access was primarily directed to higher-level accountability by looking back up the spending chain to the monitoring and other responsibilities of the funding bodies, rather than direct critical examination of the activities and expenditures of the lower-tier bodies and grant recipients.

On contracts with industry, pressure for more access and accountability was frequently met with reluctance by the companies concerned on the grounds of commercial confidentiality. However, progress was made with the publication in March 2014 of the PAC's 47th Report of Session 2013–14 on 'Contracting out Public Services to the Private Sector' (HC77). The Report examined a number of serious failures in government control over the increasing volume of business placed with contractors for a wide range of services, including four large contracts reported on by the C&AG. The PAC concluded that there was a far greater need for transparency in government, Parliament, and the public, and recommended measures to ensure that the C&AG had adequate rights of access to contractors. The Committee also made a number of other recommendations to tighten systems of monitoring and control within departments and other bodies in the placing and management of contracts. After the PAC had taken evidence, but shortly before publication of its report, the Confederation of British Industry (CBI) on 5 March 2014 issued its own report on these matters, including a parallel recommendation that the NAO should be able to audit government contracts with the private sector.[19] A further meeting between the Cabinet Office, the CBI, and senior industry representatives on 1 May 2014 confirmed a strong and united backing for all necessary measures in order to strengthen audit and accountability. This was part of the ongoing debate on the extent to which companies dealing with government should be expected to recognize a duty of care to the taxpayer. Here the position of the contracting industry has changed significantly; they now accept the notion of a duty of care and the need for transparency on cost and performance, with a line of accountability to Parliament. The work of the NAO has an important part to play in helping to carry forward these developments.

Competition and Contracting Out

The exclusive authority given to public sector audit at both national and local level has often attracted the criticism that it is never subject to the discipline and stimulus of competition. This encouraged suggestions that private sector alternatives could provide important benefits, particularly the larger accountancy and management consultancy firms. A preference for the private sector over the public sector was motivated by political ideology, rather than being based on any close appraisal of the respective skills and experience of public sector and private sector auditors. There are special demands in the accountability and audit of public funds and other resources in the highly regulated environment of government operations and parliamentary business, most especially when handling sensitive or secret government material. There is also the expectation of rigorous confidentiality when dealing with matters related to personal and company taxation.

---

[19] Confirmed in a government press release issued 2 May 2014.

Despite similar, but less significant, concerns at local government level, the Thatcher government in 1983 decided to replace the local government District Audit Service with a new Audit Commission, which was required to contract out a significant proportion of audits, including value-for-money examinations, to the private sector. In 2010 the government announced proposals to abolish the Audit Commission altogether, which was accomplished with the Local Audit and Accountability Act 2014. The Act gave local authorities, police authorities, and local health bodies the right to choose their own auditors and established a new decentralized audit regime. The Financial Reporting Council would become the primary regulator within the new framework and the NAO would prepare and maintain a Code of Audit Practice and associated guidance to auditors. The NAO also has powers to report on the operation of the Code, and associated matters.

The compulsory introduction of private sector accountancy into local government audit in order to provide greater competition was not extended to central government audit, for a number of reasons. The E&AD was a stronger, more influential, and independent organization than the Audit Commission and, given past history, the imposition of government requirements on the C&AG would inevitably have been contentious. As already noted, shortly before the election of the Thatcher government in 1979 the management review set up by C&AG Sir Douglas Henley had completed a major examination of all aspects of E&AD management and the conduct of audit, leading to many improvements being introduced. Importantly, the review and the consequent changes had the participation and support of the Executive in the form of the Treasury, the Civil Service Department, the Government Accounting Adviser, and a departmental Accounting Officer, as well as accountants from the private sector. At the same time, there was a growing recognition within the Executive and Parliament of the need for statutory changes that was to lead to the 1983 Audit Act. Clearly this was not the time for a fundamental transfer of C&AG responsibilities to the private sector. It was also recognized that the C&AG and his staff had from 1866 provided a well-established, effective, and trusted single source of support and advice for the PAC, whereas there would be a large number of different points of contact if the audit was to be dispersed amongst several providers. Any contracting out of work to the private sector was therefore left to the discretion of the C&AG.

Contracting out of selected individual audits or particular examinations, in whole or in part, by the NAO to the private sector, with the NAO retaining overall control or supervision and responsibility for reports to Parliament, has provided a bridge over an unnecessary public sector/private sector divide and secured the advantages of both public and private sector skills and experience. Developments of this kind have significantly increased in recent years as part of a continuing process of drawing upon outside resources and special skills to control the level of staff numbers within the NAO itself and to target in-house resources on core NAO activities rather than setting up specialist units within the Office. Specialist skills that might be needed on the most complex or demanding examinations would be accessed from the market.

Devolution

When greater legal and financial autonomy was devolved to the Scottish Parliament in 1998 the post of Auditor General for Scotland was created and the Public Finance and Accountability (Scotland) Act 2000 set out the Auditor General's formal position, powers, and responsibilities for the audit of expenditure on functions devolved to the Scottish Parliament. The Act also set out in extensive detail the framework of departmental accountability within which the Auditor General would work. These arrangements applied also to Audit Scotland, which was established to carry out the audit of accounts and value-for-money examinations on the Auditor General's behalf. In many respects, except for some matters arising from constitutional differences, these provisions were similar to those applicable to the C&AG. The Auditor General's reports to the Scottish Parliament are similarly considered by the Scottish Public Audit Committee. The audit of Scottish local government expenditure remained the responsibility of the Audit Commission, also carried out on the Commission's behalf by Audit Scotland. The audit of expenditure on reserved functions not devolved to Scotland, in general those with a UK-wide or international impact—including defence, foreign affairs, central government taxation, and social security—remain the responsibility of the C&AG.

In Wales, the accounts of the Welsh Assembly and its sponsored bodies are audited by the Auditor General for Wales, created by the Government of Wales Act 1998 and reporting to the Audit Committee of the Welsh Assembly. The Wales Audit Office was established in 2005 under the Public Audit (Wales) Act to take over the responsibilities of the Audit Commission and the NAO in respect of expenditure controlled by the Welsh Assembly. The C&AG retains access rights to the Welsh Assembly and public bodies in Wales for the purposes of reporting to Parliament.

Accrual Accounting and Resource Accounts

The merits of preparing departmental accounts on an accruals basis rather than a cash basis had been considered at various times since at least 1917. The trial introduction of accrual accounts for the Army on an experimental basis in the period 1919–25 incurred heavy costs for little benefit. As a result it was abandoned and appropriation accounts on a cash basis were reintroduced. A detailed debate on the advantages and disadvantages of accrual accounts for government departments emerged again in the late 1990s. As before, the matters raised covered general issues arising from fundamental differences between the objectives, functions, and priorities of government programmes and services and those of private sector manufacturing and trading entities where accrual accounts were most obviously relevant. There were also concerns about the subjectivity and inevitably high costs, both initially and subsequently, of moving to an entirely different and more complex system, most especially whether existing departmental financial records, asset registers, and accounting systems were sufficiently strong and reliable to meet the extra demands.[20]

An important argument put forward for accrual accounting was the ability to match departmental activities within an accounting period with the full costs incurred on those activities, including the capital and other resources involved. This would improve completeness and transparency. It was maintained that accrual accounts would encourage closer financial control of non-cash and, therefore, less obvious costs. Other advantages claimed included better allocation of scarce resources, improved asset management, and more safeguards against such dangers as retention and maintenance of surplus or redundant assets. It was also claimed that there would be more general benefits from improved financial and accounting disciplines, and that there would be a welcome shift in focus from inputs to outputs. Some argued that accrual accounting would significantly improve internal and external accountability, while others saw risks in unnecessarily complicating an existing system that was simple, long-standing, and well-understood, particularly when there was no clear or compelling pressure or priority for change.

The Government Resources and Accounts Act 2000 overrode objections about accrual accounting by introducing resource (accrual)-based accounting and budgeting for all departmental accounts, to be audited by the C&AG. The Act also provided for the preparation of consolidated accounts for the whole public sector, also to be audited by the C&AG. These 'Whole of Government Accounts', the largest consolidation of public sector accounts in the world, were introduced to provide a more comprehensive picture of the public expenditure and the financial position across the whole of the UK public sector.[21] In contrast to some earlier expectations from accrual accounting, a later NAO examination has confirmed that:

> while resource accounting and budgeting was intended to help government move away from a focus on the annual expenditure cycle towards longer-term strategic

---

[20] The number of qualified accountants in UK central government rose from 600 in 1989 to 2,200 in 2003.

[21] C&AG Report, HC 849, Session 2015–16, p. 41, para. 2.5.

planning and focus on the balance sheet, in fact much of the accountability for government's financial performance still focuses on a retrospective view of annual expenditure, rather than the financial position and management of assets and liabilities.[22]

The preparation of accounts on an accruals basis, and the requirement that they should present a 'true and fair view', significantly changed the basis of the C&AG's audit and required consequential amendments to the accounting and audit provisions of the Exchequer and Audit Departments Acts 1866 and 1921 and of the National Audit Act 1983.

NAO Corporate Governance and Independence

The attention of Select Committees, Parliament more generally, the press, and the public had always focused on the C&AG's audit responsibilities, the work carried out, and the reports and other results produced. Except during the passage of the National Audit Act in 1983, there was little interest or concern over the conduct of internal NAO business, management, and relationships, other than individual aspects that might arise in budget discussions with the Public Accounts Commission. This changed in 2007. Following a Freedom of Information request from the satirical magazine *Private Eye*, the NAO released information on expenses claimed by C&AG Sir John Bourn showing that for the three years from April 2004 he had incurred expenses of £365,000, mainly on international travel, and hospitality expenses of £27,000 over the same period. This disclosure was pursued widely by the press, not only because of the nature and size of the amounts involved but also because expenses at that level were seen as conflicting with the C&AG's 'public watchdog' role of curbing extravagance in public spending.

Concerns were also raised in Parliament, involving particularly the members of the Public Accounts Commission. Although the expenses concerned were funded from the NAO resource budget, voted by Parliament on the recommendation of the Commission, the Commission was quick to point out that the 'C&AG's decisions to incur expenditure from the resource budget are not subject to approval by staff of the National Audit Office, of which the C&AG is the head, nor by the Treasury'. The Commission acknowledged, however, that the disclosures now raised were within its field of responsibility and in July 2007 it confirmed that steps had been taken to establish new procedures for reviewing the C&AG's expenses. These include the requirement

---

[22] C&AG Report, HC 849, Session 2015–16, p. 41, para. 2.5.

that the NAO will provide every six months a report of actual expenditures, audited externally.[23]

The Commission also reported that there was to be a wider review of the NAO's corporate governance. Stronger corporate governance had become increasingly recognized as an important means of better controlling the dominant power of a sole executive head of, or a small group within, an organization, whilst maintaining probity and propriety, the effective management and conduct of its business, and the proper discharge of its responsibilities. Targeted initially at larger companies and organizations in the private sector, it had become increasingly recognized that there were valuable lessons to be transferred to bodies in the public sector. In July 2005 the Treasury had for the first time issued a code of practice, *Corporate Governance in Central Government Departments*, to be applied where appropriate to other bodies. The disclosures on expenses by *Private Eye* and the dominant position of the C&AG in the management and conduct of the NAO had made it an obvious candidate for a corporate governance review.

The open-ended period of service of the C&AG under the continuing provisions of the 1866 Audit Act, which at the time had been considered a necessary safeguard of independence, was also relevant to matters of governance. Modern practice, in contrast to the nineteenth century, was for broadly similar appointments to be for a fixed term, normally up to a maximum of ten years. Although the question of a fixed-term appointment had been given some prominence with Sir John Bourn's near-record twenty-year period in office, open-ended tenure had not in practice been a significant issue with any of the previous thirteen C&AGs since 1888. Only two had served more than ten years, both reflecting wartime circumstances. The average period of service was seven and a half years and the average time for the previous five C&AGs was under six years (see Appendix 1). Nevertheless, it became an almost foregone conclusion that future C&AGs would be appointed for a fixed term. The Chairmen of the Public Accounts Commission and of the PAC were already in favour of a fixed-term appointment, as was Sir John Bourn himself.[24]

In October 2007 the Public Accounts Commission announced its terms of reference for a review of the governance of the NAO. The review would:

identify the extent to which the NAO's corporate governance arrangements are consistent with the best practice elsewhere (including the arrangements set out in the Combined Code on Corporate Governance and the Treasury's Corporate

---

[23] Public Accounts Commission 13th Report, 2006–7, HC 915, paras 3–4.
[24] HC Debate, 23 January 2008, c.1523.

Governance in Central Government Departments: Code of Practice) and to pro-
pose any necessary improvements, taking account of the need to protect the
Comptroller and Auditor General's statutory discretion in carrying out his duties.
The review should focus on the role of the C&AG and his relationship with the
NAO, and should cover the role of the NAO's Senior Management Board.

The government also announced in October 2007 that 'space will be made
available in the forthcoming constitutional reform Bill for any agreed changes
to the corporate governance of the National Audit Office emerging from the
review'.[25] John Tiner, Chief Executive of the Financial Services Authority from
2003 to 2007, was appointed to lead the review. His report was published on
12 February 2008 as the 14th Report of the Public Accounts Commission.[26]
Based on a comparison of the existing NAO governance arrangements with
those of a range of similar organizations, the report concluded that 'there was
an overwhelming case for strengthening the governance of the NAO' and
made a series of recommendations for change. Possibly the most controversial
change suggested was the creation of new arrangements for the management
of the NAO, with a new Chairman and NAO Board.

The Public Accounts Commission responded to the Tiner proposals in
March 2008.[27] It substantially accepted the recommendations, although
with some reservations and modifications. The Commission emphasized
'the fundamental importance of preserving the independence of the C&AG
in deciding what audits to carry out and in making audit judgements, and
above all in preserving his or her independence from the Executive'. Looking
forward to the legislative changes that would be needed, the response focused
on what the Commission saw as 'the central problem' of how to meet the
objective of strengthening the NAO's corporate governance and internal
controls without compromising the key objective of preserving the C&AG's
independence. To strike that difficult balance there would need to be careful
delineation between the respective roles, responsibilities, and powers of the
C&AG and those of the proposed Chairman of the NAO. On this issue the
Commission emphasized that:

> There is general agreement that it would be unacceptable if the Chairman were
> able to constrain the C&AG's audit decisions (including decisions on what audits
> to conduct) or to act as an alternative figurehead for the NAO, given that the
> Chairman would not be responsible for what the NAO actually produces, which is
> audit judgements. With this in mind, we agree to the proposal for a Chairman on
> the basis that he or she would have only an internal role, and would speak in
> public only about governance matters, and in particular would not comment on

---

[25] HC Debate, 26 October 2007, c.408.   [26] HC 328, 2007–8.
[27] HC 402, 2007–8 The Public Accounts Commission, *Corporate Governance of the National Audit
Office; Response to John Tiner's Review*, 4 March 2008.

the audit reports or the audit programme of the C&AG. Given that the role would be largely internal, the Chairman's interventions in public would be rare. We would prefer the Chairman to be Chairman of the NAO Board rather than of the NAO, if legally possible. The C&AG would act as Chief Executive of the NAO, would lead the NAO executive, would manage the NAO's resources ... and would be the public face of the NAO.[28]

The Commission considered that the independence of the C&AG was such an important principle that the Board should not be able to prevent the C&AG conducting an audit that the C&AG considered necessary or require the C&AG to undertake an audit that the C&AG did not regard as of sufficient priority. However, the inclusion of non-statutory work in the NAO strategy, for example international work, would require the agreement of the Board. In August 2008 the Commission published its sixteenth report,[29] containing draft clauses for the proposed legislation that had been drawn up by the NAO and endorsed by the Commission. These draft clauses, with some further amendments, were reflected in the subsequent provisions of the Budget Responsibility and National Audit Act 2011.[30]

Sir John Bourn retired in 2008 and was followed as C&AG on an interim basis by Tim Burr, the Deputy C&AG, pending the outcome of the governance review. A new C&AG, Mr (later Sir) Amyas Morse, was appointed in January 2009. He was only the second professional accountant in more than 100 years to become C&AG, bringing with him extensive high-level experience in the profession, both in the UK and internationally. Since July 2006 he had served in the Ministry of Defence as Defence Commercial Director. The appointments of both Tim Burr and Amyas Morse were made under the provisions of the National Audit Act 1983, involving the Chairman of the PAC and the Prime Minister. The House of Commons debate on the interim appointment of Tim Burr produced, yet again, a brief rehearsal of the concerns of some Members of Parliament about any government involvement in the appointment process and the need to maintain the independence of the C&AG.

The Chairman of the PAC, Edward Leigh, once again confirmed the Committee's view that, on balance, and given the C&AG's extensive rights of access to government documents and files, this joint participation reflected the legitimate interests of both the Executive and the House of Commons.[31] He further reassured the House by underlining the crucial difference between

---

[28] HC 402, 2007–8, The Public Accounts Commission, *Corporate Governance of the National Audit Office; Response to John Tiner's Review*, 4 March 2008, para. 8.

[29] HC 1027, 2007–8.

[30] Standard Note SN/PC/4595 written by Oonagh Gay and published on 12 May 2008 for the information of Members of Parliament by the Parliament and Constitution Centre provides a detailed step-by-step account of the developments on governance and the proposed legislation.

[31] HC Debate, 23 January 2008, c.1527.

the *selection* stage in the appointment process, which was conducted by the Chairman of the PAC as the basis for his final choice of the person to be presented to the Prime Minister for submission to the House of Commons, and the *appointment* stage, which required a motion submitted to the House and was therefore the point at which the government had to be involved. He confirmed that both the Prime Minister and the Opposition Chairman of the PAC:

> need to be involved in the appointment, but not in the selection. That should be the job of the House . . . and I would need to be advised by a senior board . . . (that) would consist of a recently retired very senior servant—perhaps a former permanent secretary—a senior accountant from private practice and perhaps a recently retired officer from the NAO. I would need to listen to and consider their advice, but the Government do not need to be involved in that part of the process; otherwise there is the danger that I could find myself steered in classic Whitehall fashion in the direction of a safe candidate. I am sure that that would not be good for the future independence of the position. The Government do not have a right to a final veto.[32]

These changes to the method of appointing the C&AG were consistent with the revised arrangements for senior public sector appointments introduced in 1995 to ensure the integrity of the public appointments process. The appointment of Amyas Morse as C&AG was considered by a selection panel chaired by Edward Leigh, Chairman of the PAC, sitting with Sir Nicholas Macpherson, Permanent Secretary at the Treasury, and with Tim Burr, the outgoing C&AG, as an observer. The need for transparency in the appointment was recognized by a separate pre-appointment hearing by the PAC and information on the selection process being published by the PAC in February 2009.[33] The Public Accounts Commission also noted that the C&AG should be subject to the regulation of the Advisory Committee on Public Appointments when leaving the post, to avoid potential conflicts of interest.

New NAO Legislation

In the light of the findings on governance, the subsequent Budget Responsibility and National Audit Act 2011 introduced significant changes in the structure, management, and conduct of business in the NAO. These new provisions revised, and in some respects reduced, the independence and previous powers of the C&AG whilst retaining the C&AG's complete discretion on professional and operational decisions. The NAO became a body

---

[32] HC Debate, 23 January 2008, c.1527.   [33] HC 256, February 2009.

corporate with nine members: a non-executive Chairman and four non-executive members, the C&AG, and three NAO employee members. This gave the non-executive members the majority. Each member has a single vote, with the Chairman having a casting vote where necessary. The C&AG and the NAO Chairman, initially Professor Sir Andrew Likierman and later Lord Bichard, have effectively the same status of appointment and removal. Both are appointed by Her Majesty by letters patent exercisable by an address by the Prime Minister to the House of Commons. The removal of either the Chairman or the C&AG requires an address by both Houses of Parliament. The Chairman has an initial period of tenure of three years, renewable to six years, and the C&AG a maximum period of tenure of ten years. The C&AG became the Chief Executive, but not an employee, of the NAO.

The four non-executive members of the Board of the NAO are appointed by the Public Accounts Commission on the recommendation of the NAO Chairman. Their appointment may be terminated by the Commission. The NAO employee members are appointed by the Chairman and non-executive members of the Board on the recommendation of the C&AG. Their appointment as Board members may be terminated by the Chairman and non-executive members. The staff of the NAO, who are no longer employees of the C&AG, are appointed by, and their remuneration and terms of service determined by, the Board of the NAO.

A schedule to the Act detailed the new relationship between the NAO and the C&AG and arrangements for the provision by the NAO of resources as required by the C&AG. It also provided that 'the NAO must, in such manner as it may consider appropriate, monitor the carrying out of the C&AG's functions'. The C&AG must have regard to any advice the NAO Board may give on the carrying out of those functions. These and related matters were to be set out in a code prepared jointly by the NAO and the C&AG, after consulting the Treasury, and submitted for approval by the Public Accounts Commission. Certain services provided outside the C&AG's main statutory functions, for example international audit work, require the approval of the NAO and it is for the NAO to determine the maximum amount of resources that such services require.

The NAO and the C&AG must jointly prepare a strategy for the national audit functions, including a plan for the use of resources on those functions. The NAO Chairman and the C&AG must jointly submit the strategy to the Public Accounts Commission for approval. Performance against the strategy is to be reviewed and reported each year, and the strategy revised and updated as necessary. For each financial year the C&AG and the NAO must jointly prepare an estimate of the NAO's use of resources. The estimate is submitted jointly by the C&AG and the Chairman of the NAO to the Public Accounts Commission for approval by the House of Commons. An annual report on the work of the C&AG and the NAO is to be presented to Parliament with the annual accounts, including a range of indicators of performance.

On direct operational matters, the 2011 Act importantly confirmed the C&AG's complete discretion in carrying out the professional functions of the office. On the audit of accounts, investigations under rights of access and inspection, examinations of value for money, economy and effectiveness, and reporting of results, the C&AG essentially retained all previous powers. The Act added that the C&AG must aim to carry out these functions efficiently and cost-effectively and must, as the C&AG considered appropriate, have regard to the standards and principles that an expert professional provider of accounting and auditing services would be expected to follow.

In the interests of corporate governance the 2011 Act deliberately removed or reduced some of the C&AG's long-standing powers of exclusive authority and freedom of action. Changes in some respects have reduced the independence of the C&AG. Any risks that this may involve have to be balanced against the ways in which an effective partnership between the C&AG and the NAO Board would enhance public confidence and provide valuable external advice and a broader basis of support on key issues affecting the audit, especially budget discussions with the Public Accounts Commission, and relationships with departments, the Treasury, and with the PAC and Parliament. The real test of the Act will not be the wording of the legislation but whether in practice, and in the longer term, the right balance is struck between the NAO Board and C&AG responsibilities, powers, priorities, and concerns, to ensure the highest professional standards of audit and the proper and effective conduct of business, in the interests of Parliament.

NAO Performance 2014–15

The NAO's current achievements are widely recognized, both nationally and internationally, and it continues to be strongly supported within Parliament, from Select Committees and individual MPs. The benefits of its work have been praised within the United Nations (UN) and by countries to which the Office had provided assistance. The C&AG also continued to be a major auditor of UN bodies with income from UN work amounting to £3.2 million and income from other international work generating £0.7 million. In the financial year 2014–15 the C&AG certified more than 440 accounts, spread over 344 organizations and covering all government departments and many other public sector bodies, including some operating as private sector companies. The combined revenue and expenditure of the bodies audited was more than £1 trillion a year. NAO examinations in 2014–15 helped to secure savings and efficiency benefits amounting to £1.15 billion, representing a return of £18 for every £1 spent. Savings and efficiency benefits over the five years 2010–15 amounted to £5.5 billion.[34]

In 2014–15 the NAO presented sixty-five major audit reports to Parliament, including forty-nine reports on value for money, thirteen reports on other investigations, and three financial information reports. In pursuing the issues raised, the Office supported sixty hearings of the PAC. Briefings and support were provided to another twenty-four parliamentary committees, including seventeen departmental overviews. The Office also responded to a wide range of specific tasks commissioned by Parliament, including providing advice on a new governance and management structure for the House of Commons. Advice and assistance provided to departments and other bodies extended to fifty-seven good practice guides and briefings. Over the period 2010–15 the Office completed 298 value-for-money studies and thirty-eight other investigations, and supported 276 PAC evidence sessions. The government accepted 88 per cent of the resulting PAC recommendations, with 636 recommendations implemented. To carry out its work, the NAO in 2014–15 employed 779 full-time equivalent permanent staff, which was less than the 822 staff in the previous year. Staff numbers have been progressively reduced since 2010.

Conclusion

The 1990s and the early 2000s saw continuing developments to meet challenges and opportunities on both certification audit and value-for-money examinations. On certification audit there were increasing demands to meet the proliferation of professional accountancy and audit standards, the increasing number and variety of accounts, and associated staff training. The newer bodies becoming involved in the delivery of programmes and services previously handled by departments meant that, on certification work and when exercising rights of access and inspection, additional attention had to be given to issues of regularity, propriety, and the proper conduct of public business. Towards the end of the 1990s additional demands arose from preparations for the introduction of resource accounts across government.

With value-for-money examinations there was a widening range and depth in the subjects covered and the variety of bodies in which the work was carried out. Increased penetration in the reports and conclusions brought with it a

---

[34] The facts and figures quoted are from the NAO Annual Report and Accounts, 2014–15. HC 190, Session 2015–16, 16 June 2015. The basis for calculating the financial impacts of the NAO's work are set out in the Annual Report and the figures are validated by the Office's statutory external auditors.

corresponding increase in the attentions of the PAC and, in some cases, other Select Committees. Some of the work also required more expertise in non-audit disciplines, obtained on a study-by-study basis by contracting in specialists from outside bodies. There was also recruitment to strengthen in-house skills in economics, statistics, operational research, and sampling and survey techniques. These were important both in the planning and selection of examinations and in collecting independent evidence to complement material from departmental files and reports and to provide a wider perspective.

Reports were venturing into a wider and more ambitious range of subjects and issues, with findings and conclusions dealt with in different ways. They were also being increasingly carried out at earlier stages in the programmes and projects concerned. More was being done to ensure that audit provided added value, and to use audit findings and conclusions to help spread good practice and improve service delivery at national and local levels. This improvement mandate has been a key part of the NAO's forward strategy. These developments were part of the process of moving the NAO towards a more collaborative rather than an adversarial role, whilst continuing to report strong criticisms where necessary.

Some of the subjects and issues covered in NAO reports from 2000 onwards, the objectives pursued, and the conclusions reported might have been regarded thirty years before as venturing too far into uncharted territory and liable to be challenged by the Executive as falling outside the E&AD's accepted remit. Yet not everything was breaking new ground. A number of examinations would in many respects be familiar to an earlier E&AD auditor. Some reports from the 1960s to the early 1990s would have sat comfortably alongside reports in 2000 and beyond. While recognizing the innovative nature of much of the work of the NAO today, there are still features that recognize the contributory legacy of the past.

The NAO from 2000 onwards was in many respects a very different organization from the E&AD of the 1950s and 1960s, and even that of the NAO in the 1980s and early 1990s. Fundamental statutory changes had been introduced in NAO structure and allocation of responsibilities. Relationships with Parliament, with departments, and with other bodies had been enhanced. The culture and style of the NAO itself had also changed for it no longer demonstrated the same degree of 'family' spirit that had been a strong feature of the E&AD. The NAO was more obviously demanding and disciplined, expectations were higher and there was a stronger outward focus. Changes of this kind were inevitable and indeed essential if the NAO was successfully to face the challenges and opportunities of the millennium and the more demanding environment in which it was increasingly operating. Nevertheless, the differences should not be exaggerated. The E&AD had made many advances and the NAO retained a supportive corporate identity and pride in its constitutional responsibilities that added a valuable dimension to the increased emphasis on professionalism and performance.

There would be further opportunities to improve management and systems in the audited bodies, provided on an advisory basis and without compromising audit independence. Wider-ranging examinations would be directed specifically at cross-government management and financial control issues, with the results not necessarily communicated in formal reports. As the millennium continues there will be a continuing range of important matters to be addressed.

11

Recurring Themes and Continuing Change

'A state without the means of some change is without the means of its conservation.'

Edmund Burke, *Reflections on the Revolution in France* (1790)

The 900-year pursuit of accountability has not been a steady and consistent process. Themes important to its eventual success have emerged, faltered, and re-emerged over the centuries in the flux of constitutional, parliamentary, and political pressures. The history of the National Audit Office (NAO) and its predecessors is interwoven with these themes and pressures. Ensuring the formal and operational independence of the Comptroller and Auditor General (C&AG) remained the priority, especially as the remit of the C&AG moved into areas where the contours of the public business and the public interest were less certain. This process of change has required both a strengthening of traditional relationships with Parliament and the Public Accounts Committee (PAC) and redefining relationships with the Treasury and departments. Many of today's audit objectives, priorities, challenges, and opportunities share key elements with those of the past and, as part of an audit continuum, with lessons learned, they offer a prospect of future developments.

Appropriation

Appropriation to ensure that funds are spent only on the services for which they were approved and within the totals voted is a thread that has run through the fabric of accountability for hundreds of years. Appropriation applies only to expenditure by government departments from funds voted by Parliament. Though non-departmental bodies, agencies, and others supported by substantial grants or grants-in-aid are similarly required to spend funds only on intended purposes and within the limits approved and in accordance with any other conditions imposed, these are part of the financial controls operated by the funding departments. Appropriation applies to expenditure, not revenue. Revenue from taxation, for example, is part of the total funds available to the Executive to be spent as it decides. It has from time to time been suggested that revenue from specific taxes should be appropriated towards spending on related activities, such as revenue from Road Fund licences to be spent on roads, but this has never been accepted.

For the first 250 years of the medieval Exchequer the King was not required to account for the spending of his traditional revenues or the proceeds of taxation. It was not until the middle of the fourteenth century that the initial stirrings of appropriation began when the King was no longer able 'to live of his own' and required grants and aids that came with conditions attached. Yet, for another 250 years development was haphazard; measures moving in some ways towards the system of appropriation that Parliament expects today did not emerge until the introduction of the Civil List at the end of the seventeenth century. These were developed significantly under the provisions of the 1832 Audit Act, which required more informative estimates and appropriation accounts to be presented to Parliament. There were still important deficiencies in the degree of accountability provided and the changes introduced were less successful in some of the larger spending departments. Matters were not put on their comprehensive modern footing until the provisions of the 1866 Audit Act.

Appropriation developed in ways that provided a degree of flexibility in its practical application. Increasing the level of detail in estimates had been recognized as important to provide Parliament with the information it needed for an informed decision on the funds to be voted. To hold the Executive accountable for compliance with all levels of that detail would have been rigid and bureaucratic, given the unpredictability of the scale and timing of some expenditure. Virement was therefore introduced as a limited measure to allow the Treasury to switch funds in particular circumstances between expenditure subheads as set out in the estimates. This was a technical breach of the House of Commons' powers of supply and was closely monitored during audit, with more doubtful cases brought to the attention of the PAC. The unpredictability of the scale and timing of expenditure vastly increased during the First and Second World Wars and appropriation was modified further by the introduction of Votes of Credit that gave the Treasury power to appropriate military and some civil expenditure in subsequent accounts. Post-war, appropriation returned to its key place in parliamentary accountability. The principle of appropriation remains today, though appropriation accounts themselves were replaced with resource accounts under the provisions of the Government Resources and Accounts Act 2000.

Accounting Officers

The success of appropriation relied upon the allocation of a direct personal responsibility to named individuals. Heavy penalties were imposed for breaches of the many regulations governing the conduct of business and, although these diminished over time, an element of personal financial sanction remained until the twentieth century. The principle of direct personal accountability was reinforced in the appointment of departmental Accounting Officers following the 1866 Audit Act, although there were continuing uncertainties over the level at which Accounting Officers should be appointed. The Treasury believed that proper accountability and concern for finance would only come if responsibility for expenditure—and responsibility for policy and administration giving rise to that expenditure—were combined at the highest level, that is by making the Permanent Head the Accounting Officer. Departments, however, fought for Accounting Officer responsibility to be assigned at lower levels. Permanent Heads as Accounting Officers were eventually approved by the Cabinet and endorsed by the PAC in the discussions leading up to the formulation of the 1921 Audit Act.

The 1866 Audit Act provided that Accounting Officers were responsible only for matters of appropriation accounting and regularity. Responsibility for economy and efficiency was deliberately not mentioned in the Act. This limited approach was increasingly challenged in reports by the early C&AGs, strongly supported by the PAC, which promoted the need for audit to encompass matters of economy and efficiency that were already starting to be referred to as 'value for money'. Significant changes in Accounting Officer responsibilities were later introduced, which reflected the growing spread and devolution of the management and delivery of programmes when services that were previously the responsibility of departments were given to a growing number of non-departmental bodies and agencies.

Audit Independence

The ebb and flow of the battle to secure audit independence has been a dominant theme of developments since a coherent structure of parliamentary audit was first introduced with the appointment of the Commissioners for Examining the Public Accounts in 1780. Audit examinations in the medieval Exchequer, when carried out at all, were essentially internal procedural checks on behalf of the Executive. Consequently, independence as viewed today was not then a recognized concept. The work of the Auditors of the Imprests appointed in 1589 was not only fallible but also wholly directed by the Treasury for almost 200 years.

It has never been difficult to secure formal recognition of the importance of audit independence, at least in terms of formal provisions safeguarding the appointment, status, tenure, and conditions of service of Commissioners of Audit, C&AGs, and other senior officials. In themselves, however, such provisions, even when expressed in statute, have never been sufficient to ensure independence in practice. This was exemplified by the dominance of the Treasury over the work of the statutorily appointed Commissioners and Board of Audit 1785–1866. True independence lies in the professional freedom to select, conduct, and report audit examinations. From its establishment in 1866 the Exchequer and Audit Department (E&AD) fought for and progressively established operational independence, led by successive C&AGs and with growing parliamentary support. Nevertheless, there continued to be an Executive predisposition to retain some controls or influence over the C&AG's audit that was not finally dispelled until the provisions of the National Audit Act 1983.

While recognizing the fundamental importance of independence, too vehement a determination to remain independent in all areas and at all times had adverse effects. A balanced view of the achievements of the E&AD would have to accept that at times this attitude contributed to a reluctance to engage closely and constructively with audited departments and other bodies. The NAO later recognized the importance of more cooperative relationships with the Treasury and departments and the wider benefits this provided, not only across an increasingly devolved public sector but also to the audit itself. These developments were careful to retain the C&AG's ultimate freedom of action and power of final decision.

The transformation of public sector practices, demands of accountability, and greater corporate governance were recognized in the 2014 Budget Responsibility and National Audit Act, which reduced the C&AG's dominant position in the NAO. The new NAO board includes the C&AG and other NAO members but with a voting majority given to outside members and it is headed by a NAO Chairman appointed, like the C&AG, by royal letters patent. The C&AG became the Chief Executive of the NAO and, crucially, retains full independence on all the professional functions of the Office, including: the audit of accounts; investigations under rights of access and inspection; examinations of economy, efficiency, and effectiveness; and the presentation of reports to Parliament and their examination by the PAC. The Act made a very clear requirement that the 'NAO must, in such manner as it may consider appropriate, monitor the carrying out of the C&AG's functions' and the C&AG must have regard to any advice the NAO may give on the carrying out of those functions.

Audit Remit

The dominance of the Treasury over the Commissioners and Board of Audit undermined not only their independence but also the extent and nature of their audit. The Treasury decided which accounts should be sent to the Commissioners for audit and which excluded, how far the Board of Audit's examination should extend, and any action to be taken on audit findings. Parliament was singularly uninformed on these matters; many MPs happily believed that the Board of Audit examined all departmental spending. These gaps in accountability were increasingly criticized in the years leading up to 1866, mainly by parliamentary committees and individual MPs rather than by a disappointingly passive Board of Audit, before being finally remedied in the 1866 Audit Act.

With the C&AG's strong new powers under the 1866 Act another recurring battle over the C&AG's remit was the determination of the auditors to extend the scope of their work and carry it into new areas of departmental business. These included stores audit and manufacturing and trading activities but the most obvious, and certainly the most heralded, development was the examination of value for money in its various aspects. Prompted by its intrinsic merits, and fuelled by recurring economic difficulties and resulting pressures on public funds and resources, particularly as a result of the First and Second World Wars, this was progressively extended into increasingly important areas. In retrospect this development was inevitable, despite determined and, at times, vehement opposition by the audited departments and other bodies. The key to its success was the strong and enthusiastic support of the PAC, and in some cases even that of the Treasury as part of its determination to curb departmental spending.

Though earlier value-for-money examinations had provided many successes, it was progessively recognized from the early 1970s that the objectives and methods of this work needed to change to reflect developments in the public sector environment within which the E&AD was now operating. While maintaining the critical edge where necessary, steps were needed to revise relationships with departments and to extend the added value and wider benefits of audit work through closer collaboration with departments and other bodies. This is now a major feature of present work by the NAO. Without such developments there was a growing risk that audit and reports directed largely towards criticism, forcefully pursued by the PAC and highlighted by the press, would contribute to the culture of risk aversion and fear of failure that was already being criticized in the civil service.

Rights of Access and Inspection

Although the 1866 Audit Act gave the C&AG powers to examine the books and records of the departments and other bodies where he was the appointed auditor, it became increasingly recognized that there would be significant gaps in accountability if similar rights of access were not granted to carry the audit into the growing number of bodies supported from public funds. Many of these bodies were brought into the net by agreement and without much difficulty. It became accepted practice, endorsed by the PAC, for access to be agreed in all cases where public funds provided a substantial part of the income of the bodies concerned. Examinations were not directed towards scrutinizing or double-checking the work of the appointed auditors. Instead, examinations were concerned with compliance with the terms and conditions attached to the public funds provided, with matters involving the 'proper conduct of public business' and, increasingly, with questions of value for money. These examinations provided a significant number of reports dealt with by the PAC.

There have been some long-running battles to secure and maintain rights of access and inspection to other bodies receiving substantial public funds. Perhaps the most notable examples of successful persistence and determination were when rights of access were secured in 1966 to the books and records of the University Grants Committee and all universities and in 2010 to the BBC. In both of these cases, access had been pursued at various times since the 1930s and was secured in the face of strong opposition by the determined advocacy of the C&AGs concerned. Securing and maintaining rights of access and inspection was also protecting the PAC's interests, for the Committee's investigations under its Standing Orders are largely dependent on the presentation of C&AG reports to Parliament. Thus, limitations on the C&AG's rights of access would have weakened the PAC's examinations.

The NAO's access to the BBC which was established under the 2011 framework agreement on rights of access allowed the NAO to conduct value for money investigations only in specific areas of BBC activity, by agreement with the BBC Trust. These limitations were recognized when, in February 2015, the Culture, Media, and Sport Select Committee recommended in its 'Report on the Future of the BBC' that the NAO should have 'unfettered access' to the BBC in carrying out value-for-money investigations and that NAO rights of access should be made statutory.[1] In reaching its conclusions the Committee took into account concerns expressed by C&AG Sir Amyas Morse on difficulties and delays experienced in carrying out and reporting on investigations

---

[1] HC 315, Session 2014–15, Fourth Report, *Future of the BBC*, paras 315 and 330.

under the terms of the NAO's existing non-statutory rights of access.[2] Continuing concerns on the accountability and governance of the BBC and the need for independent scrutiny were expressed in March 2016 in Sir David Clementi's 'Review of the Governance and Regulation of the BBC'.[3] The NAO was amongst the bodies consulted during the review but any proposals on possible changes in the NAO's role were outside the scope of the review. However, on 12 May 2016 when announcing the publication of the Government's White Paper on 'A BBC for the Future'[4] the Minister for Culture, Media, and Sport confirmed that in considering the renewal of the BBC's Charter, which was due to expire at the end of 2016, the Government proposed that 'the National Audit Office, which has an outstanding track record, will therefore become the financial auditor of the BBC and will have the power to conduct value for money investigations of the BBC's activities, with appropriate safeguards for editorial matters.'[5] In response, the Opposition fully endorsed the views expressed on the value of the NAO's work and confirmed that it would not object to the proposal.

Efforts to secure rights of access were not always successful. The long campaign to secure C&AG access to nationalized and other public corporations, pressed largely within Parliament rather than with enthusiastic C&AG support, was finally denied in the negotiations leading up to the passage of the 1983 National Audit Act. The Act itself, though clear on retaining existing rights of access, was less reassuring on procedures for securing future rights of access, which led to some later difficulties in ensuring coverage of the growing number of bodies involved in the management and delivery of government programmes and projects through the 1990s. These were largely resolved following the strong recommendations on access in the 2001 Sharman Report. Another major advance was the C&AG's access to the books and records of government contractors, which had been urged in many reports during and after the First and Second World Wars, particularly on contracts for military expenditure, and was finally agreed with the Council of British Industry in 2014.

Relationships with the PAC and Parliament

While some of the themes pursued over the years have involved differences of view between the E&AD and the Treasury and departments, there has always

---

[2] HC 315, Session 2014–15, Fourth Report, *Future of the BBC*, paras 325–9.
[3] Cm 9209, presented to Parliament March 2016.
[4] CM 9242, presented to Parliament May 2016.
[5] In confirming that the C&AG should become the BBC's appointed auditor, pp. 87–8 of the White Paper summarized the benefits from the work and achievements of the NAO, both on the BBC and more generally across the public sector.

been a strong mutual desire that audit examinations should stay well clear of issues relating to policy and politics. The determination of successive governments that audit should not become involved in these matters was matched by the C&AG's determination not to do so. This understanding was easily maintained on certification audit and by ensuring for the many years that value-for-money examinations were directed essentially towards questions of economy and efficiency. When the emergence of examinations of effectiveness raised the spectre of audit trespassing on matters of policy, both sides quickly arrived at the mutually acceptable provision in the National Audit Act 1983 that the C&AG was not entitled to question 'the merits of policy objectives'. This did not exclude all examinations involving policy issues but set boundaries to such work. There was also a shared view on the importance of audit examinations and reports avoiding issues with a party political dimension, most importantly because of the risk that this could damage the bipartisan approach of the PAC that was an invaluable strength in the effectiveness of its investigations and reports.

The symbiotic relationship between the PAC, the E&AD, and the NAO since 1866 has been a persistent feature of parliamentary accountability and an essential factor in the success of each. The nature and strength of this relationship has reflected at times the different personalities and priorities of C&AGs and those of the Chairmen of the PAC, but also those of the members of the PAC. The final selection and reporting of audit examinations have always been matters entirely for the C&AG. This was deliberately reinforced, at the insistence of the government, in the provisions of the National Audit Act 1983, in part to counterbalance the requirement that the C&AG was to consult the Committee on the NAO's forward programme and also the new role of the PAC in advising the Public Accounts Commission on the NAO's budget. The provision in the 1983 Act allowing the C&AG's reports to be presented to Parliament throughout the year, separately from the accounts, provided immediacy, impact and a strong showcase for the NAO's own achievements. The opportunity was increasingly taken to improve reports and raise the NAO's profile by presenting more information on the objectives, findings, conclusions, and recommendations of NAO work.

Constitutionally and statutorily the C&AG's responsibilities and relationships are with the House of Commons as a whole, but from the outset these have always been dominated by the relationship with the PAC. As a result, this has been the focus through which the majority of MPs have over the years viewed the work of both the E&AD and the NAO. Other than occasional interest in individual issues or reports of particular concern, there has rarely been much evidence of a close and consistent interest in audit matters by individual MPs, other than members of the PAC and a limited number of other MPs. The annual House of Commons debates on the PAC's reports have rarely been well-attended by MPs other than those directly involved. Audit is not glamorous, it has a low political profile, and it is not an area of much concern to an MP's constituents. However, MP responses to recent NAO surveys indicate an encouraging level of awareness of the contribution of NAO work to parliamentary accountability and, more specifically, to matters in which individual MPs have a special interest.

Relationships with the Treasury and Departments

Although it took many years, E&AD and NAO relationships with the Treasury changed dramatically in favour of the auditors. It shifted from a position of almost total domination by the Treasury up to and including the work of the Commissioners and Board of Audit 1785–1866, to the final removal of all Treasury controls by the National Audit Act 1983. From the early years following the 1866 Audit Act successive C&AGs, starting with Sir William Dunbar, refused to subordinate audit to the Treasury, as envisaged by William Gladstone in the genesis and framing of the Act. They did so not by high-level appeals or manoeuvres but by developing and improving the day-to-day conduct of both certification and value-for-money examinations in ways that earned the support of the PAC and the House of Commons. In this way, the C&AGs were able to establish a distinct audit persona and a reputation for revealing waste and extravagance and pursuing economy and efficiency at a time of growing public expenditure. The E&AD's work enhanced this position throughout the First World War, the economic difficulties of the 1930s, and the challenges of the Second World War, with a resurgence during high levels of post-war expenditure arising from continuing military procurement and the introduction of new health and welfare programmes.

By the 1960s the status of the E&AD, its reputation within Parliament, and more widely, was such that, whilst still subject to Treasury controls on budgets and staffing, the E&AD was well past being an organization that the Treasury could expect to dominate or successfully ignore. A more balanced relationship reached in the respective positions of the E&AD and the Treasury was also the result of changes in the Treasury's own priorities; from the 1960s onwards these were increasingly focused on urgent matters of economic management and expenditure control, and audit issues were less important. The position today, though subject to occasional strains, reflects overall a joint interest in, and closer working on, matters of common concern.

The E&AD's relationships with departments and other audited bodies on certification audit were generally satisfactory, with only occasional problems. On value-for-money examinations, relationships were always more difficult and at times confrontational. This was especially so with the large spending departments when their Accounting Officer faced the prospect of aggressive questioning by the PAC on a critical C&AG report. These concerns increased with the more penetrating developments of examinations of economy, efficiency, and effectiveness following the 1983 Act. Accordingly, the NAO took a number of initiatives with Accounting Officers, Principal Finance Officers, and the Treasury to improve understanding on both sides. In 2014–15, NAO surveys confirmed that many audited bodies recognized the benefits of the Office's work on issues of accounting, financial management, and control. At the same time, although there were still significant reservations about examinations of economy and efficiency, there was clear appreciation of the constructive and responsive approach by NAO staff in conducting examinations and when dealing with the results. Examples of continuing unease are not surprising. In some respects they are inevitable given the importance to both sides of the issues being pursued.

Clarifying and Strengthening Accountabilities

Continuing changes in departmental management and in service delivery meant that, for some time, strains had been developing in the framework of accountability, particularly in maintaining the necessary balance between the effective discharge of the separate, but related, responsibilities of Permanent Secretaries. They serve ministers in the management of their departments and with the formulation and implementation of policy. They are also Accounting Officers accountable to Parliament for safeguarding regularity, propriety, and value for money in public spending and for stewardship of resources. These separate responsibilities sometimes conflict. Emerging concerns, the risks involved, and the need for improvement were the subject of PAC reports in 2011 and 2012.[6]

In its 2011 report the PAC identified five fundamentals of accountability. In all departments the Accounting Officer is personally and ultimately responsible to Parliament for the spending of taxpayers' money and must be undeterred in the discharge of these responsibilities. Where a department provides funding to other bodies, the Accounting Officer is responsible for ensuring that there is an appropriate framework in place to provide him or her with the necessary assurances and controls. At the same time, responsibilities and authority for policy and operational decisions are clear throughout the delivery chain and there must be a clear process for measuring outcomes,

---

[6] HC 740, Committee of Public Accounts, *Accountability for Public Money*, Twenty-eighth Report. Session 2010–11, April 2011. HC 1503, Committee of Public Accounts, *Accountability for Public Money—Progress Report*, Seventy-ninth Report, Session 2010–12, April 2012.

evaluating performance, and demonstrating value for money, which allows organizations to be held to public account. This would enable reliable comparisons to be made across organizations delivering the same or similar services. All bodies that receive public funds are expected to be well governed and have robust financial arrangements in place. Though these fundamentals of accountability are clearly stated, there are significant difficulties and ambiguities in ensuring that they are applied effectively and consistently across an increasingly varied and devolved public sector, at departmental level and, particularly, at lower points of delivery of programmes and services.

Difficulties and ambiguities of accountability at departmental level have involved a number of factors. Ministers in successive administrations were taking a closer interest in the delivery of their policies and programmes and were becoming increasingly involved in decisions on implementation that were previously left to officials. Accounting Officers were then in the position of being accountable to Parliament for the financial and other outcomes of decisions outside their control. The 'ministerial directions' that were in principle designed to protect Accounting Officers in this situation were fallible in practice, partly because of a reluctance to call for them. The involvement of ministers' political advisers, themselves unaccountable to Parliament, added to the complications. Programmes that were not exclusive to one department, and joint enterprises involving departments and other bodies in multi-agency arrangements, though designed to save money and improve performance, could also create uncertainties in relation to the accountability of the individual Accounting Officers involved.

At the other end of the accountability spectrum, detailed decisions on service delivery were being pushed further and further down the line, involving a range of bodies at lower level with autonomous or semi-autonomous powers for the spending of public funds. Thus, more extensive devolved powers and funding were being agreed for local authorities. Central government was also expanding delivery of public services through semi-autonomous local bodies such as academies and foundation trusts, with the former to be substantially increased under proposals in the 2016 Budget. More public services were being delivered by setting up arm's-length limited companies, with an estimated sixty-six new companies since 2010, and contracts were being placed with private and voluntary sector bodies to deliver front-line public services and other forms of support. The position and responsibilities of some of these bodies within the existing framework of accountability was not always clear. Funding in some cases was blurred by the involvement of both public funds and financial support from charities and other private sector organizations. In the case of some of the newer bodies involved there were reservations expressed about their experience with the requirements expected in relation to the proper conduct of public business, achieving value for money, the strength of their financial controls and management systems, and matters of governance. For example, the NAO reported in October 2014 that although there had been some improvements with academy trusts and maintained schools more needed to be done to clarify and strengthen arrangements for monitoring and intervention to ensure that greater school autonomy was coupled with effective oversight and assurance.[7] In this situation any uncertainties are clear risks to the accountability of the Accounting Officers ultimately responsible. Sir David Clementi, in his review of the BBC referred to above, emphasized that:

> Accountability should be thought of not as a function separate from governance and regulation, but as an inherent part of a good governance and regularity system. The interests of accountability are well served by a model in which parties have clear responsibilities; and poorly served by a model in which parties have overlapping responsibilities with the potential for confused accountability.[8]

In response to these and related issues, in February 2016 the C&AG issued a wide-ranging sixty-page report to the House of Commons: *Accountability to Parliament for Taxpayers' Money*.[9] The report reviewed what accountability to Parliament means in the twenty-first century, the role and responsibilities of Accounting Officers, the robustness of the Accounting Officer role as a control over value for taxpayers' money, the health of current accountability to Parliament, and challenges to existing accountability. The report was based on analysis of evidence collected between July and October 2015, including a detailed review of 171 published NAO and PAC reports on accountability issues. The NAO also examined Treasury and other guidance to Accounting Officers, analysed the number and value of all ministerial directions since 1990, and conducted interviews with officials and expert commentators on government accountability and public finance.[10]

At the time this book was being finalized for publication the C&AG's 2016 report had just been presented to Parliament. The report was clearly a key step in bringing accountabilities more closely in line with the ways in which public sector business was now being conducted and public funds spent. Although the report expressed a substantial number of concerns and specific criticisms on a wide range of issues, there had been insufficient time for a government response and the PAC had yet to consider the many issues raised and recommendations for action.

---

[7] HC 721, 2014–15, October 2014, Academies and Maintained Schools: Oversight and Intervention.
[8] Cm9209, chapter 1, para. 7.   [9] HC 849, Session 2015–16, 23 February 2016.
[10] HC 849, Session 2015–16, 23 February 2016, p. 57.

Conclusion

The 900-year history of British national audit is a history of challenge and change. Change has at times been clear and positive: at other times less so. The pursuit of accountability has nevertheless been a continuing theme. The aims, objectives, management, and delivery of public sector programmes and projects are still changing and public sector auditors have to match and support these changes. This is a key responsibility in the interest of good government and to help provide the services the country deserves. To repeat Edmund Burke, 'A state without some means of change is without the means of its conservation.'

Throughout the changes to British national audit the twin pillars of public accountability remain the presentation and publication of accurate accounts of revenue and expenditure of public funds, independently audited on behalf of Parliament, and independent reports on the economy, efficiency, and effectiveness of public spending and use of resources in the delivery of public services. The latter have a higher profile and receive the most attention in Parliament, in the press, and in the mind of the general public. The former, though less heralded, nevertheless play a vital part in Britain's democratic and constitutional framework and the processes upon which all accountability and, ultimately, public trust depends.

Sixteen years into the millennium the NAO remains at the forefront of developments in the conduct of public business. With recent changes in its organization and powers it has a widening range of responsibilities in central and local government and, ultimately, how well services are delivered to those in need. The C&AG's recent reports confirm that there remain important tasks in strengthening public accountability and performance at all levels. Responding successfully to these challenges and opportunities will require ambition, determination, and persistence, as they were required for the successes of the Exchequer and Audit Department and its predecessors.

Appendices

Comptrollers and Auditors General

Sir William Dunbar (Bart.)	1867–88
Sir Charles Ryan KCB	1888–96
Sir Richard Mills KCB	1896–1900
D. C. Richmond CB	1900–4
Sir John Kempe KCB	1905–11
Sir Henry Gibson KCB	1911–21
Sir Malcolm Ramsay KCB	1921–31
Sir Gilbert Upcott KCB	1931–46
Sir Frank Tribe KCB, KBE	1946–58
Sir Edmund Compton KCB, KBE	1958–66
Sir Bruce Fraser KCB	1966–71
Sir David Pitblado KCB	1971–6
Sir Douglas Henley KCB	1976–81
Sir Gordon Downey KCB	1981–7
Sir John Bourn KCB	1987–2008
T. J. Burr CB	2008–9
Sir Amyas Morse KCB	2009, to date

APPENDIX 2

Exchequer Tallies: 'Preposterous Sticks'

Tallies were for eight centuries the iconic image of Exchequer business, from before the Norman Conquest until they were finally abolished in 1826. They symbolized an absolute determination to cling to tradition and the arcane procedures of 'The Course of the Exchequer', with all its inefficiencies and delays.

The tallies were lengths of hazel wood, chosen for its straightness and ability to split evenly, and notched across the face at defined intervals to identify the sums to be accounted for. For example, 'a thousand pounds is signified by a cut the thickness of the palm of the hand; a hundred pounds by the breadth of the thumb; a score of pounds by the breadth of the little finger; a single pound by the width of a fat barleycorn; etc'. They were inscribed along their length in 'barbarous abbreviated Exchequer Latin' to identify the transaction involved and the person to whom they had been issued. They were then split in half along their length, with one half (the foil) given to the person to be held accountable and the other (the counterfoil) retained in the Exchequer. When the account was due to be settled the two halves were brought together and the notches matched. Before they were finally abolished, tallies were being used to account for sums running into seven figures, and could be four feet long.

Tallies have been described as 'resembling more the rude contrivance of the denizens of a wilderness than a voucher issued from the Exchequer of one of the most powerful monarchs reigning over one of the most polished nations of the globe'. They were mocked even more scathingly by Charles Dickens in a speech on administrative reform at the Drury Lane Theatre on 27 June 1855:

Ages ago a savage mode of keeping accounts on notched sticks was introduced into the Court of the Exchequer, and the accounts were kept much as Robinson Crusoe kept his calendar on the desert island. Official routine inclined to these notched sticks as if they were pillars of the Constitution. In the reign of George III, an inquiry was made by some revolutionary spirit whether pens, ink and paper, slates and pencils being in existence, this obstinate adherence to an obsolete custom ought to be continued. All the red tape in the country grew redder at the bare mention at this bold and original conception. At last abolished in 1826, what was to be done with this considerable accumulation of worn-out, worm-eaten, rotten old bits of wood? In 1834 they were burnt in a stove in the House of Lords; overgorged with these preposterous sticks the stove set fire to the panelling; the panelling set fire to the House of Lords; the House of Lords set fire to the House of Commons; and the two Houses were reduced to ashes.

As well as their part in the burning of Parliament, these derided 'preposterous sticks' had a final sweet revenge. In June 1992 *The Times* newspaper reported that a bundle of surviving tallies, slightly scorched, had been sold at Sotheby's in London for £17,000.

Dialogus de Scaccario, and Sir Ernest Clarke, *An Old Exchequer Tally (Journal of the Royal Statistical Society*, Vol. 75, Part 1, December 1911).

Bibliography

Primary Sources

Advisory Board, *Report of the Advisory Board, London School of Economics, on the Fifth Course at the London School of Economics, 3rd October 1910 to 22 March 1911, for the Training of Officers for the Higher Appointments on the Administrative Staff of the 'army and for the Charge of Departmental Services* (London: HMSO, 1911)

Advisory Board, *Report of the Advisory Board, London School of Economics, on the Sixth Course at the London School of Economics, 5th October 1911 to 27 March 1912, for the Training of Officers for the Higher Appointments on the Administrative Staff of the 'army and for the Charge of Departmental Services* (London: HMSO, 1912)

Burke E., 'Speech on presenting to the House of Commons a Plan for the Better Security of the Independence of Parliament, and the Oeconomical Reformation of the Civil and Other Establishments', House of Commons, 11 February 1780

Comptroller and Auditor General, 'Memorandum presented to the Public Accounts Committee', *Fifty Years of the Exchequer and Audit Departments Act 1866*, Cmnd 8337 (1916)

Comptroller and Auditor General, *The Financial Management Initiative* (1982)

Comptroller and Auditor General, *The Rayner Scrutiny Programmes 1979–1983* (1986)

Comptroller and Auditor General Report, *The Next Steps Initiative* (1989)

Civil Service Committee (Fulton Committee), 'Report', *British Parliamentary Papers*, Cmnd. 3638 (1968)

Civil Service Inquiry Commission (Playfair Commission), 'First Report', *British Parliamentary Papers*, vol. 23, pp. 1–47 (1875)

Commissioners for Examining the Public Accounts, 'Fourth Report', *Journals of the House of Commons*, 6–9 April 1781

Committee on Estimates, 'Sixth Report', *Recruitment in the Civil Service* (1964–5)

Committee on Expenditure, 'Eleventh Report', HC 535 (1976–7)

Committee on Expenditure, 'Fourteenth Report', HC 661, *Financial Accountability to Parliament* (1977–8)

Committee on Finance, 'Fifth Report', *British Parliamentary Papers*, vol. 2 (539) (1819)

Committee on Miscellaneous Expenditure, 'Minutes of Evidence', *British Parliamentary Papers*, Q.692, 693 (1860)

Committee on National Expenditure, 'Appendix 13: Memorandum by Lord Welby, The Control of the House of Commons Over Public Expenditure', Report, *British Parliamentary Papers*, vol. 7, pp. 228–55 (1902)

Committee on Procedure, 'First Report', *British Parliamentary Papers*, HC, Sessional Paper 588, vols. 1–3 (1977–8)

Committee on Public Monies, 'Appendices to the Report of the Select Committee on Public Monies', *British Parliamentary Papers*, vol. 34, p. 377 (1857–8)

Committee on Public Monies, 'Appendix 25, Report of the Audit Office on the Functions of the Commissioners of Audit', *British Parliamentary Papers*, vol. 34 (1857)

Committee on Public Monies, 'Confidential Submission of the Chancellor of the Exchequer to the Select Committee on Public Monies', *Memorandum on Financial Control* (1857)

Committee on Public Monies, 'Observations upon the Memorandum on Financial Control by the Treasury', Appendix 3 to the Report of the *British Parliamentary Papers*, Session I, vol. 1, p. 761 (1857)

Committee on Public Monies, 'Report', *British Parliamentary Papers*, vol. 34, p. 385 (1857)

Committee on Treasury and Civil Service, 'Third Report' (1982)

Committee to Consider Decentralisation of War Office Business (Brodrick Committee), *British Parliamentary Papers* (C.8934) vol. 12 (1898)

Estimates Committee, Sixth Report, *Recruitment in the Civil Service* (1964–5)

Fulton, Lord, *The Civil Service: Report of the Committee 1966–68*, Cmnd 3638 (1968)

House of Commons, 'Green Paper', *The Role of the Comptroller and Auditor General*, vols. 1–3, Cmnd 7845 (1980)

House of Commons, *Public Income and Expenditure 1688–1869* (London: King & Co., 1869)

House of Commons, *The Reorganisation of Central Government*, Cmnd 4506 (1970)

National Audit Office, *Annual Accounts and Report, 2013–14*, HC 230 (2014)

National Audit Office, *Annual Report and Accounts, 2014–15*, HC 190 (2015)

National Audit Office, *Report by the Comptroller and Auditor General, Accountability to Parliament for Taxpayers' Money*, HC 849 (2016)

Public Accounts Committee, 'Memorandum to the Public Accounts Committee Inquiry', vol. 39, p. 184 (1867)

Public Accounts Committee, 'Report', HC 301 (1870)

Public Accounts Committee, 'Second Report', HC 198 (1872), and Treasury Minute, 5 April 1872

Public Accounts Committee, 'First Report', HC 110 (1873), and Treasury Minute, 14 August 1872

Public Accounts Committee, 'Report', HC 242 (1874), and Treasury Minute, 20 December 1873

Public Accounts Committee, 'First Report', HC 83 (1878), and Treasury Minute, 25 September 1878

Public Accounts Committee, 'Third Report', HC 350 (1881), and Treasury Minute, 1 February 1882

Public Accounts Committee, 'Report', HC 269 (1882), and Treasury Minute, 23 December 1882

Public Accounts Committee, 'Second Report', HC 187 (1883), and Treasury Minute, 31 October 1883

Public Accounts Committee, Second Report, HC 237 (1884), and Treasury Minute, 13 November 1884

Public Accounts Committee, 'Second Report', HC 169 (1886), and Treasury Minute, 15 November 1886

Public Accounts Committee, 'Second Report', HC 317 (1888), and Treasury Minute, 10 January 1889

Public Accounts Committee, 'Second Report', HC 180 (1892), and Treasury Minute, 5 November 1892

Public Accounts Committee, 'Second Report', HC 255 (1893), and Treasury Minute, 24 November 1893

Public Accounts Committee, 'First Report', HC 227 (1896), and Treasury Minute, 16 November 1896

Public Accounts Committee, 'Third Report', HC 248 (1905), and Treasury Minute, 30 December 1905

Public Accounts Committee, 'Second Report', HC 296 (1906)

Public Accounts Committee, 'Fourth Report', HC 352 (1906), and Treasury Minute, 15 December 1906

Public Accounts Committee, 'Third Report', HC 126 (1909), and Treasury Minute, 10 June 1909

Public Accounts Committee, 'Fifth Report', HC 284 (1909), and Treasury Minute, 21 December 1909

Public Accounts Committee, 'Third Report', HC 144 (1910), and Treasury Minute, 11 December 1910

Public Accounts Committee, 'Second Report', HC 110 (1911), and Treasury Minute, 8 December 1911

Public Accounts Committee, 'Second Report', HC 119 (1912), and Treasury Minute, 18 December 1912

Public Accounts Committee, 'Third Report', HC 156 (1912), and Treasury Minute, 10 December 1912

Public Accounts Committee, 'Second Report', HC 179 (1913), and Treasury Minutes, 7 January and 2 February 1914

Public Accounts Committee, 'Report', HC 249 (1914)

Public Accounts Committee, 'Second Report', HC 270 (1915), and Treasury Minute, 1 November 1915

Public Accounts Committee, 'First Report', HC 83 (1916), and Treasury Minute, 1 September 1916

Public Accounts Committee, 'Second Report', HC 115 (1916), and Treasury Minutes, 8 December 1914 and 29 January 1915

Public Accounts Committee, 'Report', HC 123 (1917), and Treasury Minutes, 1 November 1917 and 31 December 1917

Public Accounts Committee, 'Report', HC100 (1918), and Treasury Minute, 11 September 1918

Public Accounts Committee, 'Second Report', HC 145 (1919)

Public Accounts Committee, 'Third Report', HC 223 (1919), and Treasury Minute, 2 February 1920

Public Accounts Committee, 'Third Report', HC 182 (1920), and Treasury Minute, 1 December 1920

Public Accounts Committee, 'Fourth Report', HC 231 (1920), and Treasury Minute, 1 February 1921

Public Accounts Committee, 'Third Report', HC 212 (1921), and Treasury Minute, 24 November 1921

Public Accounts Committee, 'Third Report', HC 167 (1922), and Treasury Minute, 18 November 1922

Public Accounts Committee, 'Report', HC 125 (1923), and Treasury Minute, 1 November 1923

Public Accounts Committee, 'Second Report', HC 138 (1924), and Treasury Minute, 1 December 1924

Public Accounts Committee, 'Second Report', HC 196 (1925), and Treasury Minute, 1 January 1926

Public Accounts Committee, 'Special Report', HC 97 (1934)

Public Accounts Committee, 'Report', HC 99 (1935), and Treasury Minute, 30 January 1936

Public Accounts Committee, *Epitome of the Reports from the Committees of Public Accounts 1857–1937, and of the Treasury Minutes thereon*, HC 154 (1938)

Public Accounts Committee, 'Report', HC 105 (1941), and Treasury Minute, 12 February 1942

Public Accounts Committee, 'First Report', HC 104 (1942), and Treasury Minute, 3 February 1943

Public Accounts Committee, 'Second Report', HC 127 (1942)

Public Accounts Committee, 'Report', HC 116 (1943), and Treasury Minute, 12 February 1944

Public Accounts Committee, 'Second Report', HC 115 (1946–7), and Treasury Minute, 28 January 1948

Public Accounts Committee, Third Report, HC233 (1948–9), and Treasury Minute, 27 February 1950

Public Accounts Committee, 'Fourth Report', HC 241 (1950–1), and Treasury Minute, 29 November 1951

Public Accounts Committee, 'Third Report', HC 253 (1951–2), and Treasury Minute, 18 November 1952

Public Accounts Committee, 'Second Report', HC 132 (1963–4), and Treasury Minute, 19 November 1964

Public Accounts Committee, 'Third Report', HC 265 (1964–5), and Treasury Minute, 17 November 1965

Public Accounts Committee, 'Special Report', HC 290 (1966–7), and Treasury Minute, 8 November 1967

Public Accounts Committee, 'Second Special Report' (1966–7), HC 571, and Treasury Minute, 8 November 1967

Public Accounts Committee, 'Memorandum by the Treasury on the Responsibilities of Accounting Officers and the scope of Departmental and Treasury Responsibility', *Epitome of PAC Reports*, 1938–69 (1969)

Public Accounts Committee, *Epitome of the Reports from the Committees of Public Accounts 1938–1969, and of the Treasury Minutes thereon*, HC 187 (1970)

Public Accounts Committee, 'Second Special Report,' *Management Review: Report of the Steering Committee* (1979)

Public Accounts Committee, 'The Work of the Committee of Public Accounts and the Status and Functions of the Comptroller and Auditor General', *Second Special Report from the Committee of Public Accounts, 1978–9*, 2 April, Sessional Paper 330 (1979)

Public Accounts Committee, 'First Special Report', *The Role of the Comptroller and Auditor General* (1981)

Public Accounts Committee, 'Report', HC 117 (1985–6)

Public Accounts Commission, 'Thirteenth Report', HC 915 (2006–7)

Public Accounts Commission, *Corporate Governance of the National Audit Office; Response to John Tiner's Review, 4 March 2008*, HC 402 (2007–8)

Public Accounts Commission, 'Fourteenth Report', *Corporate Governance of the National Audit Office*, HC 328 (2007–8)

Public Accounts Committee, *Appointment of the Comptroller and Auditor General*, HC 256 (2009)

Public Accounts Committee, *Accountability for Public Money*, Twenty-Eighth Report (2010–11)

Public Accounts Committee, *Contracting out Public Services to the Private Sector*, Forty-Seventh Report, HC 77 (2013–14)

Public Expenditure Committee, 'Fifth Report (second part)', *British Parliamentary Papers*, vol. 2 (216), p. 381 (1810)

State Comptroller's Office, *State Audit and Accountability* (State of Israel, State Comptroller's Office, Jerusalem, 1991)

Treasury and Civil Service Committee, 'Third Report' (1982)

Trevelyan and Northcote Report, 'Report on the Organisation of the Permanent Civil Service', *British Parliamentary Papers*, vol. 27, pp. 1–31 (1854)

Secondary Sources

Amery, L., *The Times History of the War in South Africa*, 7 vols. (London: Sampson Low & Co., 1900–9)

Aristotle, *Constitution of Athens, Chapter 48*, trans. T. Dynes (London: Seeley & Co, 1891)

Badcock, G. (Lt.-Col), *The Army Course at the London School of Economics* (LSE Archives, Unregistered Documents 20/5/36, 1925)

Badcock, G. (Lt.-Col.), 'The London School of Economics', *The R.A.S.C. Quarterly*, July (1926), pp. 104–6

Beales, D., *From Castlereigh to Gladstone, 1815–1885* (London: Nelson, 1969)

Bentham, J., *Fragment of Government, Being an Examination of What is Delivered on the Subject of Government in General* (1776)

Binney, J., *British Public Finance and Administration 1774–92* (Oxford: Clarendon Press, 1958)

Blackstone, W., *Blackstone's Commentaries*, vol. 1 (Philadelphia: William Young Birch, 1803)

Bowsher, C., *General Management Reviews: Building Government's Management Capacity.* In *State Audit and Accountability* (Jerusalem: State of Israel, State Comptroller's Office, 1991)

Bradbury, Sir J., *Inquiry into the Organisation and Staffing of Government Offices* (1919)

Bromley, R., *On the Establishment of an Audit of the Public Accounts* (Audit Office internal information paper, 1850)

Bullock, A. and Shock, M., *The Liberal Tradition: From Fox to Keynes* (London: Adam & Charles Black, 1956)

Burke, E., *Reflections on the French Revolution* (London: J. M. Dent and Sons, 1935)

Burke, E., *Speeches and Letters on American Affairs* (London: J. M. Dent and Sons, 1942)

Buxton, S., *Finance and Politics*, 2 vols. (London: John Murray, 1888)

Buxton, S., *Mr. Gladstone as Chancellor of the Exchequer* (London: John Murray, 1901)

Chester, N., *The English Administrative System* (Oxford: Clarendon Press, 1981)

Childers, C., *Life and Correspondence of the Rt. Hon Hugh C. E. Childers* (London: John Murray, 1901)

Chubb, B., *The Control of Public Expenditure* (Oxford: Clarendon Press, 1952)

Clarke, Sir E., 'An Old Exchequer Tally', *Journal of the Royal Statistical Society*, vol. 75, part 1 (1911), pp. 38–52

Clode, C., *The Military Forces of the Crown; Their Administration and Government*, vols. 1–2 (London: John Murray, 1869)

Cohen, E., *The Growth of the British Civil Service 1780–1939* (London: Frank Cass & Co., 1965)

Coleman, G. and Starkey, D., *Revolution Re-assessed: Revision in the History of Tudor Government and Administration* (Oxford: Oxford University Press, 1986)

Cromwell, V., 'The Losing of the Initiative by the House of Commons', *Royal Historical Society Transactions*, 5th series, vol. 18 (1968), pp. 1–25

Cruichshanks, E., Handley, S., and Hayton, D., *The History of Parliament: The House of Commons 1690–171* (Cambridge: Cambridge University Press, 2002)

Dahrendorf, R., *A History of the London School of Economics and Political Science* (Oxford: Oxford University Press, 1995)

Davenport, E., *Parliament and the Taxpayer* (London: Skeffington & Son, 1918)

Dewar, D., 'Environmental Auditing: The Fourth "E" ', *Managerial Auditing*, vol. 6, no. 5 (1991), pp. 7–13

Dewar, D., 'The Auditor General and the Examination of Policy', in *State Audit and Accountability* (Jerusalem: State of Israel, State Comptroller's Office, 1991)

Dicey, A. V., *Introduction to the Study of the Law of the Constitution* (London: Macmillan and Co., 1926)

Dictionary of National Biography (Oxford: Oxford University Press, 1961)

Donajgrodzki, A., 'Sir James Graham at the Home Office', *The Historical Journal*, vol. 20, no.1 (1977), pp. 97–120

Downie J., 'The Commission of Public Accounts and the Formation of the Country Party', *English Historical Review*, vol. 41 (1976), pp. 33–51

Einzig P., *The Control of the Purse* (London: Secker and Warburg, 1959)

Elofson M., Woods J. and Todd W. (eds), *The Writings and Speeches of Edmund Burke* (Oxford: Oxford University Press, 1996)

Elton G., *The Tudor Revolution in Government: Administrative Changes under Henry VIII* (Cambridge: Cambridge University Press, 1953)

Elton G., *England under the Tudors* (London: Methuen & Co., 1956)

Erickson A., *The Public Career of Sir James Graham* (Oxford: Basil Blackwell, 1952)

Finer A., *The British Civil Service* (London: George Allen and Unwin, 1937)

Fitz-Nigel R., *Dialogus de Scaccario*, ed. and trans. Charles Johnson (Oxford: Clarendon Press, 1983)

Flegmann V., *Public Expenditure and the Select Committees of the House of Commons* (Aldershot: Gower Publishing, 1986)

Foord A., 'The Waning of the Influence of the Crown', *The English Historical Review*, vol. 62, no. 245 (1947), pp. 484–507

Funnell W., 'Why 1866? Historical Notes on the Passage of the Exchequer and Audit Departments Act', *ABACUS*, vol. 32, no. 1 (1996), pp. 102–10

Funnell W., 'Victorian Parsimony and the Early Champions of Modern Public Sector Audit', *Accounting History*, vol. 9, no. 1 (2004), pp. 25–6

Funnell W., 'Accounting on the Frontline: Military Efficiency and the South African War', *Accounting and Business Research*, vol. 35, no. 4 (2005), pp. 307–26

Funnell W., 'National Efficiency, Military Accounting and the Business of War', *Critical Perspectives on Accounting*, vol. 17 (2006), pp. 719–51

Funnell W., 'The Reason Why: The English Constitution and the Latent Promise of Liberty in the History of Accounting', *Accounting, Business and Financial History*, vol. 17, no. 2 (2007), pp. 265–83

Funnell W., 'The Proper Trust of Liberty: The American War of Independence, Economical Reform and the Constitutional Protections of Accounting', *Accounting History*, vol. 13, no. 1 (2008), pp. 7–32

Garrett J. and Sheldon R., *Administrative Reform: The Next Step* (London: Fabian Tract 426, Fabian Society, 1973)

Gilbert E., *Sir Halford Mackinder 1861–1947: An Appreciation of His Life and Work* (London: G. Bell and Sons, 1961)

Gladwin I., *The Sheriff: The Man and his Office* (London: Victor Gollancz, 1974)

Gleig G., *The Life of Robert, First Lord Clive* (London: Longman, 1848)

Goodwin D., *Team of Rivals: The Political Genius of Abraham Lincoln* (London: Penguin Books, 2013)

Griffith J. and Ryle M., *Parliament: Functions, Practice and Procedure* (London: Sweet and Maxwell, 1982)

Grimwood J. (Lt.-Col.), 'Costing in Relation to Government Control, Efficiency and Economy', *The Incorporated Accountants Journal*, March 1919, pp. 114–20; April, pp. 133–8; May (1919), pp. 156–61

Guedalla P., *Gladstone and Palmerston: The Correspondence of Lord Palmerston and Mr. Gladstone 1851–1865* (London: Victor Gollancz, 1928)

Haldane, Lord, *Report of the Machinery of Government Committee*, Cmnd 9230 (1918)

Harris, C., 'Army Finance', *Army Review*, vol. I, July (1911), pp. 55–76

Harris, C., 'Financial Control in Administration', *Public Administration*, vol. 9 (1931), pp. 312–22

Harrison, A., *The Control of Public Expenditure 1979–1989* (Newbury: Policy Journals, 1989)

Hart, J., 'Sir Charles Trevelyan at the Treasury', *English Historical Review*, vol. 75, January (1960), pp. 92–110

Hatsell, J., *Hatsell's Parliamentary Precedents* (London: 1781)

Hawkins, A., 'Parliamentary Government and Victorian Political Parties', *English Historical Review*, vol. 104 (1989), pp. 638–69

Henley, D., *Unpublished Memorandum* (1996)

Hennessy, P., *Whitehall* (London: Fontana Press, 1990)

Hennessy, P., *The Prime Minister: The Office and its Holders Since 1945* (London: Allen Lane, Penguin Press, 2000)

Hirst, F., *Gladstone as Financier and Economist* (London: Ernest Benn, 1931)

Hogan, J., 'Party Management in the House of Lords', *Parliamentary History*, vol. 10, part 1 (1991), pp. 124–50

Hoskin, K. and Macve, R., 'Accounting and Examination: A Genealogy of Disciplinary Power', *Accounting, Organizations and Society*, vol. 11, no. 2 (1986), pp. 105–36

Hughes, E., 'Civil Service Reform', *History*, New Series, vol. 27, June (1942), pp. 51–83

Hughes, E., 'Sir Charles Trevelyan and the Civil Service Reform, 1853–55', *English Historical Review*, vol. LXIV (1949), pp. 53–88

Jenkins, R., *Gladstone* (London: Macmillan, 1996)

Jenkins, W. and Gray, A., *Policy Evaluation in British Government: From Idealism to Realism*, Discussion paper, University of Kent at Canterbury (1987)

Latham, R., *The Shorter Pepys* (London: Bell & Hyman, 1985)

Macaulay, C., *Observations on Appropriation Audit*, Appendix to the Report of the Committee of Public Accounts, HC 413 (1865)

Macaulay, C., *Confidential Memorandum to The Treasury, 29 April 1867, on the Consolidation of the Offices of Controller General of the Exchequer and the Audit Board* (1867)

Macaulay, T. B., *Critical and Historical Essays*, vol. 1, 1907 (London: Dent, 1966)

MacDonagh, O., *Early Victorian Government, 1830–1870* (London: Weidenfeld and Nicolson, 1977)

Madox, T., *The History and Antiquities of the Exchequer* (1796) (New York: Greenwood Press, 1969)

Magnus, P., *Gladstone: A Biography* (London: John Murray, 1954)

Matthew, H., *The Gladstone Diaries*, vols. 1–7 (Oxford: Clarendon Press, 1978)

Metcalf, L. and Richards, S., *Improving Public Management* (London: Sage Publications, 1987)

Middleton, J., *Records and Reactions 1856–1939* (London: Murray, 1939)

Mill, J., *Autobiography of John Stuart Mill* (London: Oxford University Press, 1963)

Morley, J., *Burke* (London: Macmillan and Co., 1909)

Myers, A., *England in the Late Middle Ages* (London: Penguin Books, 1971)

Normanton, E., *The Audit and Accountability of Governments* (Manchester: Manchester University Press, 1966)

Norris, J., *Shelburne and Reform* (London: Macmillan and Co., 1963)

Northcote, S., *Twenty Years of Financial Policy* (Private Printing, 1862)

O,'Halpin, E., *Head of the Civil Service: A Study of Sir Warren Fisher* (New York: Routledge, 1969)

Parker, C., *Life and Letters of Sir James Graham* (London: John Murray, 1907)

Pepys, S., Diary (London: Alexander Murray, 1870)

Pocock, J., 'Burke and the Ancient Constitution: A Problem in the History of Ideas', *The Historical Journal*, vol. 3, no. 2 (1960), pp. 125–43

Pollitt, C., 'Beyond the Managerial Model: The Case for Broadening Performance Assessment', *Financial Accountability and Management*, vol. 2, no. 3, Autumn (1986), pp. 155–70

Poole, R., *The Exchequer in the Twelfth Century* (Oxford: Clarendon Press, 1912)

Reitan, E., 'The Civil List in Eighteenth-Century British Politics: Parliamentary Supremacy versus the Independence of the Crown', *The Historical Journal*, vol. 9, no. 3 (1966), pp. 318–37

Roberts, C., 'The Constitutional Significance of the Financial Settlement of 1690', *The Historical Journal*, vol. 20, no. 1 (1977), pp. 59–76

Roseveare, H., *Treasury: The Evolution of a British Institution* (London: Allen Lane, 1969)

Thomas, P., *The House of Commons in the Eighteenth Century* (Oxford: Clarendon Press, 1971)

Schama, S., *A History of Britain: Fate of Empire 1776–2000* (London: BBC Worldwide Ltd, 2003)

Shannon, R., *Gladstone*: Vol. 1, *1809–1865* (London: Hamish Hamilton, 1982)

Sharman, C., *Holding to Account; Review of Audit and Accountability for Central Government* (London: 2001)

Steel, A., *The Receipt of the Exchequer 1377–1485* (Cambridge: Cambridge University Press, 1954)

Stephenson, C. and Marcham, F., *Sources of English Constitutional History: A Selection of Documents from A.D.600 to the Present* (New York: Harper & Brothers, 1937)

Thatcher, M., *The Downing Street Years* (New York: Harper Collins, 1993)

Tomkins, C., *Achieving Economy, Efficiency and Effectiveness in the Public Sector* (London: Kogan Page, 1987)

Various, authors, *The History of the Prince of Wales' Own Civil Service Rifles* (London: Reprinted by Naval and Military Press, 2002)

Ward, I., *The English Constitution: Myths and Realities* (Oxford: Hart Publishing, 2004)

Ward, J., *Sir James Graham* (London: Macmillan, 1967)

Wright, M., *Treasury Control of the Civil Service 1854–1874* (Oxford: Clarendon Press, 1969)

Wright, M., 'Public Expenditure in Britain: The Crisis of Control', *Public Administration*, vol. 55, Summer (1977), pp. 143–69

Index